Memorial Book of Kolomey
(Kolomyya, Ukraine)

Translation of *Pinkes Kolomey*

Original Book Edited by:
Shlomo Bickel

Published in New York, 1957

Published by JewishGen

An Affiliate of the Museum of Jewish Heritage—A Living Memorial to the Holocaust
New York

Memorial Book of Kolomey (Kolomyya, Ukraine)
Translation of *Pinkes Kolomey*

Copyright © 2021 by JewishGen
All rights reserved.
First Printing: September 2021, Tishrei 5782

Editor of Original Yizkor Book: Shlomo Bickel
Project Coordinators: Claire Hisler Shefftz z"l and Dr. Ben Nachman
Layout and Name Indexing: Jonathan Wind
Reproduction of Photographs: Sondra Ettlinger
Cover Design: Rachel Kolokoff Hopper

Published by JewishGen, Inc.
An Affiliate of the Museum of Jewish Heritage
A Living Memorial to the Holocaust
36 Battery Place, New York, NY 10280

Printed in the United States of America by Lightning Source, Inc.

Library of Congress Control Number (LCCN): 2021946111

ISBN: 978-1-954176-19-5 (hard cover: 342 pages, alk. paper)

Translator's Note

My parents, Aaron and Mary (Miriam Shuster) Hisler came from Kolomey and my father was on the Kolomeyer Memorial Book committee and in charge of the book's distribution. The book was copyrighted in care of his name and address. I was encouraged to read the book but never quite managed to get much beyond the first page when my parents were alive. In the years since their deaths, I have observed Yom Hashoah each year by slowly translating some of the section of the Holocaust as best I could and writing it down.

Many years ago, my father expressed the wish that the book be translated into English and published; I thought that very unlikely. But now this website has made his wish possible in a way he could never have imagined.

Claire Hisler Shefftz z"l

Credits for Book Cover

Front Cover Illustration: *The Tall Synagogue* page 85 (129).

Front and Back Cover Background Illustration: *The Tall Synagogue*, page 85 (page 129)

Back Cover Illustration: From the cover of the original book, page 1.

Back Cover Photographs from Left to Right:
    Emanuel Feuermann, page 190 (266).
    Efroim Klarman, page 223 (303).
    Yakov Biter, page 221 (301).

Poem on the Back Cover: *Between Stopchet and Kolomea* by Itzik Manger, page 180 (256)

JewishGen
Yizkor-Books-in-Print Project

This book has been published by the **Yizkor-Books-in-Print Project**, as part of the **Yizkor Book Project** of JewishGen, Inc.

JewishGen, Inc. is a non-profit organization founded in 1987 as a resource for Jewish genealogy. Its website [www.jewishgen.org] serves as an international clearinghouse and resource center to assist individuals who are researching the history of their Jewish families and the places where they lived. JewishGen provides databases, facilitates discussion groups, and coordinates projects relating to Jewish genealogy and the history of the Jewish people. In 2003, JewishGen became an affiliate of the **Museum of Jewish Heritage—A Living Memorial to the Holocaust** in New York.

The **JewishGen Yizkor Book Project** was organized to make more widely known the existence of Yizkor (Memorial) Books written by survivors and former residents of various Jewish communities throughout the world. Later, volunteers connected to the different destroyed communities began cooperating to have these books translated from the original language— usually Hebrew or Yiddish—into English, thus enabling a wider audience to have access to the valuable information contained within them. As each chapter of these books was translated, it was posted on the JewishGen website and made available to the public.

The **Yizkor-Books-in-Print Project** began in 2011 as an initiative to print and publish Yizkor Books that had been fully translated, so that hard copies would be available for purchase by the descendants of these communities and by scholars, universities, synagogues, libraries, and museums.

These translated Yizkor books have been produced almost entirely through the volunteer effort of researchers from around the world, assisted by donations from private individuals. The books are printed and sold at near cost, to make them as affordable as possible. Our goal is to make this important genre of Jewish literature and history available in English in book form, so that people can have the personal histories of their ancestral towns on their bookshelves for themselves and for their children and grandchildren.

A list of all published translated Yizkor Books in the project with prices and ordering information can be found at: http://www.jewishgen.org/Yizkor/ybip.html

Yizkor Books Project Manager: Lance Ackerfeld
Yizkor-Books-in-Print Project Coordinator: Joel Alpert
Yizkor-Books-in-Print Associate Project Coordinator: Susan Rosin

Please send donations to: Yizkor Book Project, JewishGen, Inc., 36 Battery Place, New York, NY, 1280

JewishGen, Inc. is an Affiliate of the
Museum of Jewish Heritage - A Living Memorial to the Holocaust

Notes to the Reader

The images in the original book were scanned from photographs from the time of the first edition. Already of poor quality, being pre-war, and at least 30 or more years old, these photographs had started to decompose. A special process of scanning and photographing the photos in the book produced images that in many cases were significantly improved from the original book and for that we thank our photographer.

A reader can view the original scans of the book on the web sites listed below.

The original book can be seen online at the New York Public Library site:

https://digitalcollections.nypl.org/items/a4106400-7a6b-0133-5735-00505686a51c

or

at the Yiddish Book Center web site:

https://www.yiddishbookcenter.org/collections/yizkor-books/yzk-nybc313822/bickel-shlomo-pinkes-kolomey-geshikhte-zikhroynes-geshtaltn-hurbn

To obtain a list of all Shoah victims from Kolomey (Kolomyya), the reader should access the Yad Vashem web site listed below; one can also search for specific family names using family name option. These lists are continually updated by Yad Vashem, so it is worthwhile to periodically search these lists.

There is more valuable information (including the Pages of Testimony, etc.) available on this website: http://yvng.yadvashem.org

A list of all books available from the Yizkor-Book-In-Print Project along with prices is available at: http://www.jewishgen.org/Yizkor/ybip.html

Geopolitical Information:

	Town	District	Province	Country
Before WWI (c. 1900):	Kołomyja	Kołomyja	Galicia	Austrian Empire
Between the wars (c. 1930):	Kołomyja	Kołomyja	Stanisławów	Poland
After WWII (c. 1950):	Kolomyya			Soviet Union
Today (c. 2000):	Kolomyya			Ukraine

Alternate names of the Town:

Kolomyya [Ukr, Rus], Kołomyja [Pol], Kolomea [Yid, Ger], Colomeea [Rom], Kolimeya, Kolimia, Kolomai, Kolomey, Kolomyia

Nearby Jewish Communities:

Pechenizhyn 7 miles W
Yabluniv 10 miles SSW
Dzhurkiv 10 miles NE
Pistyn 12 miles S
Hvizdets 12 miles ENE
Zabolotiv 12 miles ESE
Lanchyn 13 miles W
Obertyn 13 miles NNE
Demiche 13 miles ESE
Rozhniv 15 miles SE
Khotymyr 15 miles N
Banya Bereziv 15 miles WSW
Kosiv 15 miles SSE
Bili Oslavy 15 miles W
Dzhuriv 16 miles SE
Otyniya 16 miles NNW
Chortovets 16 miles NE
Moskalivka 16 miles S
Miliyeve 18 miles SE

Delyatyn 18 miles W
Vynohrad 18 miles NW
Tyshkivtsi 19 miles NE
Banyliv 19 miles SE
Kuty 21 miles SSE
Vyzhnytsya 21 miles SSE
Dora 21 miles WSW
Chernyatyn 21 miles ENE
Korytne 21 miles SE
Knyazhe 21 miles ESE
Mykulychyn 21 miles WSW
Nadvirna 22 miles WNW
Vyzhenka 23 miles SSE
Tlumach 23 miles N
Yaseniv-Pilnyy 23 miles ENE
Horodenka 23 miles ENE
Hrabovets 24 miles NW
Roztoky 24 miles S
Stetseva 24 miles E

Vashkivtsi 24 miles ESE
Tatariv 25 miles WSW
Snyatyn 25 miles ESE
Tysmenytsya 27 miles NNW
Chernelytsya 27 miles NE
Starunya 27 miles WNW
Berehomet 28 miles SSE
Koropets 28 miles NNE
Verkhovyna 29 miles SSW
Nyzhni Stanivitzi 29 miles ESE
Ust'-Putyla 29 miles S
Nyzhniv 29 miles N
Potochyshche 29 miles ENE
Bohorodchany 29 miles NW
Nepolokivtsi 29 miles ESE
Zolotyy Potik 30 miles NNE
Lysets' 30 miles NW
Solotvyn 30 miles WNW
Ustechko 30 miles ENE

Jewish Population in 1900: 16,568

Present Day Map of Ukraine with **Kolomyia** indicated

Cover page of Original Hebrew Book

Translation of Previous page

Pinkas
Kolomey

History
Memories
Characters
Destruction

5717   New York   1957

TABLE OF CONTENTS

Khurbn [Holocaust]

In Memory of Our People

Kolomear Organizations in New York

פנקס קאלאמיי

געשיכטע
יכרונות
געשטאלטן
חורבן

תש"ין
ניו-יארק
1957

[Pages VII- X]

Preface

by Shlomo Bickel

Translated by Claire Hisler Shefftz
with reference to the translation of the first part by Adele Miller

The idea of a "pinkas Kolomey," which would tell about the once splendid past of our now, in the Jewish sense, destroyed native city, and which would, through the accounts of eye-witnesses, victims who miraculously survived, mourn the annihilation of the Jewish Community of Kolomey - arose silmultaneously among the "olei Kolomey" in Israel and among the "sharit haplita," the survivors in New York.

Here, in New York, the concept of a "pinkas Kolomey" was nurtured with deep love and devotion by the poet Naftali Gross. He, together with the writer of these lines, were to be the editors. We had an understanding that he, Naftali Gross, would be the chief editor and bear the major responsibility of reading and preparing the manuscript for publication.

First of all, he was much more involved, and with eager and sad interest, sought out every Jewish writer who had something to tell about the past joys and the later heavy sorrows of his Kolomey.

Secondly, the serious heart disease of his last few years which kept him from his regular editorial position, forced him to stay at home and thus gave him more time (how comic and how tragic was our optimism!) to be involved with the yizkor book project.

His illness gave Naftali Gross "more time" but not enough time to begin the selection and editing of the manuscript. He left us suddenly and unexpectedly on the night between Shabbos and Sunday, on April 8, 1956.

The yizkor book for which the living Naftali Gross was to have been the chief editor was dedicated by him to the martyred community of Kolomey; he had been the poetic voice of their lives and deaths. At the end of the section "Stories and Memories," we placed Naftali Gross's poem, "Yosl Klezmer Saves Kolomey from a Terrible Fire" and thereby memorialized both the poet and his hero, Yosel Klezmer, who was his literary alter ego.

We ended the section "Stories and Memories" with Gross's poem and began the section "Portraits" with poems of Naftali Gross and Itzik Manger (a Kolomeyer through his mother's family). To Naftali Gross's biography in that section, we added a brief review of his work; also added was the eulogy this writer delivered at the poet's funeral. I could not muster the energy and patience for a more complete evaluation.

In the section "Portraits," we tried to create a panorama of ideas and movements in the Jewish community and the achievements of its members. We included only those who were no longer living since we could better see how their efforts led to the achievement of their goals.

We did make one exception for the sculptor Chaim Gross. With him, with our Chaim, long may he live, we began the "Portraits."

We believed that we couldn't leave out Chaim Gross, our Kolomear sculptor, who had achieved a world renown for his artisitic creations and was now, in his later years nearly half of his hundred and twenty.

We know that we did omit quite a few Kolomeyer who deserved to be included in this section, and we left them out only for their "sin" of still being alive. We hope that they will all continue with this "sin" for many long, healthy, and creative years and this will certainly put our minds at rest.

And now, for a blessing, for all those without whose help this book would never have been completed:

First of all, the Kolomeyer in Haifa, Itzchak Teitelbaum, who with his hard work, his devotion, and his attention to detail prepared most of the material that is included in the book. He descended upon writers, he found people who knew how to write and he sought out all the photographs of long ago Kolomey. The dispersed Kolomeyer in Israel and America owe him a debt of thanks that can never be repaid.

And from the landsleit in Israel, I want to especially remember the walking encyclopedia about Kolomey, Levi Grebler. All that he knows and remembers about Kolomey would fill not just one but several volumes. We used a great deal of his material under his own name, under his initials, and also in some articles under other initials. Levi Grebler certainly earned himself much thanks from the Kolomeyer yizkor book.

And now, my kinsmen, those near to me, whom I saw here at work in New York with the burdens they carried on their shoulders and their worries about the budget. They were, in alphabetical order, the members of the yizkor book committee: the self-sacrificing devoted Aaron Hisler; the dynamic and in Kolomeyer circles, beloved Leib [Louis] Weitz who together with Naftali Gross established the yizkor book committee in New York; the reliable and always stimulating young friend of mine, Yitzchak [Isaac] Susskind; and the lively, friendly Isaac Feuerstein [Edward Firestone]. These four did not begrudge any effort or time to get the Kolomeyer landsmanshaften in New York interested in the book as well as Kolomeyer landsleit throughout the world.

The writer of these lines who took upon himself the heavy task of editorship after the death of Naftali Gross, z"l, is certain that without the previously mentioned four friends and comrades, all his editorial work would have been overwhelming. Without their efforts, this book could not have been published.

And finally, I want to thank my friend, Baruch Tchuvinsky, who helped me with the editorial work and took upon himself the extra work of binding in addition to editing and printing.

Shlomo Bickel

New York, June, 1957

[Page 13]

History of the Jews of Kolomea [1*]

Dr. N. M. Gelber (Jerusalem)

Translated by Gloria Berkenstat Freund

1.

Jews were already in Raysn [2*] in the days of King Lev the First, who permitted Jews and Armenians to settle within his realm. However, there are no official documents that can confirm that Jews settled in Kolomea and its vicinity at that time.

There is a document from 1466 from which we learn that the Polish Lord Kastelan of Podolya and the provincial governor of Snyatyn and Kolomea, Mikhal Moszila Buczacki, leased the salt mines and estates in Kolomea to the well known Jew, Shimshon (Pamozo Samsoni Judeo), who was a lessee in Zidiczow [Zhidachov]. In addition, in 1469 a lessee agreement was signed between them. This Shimshon was a lessee of great prominence. He leased entire cities in the Halych area [1]. Shimshon of Zidiczow was the largest holder of the right to collect taxes, lease holder and merchant, as well as the main banker in Raysn. He carried out commerce with noblemen and also leased estates from the king and from noblemen. He gave loans on pledges in Lemberg [Lviv] and in other cities. The lessee died in 1474 and after his death his wife, Sarah, and his son, Yehoshua ("Owsha"), took over the businesses [2].

The fact that Shimshon held various leases in Kolomea does not mean that there was a Jewish settlement in the city itself.

At the beginning of the 16th century Jews began to settle in the vicinity of Kolomea.

At that time the trade highway on which one

[Page 14]

transported goods to Wallachia [region of Romania] drew many Jews to settle there. During the years 1521-1540 the Jews of Kolomea and Snyatyn were known in Wallachia, Raysn and also in Turkey, where the flow of many goods shipments were in evidence with goods from Wallachia [3]. Lemberg Jews, who settled in Kolomea, enjoyed the privilege that was also confirmed by the constitution, namely: they were placed under the rule and jurisdiction of the city and they were obliged to participate in all city responsibilities, including – the city taxes. Therefore, they enjoyed all of the city freedoms and the principles of equality applicable to every citizen without any restriction not only in the economic realm, but also – in a certain measure – in the realm of political rights. Jews received passive voting rights in Kolomea and they also had the right to take part in the voting for city officials, and even for the city president. They also had the right to take part in the audit of city finances and even to send a representative or two to the session of the city-council, where reports about the city finances were given. The granting of this right was motivated by the fact that the Jews took part – according to an evaluation – in two-thirds of the city expenses. The Jews could live in the center of the city ("Rynek"); however, they could not put out any tables of goods on the market days that would be held every week on Friday, unless on the central square of the city [4]. Of the Lemberg Jews who lived in Kolomea, Mordekhai Yehuda, the holder of the lease to collect tolls, was well known in 1599.

Jews also lived in the villages in the Kolomea district and were employed running taverns and distilleries. We learn from the tax list of 1569 that 10 Jewish houses were found in the villages in the Kolomea district. If we take as a count that 12 Jews lived in each house, we will reach a number of 120 Jewish souls [5]. In 1616, the Jews received – according to the decree of the commission for tax registration – a suitable location to build a shul and a location for a cemetery outside the city [6]. Permission was given to erect a residence there for a grave digger. These locations and their buildings were freed of tax payments. The Jews made a 20 dollar yearly payment for a staroste [village chief]. The

[Page 15]

Jewish butchers along with the Christian butchers were obligated to provide him with 40 stones (a stone equaled 32 pounds) of fat. In addition, the Jews along with the Christian residents had to grind straw from the field as fodder. In 1621, they suffered a great flood and from an ambush by the Tatars. In that year the Jews received written confirmation that all of their rights and duties remained in force.

In the year 5408 (1648), attacked the city and his troops murdered the 300 Jewish residents [7].

After the Chmielnicki destruction, Jews again came to Kolomea and, in the course of several years, the Jewish settlement grew, thanks to the fact that the number of non-Jewish residents was small and their economic position was insignificant. The Jews so developed their trade that in 1715 an agreement was signed between the city hall and the kehile [organized Jewish community] that the Jews were required to contribute two-thirds of all city taxes. In addition, in 1717-1719, the Jews paid a head tax. Of the contribution of 33,857 gildn that was required of the Jews in Raysn, the Jews of Kolomea participated with a sum of 1,040 gildn and 21 groshn [8].

Lessees and holders of a lease to collect customs duties had the highest standing in the Jewish settlement. From time to time conflicts broke out between them and the kehile, particularly in matters concerning taxes. Such quarrels were brought to the Council of the Four Lands.

As can be seen by the decision of the council in Tammuz 5387 ([June or July] 1627), it was decided: "In regard to the matter of a lessee [9] from Kolomea, we have found that whoever holds the lease will give the kehile a sum of 300 gildn each year for the first three years and the money will serve to support the rabbi and the khazan [cantor] and shamas [sexton] and the poor people. And he who will hold the lease will have the contract for three years. If the contract holder wishes to participate in the Gramnitz fair, the Jewish community in Kolomea may agree and is entitled to certain payments [10]."

This internal life of the kehile was the same as in all of the organized Jewish communities in Poland. The legal power and the task of the kehile was administrative and fiscal, as well as jurisdictional and included the educational system.

At the head of the kehile stood the elected heads of the community, or leaders, who

[Page 16]

Kolomea.
Kolomyja.

[Page 17]

Kolomey Town Hall

[Page 18]

constituted the guiding administrative body. It consisted of three to five members who were responsible for relations with the state for the entire kehile. They swore a loyalty oath after their election – in the presence of the representative of the regime – to the king and to the state. They were required to receive confirmation from the staroste [village chief] in Kolomea, or from his assistant.

Every month the parnosim [elected heads of the community] changed their roles and the acting parnes [elected head] was called the parnes khodesh [monthly head]. In addition to the parnosim, two elders from the cities sat in the kehile council, according to the pattern of boni viri [Latin for "good men"].

The third administrative office consisted of members of the kehile and of the kehile committees. The number of members was not fixed. The committees dealt with matters of charity (charity trustees), with audits of the accounts, with market matters, supervision of cleanliness in the Jewish quarter, provided a guard to supervise kashrus [observation of the kosher laws], supervision of weights and measure, with matters of educational institutions and schools (four to seven trustees for schools).

There were also trustees concerned with Eretz-Yisroel from the 17th century on, as well as tax evaluators and guardians of the unions of artisans (guilds) that represented their affairs in the leadership of the kehile and their number was tied to the number of artisan unions. The elections were carried out by the mediation of "honest men" (voters), who were chosen by lot so as to be nominated by the kehile.

The kehile, which had an office room at its disposal, consisted of the city rabbi who was the first to be hired and was the religious-spiritual leader of the kehile; the magid [preacher], known under the name, Magid Mishorim [righteous preacher]; and the secretary who was the administrative representative of the kehile. The latter largely filled the role of the kehile intercessor. The kehile took care of all matters for its residents – economic, communal, cultural and educational. It set and collected the necessary taxes in order to cover the kehile budget that included the salaries of the administrative apparatus, payments for state officials, such as the staroste (village chief) and so on, for the clergy in the schools, for City Hall and the remaining taxes that were placed upon the Jews.

Direct and indirect taxes also served to cover

[Page 19]

payments for proprietorship and to pay for weddings, funerals, dowries, and for titles, khover [title given to learned, middleclass men], moyreyne ["our master" – title conferred by Talmudic academies in Poland].

Kolomea belonged to the Vaad haMedine Rayzn [Council of the Raysn Nation], which was directed by the Lemberger kehile; but its influence became much less and its place was taken by the Zholkev [Zhovkva] kehile.

As is known, the Vaad haMedine [Council of the Nation] had the power to elect the representatives to the Council of the Four Lands, to divide the taxes among the kehilus and the small communities attached to them, as well as to regulate conflicts which took place among the individual communities.

We do not actually possess any precise information – due to a lack of sources – about their exact activities. The first Vaad haMedine was established in 1519 in Greater Poland [west-central Poland]. In Lesser Poland [the area of southern Poland], the first Vaad haMedine was founded in the middle of the 17th century and also in Raysn. The activity of the Vaad haMedine in Raysn began after 5408 (1648) with the decline of the Lemberger kehile. In 5424 (16th June 1664), the heads of the Zholkever kehile assembled along with the influential people and the envoys and those elected from the remaining kehilus of the Raysn Vaad haMedine in Svirzh (near Boiberik [Bobrka]); from Brod [Brody], Buczacz, Kolomea – all former small communities attached to the Lemberger kehile which mutinied against it. At the session of the Vaad in question, improvements were made "in the order of electing the kehile" and "in nominating the tax collectors and the setting of the head-tax." Rabbi Reb Avraham, son of Reb Wolf, who signed the rules that were adopted, took part in these sessions in the name of the Kolomea kehile with the approval of Reb Shimshon Ginzburg of Przemyśl, Reb Josef Aizik of Jaworów, Reb Shmeul Zaynwl Segal of Lemberg and Reb Dovid Preger of Buczacz, who was the main Bund organizer against the Lemberg kehile.

Reb Avraham Reb Wolf's (Reb Avraham, the son of Reb Wolf], who did a great deal for the establishment of the kehile, served as rabbi in Kolomea. However, it is not known how many years he was the rabbi and in what year he died.

Reb Avraham ber [son of] Josef Kac stood at the head of the yeshiva during the period of his rabbinate. He spent time in Lemberg in 5424 (1664) and was murdered there during the pogroms that took place there on Shabbos, 8 Iyar [3 May] [11].

[Page 20]

Following Rabbi, Reb Avraham, Wolf's son, the rabbi was Reb Haim ber Yehoshua of Krakow (1590-1648) (the author of Meginei Shlomo [Shlomo's Sorrow] and Pnei Yehoshua [Yehoshua's Face]), the well known head of the yeshiva during the course of 1639-1648. In 5431 (1671), he was at the Jaroslower fair at the time when the Council of the Four Lands came together. He was received as the head of the yeshiva in Lemberg and died there on 9 Adar 5533 ([4 March] 1673). He supported yeshivus in various places and particularly in the "important Jewish cultural center of Kolomea." He left behind two sons, Efraim Fishl, chairman of the rabbinical court in Kolomea, who died in 1683. His second son, Tzvi Hirsh, was the rabbi in Berezan, Drobich [Drogobych], Tismenitz [Tysmenytsya], Brod and Liske.

In that era (1690) the Rabbi, Reb Dovid Kohan was also the chairman of the rabbinical court in Kolomea [12].

After Efraim Fishl, his son-in-law, Rabbi Meshulem ber Yeshayahu, who was the head of the yeshiva in Lemberg for more than two years, sat on the rabbinical chair. He died on Sukkos 5506 (1746) and his place was taken by his son-in-law, Reb Noakh Efraim Fishl ber Moshe, who was the rabbi in Kolomea until 1783.

Life in the kehile was normal, without special events, until the Shabbatai Tzvi [3*] movement. The majority of the population supported itself with small businesses, with taverns, peddling and crafts. Individuals carried out wholesale-trade with Moldava and Wallachia – there and back.

On 2 January 1765, a census was carried out for the purpose of collecting a head-tax by the commissar of the Halych district and the counties of Trembowla [Terebovlya] and Kolomea, Juzef Paradowski, who was the judge in matters of water boundaries in Halych, Matsei Korovosiecki ("Lovczi Platski"). The census authenticated by an oath of the rabbi, two kehile-parnosim [elected heads of the kehile] and the writer for the kehile [13].

Rabbi Fishl Moshkowitz (Fishko) signed the census in Kolomea and this was the rabbi, Reb Noakh Efraim Fishl ben Moshe.

According to the census, there were 985 Jews and 87 children under a year old in Kolomea. In the villages that were members of the Kolomea kehile, 74 Jews and four children under a year old were counted. And these are the villages: Piedik [Pidhaychyki] – two and a child, Dietkovin [Dyatkovtsy] – six, Kniazdwor [Nizhneye] – 12 and one child, Spas – four, Krinitsa –

[Page 21]

13 men and two children, Wiskrisnits [Voskresentsy] – two and one child, Markowitz [Markoviche], – 10, Tzienewe [Tsenyava] – four, Hantsherev [Goncharov] – seven, Diletin [Dilyatyn] – two, Oslave – four, Zalitshe [Zaliztsi] – four.

All together, there were 1,059 Jews and 91 children under one year old.

There was a total of 10,987 souls, including 714 children under a year old in the entire Kolomea county. It must be noted that these cities belonged to the Kolomea county: Solotvine [Solotvyn] – 471 and 19 children, Pystin [Pystan] – 233 and 17 children, Yablonov – 467 and 49 children, Snytyn [Snyatyn] – 1,123 and 102 children, Kitev – 1,013 and 26 children, Gvazdziets [Gvozdets] – 659 and 27 children, Zabletov [Zabolotiv] – 946 and 63 children, Kamineki Vielkye [Velyka Kam"yanka] – 56 and five children, Otynye [Otyniya] – 345 and 51 children, Lysiec [Lysets] – 171 and 16 children, Nadverne [Nadvirna] – 1, 196 and 75 children, Obertyn – 419 and 30 children, Horodenka – 906 and 67 children, Kolockovtse [Kulachkovtsy] – 150 and 13 children.

The economic situation worsened during the last years of the Polish regime. The trade in grain – the main commerce in Pokucie [4*] – lost its value on the European market and exports from Poland declined to half their amount in the beginning of the 18th century.

Poverty reigned in the cities, which led to a decline in commerce because trade increasingly dwindled – particularly in eastern Poland. It should be understood that these conditions also had a bad effect on the economic conditions of the Jews of Kolomea.

At the beginning of the 18th century, southeastern Raysn and Podolya were under the marked influence of the Shabbetai Tzvi movement and its messenger, the Kabbalist Haim Malakh. The cities of Zolkiew [Zhovkva], Buczacz [Buchach], Horodenka, Zbaraz [Zbarazh], Zloczew [Zolochiv], Podhajce [Pidhaytsi] were known nests of Shabbetai Tzvi followers.

It is not known if Shabbetai Tzvism penetrated into the Kolomea kehile and how much. It must be assumed that the propagandists of Shabbetai Tzvism, the followers of Reb Yehuda the Hasid and of Haim Malakh, such as: Moshe Meir Kaminsker of Zhovkva, Elihu Shor of Rohatyn and Fishl of Zolochiv, who visited the area of Kolomea and wandered from city to city, spreading the teachings of Shabbetai Tzvi, were probably also in Kolomea.

[Page 22]

It is particularly possible because the Kolomea district contained such cities as Horodenka and Nadvirna where many followers of Shabbetai Tzvi were found who would leave their city on Tisha b'Av [the day commemorating the destruction of the Temple in Jerusalem], steal a sheep and slaughter it not in accordance with Jewish law and roast it on a fire and eat it on Tisha b'Av. [5*] Yehuda Leib ben Note Kris, the head of Yakov Frank's [6*] "gabbaim [assistants]," would visit the nearby shtetlekh and preach Shabbetai-Tzvism, as well as Wolf Bendits who was sent by Shabbetai's followers from Nadvirna to Saloniki [Thessaloniki or Salonica] to Brukhia, the head of the Shabbetai Tzvi followers.

We do not have any exact information if Frank had any followers in Kolomea itself. We see that among those on a list of Frankists who converted to Christianity after the debate in Lemberg (1779) there is not even one Jew from Kolomea.

Therefore, an extensive range of Hasidim were found here who created and strengthened the triangular area in which Kolomea is located.

In the first half of the 18th century, the number of "miracle workers in the area of South Raysn and Podolya," who were known only within the limits of their city and their region, increased. The majority of them were healers who healed with herbs, with incantations over the spleen, with amulets and conjuring; they would also drive out dybukim. [7*] These miracle workers had a visible influence on the common people who were inclined to passions and simple faith.

The Jewish miracle worker who settled in this era in the city of Toust revealed his new teachings and traveled to the nearby communities: Norodenka, Kitev and others and he was known as the Baal Shem-Tov [Master of the Good or Devine Name] (the Besh"t [an acronym of Baal Shem-Tov]).

Kolomea was mentioned in Shivhei Besh"t [In Praise of the Baal Shem Tov], the book that declares his praises.

There is a story about a magid [preacher] named Reb Dovid ber Moshe from Kolomea who traveled to collect Chanukah money and became lost on the way and came to the house of the Besh"t. The Besh"t was himself in his secluded shtibl. The preacher asked about the master of the house, his wife answered that he had gone to the holder of the tax collection lease in order to help him water the cattle. The Besh"t returned to the house and attended to the preacher. He

[Page 23]

made the bed for him and prepared the dishes with water to wash himself when he woke up.

At midnight, the Besh"t arose for khtsos [midnight study and prayer commemorating the destruction of Jerusalem] and sat quietly behind the oven and performed khtsos.

Reb Dovid woke up from his sleep and saw a great light from behind the oven. He thought that the wood on the oven had caught fire. He went down from his bed and took the dish of water that stood near him and went to put out the fire. As he neared the oven, he saw to his astonishment that the Besh"t was sitting and a light shone on him like a rainbow. The preacher fainted from fright. As he revived, he asked the Besh"t what this signified. The Besh"t answered that he did not know; he had preformed khtsos and it was possible that "I had been one with the Lord. Therefore, I shone thus."

From that night, the preacher from Kolomea became one of the Besh"t's Hasidim, but before the Besh"t was revealed, he would travel to him to hear words of Torah [14]. Reb Dovid then spread the Besh"t's teachings. And when he was asked from whom he gets his learning, he would answer: "From one, a secluded poor man." When Reb Dovid once heard how the Rabbi, Reb Gershon of Kitev, rebuked the Besh"t for his stories, he said to him: "Leave him alone, because he is smarter than you." He did not say anything more because the Besh"t had decreed that he not tell what he had seen.

According to Hasidic legend, the Besh"t would come to Kolomea before going to Toust [Tolstoye] from the village of Koshylovtse (near Jaz³owiec) and here he was revealed. He designated his seat in the synagogue, after which this was called the Kosover shulekhl [small Kosovo [8*] synagogue]. He would immerse himself in the mikvah [ritual bath] of the old bathhouse, which was later referred to as "the Besh"t's mikvah." Hasidic legend assigns one Hasidic story to Kolomea, which is connected to the Kuntshi's family (from the name of Mrs. Kune). Someone in the family argued with the Besh"t. One Friday night, one of the Kuntshis sat with his wife and spoke mockingly of the Besh"t and his stories. In the morning the Besh"t went to the mikvah and met that person standing on the doorstep of his house. The Besh"t asked him if this is how one pays respect on a Friday night, by speaking

[Page 24]

slander and loshn hora [prohibition about speaking badly of someone]? The person answered him that he did not know who told the Besh"t or if the angels were speaking slander. The Besh"t said to him that by speaking slander one created an angel and this angel can speak slander.

Reb Dovid ber Moshe, already mentioned above, was known as one of the Besh"t's first Hasidim in Kolomea. He died in 5492 (1732) in Skala. Reb Leib of Pystin was even more well known, [15] who was embraced by the leader of Hasidus in the first era. He died in Kolomea, 3 Iyar [12 May] 5505 (1745)[16]. Reb Jakov Kopl ber Nehemiah Feiwl, who was know as Kopl Hasid, was also among the well known Hasidim. He was the father of Reb Menakhem Mendl of Kosov, the author of Ahavas Shalom [Lover of Peace]. Reb Kopl then left for Tismenits [Tysmenytsya] and died there on the 15 Elul [29 August] 5547 (1787). His daughter married Reb Uri of Strelisk, who was known by the name, "the Seraph," the student of Reb Shlomo of Karlin. His son, Reb Menakhem Mendl lived in Kolomea for many years before moving to Kosov. There his wife, Sheina Ruchl had a shop and with it was the source of support for them. He was the founder of the Hager Hasidic Dynasty.

At that time, the well known tzadekus [pious woman] Nekha, the daughter of Reb Yitzhak Drobicher and the sister of Magid Yeheil Mikhl of Zlotshev, who was considered one of the first followers of the Besh"t, lived in Kolomea, Her husband, Eliezer ben Josef Katvan [17], went to Eretz-Yisroel and died there.

2.

Changes took place in the life of the local kehilus [organized Jewish communities] with the political union of Galicia and Austria after the first division of Poland in 1772.

According to the "Juden Ordenung" [Jewish arrangement or order] of the Empress Maria Theresa in 1776, the Jews of Galicia were organized into a special administrative body at whose head stood the chief leader of the Jews in Galicia. It was put together from the kehilus with six to 12 parnosim [elected heads of the community] at the head. The kehilus in each districts in Galicia were divided into six districts. They were under the direction of a parnes [elected community leader; plural, parnosim]. Six parnosim from throughout the country had control of them, along with

[Page 25]

the chief rabbi of the country.

The six district parnosim and the six country parnosim, with the chief rabbi of the country at the head, formed the main leadership of the Jews in Galicia.

In 1785 this organization was liquidated. Only the parnosim from the local communities remained. Except for the communities of Lemberg and Brod, where seven parnosim stood at the head, Kolomea, at the head of the remaining communities, brought in three parnosim. Their task was to represent their communities before the regime, to provide for the community's poor, to have supervision with the rabbi over the registration of those born, married and the dead, to collect the community taxes and to direct all kehile business. Actually, the parnosim were dependent on the district regime and they were subject to their orders.

Kolomea was surrounded by much uncultivated and unbuilt stretches of land. The thick forests around the city were used without any economic considerations. The majority of houses in the middle of the city and in the main streets were in Jewish hands, which constituted the predominant majority of the population. The Christians for the most part lived in the suburbs where they were employed in handiwork and agriculture. Because many fires broke out and many wooden houses were burned, the regime forbid the building of new wooden house and only permitted buildings of brick and stone. At the end of the 1780's, Kolomea began to build buildings of brick and stone and in this way, the city began to receive the character of a large urban city. [18]

The city of Kolomea and vicinity constituted a special district until 1782. However, based on the law of the 22nd of March 1782, this district was combined with Tisminitz [Tysmienica] as the united district of Stanislaw.

During the first period of its rule in Galicia, Austria considered the Jews as a foreign element that needed only to be tolerated and protected. This protection and tolerance they had to buy with taxes and special payments. As foreigners, they were excluded from the area of defense and they had to pay many taxes that were higher than for the other parts of the population. The Austrian administration intended to slowly

[Page 26]

change the Jews and have them adapt to new conditions. But the innumerable injunctions, regulations and decrees with which they flooded the Jews in Galicia as a result of parliamentary motions and as a result of the initiative of the government in Lemberg, and according to the confirmation of the central government in Vienna, created only chaos.

In the course of time, the Austrian bureaucratic apparatus began to understand little by little that the decrees and injunctions were not reforming Jewish life.

The fate of the Kolomea kehile was exactly the same as all of the other kehilus in Galicia.

Despite various difficulties, the Jewish population began to develop here in the economic sense and also began visibly to progress.

In 1776, the Kolomea Jews lived in a small number of houses, that is, 10 or 11 souls lived in each house. The houses at that time were small and badly built and the Jewish apartments were crowded.

The majority of the Jewish population consisted of retail merchants, shopkeepers and tavern owners.

One of the purposes of the administration was to close the Jewish taverns in Galicia, which were seen as the essential factor preventing the development of the standing of the peasants.

On the basis of a questionnaire that was circulated among the 18 district leaders, the central government arrived at this decision, although only eight district leaders said yes to the closing of the taverns. It was the intention that the liquidation of the taverns would force the Jews to be employed in a productive manner. The same point of view was held by those in power in Kolomea.

However, in addition to the decree and the attempts that were made based on the initiative from above, a positive result and a bettering of the economic life of the Jews in Kolomea did not occur under the reign of Maria Theresa. Therefore, it is no wonder that the economic situation of the Jews in Galicia under the reign of her successor, Emperor Josef the Second, was also bad, so that the government

[Page 27]

posed the difficult question: what can be done to improve the precarious circumstances of the Jews?

Various prohibitions were placed upon the Jews as a supplement to their taxes. The most difficult prohibition was related to getting married. When there was an income of 100 gildn a year, there was a payment required of three dukats for the marriage of the first son, six for the marriage of the second son and 12 dukats for the third son. The father had to pay not less than 30 dukats for permission to marry for each additional son.

Woe to those who married off their children without permission from the regime. Thus, in 1774, for example, the possessions of two Jews who had married off their children without government permission were confiscated. Their possessions were given away to Simonowitz, a convert. And they, the two Jews, were driven out of Galicia.

Heavy penalties were placed for even taking part in an illegitimate wedding.

In connection with the ban, the ban against marrying relatives (1785) and against burying bodies before two days should be remembered. It was also decreed that a divorce must be carried out in a government court.

The remnants of kehile autonomy were eliminated in 1875 and all political and legal privileges were annulled. Taxes were not placed on the entire kehile, but on each Jew individually and the collection was transferred to government officials. The Jewish population was placed under the jurisdiction of city hall in policing matters. The kehile thus was robbed of its civil character and converted into an exclusively religious organization.

Josef the Second was a follower of political-economic beliefs according to which he believed that he would solve the Jewish problem by settling the Jews on the soil as farmers. In 1782 a decree was issued from Vienna that the Jewish agricultural workers would pay only half the marriage tax and would be completely freed from this payment in a short time. However, the founding of the Jewish colonies

[Page 28]

first began in 1785; after a royal decree of 16 July, in the spring [12*] of 1786, the first Jewish colony in the village of Dombrovke [Dubivka] near Ney-Sandez [Nowy Sacz) was created. After this, the colony, "Babylonia," was founded near the city of Bolechov. Several small colonies were also founded, but they did not exist for very long.

According to the registration program, it was decided that Kolomea had to provide 20 Jewish families of the total number of colonists – 1,410 – in Galicia. However, up to the end of 1794, only 10 families from Kolomea – 20 men, 36 women and 62 children under 18 (35 boys and 27 girls) – actually moved. The possessions of these colonists consisted of 20 houses, 20 barns and stalls, 248 parcels of land, 20 agricultural tools, 25 horses, 46 oxen, 56 cows. [19]

The budget for colonization had to be covered by the kehile. The expense for one family was estimated at a high of 250 florins. Each 25, 30, 40 families were obligated to pay for the colonization of one needy family.

The general number of colonists reached 91 families in the entire Kolomea district, which it should be understood also included the city of Kolomea itself. In 1822 there remained only 83 families on the soil and all were supported by the kehilus. (Not one family settled on the soil of its own accord.)

Just as in all communities in Galicia, the Jews in Kolomea also suffered from the yoke of taxes that in no small part resulted in a difficult situation. In addition to the tolerance taxes, the Jews also paid various other taxes and fees.

As was already mentioned above, the majority of Jews were involved with taverns; often the number of Jewish families was identical to the number of taverns. There was a special official to take care of all matters that were connected to the collection of the meat tax. His yearly salary reached a sum of 200 florin and there was a Jewish secretary who received yearly support of 350 florin.

Sadly, we do not possess any exact facts about the number and the composition of the Jewish population in Kolomea itself. In 1788 a count was carried out in all of Galicia. There

[Page 29]

were facts about the number of Jews in the Stanislaver District, to which the city of Kolomea also belonged. According to this count, there were 11 kehilus in Stanislawer District, namely: Stanislav, Tiseminc [Tyśmienica], Boroszyn, Kolomea, Jablonow, Kosiv, Kitev, Obertyn, Narwerne, Maryampol [Mariampol] and Monasterzyska [Monastyriska]. These kehilus consisted of 3,530 families, comprised of 17,342 souls, of them – 8,584 men and 8,758 women.

In 1790, there were 3,351 families in the Stanislaver District and they paid 13,404 florins in tolerance taxes. In 1792, these taxes were paid in the Stanislaver District by 3,252 families, which consisted of 15,420 souls.

In addition to running taverns, retail trade and peddling, the Kolomea Jews were occupied in the wood business, excluding the leasing of the forest estates that was forbidden to Jews since 1780, and with potash and salt. However, the Jews were forbidden to transport the salt from its production place to the market place. Kolomea Jews were also employed with tobacco plantations that were a very important part of the economy. Three story tobacco warehouses were erected in Kolomea. [20] A Jewish company in which the brothers Avraham and Shlomo Krigshaber and Moshe Lew took part would sell 2,500 50 kilo [bundles] of tobacco leaves each year to the Jewish lessees of the tobacco administration in Galicia, Moshe Honik and Josef Szrenk. [21]

Feywl Hershl was also a well known tobacco merchant. Feywl Hershl was the type of community leader who took advantage of every opportunity. In August 1784, the regime notified him that he could receive his wages at the district office in Zaleshchik [Zalishchyky] for his information about the secret weddings among Jews. However, he was not alone among the Jews of his generation. There was no kehile in Galicia where one of its leaders was not employed in the craft of denunciations and giving secret information to the regime. Such a phenomenon was the product of the administration. The same Feywl Hershl was one of the leaders of the kehile and he was himself implicated in an investigation that was carried out against him and Shmuel Nota, the secretary and treasurer of the kehile, because of kehile accounts. True, they both complained to Ertl, the district governor of Stanislaw, that it was because of a campaign of agitation being waged against them by the broker Mendl Markus that he had involved

[Page 30]

them in a trial about disarray in the kehile treasury. As a consequence of this investigation, the secretary of the kehile, Shmuel Nota, was removed from his office, as well as Wolter [113*], the Jewish scribe in Kolomea.

In their accusation against Ertl, they complained about the turmoil from which they suffered and that he had conducted an investigation without any proof. Besides these complaints, there were grievances against this Ertl on the part of Jews in Nadwerne and in Kolomea. On the 30ᵗʰ of December 1784, the government demanded from Ertl an exact report about this question and simultaneously told him that it would be sent to Stanislaw to the attention of the district governor, to a provincial council, in order to investigate the entire matter. During the course of the investigation, it was stated that Commissars Rimain and Gors were also involved as well as a number of employees, due to the taking of gifts and bribes from Jewish brokers. The central government in Vienna also became involved in this matter and demanded an end of the "shortage in the managing committee" and to the taking of bribes, as well as a ban on the use of Jewish agents who fill the role of intercessors with the regime. The investigation of Ertl lasted several months and ended in June 1786 with the resignation of Walter and with blame placed on Ertl. [22]

The kehile in Kolomea and the kehilus in Tismenic, Nadwerne and Kitev complained in connection with this investigation of the matters of sub-lessees [114*] for meat taxes in Bord, as well as about the matter of the Jewish tax lessees Kopler and Wofstal. [23]

An important economic sector that was in Jewish hands was wax, honey and tallow. In 1786 Leizer Leibl received the lease [or concession] for wax, honey and tallow for a payment of 200,000 florins. It was worthwhile for him to pay 10 florins for 50 kilos of honey, although the market price was then six to seven florins. [24]

Trade relations with Walachie and Moldava were expanded during the era of the Austrian regime, particularly after the conquest of Bukovina, thanks to the geographical position of Kolomea. Austria was interested in continuing the

[Page 31]

trade relations with these nations in order to import livestock and various agricultural products.

The Jews concentrated in their hands the important fields of buying and selling of livestock and horses, as well as the sale of agricultural products. Their dealings went as far as Bukovina through Kolomea to other cities in Galicia and from there they all carried on the salt trade with Bukovina and Moldova. The commerce in horses of southern Galicia and Moldova actually was mainly concentrated in the hands of Armenian livestock traders from Stanislaw. However, the majority of the contractors were Jewish merchants from Kolomea. [26] It is interesting that Hake Baltazar, a professor from Lemberg University, who would make brief visits across Galicia every year, reported that in Kolomea, which is one of the most important cities in Galicia, all of the economic sectors were in Jewish hands.

As a result of Joseph the Second's "Juden Ordenung," dated the 20th of March 1786, which placed many obligations on Jews, particularly that they were obligated to erect secular schools for the Jewish youth, the emigration of Jews located in the counties near the Walachie-Moldova border increased. The Jews of Kolomea were also drawn to this border. It became so widespread that the Viennese government gave instructions to its consulate in Jas not to give these emigrants any consular support. [27]

As in other communities in Galicia, a Jewish public school was founded in Kolomea in 1788, according to the program of Herc Homberg and was certified by the government. Leizer Fryd served as a teacher here and his yearly salary was 200 florin.[28]

However, the harshest decree was on the 17th of February 1788 that obligated Jews to military service. This decree intensified the flight of young men to Poland and Moldova. The asentirung [military conscription] law was only repealed two years later, after the regime became convinced that the Jews would not appear for military service. Instead of military conscription, a sum of 30 gildn was required to be paid for every young man obligated for service. This situation lasted until 1804.

A bitter chapter, full of oppression of the Jewish masses,

[Page 32]

began in the life of Galicianer Jews on the 11th of November, 1797 with the initiation of a candle tax. The period of the "candle lessees" [the right of individuals to sell candles] is sadly engraved in the life of all kehilus.

The yoke of taxes grew larger year by year, so much so, that in 1811 there was a large debt for the taxes for meat and for Shabbos candles, as well as a debt from the state that the Jews were obligated to pay off. In 1815 accusations were made to the state against the heads of the kehile. The parnosim were accused of dishonest management of the kehile money and in using the taxes for their own good and of working with the lessees. The county officials removed the kehile leadership – the same thing happened in Stry and in Brod – and nominated new kehile parnosim.

The Jews of Kolomea especially complained about the manner of the tax distribution, that a greater number of the taxes were placed on the poor residents and the rich strata was spared. Tax debts accumulated due to this situation. However, the regime paid no attention to the plea of the Kolomea Jews and demanded payment of the tax debts.

In 1812 there were 427 Jewish families in Kolomea, which numbered 2,003 souls, 986 men and 1,047 women. There were 2,484 Jewish families in the entire Kolomea district, which numbered 11,205 souls. Of them – 5,514 men and 5,691 women. The number of Jews in Kolomea district did not change very much in those years. In 1819 2,473 Jewish families were counted and of them 91 families that were employed in agriculture.

It would be interesting to learn of the professional structure in 1820.

There were 757 Jewish merchants in the entire district who were involved with the trading of wheat and with various agricultural products, food, hides, tanning, salt, livestock, wax, malt and hops. There were 334 retail merchants counted in the entire district and there were 488 proprietors of workshops and small factories, of them – 201 whiskey producers (out of 2,015 in all of Galicia), 20 carpenters (of 69 in all of Galicia), nine candlemakers (38 in all of Galicia), three roof weavers who were

[Page 33]

then the only ones in all of Galicia, 252 various craftsmen, such as tailors, shoemakers, furriers and ropemakers.

We can learn from these figures that the economic condition of the Kolomea Jews improved considerably at the beginning of the 19th century. There were 67 Jewish wholesalers out of 72 wholesale firms in Kolomea district in 1826. According to the count, the Jews in Kolomea then made up half of the general local population.

In 1818-1819, a struggle broke out in the kehile against the Vad HaKehilus [Council of the of Jewish communities]. At the head of the opponents stood Moshe Lajbrajkh, who pelted the regime with memoranda and letters in which he complained about the parnosim of the kehile and their actions against the population, whom they treated severely in the distribution of taxes. The district office carried out long investigations, in which the tax-lessees and their agents were implicated. In 1819, the parnosim were removed and new ones were nominated in their place. But conditions did not change.[30]

In 1820, thanks to the efforts of the then rabbi in Kolomea, Reb Gershon, the holy society, gmiles khesodim [15*], was founded, "because the old were gone and the young people" had begun to neglect the mitzvah [commandment] of taking care of the dead, particularly with carrying the mite [board on which a corpse was placed]."

The duties and the tasks of the members were stated in the statutes of the society. A vote was taken on every Khol Hamoed Pesakh [the intermediate days of Passover, during which work is permitted]. Five kosher [i.e. honest and pious] arbitrators elected three gabbaim [those who assist with synagogue work] by majority vote. The gabbai was obligated to provide a banquet for the society on holidays.

In addition to the matter of burials and everything related to the corpse, the society was also concerned with the sick in the hospitals and took care of their comfort and "restored" them.

In cases in which a corpse was a very wealthy man in life, the gabbai did not have sole authority to decide the cost of his grave without the knowledge of the other gabbaim from the society. Donations for the society had to be collected in a special pushke [a box or can used to collect money for charity]. The duties and the rights of gabbaim were arranged in special statutes in one-two order.

[Page 34]

3.

In the history of the Jews in Galicia, the period of the Austrian revolution in 1848 was symbolized by the severe conflicts between the pious Jews and the Hasidim on one side and the emerging maskalim [followers of the Enlightenment] on the other side.

The Hasidim succeeded in planting widespread roots in Kolomea and administered kehile [organized Jewish community] life. The Haskalah [Enlightenment], in opposition, began to spread with slow steps; it was not strong enough and did not have any known personalities, as did the followers of the Enlightenment in Brod, Tarnopol, Lemberg, Tismenitz and Bolekhov.

Kolomea did not have a distinct role in the struggle to spread general culture that flared up in all of the communities during those years. Still more: it was almost entirely outside the struggle between the pious and the followers of the Enlightenment. There was no sign of any followers of the Enlightenment who strove to bring in reforms and changes in the internal life of the Jews. There were also no attempts made to break away from the existing synagogues and houses of prayer and build a synagogue for the progressive thinkers as was done by the followers of the Enlightenment in Tarnopol in 1820. A stable Hasidic life took shape here. It is therefore no wonder that the Hasidim from Kolomea made efforts to influence the tzadek [righteous man] from Sadigere [Sadagora, Bukovina], Rav Yisroel Friedmann – when the regime of Bukovina issued a deportation order from Sadigere against him – to settle in Kolomea. In fact, they succeeded in obtaining the right of residence in Kolomea for him. There was great joy among the Hasidim. They sent a delegation to Sadigere and the rebbe promised them that he would settle in Kolomea. However, in the meantime, the entire matter in Bukovina became quiet and there was no longer any obstacle to the rebbe remaining in Sadigere.

The events of 1848 were not particularly apparent in the life of the Jews, except that the medical doctor, Dr. Rosenheck, became one of the few active participants in the events. We do not have any information about the participation of the Jewish population in the National Guard or something similar.

[Page 35]

Dr. Rozenhek of Kolomea was elected to the Sejm [lower house of the Polish parliament] that was called by the government in Lemberg on the 20th of April 1848 – against the will of the National Committee. But the Sejm never met then.

During the years 1848-1849 the city suffered from cholera, which claimed many victims and bankrupted the poor population from an economic standpoint.

During the second half of the 19th century, and particularly after the year 1848, Kolomea was transformed into an important place of trade for Galicia, Bukovina and Walachia. The Jewish population in Kolomea increased from year to year until it made up half of the entire city population thanks to the improved economic situation. Despite the changes brought about in the life of the Jews in Galicia after 1848, the Kolomea Jews remained devoted to tradition and they did not strive for any widespread reforms in kehile life.

The management in the kehile remained in the hands of the pious Jews. The Kolomea kehile and the Stanislaw kehile turned to the Interior Ministry with a request to permit the Jewish merchants to open their businesses on Sunday because it was difficult for them to observe two days of the week, as well as the Jewish and Christian holidays in addition to Shabbos and Sunday. They provided the details of what this means: not working 149 days a year – something that they could not endure from an economic standpoint.

In 1860 when Jews were permitted to buy permanent estates, 15 Jews from Kolomea submitted requests to be permitted to buy houses and estates. The names of the Jews whose requests were granted were:

1) Josl Chajes, a wholesaler of woolen goods and a parnes of the kehile.

2) Shlomo Wieselber[g], an agent.

3) A. Meltzer, an estate lessee.

4) Y. Ro[s]enheck

5) Chajes, an owner of a whiskey distillery.

6) Yakov Zenenzib, a wood and grain merchant, as well as a builder.

[Page 36]
7) Gugig, a building contractor

8) Litman Brettler, an estate lessee.[30]

At that time the Jews constituted half of the general population of Kolomea. In 1860 the Jewish population increased to 8,000 souls and in 1869 to 8,232 souls and the general number of residents reached 16,909. The greater part of economic life was concentrated in the hands of the Jews, both the wholesale trade and the retail, particularly the cattle and horse trade, as well as agricultural products. The industries, mills and pottery making were also mostly in Jewish hands. Jewish trade changed, especially in the year 1869 when the Lemberg-Chernowitz train line was completed with a station in Kolomea. This greatly improved the economic condition of the Jews in Kolomea and its surroundings.

Despite the changes that took place as a result of the legislation in 1848 and 1851, the law of the 25th of January 1803 according to which Jews were forbidden to employ Christians as attendants and servants, remained in force. On the 23rd of September 1853 the governor even found it necessary to declare to all county clerks that this ban was still in force, but that exceptions could be made in cases of agricultural work.

It is interesting that only the leadership of the Kolomea kehile protested to the Interior Ministry against this ban.

Thanks to this, the matter was dealt with by the government. The Interior Minister transferred the matter to the Minister for Religious Matters. This minister expressed his opinion that the order of the governor must be followed. In this way the Interior Minister rejected the protest from the Kolomea kehile[31]. That year the governor of Lemberg dealt with the question of founding a rabbinical seminar and the problem of Jewish clothing. In 1851, the rabbi of Sambor, Shmuel Daitch, sent the government a memorandum about reforming Jewish life in Galicia. He proposed that the Galicianer Jews renounce their traditional clothing, that an assembly of esteemed Jewish representatives be called together and that the suppression of Hasidism and of rebbes [Hasidic rabbis] begin. Against this plan emerged

[Page 37]

the rebbe, Reb Tzvi Hirsh Chajes from Zolkiew, who opposed the forced methods. He proposed that more rabbis be invited to this assembly than worldly representatives.

On one side it was proposed that the Lemberg city governor should call together an assembly of 16 representatives, of them only six county rabbis who had graduated from a faculty of philosophy. The six should be: the county rabbis from Slotew-Brod (Kristiampoler), Zolkiew (Chajes), Czernowitz [Chernivtsi] (Dr. Ingl), Sambor (Daitch) and Kolomea. Reb

Nakhum ben-Yitzhak Tojbsz was then the rabbi in Kolomea. It is hard to believe that Tojbsz had graduated from a faculty of philosophy.

In 1854 a Jewish hospital was founded in Kolomea. There was no Jewish school in Kolomea then, as in Lemberg, Brod, Tarnopol, Bolekhow [Bolechow] and in the other communities, only private khederim [religious elementary schools, usually only for boys].

During the same years, the kehile erected a special building for the Talmud Torah [school for poor boys], where 120 children studied.

A Jewish public school was founded by the Viennese Allianz [17*] first in 1886.

It is interesting to note that in 1850 the wish to found a gymnazie [high school] in Kolomea, "in order to spread education among the Jewish population in one of the large city election districts in Galicia" was published in the press[32]. The government needed to be made interested in the founding of a gymnazie. The opinion was expressed that the founding of a gymnazie was necessary from a Jewish standpoint. The Kolomea Jews, it was said there, surpass their brothers in the other parts of the country in their "ignorance." Nothing would be so able to help the spreading of education among the Jews as an educational institution. Moreover, one can imagine with certainty that there would be gratifying results if a gymnazie were founded in Kolomea. This wish was only fulfilled 10 years later.

In 1861, a gymnazie was founded in Kolomea and Jewish students began to be taught there.

Kolomea elected its own deputy to the Galician Sejm the same year. The well known Jewish community worker, Dr. Eliezar Duks, was elected

[Page 38]

who fulfilled his functions as a Sejm deputy until his death in the beginning of 1865.

After his death, the mayor filed a memorandum to the regional government with a demand that no by-election be arranged in Kolomea "because the majority of voters are Jews and there is no doubt that Jews will again elect a Jewish deputy." If it was not possible to annul the by-election, the municipal administration asked to change the voting arrangements so as to enable another respected resident from the city of Kolomea to be elected and his election would be recognized only if a third of the votes were from Christian voters.[33] The municipal administration rejected this request because it was in contradiction of the constitution.

Maximillian Landesberger, the Jewish candidate, received 353 votes against 226 votes received by the Polish candidate. Dr. Landesberger was elected in this manner. He was a well known lawyer in Lemberg and in 1840 took an active role in the life of the Lemberg kehile. He was one of the founders of the temple in Lemberg and in 1848 he was numbered among the community workers of the Lemberg Jewish intelligencia in political life and he was an adherent of the centrist direction. For a time he belonged to the wing of the pious Jews in Lemberg, under the direction of Meir Minc. He was a member of the Galician Sejm until 1870 and he took an active role in the negotiations that were then being carried on in connection with the Jewish problem.

Dr. Landesberger represented the Galicianer Sejm in the Viennese Parliament from 1867. He was the only Jewish representative. No direct elections to the parliament took place from 1867-1873, but the Sejms would send delegates. On the 7th of April 1870 the Poles left the Viennese

Parliament and Dr. Landesberger resigned. He also left the Sejm a short time later and withdrew from political life.

In 1865 (May 2nd), a terrible fire broke out in the city that made a ruin of 500 houses with a thousand families, mostly Jewish. Those suffering remained without a roof over

[Page 39]

their heads. Little by little the burned quarter was rebuilt and the victims had their lives restored.

In the 1870's changes came to the composition of the Vaad haKehile [Council of the Jewish community]. Little by little, parnosim [elected leaders of the Jewish community] were also elected from the intelligencia and they tried to carry out reforms in the structure of the kehile. While the Lemberg kehile worked out sample statutes for the kehilus in 1877, Kolomea was one of the first communities in eastern Galicia that brought in these statutes and conducted community business according to them.

Arguments and conflicts broke out in the kehile between Hasidim from Vizhnitz [Vyzhnytsia, Ukraine] and Sadigere. These arguments were also a product of the events in the neighboring kehilus. So in 1875 the election of a rabbi in Snytyn gave rise to arguments among the Hasidim in Kolomea.

The Kolomea Jews took a much greater part in general communal life during the second half of the 19th century, particularly on the city council. In 1873, the Jews offered their own list, with Dr. Rash as mayor, in the election to the city council. In addition, according to the number of residents, the Jews should have received 36 electoral positions; only 14 Jews [33] were elected as members of the city council. A non-Jew was elected as mayor. In 1878, the Jews also came out with an independent list against the Poles. At this election, the Jews received the majority. At the session of the city council on the 24th of September 1878, the Jewish lawyer, Dr. Maximillian Trachtenberg was elected as mayor. He was born in 1846 in Tarnopol. After finishing his studies, he settled in Kolomea and was a beloved lawyer there. He was the mayor until 1885. In 1893 he was elected as president of the kehile[34].

In 1873, the first elections to the Austrian Parliament in Vienna took place. In view of the fact that the Poles in the Galician Sejm did not envision the interest of the Galicianer Jews, and during the years 1870-1873 there was not even one Jewish representative in the Vienna Parliament, the organization Shomer Yisroel [Guardian of Israel] in Lemberg decided to enter the election with an independent Jewish list and on the 28th of May 1873, constituted itself a central

[Page 40]

Jewish election committee that was composed of the representatives of the city under the leadership of Dr. Julius Kulisher and Dr. Emil Byk as secretary.

Shomer Yisroel decided to present as its political program of the Jews, "the carrying out of the constitution and their devotion to it."

In Kolomea itself, the majority of the Jewish voters wanted to present a candidate who was devoted to the constitution[35]. The Kolomea Jews and the Jewish county election committee published their first program on the 20th of August 1873, in which the Jewish demands were formulated in relation to the elections to parliament. This was the first such declaration in Galicia.

It was established in the declaration:

"The representation of the Galician Jews in the Galician Sejm and Parliament is not representative of their numbers, their status and their tax payments. Therefore, it is necessary to present a Jewish candidate in the Kolomea district, who would especially represent the important life interests of the Jews.

"The Kolomea Jews demand devotion to the state constitution and are opposed to the independent oligarchy and opposed to the decentralization of Austria which would only lead to the rapid breakdown of the monarchy and to changes that could not be favorable to the Jews in Galicia.

"They are also against the removal of the German language from the folks-shuln [secular public schools] and the middle schools. Taking into account the fact that the Slavic languages do not possess any capability for scholarly expression and are only spoken by a limited stratum, the young who are studying would not be proficient in absorbing the subjects and preparing for higher studies – as a result of the removal of German as an instructional language.

"True, the Kolomea Jews want the constitution to take into account the interests of the various national groups and religions, how much these interests are in agreement with the interests of the state and of its development. By this means, they want their candidate to be particularly acquainted with economic life in order that his position would be appropriate for representing them [36]."

Dr. Oscar Henigsman, was chosen as the candidate in Kolomea, by agreement of dozens of Jewish election committees. Against him,

[Page 41]

the Poles presented Dr. Florian Ziemiakowski. But after negotiations with dozens of Polish election committees, Dr. Ziemiakowski withdrew from his candidacy in Kolomea.

Dr. Henigsman was elected and was the first Jewish deputy from Kolomea in the Austrian Parliament in the years 1873-1879. He was born on the 10th of March 1824, in Rajcza and he died in Vienna, the 27th September 1880. He studied jurisprudence in Vienna, settled in Lemberg as a lawyer and there took an active part in Jewish life. He was a member of the Vaad haKehile [Council of the religious community] and the city council in Lemberg during the years 1861-1866 and he was a deputy in the Galician Sejm from Brod starting in 1867. He was a magnificent speaker, one of the main speakers in the Sejmbecause matters of Jewish equal rights were considered there.

He was one of those who founded the Jewish-Polish union, Shomer Yisroel; and thanks to this union, he was elected as a deputy from Kolomea, after the agreement with the Ukrainians. In parliament, he belonged to the "Writers' Party" along with the other Jewish deputies from Galicia: Nusen Kalyu, Dr. Yaakov Landau and Herman Mieses.

[Page 41]

History of the Jews of Kolomea (cont.)

4.

At the time of this political struggle, Rabbi, Reb Hillel Borukh Bendit Lichtenstein was the rabbi in Kolomea, a man with a great reputation in the Jewish world.

Reb Hillel Lichtenstein came from Hungary. He was born in 1815 in Vag Vecse [Veèa, Slovakia], where his father was the rabbi and chairman of the Beis Din [rabbinical court]. In 1867, Reb Hillel was received as rabbi in Kolomea. In his youth he excelled with his particular abilities. He was one of the most distinguished and most zealous students of the Chasam Sofer [18*] (Reb Moshe Sofer). He [Reb Moshe Sofer] wrote about him: "He was one of the best yeshiva students in the Petersburg Yeshiva, filled through and through with Gemara [Talmudic rabbinical commentaries] and pusokim [post Talmudic commentaries], rishonim and acharonim [rabbinical scholars from the 11th century to the present], his sense – clear and polished – and his fear of God was great."[37]

In the course of many years Reb Hillel was active in the yeshiva of Chasam Sofer in Petersburg where he was valued because he was a God-fearing person, because of his diligence and his capabilities as a great preacher. From 1850

[Page 42]

he was the rabbi in various kehilus [Jewish communities] in Hungary. In 1852 he was accepted as the rabbi of Klozenberg. There he was involved in a quarrel with Rabbi, Reb Avraham Fridman, chairman of the Beis-Din of Karlsburg. He also was the rabbi of the state from 1846. The kehile did not order his certification according to the law. Rabbi Fridman waited for a long time. When no request came on the part of the Klozenberg kehile, Rabbi Fridman complained to the governor and on the 2nd of March 1853, he received his decision according to which Reb Hillel Lichtenstein was removed from his rabbinical seat. Then Reb Hillel left Klozenberg.[38] He was the rabbi in Szikszo [Hungary] during the years 1865-1867.

Reb Hillel Lichtenstein belonged to the extreme and he placed himself against every reform of Reb Azriel Hildesheimer who tried to spread general education. Reb Hillel was against the sermons in the German language that Hildesheimer gave in Western Hungary.

The question of presenting a national seminar [school] for rabbis in Budapest emerged on the agenda. He was the strongest opponent at the rabbinical assembly in Nyíregyháza, in 1864. He was a member of the rabbinical delegation that was sent to Kaiser Franz Josef I to deliver the negative opinion concerning the plan to found a rabbinical seminar.

In the years 1868-1869 he took part in the Jewish Congress in Pest, although he was then already a rabbi in Kolomea. Following his lead, the pious representatives took an extreme attitude.

He was one of the most extreme at the Jewish Congress in 1868-1869. He was a magnificent preacher and traveled to all of the kehilus [organized religious communities] and spoke against the new reforms. He was a moralist and a Hasid of Reb Chaim Halberstam of Sandz. He led his life according to the customs of the Hasidim. After the death in 1863 of Rabbi, Reb Gershon Ben Yehudah, the author of Avodas HaGershon [The Works of Gershon], the son-in-law of Reb

Menakhem Mendl of Kosev, Reb Hillel Lichtenstein became rabbi of Kolomea in 1867. He brought about the opposition by the progressive people and followers of the Enlightenment because of his extreme attitude toward the question of education and his opposition to the achievements of the emancipation. They, in his opinion, caused

[Page 43]

the discarding of the yoke of tradition [and adherence] to heresy and to the Enlightenment. He preached that they wait patiently for the coming of Moshiakh [the Redeemer or Messiah].

When he acquired the rabbinical seat in Kolomea, he also began to exert influence on the rabbis and rebbes, that they should call together an assembly of rabbis in the manner of the Hungarian Orthodox in order to enact rules about separating "the pious from the destructive." In 1883 an assembly of rabbis was called in Lemberg and as a result of this assembly the Khevra Makhzikei haDas [Society to Uphold the Faith] was created.

All of his thoughts were focused on the damage to religious Jewry according to the style of the Hungarian orthodoxy. He strongly opposed orthodoxy in the style of Reb Azriel Hildesheimer and his heirs. He came out especially against his son, Hirsh Hildesheimer, because he recommended the founding of schools in Eretz-Yisroel. He saw "sinners and villains" in support of this plan that would cause greater wickedness than Christian clergymen who try with much money to catch [Jews] in their nets, but their success is very small.[39] In Galicia it was thought a sin that he took part in the Congress of Hungarian Orthodoxy.

During the days of the Tisa Eslar Proces [blood libel and trial in Tiszaeszlar, Hungary involving the death of 14-year old peasant girl], he accepted that the anti-Semites and their stories were just "God's messengers" and "the sinful Jews spoke uselessly, that their entire hatred and intention was to corrupt, God forbid, God fearing persons, because they are "...am le'ba'dad yish'kon..." [Numbers, 23:9 – "...lo, it is a people that shall dwell alone..."] and do not mix with the gentiles, do not eat and drink with them and they have no complaints about them."

In his thoughts and beliefs about fundamentals (precepts) of Yidishkeit [Jewish way of life], Eretz-Yisroel occupied a central position. He had an absolute hatred for the exile.

"In some nations there were good kings and their rulers and residents were people of mercy, as in other nations and in all of the nations of our King, may his glory be enhanced. However, we see ourselves as strangers who are called 'patient ones' and those who say the opposite are non-believers in the dogma of dogmas of the faith and do not take into account the Jewish nation that believes and is devoted to the faith in God." However, he was an opponent of the Ahavat Zion [Lovers of Zion] and of Baron Rothschild's work in Eretz-Yisroel.

He was against erecting schools in Eretz-Yisroel and he turned to the supervisors of all the communities in Jerusalem with an appeal

[Page 44]

in which he publicly came out against Hildesheimer, "who wanted to create szkoles [szkole is the Polish word for secular schools] (schools) in Jerusalem, the Holy City," because, according to his understanding, it was incomprehensible: "If he truly wants the colonization of Israel, why does he need szkoles and to dress Jews in French clothing, as this is not necessary for agricultural work?"

He was against cooperation with those who, according to him, would bring shame upon the Jewish people and "for whom all mitzvahs that were connected to the land were worth nothing" and "they put on French clothing so that we no longer recognize that they are Jews."

"Therefore we said: It is time to do for God, a time to build and to create unions for Eretz-Yisroel according to the Torah and mitzvah [commandment] that this is the practical purpose of a true Eretz-Yisroel and to appoint as leaders the great men of Israel who will serve as eyes for the congregation, so that it does not yield a hair of the Shulchan Aruch [book codifying Jewish laws] and of Jewish customs. And they will attempt to establish colonies and to employ God fearing appointees so that they will be seen to be keeping the mitzvus [commandments] that are connected with the land."[41][The designation for footnote #40 is missing.]

In the course of his talk he was not deterred even from criticizing the earlier settlers and the Lovers of Zion stating that their purpose "was not to found villages in the land of our forefathers, but their intention was to increase the denial of existence of God, filling the land with secular schools and houses of prostitution – this was their tendency."

In exile he saw – a deviation from the way of Torah. In the Jews taking root in lands of exile he saw the danger of their complete assimilation. Because of this he was opposed to learning the language of the land. And "if the dignitaries of the country demand this of us, explicitly saying to us that only with this condition could the respect and freedom that is called equality be given to us, then we need to do everything that is possible in order not to agree to this. We also need to tell them that we do not want any freedom that causes our slavery for eternity and that we have a country that is ours by inheritance, a land that is called the holy land and only this rosy land is called Palestine by us, about which we pray and every day look to return there, although we have respect and freedom in other nations."

The basis of his conception of the world was the conclusion that during this long exile we went through various times, bad and good. It was now a time when the Jews had become very

[Page 45]

loathsome to the gentile nations who pursued all kinds of persecutions and the Jews withdrew from them and they were abused in all matters and the exile from this standpoint had for each generation good and bad, but the good side was outweighed; the bad was that which was against common sense and against the habits of human spirit; because one God had created us and we all have one God; yet he created me and him from one belly. Then how can we betray him? And the good is by which we are belittled and estranged from them, and it does not even suit them to speak with us and those who do talk are unified with us, brought closer and mix with us – thanks to this, Jews remain an "am l'vadad yishkon [a nation that lives alone - Numbers 23:9]."

Rabbi Lichtenstein was convinced that no foundation for the traditional life was present in the lands of exile, but that the Jews needed to avoid every contact with the non-Jews and avoid every move towards their life. The young must not learn anything other than – Torah or a trade – and not the wisdom and not the writing in the language of the people. His worries about his beliefs about the religious way of life can be found in judgments carved with a lead quill in the memory of generations. This was embraced in great part, at his initiative, at the rabbinical conference in Michalovce [Nagymihály, Hungary] in 1866.

He rose above all afflictions of the world and in his eyes all of human life was a matter of suffering: a person was tested through all kinds of trouble and he became refined by poverty in order to be able to better his way. And the Torah was the rope with which God lowered us from heaven to the earth. And "whoever holds it will not sink in the depth of the sea of afflictions in exile."

He held in esteem the ways of the Hasidim and the rebbes and believed that they were the tzadikim [righteous men] of the generation. In his program for Eretz-Yisroel, he was strongly influenced by Reb Akiva Josef Schlesinger (1838-1922), who married his daughter in 1860 and was with him in Kolomea oyf kest [support given by her father to a daughter's husband so that he could study Torah] for approximately 10 years.[42] Reb Akiva helped a great deal in the leadership of the yeshiva and in his communal activity. Following Rabbi Lichtenstein's initiative, Reb Akiva Josef Schlesinger was chosen as a member of the Beis Din [rabbinic court] in Kolomea. In his old age, Reb Hillel Lichtenstein wanted to emigrate

[Page 46]

to Eretz-Yisroel. His Hasidim collected money in order for him to be able to fulfill his desire. But he did not emigrate to Eretz-Yisroel.

When Schlesinger's son-in-law and brother-in-law worked on the creation of Petah Tikva and laid the cornerstone, Rabbi Lichtenstein sent money to buy building lots in order to settle two families of pious Jews there.

Rabbi Lichtenstein himself was involved in a quarrel about the shoykhet [ritual slaughterer] who was accepted in Kolomea that broke out at that time in Kolomea between him and the Wisznicer Rebbe. The quarrels lasted a long time and the kehile was divided. The two sides struggled in the synagogues and in the bati-medrashim [houses of prayer]. It was such an embittered struggle that the police had to become involved in the matter and it was even necessary to call the army to help. In such a situation, it was difficult for Rabbi Lichtenstein to help his son-in-law and he devoted himself to collecting money for the settlements in Eretz-Yisroel. In addition, the Wisznicer Rebbe expressed his opposition to Schlesinger who in 1884 visited rabbis and admorim [our lords, teachers and masters – title of Hasidic rabbis] in Galicia about help in the matter of settling pious Jews in Petah Tikvah, and warned him to stop spreading propaganda on the part of the agricultural settlement in Eretz-Yisroel. This threw fear into Rabbi Lichtenstein who already knew the strong hand of the Wisznicer Rebbe and did not want to enter a new quarrel in his old age.

Rabbi Lichtenstein gave the bill of sale for the lots of land in Petah Tikvah as a documented gift to the leaders of the Kolel Ungarn [union of kehiles from Hungary] in Jerusalem, Chaim Zonenfeld and Yakov Blumental. It was said in their declaration that was published in the Orthodox press: "If for now we will not have anything to do with the lots, is it because bavoynese ynu-ho ra'bim [in the view of our many sins – said with the presumption of an unfavorable development] an appropriate time has not yet arrived so that Israel's children can sit in the Holy Land in joy and calm, each one under his vineyard and rainbow? Or because every step is surrounded by cliffs of temptation and stumbling blocks? However, we accepted the lots for the coming day (may it be God's will) that will, quickly in our days, bring salvation and relief for Jews. The agricultural worker will build his house and work his field undisturbed. And in order to show that the gaon [brilliant man] and tzadek [righteous man] loves charity, it is our duty to announce to all brother contributors who have helped through the tzadek that this gift of money

[Page 47]

reached the correct source, the desired place and with peace for Israel."

First, Rabbi Lichtenstein gave the document to his wife and children so that they could settle on the lots. Then he heard that the lots could pass again to the authority of the Turkish government if five years pass without the payment of taxes. Therefore he returned to his first decision and gave the lots to the Kolel Ungarn as a gift with the provision that these lots should be a Karen Kamyemes [permanent fund] for always and that it be named after him.

However, his request was only half fulfilled; the supervisors of Kolel Ungarn announced their opposition to his provisions in the press.

They tried to sell his lots several times; Rabbi Lichtenstein did not permit this harsh goal to be carried out, and the lots were sold only after his death to the officials of Baron Rothschild despite the sharp protest and the declaration of his son-in-law, Schlesinger.[43]

Rabbi Lichtenstein, feeling that his end was approaching, called all of the leaders of the Kolomea kehile to him, preached musar [a stress on spiritual and ethical discipline] to them and told them how to behave after his death and that they should not stray from the path of Torah and its minutest restraints.[44]

His religious extremism was so great that, according to his student and biographer Tzwi Hirsh Heler in his book, Beit Hillel [House of Hillel], Munkacs, 1893, they had purchased a donkey for him in order to fulfill the mitzvah [commandment] of peter khamor [the redemption of the first donkey] and he also had sheep in order to fulfill the mitzvah of reishit hagez [providing the kohanim – high priests – with the first shearing from the sheep raised in Eretz-Yisroel].

He died in Kolomea on the 10th of Iyyar [18 May], 5651 (1891).

As a preacher he was a people's speaker, "whose mouth was like a torch." There was no doubt that despite his extreme views according to which he did not even fear a split in Jewish life, Rabbi Lichtenstein was one of the esteemed personalities of his generation.

Rabbi Lichtenstein left a large number of sforim [books] that were in the largest part books of sermons and musar.

And these are the sforim: 1) Lev haIvri [Heart of the Jew] two parts. The first part is a commentary on Chasam Sofers Tzava [Chasam Sofer – seal of the scribe – Chasam Sofer's Will], around 1864; 2) Maskil

[Page 48]

el Dal [Contemplating the Needy] in four parts, around 1867-1871, Lemberg, 1870-1871, a collection of sermons; 3) Avkat Rokhel [The Perfumer's Powders] Lemberg, 1883; 4) he published an appeal in Yiddish (86 pages) entitled El Haadarim - Oyfruf tsu Ale Treye Yidish Kinder [To the Flock – Appeal to All Loyal/Devoted Jewish Children], Preszburg, 1864; 5) a book, Et La'asot [It is Time – from Psalm 119:126 – "For it is time to act for God..."]. And these are the contents of the book: questions and responses, how to show the people the way in which to go, the deeds that they should do, two parts, Lemberg, 1872-1878. These teachings are the most important of all his treatises. This is a musar-sefer [book of teaching on ethical behavior], written in the form of short questions and answers in matters of musar, Yires 4 [Awe 4] as well as in concrete matters, particularly about the struggle between the Orthodox and the followers of reforms. He demanded the exclusion from the Jewish collective of each Jew who did not follow the Torah in all its details and he strongly prohibited marriage with these people and that they be counted in a minyon [10 men necessary for prayer] because all of those who do not observe the laws of the Torah and tradition are violators of the law. Despite his extremist Orthodoxy, this book is distinguished by his ethical standing and with his devotion to the principles of Jewish ethics. Other of his other treatises that should be mentioned: 1) Makre Dardeke [Teacher of Children], commentaries on the Torah, Lemberg-Kolomea, 1888-1899; 2) Beth Hillel [House of Hillel], questions and answers, Satmar, 1908; 3) Shire Maskil [Scholarly Songs], sermons, Lemberg, 1877.

After him, Reb Uri Feywl [19*] ben [son of] Yisroel Moshe haLevi Schreier, who was the rabbi in Borotshyn [Bohorodczany], the author of The Great Ones of Holiness and the Small Temple, one of the founders and leaders of communal settlement in Eretz-Yisroel, Ahavat Zion [Lovers of Zion], was chosen as rabbi. In his old age, he returned to the rabbinical chair in Borotshyn and died there in 1898. After him, Reb Yakov ben Efraim Taumim, a descendent of Chacham Tzvi, was chosen as rabbi. He was the rabbi in Wielkie Oczy, then in Tarnograd, Poland. As he was driven out of there because he was an Austrian subject, he was invited to take up the rabbinical seat in Kolomea. He was the rabbi there from 1898 until his death on 2nd of the month of Iyyar, [May 3rd] 5688 (1908).

5.

In the course of time changes took place in politics in relation to the Jews in Galicia. In 1876, the municipal administration demanded that the kehile hasten to carry out the reorgan-

[Page 49]

ization. Shomer Yisroel [Guardian of Israel] made efforts to stabilize the status of the kehilus [organized Jewish communities – kehile is the singular] by arranging a uniform status, approved by the government and uniting all of the kehilus in one national union.

For this purpose, Shomer Yisroel called together the kehilus for a kehilus- day in order to deal with all the problems that were connected to the life of the Jews in Galicia. The Kolomea kehile was represented at the kehilus-day in Lemberg, from the 18h to the 20th June 1878, by its chairman, Shlomo Hersh Wizelberg, who was elected to the presidium of the conference along with Rachmiel Mizes and Dr. [Emil] Bik. Wizelberg was the second vice president; he also was president of the charter committee and he took an active part in the debates. A standing committee that was to be involved with the organization of the kehilus was elected before the close of the conference. Wizelberg was elected as second vice president.

Meanwhile, the elections to the Viennese parliament drew near. The Shomer Yisroel circles that had approached the parliamentary elections in 1873 with the slogan of an independent Jewish politics, renounced the idea in 1879. This time they did not prepare for the elections.

The Poles made use of the situation; Rabbi, Reb Shimeon Schreiber, one of the leaders of the extreme Orthodox, who created the society, Mahazike ha-Dat [Defenders of the Faith], as an organization struggling against the enlightened was presented as a candidate in Kolomea. A Jewish journalist from Vienna, Aleksander Scharf, stood against him. But, after a short time, he withdrew his candidacy.

Rabbi Schreiber received 1,443 votes out of 2,251 at the election.

Rabbi Schreiber was elected on the condition that as president of the "Defenders of the Faith," and together with its spiritual leader, the Belzer Rebbe, he would influence the pious in all of the counties of Galicia to support the candidates of Kolo Polskje [Polish Circle].

After Rabbi Schreiber was elected, he never took part in the parliamentary debates because he did not know any other language besides Yiddish. But he always voted according to the instructions from Kolo. Once, when the vote

[Page 50]

occurred on erev Shabbos [on the eve of Shabbos], Kolo arranged for there to be a minyon [10 men necessary for prayer] in the parliamentary building so that Rabbi Schreiber could be at the voting. Rabbi Schreiber died in 1883 and elections were held in Kolomea. The Jewish intelligentsia in the voting circles of Kolomea-Buczacz-Sniatyn required a candidate to be entered who would have the standing to represent the Jews in parliament and know his way around the political problems. The election committee in these cities turned to the rabbi of Florisdorf, Dr. Josef Shmuel Block, who was born in Dukla and asked him to offer his candidacy to parliament. It is true that they placed the condition that he join the Polish faction. In his youth, Dr. Block was known for his great knowledge of the Talmud and he had a reputation as the "child prodigy of Dukla." Ten years after his death, new ideas about the Torah were issued in his name.

After he left Galicia he dedicated himself to worldly studies. He graduated from the university and was welcomed– after he had been the rabbi in several smaller kehilus – as rabbi in Florisdorf. He became famous at this time thanks to his bold struggle against anti-Semitism, and particularly because of his appearance against Prof. Rohling [22*] of Prague, revealing his egregious forgeries from the Talmud. In Dr. Block, the Galician Jews saw the fighter for Jewry. After Dr. Block agreed to the conditions of the election committee, he was officially presented as a candidate to the Viennese parliament. In Lemberg, the Jewish notables, with Dr. Emil Bik and the preacher, Bernhard Lewenstein, at the head, came out against Block. The contention was that a deputy who was connected to Galicia with an internal-national alliance (Poland) must be elected. On the 1st of May a meeting, under the chairmanship of Dr. Philip Druker, took place in the kehile house. Dr. Philip Manish, the leader of Shomer Yisroel who contended that it was necessary to have political representation and not theologians such as Dr. Block in parliament, was against Block.

At the initiative of Lemberg, several kehilus in Galicia urged the residents of Kolomea to elect Dr. Bik.[45]

The Polish central election committee recommended the

[Page 51]

candidacy of Dr. Yohatan Warszawer of Krakow and the gabbai of the Belzer Rebbe, Reb Mordekhai Pelc, recommended the candidacy of the Christian, Baron Romaszkan.

Although Dr. Block was supported by the president of parliament, Dr. Smolka, the Poles boycotted him. Despite this "all-sided" opposition, Dr. Block was elected with a majority of two-thirds of the vote, although he had not appeared even once in the voting district.

After the voting, he visited the cities of his voting district and he was received there with great enthusiasm by the Jewish masses. The leaders of the parnosim of the kehilus and the members of the city councils did not appear at the welcome in honor of Dr. Block. In particular, Dr. Maksimilian Trachtenberg, the Jewish city president [mayor] of Kolomea, boycotted him. In parliament, Dr. Block fulfilled his task as Jewish representative.

In 1885 the parliament session closed and new elections were declared. Dr. Block turned to a member of the Vaad haKehile [Council of the Jewish community] and of the city council, Shlomo Hersh Wizelberg, with an announcement that he would come to Kolomea to give a report about his parliamentary activity. True, Wizelberg was only a vinkl-advokat [23*] and although he did not have any higher legal education, he surpassed every Kolomea lawyer and he had political influence in city hall and in the kehile. Wizelberg advised Dr. Block that he should not come to Kolomea because this time he did not have a chance of being elected. Dr. Emil Bik had won over the members of the city council and the parnosim of the kehilus, as well as the government apparatus. However, Dr. Block was not scared off and he came to Kolomea. He was welcomed with enthusiasm and he became convinced that the mass of Jewish voters were with him.

In Kolomea itself a "Block party" was founded with the name "the Good Youth." This was Jakov Brelter and his entire family, which had a great influence in the city.

At that time elections also took place for the city council. The Poles worked skillfully in these elections. Their leader was Wishniewski. This Wishniewski was a man of high culture, had traveled around the European countries a great deal, was rich and a philanthropist. As a member of the city council

[Page 52]

he suggested the naming of two streets in the Jewish quarter after Spinoza and Mendelssohn. His suggestion was accepted. Wishniewski concluded an election agreement with the Block party, according to which he was obligated to support the candidacy of Dr. Block to parliament, if the members of the Block party during the election to city hall supported the election of the Polish candidate for city president [mayor].

Wishniewski and Stanislaw Szczopanowski, the authors of the book, The Desolution of Galicia, took it upon themselves to carry on propaganda for the election of Dr. Block. He was supported by Franciszek Smolka and the well known Polish deputy, Count Potocki. But the Central Polish Election Committee presented Dr. Bik. The followers of Dr. Bik carried on a hard fight against Block. Jan Dobczanski, the representative of the Central Polish Election Committee, specially visited Kolomea and warned the citizens that they should not vote for Dr. Block. In Buczacz, the Jewish city president, Berish Shtern, threatened the Jews and the Christian voters. He said that Dr. Block was an enemy of the Christians and that they must not vote for him. These elections were a great event. Enthusiasm reigned in all of the districts. The women went to the cemeteries to pray for the success of the elections. The city instilled terror at the voting boxes. But despite this, the Jewish voters in Kolomea, Buczasz and Snytyn were not scared off and they went to the voting boxes. It is true that propagandists from Dr. Bik's side falsified documents and used all kinds of schemes. In Kolomea, Wizelberg declared that Dr. Bik had promised to build a new synagogue for the Jews and a new church for the Christians if he were only elected. But all of this was of no help. Dr. Block was elected with a majority of 28 votes.

Two months after the elections to parliament, elections to the city council took place and the Jews supported Wiszniewski in the spirit of the agreement that had been made.

At the end of 1890 the term of office of the parliament session ended and the new elections were set for the beginning of 1891. The opponents of Dr. Block began to dig in against him in the voting districts. Dr. Emil Bik was not presented against him then, although he had in the last years carried out for the voters of Kolo-

[Page 53]

mea, Snytyn and Buczasz all trials in the Lemberg land courts without payment. In his place was presented Leon Meizlish, one of the grandsons of the well known Warsaw Rabbi, Reb Dov Berish Meizlish; he was the son-in-law of Brodski, the Jewish millionaire, but his wife did not want to live with him. After many years during which he filed many legal cases against her, he gave her a religious divorce and in 1890 he received compensation of a million guldn.

The initiator of his candidacy was Reb Mordekhai Pelc, the gabbai [man who assists in running of synagogue] for the Belzer rebbe, who was angry with Dr. Block because he did not want to contribute 5,000 guldn to the newspaper, Mahazike ha-Dat [Defenders of the Faith] or collect this sum among the Viennese Jews. Out of anger, he proclaimed Leon Meizlish as the candidate of Jewish Orthodoxy in Galicia.

Meizlish declared that he must receive the mandate even if it cost him hundreds of thousand of guldn. Doubts grew about his Austrian citizenship because he had lived for many years in Paris; the mayor of Buczasz, Berish Shtern, helped him sort out his Austrian citizenship and also his voting rights. Meizlish's agents spread money right and left, spread polemical writings in Hebrew and Yiddish in which the writings of Dr. Block on the subject of Biblical criticism were assaulted.

Ignatz Shreiber, the president of Mahazike ha-Dat, published a Yiddish leaflet in which he declared that the activity of Dr. Block in parliament was considered to be against the pious Jews. The Belzer Rebbe also issued an appeal against Dr. Block.

The Poles again offered their candidate, a well know enemy of Israel [the Jews], Count Staczinski, who was supported by Polish officialdom. It is interesting that the assimilated, who were concentrated around the weekly newspaper, Oczyzna [Homeland], came out against Dr. Block. The officials of the district began with various threats against the Jewish voters. The regime clearly recommended the candidacy of Staczinski. In addition to this, the Prime Minister sent a warning letter to the governor of Galicia.

This time Dr. Block was supported by Dr. Bik. The leaders of the Kolomea kehile, Shlomo Hersh Wizelberg, Yakov Bretler, Josef Funkenshtein, even publicly appealed to the voters

[Page 54]

under the name Dover Beytu [In Good Time] in which the representatives of the kehile demanded that only Dr. Josef Shmuel Block should be elected.

The kehile representatives took on a reserved attitude for as long as the struggle between Dr. Block and Dr. Bik went on. With the appearance of the candidacy of Meizlish, the kehile found it necessary to recommend Dr. Block and to declare that one must not vote for Meizlish. This appeal contributed to the unity of all voters. [24*]

The elections took place on the 4th and 5th of March, 1891. The voting passed calmly in Buczacz and in Snytyn. Terrible unrest took place in Kolomea. The peasants who supported the candidacy of Staczinski marched through the streets of the city and attacked the businesses, which closed immediately. A number of Jews were wounded and one Jew was stabbed to death. The peasants also damaged the Jewish cemetery. Despite the terror, the Jews in most of the cities in the county were not frightened off and they went to the voting boxes. Dr. Block was elected with 2,128 votes. Staczinski received 1,778 votes and only 97 voted for Meizlish who had squandered so much money.

The position of Dr. Block, who voted for Jewish interests at every opportunity, was very difficult in the new parliament. The "Social Christians," with Duke Lichtenstein at the head, began to fear the Polish faction, that it should eliminate his position. The president of the Polish Club, Zaleski, was interested in removing Dr. Block. He used the opportunity of a protest against the elections in the voting district, Kolomea, Buczacz, Snytyn and demanded of Dr. Block that he kindly decline the mandate. On the 22nd of October, 1895, Dr. Block withdrew.

New elections were held in the district. Dr. Block again presented his candidacy. The mayor, Dr. Maksimillian Trachtenberg, who was even supported by the anti-Semites, Dr. Karl Lueger and Ernst Schneider, was presented against him because they were interested in every opportunity to eliminate

[Page 55]

Dr. Block and remove him from the parliamentary political arena.

As a lawyer, Dr. Trachtenberg was convicted in 1891by the lawyers' chamber in Lemberg with a fine of 300 guldn for violating the honor of the position of lawyer and in 1892 – with a fine of 100 guldn.

The country committee determined that as the mayor he bring deposits from outside to the bank and, because of a series of swindles and abuses with these deposits, his management was considered as complete anarchy.[46] The Polish Club, with the support of the Austrian Prime Minister, the Polish Count Badeni, made every effort to disrupt the election of Dr. Block. The district executives received exact instructions to use every means possible for this purpose and they did everything they could: they demanded a tax from Jewish manufacturers of 500 guldn for Dr. Trachtenberg's election fund. The tax commission summoned Jews and warned them not to vote for Dr. Block. On election day, gendarmes guarded the entrances to the voting boxes and stopped Jewish voters.

The leaders of the anti-Semites in Vienna demanded in a telegram that in no way should Dr. Block be permitted to be elected. Thanks to such terror, Dr. Trachtenberg was elected and he sat in parliament until 1900, not achieving anything there.[46]

On the 28th of September 1900, in connection with the election in 1901, Adolf Stand proposed to Dr. Theodor Herzl that he present his candidacy to the Viennese parliament in Kolomea because the surest mandate was there. On that occasion Stand wrote to Dr. Herzl about Trachtenberg, the Kolomea deputy, that he is "a marionette in the Polish faction," but he is "adept in klabrias" (playing cards [klabrias is a card game]). His politics is – "Silent and quiet." His work program in Vienna is: he wakes up in Donacher (a well-known cabaret in Vienna) and sleeps during the parliamentary sessions.[47]

The Zionist shareholders' committee in Vienna and Dr. Herzl, himself, rejected the proposal from Adolf Stand and the Zionists did not present any candidates and did not take any

[Page 56]

active part in the elections. Dr. Natan Zejnfeld, the candidate of the Poles who represented the city during the years 1901-1906, was elected in Kolomea.

[Page 56]

History of the Jews of Kolomea (cont.)

6.

The city of Kolomea grew strongly at the close of the 1870's. There was growth both in the economic sense and in numbers. With development, the Jewish population also grew. From 8,234 Jewish residents in 1880 to 12,002 souls, or 51.9 percent of the general population, which numbered 23,109 souls.)[25*]The number of Jews in all of Kolomea County reached 19,777 souls, which represented 17.40 percent of the general population (the non-Jewish population reached 89,704 souls). Of the 19,777 Jews, 15,949 (83.2 percent) were found in the cities and shtetlekh; 2,262 Jewish souls lived in 69 villages (11.8 percent); and in estates – 966 Jews (5 percent).

In 1890, the number of Jews in the Kolomea district reached 24,116 souls who made up 18.4 percent of the general population, of them – 19,727 (84.3 percent) in the cities and shtetlekh and 4,889 in the villages. In 1900 the number of Jews reached 26,020 (19.7 percent of the general population), of these 21,893 (83.4 percent) in the cities and shtetlekh and 4,177 in the villages.

In 1890 in Kolomea itself there were 30,235 residents, of them 14,927 Jews (49.4 percent) and in 1900 there were 16,568 Jews (48.5 percent) from a population of 34,188 people. In 1910, 18,930 from a population of 42,676 people were found in Kolomea, that is, 44.3 percent of the general city population.

It should be mentioned that in comparison to the general number of residents in Kolomea, during the years 1880-1910, the percentage of

[Page 57]

the Jews was smaller than 51.9 percent in 1880 until it went down to 44.3 percent in 1910. In 1880 the general population of the number of residents in Kolomea was – 23,109, and of them – 12,002 Jews. In contrast, the general population in 1910 increased to 42,676 souls and of them only 18,930 Jews. In the years 1881-1901, the general population grew by 84.7 percent and the Jewish population by 57.7 percent.

The Jewish possession of land in the county reached 3,053 hectares in 1889 (6.2 percent) and in 1902 – 4,416 hectares.[48]

Changes in the economic conditions should be mentioned. In this era, the economic situation of the Kolomea Jews was sustained by the agricultural hinterland of the area. Besides the large land owners among the Polish magnates and the prosperity of the Ukrainian peasants, the effects of the constitutional freedom created also a visible status for the Jewish landowners and pachters [lessees] on estates, as well as in Jewish agriculture. The main trade concentrated in Jewish hands was in products: wheat, beans, oats and cows that was taken note of in the provinces of Austria and exported abroad, particularly to Germany – to the port cities of Bremen and Hamburg. This trade employed a number of Jews as agents.

The Jews were also employed in crafts in a visible mass, particularly in tailoring. The Kolomea tailors were known as tradesmen for sewing the long robes for the priests. They specialized in this, and the sewing of long coats was a separate branch of the clothing industry.

Almost all branches of trade, such as shoemaking, locksmithing, blacksmithing, tinsmithing, weaving, carpetmaking, tanning and so on, were in Jewish hands.

[Page 58]

In Werbish a Jew founded a match factory and he employed 149 Jewish workers in it and only eight Christian workers. The majority of the girls in this factory worked 12 hours a day. A girl received 25-30 Kreuzers a day or for sorting a thousand matches – 4 Kreuzers. Men received a weekly wage of 4-5 gulden.

The paraffin candle factory employed 50 Jewish workers (20 men and 30 girls) who received 20-25 Kreuzers daily (a quarter gulden) for 12 hours of work.

Various industries developed in Kolomea itself and in the surrounding area that employed Jewish workers and employees such as the candle industry and sawmills that arose at the end of the 19th century and in the beginning of the 20th century. In 1883 the talis [prayer shawl] industry also arose. Reb Shimshon Heler, a Hasid of the Boyaner Rebbe, searching for an income, ordered looms from Germany and he brought a weaving specialist from there, who in the course of several months taught the Jews the trade of weaving and knitting talisim. After the Jews had learned the trade, Shimshon Heler began to manufacture talisim. In the course of a short time he succeeded in developing favorable markets for his goods in Austria and other nations. He ran his factory in a Jewish way. In the evening he would interrupt the work in order to say the minkhah [afternoon] and maariv [evening] prayers. The majority of workers were also Boyaner Hasidim.[49]

In time another factory of this kind was founded and a number of workers who had acquired looms also worked in their homes. The well known talisim factories were those of Reb Shimshon Heler, Yona Zager and Asher Winershawer. There were a number of smaller manufacturers. They mostly employed weavers who would work in their own houses. This industry employed a significant number of talisim weavers. The talisim weavers would also knit atorus [ornamental collars for the talisim]. After their strike (a serious situation for them), the talisim weavers were organized and joined the Austrian weavers union whose central office was in Vienna. The greater number of them still worked on hand looms. The situation for the weavers was difficult. They received a wage of three gulden a week for a 15 hour day. In addition the manufacturers demanded that they work at six to seven looms. The weavers' situation was desperate. In August 1892,

[Page 59]

the weaving workers declared a strike at the rabbi's house. Four hundred weaving workers joined in the strike.

A large meeting took place on the 24th of July, 1892, in the large synagogue at which the old weaver, Hirsh Leib "Duniak," and Chaim Drisek spoke. They proposed a series of motions with demands for the manufacturers. Other workers also took part in this meeting. They were already organized in the Social-Democratic movement that had begun its activity in Kolomea in 1890. At its head stood the student, Maks Ceterboim, a founder of the P.P.S [Polish Socialist Party] in Eastern Galicia. This movement made use of this opportunity and placed the strikers under its support. Then at this meeting, when the Aron Kodesh [holy ark - cabinet holding the Torah scrolls] was opened, the weavers swore that there would be solidarity in the strike since the manufacturers would not want to agree to their three demands, namely: a) an increase in worker wages; b) an eight-hour work day; c) being paid during times of illness. The manufacturers did not want to accept these demands and, in addition, they dismissed the leaders. The weavers declared a strike.

This strike, which was organized by Mashulam Lubish, made an impression across the entire nation.

The Socialist-Democratic press in Vienna published accurate reports with pictures of the weavers in their Jewish clothing and established with great satisfaction that the socialist idea had penetrated the Jewish neighborhood in the most eastern corner of Austria. The Viennese Arbeiter Zeitung [Workers Newspaper] that strongly opposed the Zionist movement which had arisen then in Austria under the leadership of Dr. Nathan Birnboim, made use of this opportunity in order to attack the Zionists and to describe the Kolomea manufacturers, whose pictures were published with a Mogen Dovid [Star of David] on their Jewish noses, as Zionists who abuse and exploit the Jewish workers.

Dr. Birnboim did not, it should be understood, owe them any answer.[50]

The Hebrew bi-weekly, Hem, which was then published in Kolomea under the editorship of Dovid Yeshaya Zilberbush, said that the talisim weavers were very far from every [form of] socialism and it could not be determined if their strike was a

[Page 60]

class-political awakening. And that the weavers, Jews, Hasidim, who say three times a day, "May our eyes behold Your return to Zion," demand only an improved material condition. Zilberbush suggested that the Viennese Zionists collect money and enable the weavers to create their own factory on a cooperative basis. Napszud, the organ of the P.P.S. in Krakow, published detailed reports in which the weavers were portrayed as fighters with proletarian class-consciousness. However, it did not forget to underline that this strike was carried to success thanks to the rabbi of the city who implored all those striking not to return to work as long as their demands were not being fulfilled. Pobudka, the socialist newspaper of the Polish emigrants in Paris, also published an article in which it was said that this strike shows the stubborn class-struggle among the Jews.

Meanwhile the strike continued for week after week and there were even outbursts to the extent that the police mixed in and arrested several workers. The Socialist Democratic Party in Vienna sent the strike committee several hundred gulden to help the strikers and their families, and the weavers in Upper Austria received decrees not to take any work from the Kolomea manufacturers who tried to send raw material so that they would weave talisim.

Shortly after the outbreak of the strike, one manufacturer, Yona Zager, brought Jewish weavers from Russia. But they were forced by the strikers, who attacked them, to flee from Kolomea. Then the manufacturers tried to send the raw material to the Austrian weaving plants; but they were unsuccessful with this because the talisim did not turn out as well as when they were produced by the Jewish weavers. A declaration from the strikers was even published in the Social-Democratic organ, Robotnik [Worker], in Lemberg,[51] signed by Yerakhmil Blechner, Dovid Glat, Borukh Shaler, Moshe Cypser, Shmuel Dager, Shimeon Eyferman, Shmuel Schechter, Khona Hecht, Kopl Shlose, Dovid Chohen, Lipe Haker, Yisroel, Yissakhar, Moshe Berger, Meir Reich, Kopl Haber, Zeidl Haber, Wolf Hilzenfot, Shlomo Dovid Schecter, Ayzyk Rozenkranc, Gecl Frydman, Meir Wechter, Shmuel Teicher, Avraham Moshe Wolpn, Nisen Teper,

[Page 61]

Nusan Bretler, Leib Shprechman, Moshe Krel, Avraham Cwi Zalc, Chaim Grazer, Avraham Zalcman, Shmuel Shneiberg, Meri Shauder, Leizer Adolf, Noakh Zalchauer, Alter Korman, Khona Ciglrauch, Meir Shimkha Shloser, Asher Adolf and Itse Shneiberger. In this declaration it was said that the talisim weavers in Kolomea, who were being exploited by the capitalists in a dreadful manner, were convinced that the exploitation of the human work force and the solitude would not disappear as long as socialism was not victorious, that is, until the factories and all capital were in the possession of the community. Therefore, the talisim weavers declared that they were devoted to international social-democracy.

It is difficult to accept that this declaration was not sent at the initiation of the P.P.S. who wanted such a demonstration that this was the strike of socialist class-conscious workers. The weavers also organized in an independent union with the name Einikeit [Unity].

The strike ended three months later – during the course of time several workers began to work in their own homes on hand-looms and many left the city and emigrated to America. From then on a visible decline began in this industry in Kolomea.

The cleaning of swine hair was another industry in the shtetl and a visible number of Jewish workers were employed as sorters of swine hair. This hair was sent to Leipzig and there it was prepared in various factories.

These workers were organized and paid a membership fee. They also brought a designated sum to a common treasury that would serve in the case of a need during a strike.

The water carriers were a special class of workers. They were organized in a group. Their number was 14. Each one of them had a wagon with a large, long barrel and four water cans – hitched to a horse. The city was divided by them into 14 regions, according to the number of the water carriers (14). Each water carrier had an established region for his "monopoly." He sold the water there every day; two cans for one Kreuzer and for carrying the water into the home one paid

[Page 62]

from 40 to 70 Kreuzers monthly. Each water carrier employed one or two workers. They received 50 Kreuzers a day from him.

The passenger transportation in the city and outside of the city was in the hands of Jewish wagon drivers. There were 25 two-horse coaches, 38 coaches hitched with one horse and 20 cargo wagons in the city. The wagon drivers earned from 12 to 14 gulden a week. From this sum, seven gulden went to cover the expenses and to take care of the horses.

The majority of them received the money to buy the coaches and cargo wagons from Baron Hirsch's Fund.

After the weavers' strike, the P.P.S. [Polish Socialist Party] attempted to organize the bakers, the workers in the candle and match factories, only this was not successful.

At the beginning of the 20th century, Jewish merchants plunged into a new branch [of commerce], namely: selling carpets that were the hand work of the peasants in the surrounding area, particularly in Kosiv, Zablotov, Kitev, Snitin, Pechenizhyn, Horodenka. At that time, A. Hilman founded a carpet factory in Kosiv. The factory employed 60-70 trade workers, of them a number of Jews. The Kolomea Jewish agents sold these carpets in all of Galicia.

Attempts were made at the end of the 19th century to better the economic condition of the Jews. The JCA [Jewish Colonization Association], the Allianz society in Vienna and, later, also the Ezra society (aid organization for the Jews suffering from need in Galicia) worked in this area.

According to statistical figures, among the 14,000 Jews in Kolomea in the year 1898 only 100 were well-to-do.

In 1898 the JCA society created a loan office to disperse money to craftsmen, small merchants and shopkeepers. The first offices of the JCA were created in Tarnow, Stanislaw and Kolomea.

In the years 1899-1900 14,233 loans with a sum of 2,146,059 kronen were given through the loan office in Kolomea and 1,925,087 kronen were paid back.

In 1908, 2,974 people belonged to this loan fund. The sum that the members

[Page 63]

obtained reached almost 46,000 kronen. The reserve fund – over 31,000 kronen.

The sum saved reached almost 175,000 kronen. In that year 2,734 loans with a sum of over 421,000 kronen were given, and in the same year almost 396,000 kronen were paid back. Each transaction amounted to 10 kronen. The interest on the deposited savings was – three and a half percent and the members paid six percent yearly for loans. The management expenses in this year amounted to 5,580 kronen. In 1908, in order to expand and strengthen the activities of the loan office, it received a loan from the "Help Union" that reached 15,000 kronen.

In addition to the loan office of the JCA there was also the Kolomea County loan office according to Szulce's system. Actually, this was a private family bank. In 1908 there were 49 such banks with 27,693 members, of them 30 (56.3 percent) were Jewish credit funds with 16,734 members. The transactions of the members of these credit funds reached 883,493 kronen (compared with 453,907 kronen in non-Jewish funds with 10,959 members).

Because of the difficult economic situation in which the Jews found themselves during the beginning of the 20th century, a "Help Union for the Jews in Galicia" was founded in Kolomea. Its main purpose was to develop home industries and to increase the production of these industries; to found a school for artisans and to help build up agriculture. In order to draw the young, particularly the girls, to productive work, a school for housekeeping was founded in 1899 through the Baroness Klara Hirsch Fund that was led by a women's committee. In addition to work in housekeeping (cooking, cleaning, baking), the school also taught other trades and particularly tailoring. Of 108 students who studied in the years 1898-1908, 15 were employed in tailoring and 93 in housekeeping. In 1907 the "Help Union" began to found courses that taught the Jewish girls the trades of knitting and embroidery, as well as to make sheytlen [wigs worn by pious married women].

In 1908, such courses were also created in Kolomea. After a short time, the girls began to work for

[Page 64]

themselves. In all, 290 workers were educated, of them 25 were employed in making sheytlen and the rest with knitting and embroidery work. Thus a visible number of families found income and opportunities for subsistence.

In connection with the difficulties of making the Kolomea Jews productive the plan of Naftali Gelernter for erecting an agricultural school must also be remembered. He proposed this to the JCA society in 1897.

In addition, he turned to the management of JCA in Paris in the name of 278 Jewish families in whose name he brought a memorandum to Paris about purchasing an estate in the Kolomea area and settling the families there.[52] Dr. Hildesheimer of Berlin also made efforts at receiving loans for these families, according to the conditions under which JCA would give to institutions for agricultural education, as in Halem near Hanover. First of all, Gelernter was interested in having JCA found a Jewish agricultural school in Galicia. JCA answered him in September 1899 that it would be happy to help "our unfortunate brothers in religion in Galicia," but it could not agree to his proposal because it did not intend to buy any land or holdings in Galicia.

Although JCA had reacted negatively to Gelernter's plan, later, in 1901, it did buy an estate in Slobodka near Kolomea and settled scores of Jewish families there. The society also established an agricultural school on a tract of a thousand acres at this location.

The execution of this colonization work occurred thanks to Naftali Gelernter's plan.

A separate chapter is illustrated by education. The majority of the Jewish educational institutions at this time were also the khederim [plural of kheder – religious primary schools]. In 1894 there were 23 khederim in Kolomea with 37 teachers and 349 students. In 1899 – 22 khederim with 26 teachers and 364 students. In 1903 the number of khederim grew. There were then 33 khederim, 43 teachers and 691 students.

The Jewish Folks-Shule [public school], which was founded in 1886 by the Viennese Alianz, under the direction of the teacher, Wilhelm

[Page 65]

Grines, transferred to the Baron Hirsch schools in 1893. The management of the Baron Hirsch Fund built a special building for the school that cost 75,000 kronen. A local committee was created in Kolomea which administered it with the Baron Hirsch Fund. Dr. Milgrom, the lawyer, stood at the head of the committee. In 1908, 273 students studied in the Baron Hirsch School. Of the teachers, we must particularly remember Moshe Shulbaum, a well-known Hebraic philologist.

In the cultural sense, the Haskalah movement [the Enlightenment] did not penetrate Kolomea as widely as in Brod, Tarnopol or even Tysmenitsa [Tysmeytsya] and Bolechow. There was a very thin layer of followers of Haskalah here.

In the spiritual area the Kolomea Jews were governed by Hasidism and under the influence of the rebbes from the surrounding area. In addition to this Hasidic-Orthodox picture of Kolomea, the city also had hidden maskilim [followers of the Enlightenment]. There were Jews whose very religious conduct was only for appearance sake. At home, they read secular books in secret. There was even a melamed [religious primary school teacher] who was an apikoyres [heretic]. He was proficient in worldly knowledge, actually a walking encyclopedia,[53] a great expert in philosophy, literature and other knowledge.

In general, the number of maskilim who were involved with the Enlightenment was very small. In truth, the young began to study in the secular schools during the second half of the 19th century, but they were then already distant from the Hebrew cultural movement. These young people began to assimilate with the Polish culture. By the end of the century, the Zionist national movement began to return the young to Jewish culture.

Yehiel Mikhal Zaydman, the judge, who came from Jezierna [Ozërnaya, Ukraine] and was a resident of Kolomea was one of the maskilim in Kolomea.[54] He was born on the 29 Av, 5586 (1st September 1826) and he died on the 21 Elul, 5622 (14th September 1892). His father's side came from Kamenec-Podolsk. His grandfather settled in Jezierna. His grandfather's brother was the rabbi in Kamenec. However, he, himself, was an important merchant, a rich man and a scholar. His children married into aristocratic families. Yehiel Mikhal, who was simultaneously a scholar and maskil, married the daughter of one of the rich men in Kolomea. He then settled in Kolomea and was involved

[Page 66]

in financial matters. From her first marriage, his mother was the mother of the well known maskil, Shlomo Frenkel (1816-1894), who was the central personality of the Stanislaw maskilim. He founded the Union for spreading the Enlightenment among the Jews. He was one of the most important literary critics in the periodical, Kokhevei Yitzhak [The Stars of Yitzhak] and he published articles in Kohen Zedek's HaNesher [The Eagle] and in the Jewish-German press. He carried on an exchange of letters with the historian, Mordekhai Jost, and his research was accepted by Jost who used it in his history. He also influenced the education of his step-brother, Yehiel Mikhal Zaydman.

When Yehiel Mikhal lived in Kolomea, they both, he and his step-brother, Shlomo Frenkel, struggled for Enlightenment among Jews. Zaydman published original religious songs of praise and he also translated Jung's poetry.[55] He printed the letter from Jost, the historian, to his step-brother, Shlomo Frenkel, as well as an article against Kohen Zedek in the form of a letter to his relative.[56] He also wrote poems in German that were not published. One of them was translated into Hebrew by the maskil, Aleksander Chaim Shor, a resident of Drohobicz. Shor published the poem in Kokhevei Yitzhak with the name: "The Storm in the Carpatian Mountains" (Volume 31, 1865, pages 87-89). He was in conflict with Josef Kohen Zedek and he argued that his lines are laughable. Kohen Zedek also assaulted Frenkel about his historical research. Because of his attack on Frenkel, Zaydman came out against him with a strong counter-attack.

In accord with his beliefs, Zaydman belonged to the enlightened circles, whose slogans were universal and whose aspiration was: freedom for people and liberation from everything that could fall as a burden on an individual. He left the narrow frame and bound the past and the future with the present.

Coming out of this point of view, he saw the entire good fortune of Polish freedom, of the Jews coming out of the ghetto both physically and spiritually. In his poem The Blindness of Israel, he stresses with particular clarity the strength of the Jewish people and their weapons – bine [understanding] and das [consciousness]; and although it is an ancient people with an old history, it still possesses strength in its loins. As a sworn maskil he saw – in contradiction to the majority of the Galicianer maskilim

[Page 67]

of his time – in the Jewish people a carrier of a great mission in the world for all peoples; but the mission is not a religious one, as the German maskilim have seen, only a political-social one, according to which "Israel will not rest until freedom for the world and all people will be called." He was convinced that through knowing languages and secular knowledge according to the demands of the time and through the perfection in the public schools – the economic situation and the social standing of the Jews will be bettered. In contrast with the masklim of his generation, who were followers of Viennese centralism – he was a friend of the Poles and of the liberation of all of Poland and her return to her sovereign independence. In 1868 he greeted the political "period of glory" for Jews, that now, now "they will bloom and yet flourish."

Other winds began to blow on the Jewish streets at the end of the 1880's. The best minds of the Jewish intelligentsia moved closer to the Zionist movement because of the disappointment in emancipation, but he [Zaydman] was not influenced by these "winds." Despite this he remained devoted to the Hebrew language.[57] Under his influence Kolomea was transformed into a center of the Enlightenment right at the end of the 19th century. The writers Dovid Yeshayahu Zilberbush and Moshe Shulbaum concentrated around him.

Dovid Yeshayahu Zilberbush (1854-1936), born in Zaliszczik into a Hasidic family, taught secular subjects and devoted himself to Seforim Hitsonim [External Books such as the Apocrypha] after his marriage in 1898. He sympathized in secret with the Enlightenment. His wife, a rich daughter from the village of Lashkevic, died a half year after their marriage. Zilberbush returned to Zaliszczik. He often traveled to Czernovitz, where was befriended by Avraham Goldfaden, Welwel Erenkrantz (Zbarzher) and Moshe Arenshtein, the well known Hebrew writer who took over HaShahar [The Dawn – Hebrew daily in the Pale of Settlement] from Perec Smolenski. After he married for the second time, he settled in Kolomea.[58]

In 1877 Avraham Gincler (1840-1910) came to Kolomea in order to establish the publication of his newspaper, Hator that began to be published that year in Sziget. Zilberbush was one of his coworkers. In 1878 he began to publish

[Page 68]

articles and short stories in Hamabit and in HaShahar. He was in Vienna in 1880-1882 and worked there as an editor of HaShahar. After, he published the literary journal, HaOr [The Light] in Botoshan [Boto°ani, Romania] with Tzvi Eliezer Teller. After the second edition of HaOr, he left Romania and published HaOr in Lemberg. In 1883, he returned to Kolomea and became a teacher of religion in the secular schools. In 1892 he published a biweekly of Hebrew writings under the name Hem and with Leibl Toybush – a weekly in Yiddish named Dos Folk [The People]. At that time until he left for Vienna in 1893 – he concentrated around him along with Zaydman, the Jewish intelligentsia which grew into a visible group.

Moshe Schulbaum, who was on his own, also belonged this circle.

Moshe Schulbaum (1828-1918), one of the first activists for the Hebrew language in Galicia, was descended from Khokhem Tzvi on his mother's side. He received a traditional education in kheder [religious primary school] and in yeshiva [secondary school stressing Torah study], then he acquired great knowledge of many languages as an autodidact: Biblical Aramaic, Syrian, Sumerian, Arabic, Greek, Latin, German and French. He was particularly interested in the study of the Hebrew language. Starting in 1862, he took part in Kokhevei Yitzhak where he published a translation of Friedrich Schiller's poetry.[59]

In 1870 he came to Lemberg and he was the co-director of the Hebrew publishing shop there of the publisher and teacher, Mikhal Wolf. He lived in Lemberg until 1887. During the years 1871-1872, he published periodicals named Hem and Kol Het that had a national direction and whose task was to provide news of the world and to elevate the prestige of the holy language. In 1870, he founded a union in Lemberg under the name Agudat Shomrei Sfat Avar [Society to Preserve the Old Language (Hebrew)] and he called for devotion to the Hebrew language, in which he saw the absolute cultural dawn of the Jewish people. He called for the erection of Jewish schools in Galicia in his newspaper (in the year 5631 [1870]) because those who care for their faith and for the national spirituality can not send their children to a government school; and therefore, "It is our duty to prepare a

[Page 69]

school for Jewish children where they would learn Hebrew (Tanakh and Talmud) and they would know their task as people and their duty as Jews." He wrote articles in his newspaper and incomplete stories such as Nistarot Roma [The Mysteries of Rome], Der Rebbe [The Rebbe], Geheim-Rat fun Kenig [The King's Secret Council]. A literary supplement, Ruakh haEt [The Spirit of the Time] was enclosed with each edition in which there were songs, short stories, letters and commentaries on Tanakh.

The newspaper was mainly distinguished in bringing into use many words that Schulbaum had brought into the Hebrew language. After the newspaper stopped publishing, he occupied himself with teaching and with research work.

He also published his first books in Lemberg: a translation of Schiller's Die Räuber [The Robbers] (1881), Aristotle's Ethics from the German translation of Dr. Ruker (Lemberg 1877). In 1880, his General Vocabulary was published and in 1883, the first German-Hebrew dictionary German-Hebrew Words, and Treasury of Names.

As schools were founded with the help of the Baron Hirsch Fund, he settled in Kolomea and was a teacher in the school there until 1897. He belonged to the circle of Zaydman and Zilberbush in Kolomea and he had an effect on the reasoning of the Jewish intelligentsia. He called for the elevation of the prestige of the Hebrew language in the Baron Hirsch Schools; at his initiative this question was dealt with by the teaching conference that came together on the 17th-18th of July, 1894, in Stanislaw.[60] A proposal by Dr. Meir Wajsberg and Schulbaum was dealt with at a separate meeting of the Hebrew teachers. A commission was elected that would work out a plan for Hebrew education of eight hours a week, five hours for Tanakh and three hours dedicated only to the language. Schulbaum, A. Teler (Borilsaw) Toyver (Buczasz), Yakov Robinson (Stanislaw), Shpilman (Snityn), and W. Griner, the director of the Baron Hirsch School in Kolomea, belonged to the commission. Schulbaum's contribution to the Hebrew school program for the Baron Hirsch Schools was enormous. But there was not always success in carrying out the plans against the opposition of the assimilationists who stood at the head of these schools. At the beginning of 1897 he

[Page 70]

moved to the school in Mikulince [Mikulintsy, Ukraine] and in 1914 – to Tarnopol.

In 1917 he turned up Vienna as a refugee from the war.[61]

In 1887 the well known badkhin [comic poet who creates rhymes about those at a wedding], Reb Hirsh Leib Gotlib of Marmures-Sighet, who was also well known by the pseudonym, Hirsh Leib Sigheter (1829-1930), founded a twice weekly Hebrew publication named Hashemesh – in order to struggle against the extreme khederim [religious schools]. Gotlib was of the type of fighting member of the Enlightenment. He translated Schiller's poems into Hebrew (Di Gloke [Das Lied von der Glocke – The Song of the Bell], as well as Goethe's poems and several dramas by [August von] Kotzebue. He began to publish his periodical in his city of residence; but because of the ban on the part of the local Rabbi, Reb Chanayah Yom Tov Lipa Teitelbaum on the reading of a heretical newspaper, he had to move the publication to Galicia and he published it in Kolomea. He printed his organ in Bilou's printing shop in the manner of the weeklies that wanted to evade the duty to pay the newspaper tax. One week he published his newspaper under the name Hashemesh and the next week under the name HaCharsah (Sun) under the editorship of the Hebrew writer, Ruwin Asher Broydes who was driven out of Romania and settled temporally in Kolomea. Because Broydes declined to edit the periodical because of a conflict with Gotlib, he hired Gershom Bader, as editor. Zilberbush, Zaydman, Schulbaum, Shimeon Menakhem Lazar, Feiwish Melcer and others also took part in this periodical. The newspaper gave much space to literary and scientific matters and it was published until the year 1889.

7.

[Page 70]

At the end of the 1880's, individual maskilim began to become interested in the Jewish national question. Meetings and conversations about the Jewish problem from a national standpoint were influenced by Leibl Toybsh who settled in Kolomea. However, a national-Zionist organization had not yet been founded.

It is interesting to record that in 1887 a bold Pole expressed his opinion concerning a solution for the Jewish

[Page 71]

question in the manner of a national-territorial concentration. At that time in Kolomea a small brochure was published with the name Nowa Judea czyli Praktyczne załatwienie kwestyi żydowskiej i otwarty list do P.T. patryotów Irlandyi [New Judea, a Practical Solution to the Jewish Question and an Open Letter to the Irish Patriots]. This brochure was published in Kolomea, printed in Biliou's printing shop in 1887.

The name of the author is Y. Omega [Translator's note: the author was Celestyna Zyblikiewicza], an invented name. He saw the solution to the Jewish question, which troubled the people of the world, only in a national-territorial concentration of the Jewish people, that is, the founding of a Jewish state in one of the regions of America. He also proposed an elaborate plan. It is unknown how well this brochure was known by the Kolomea Jews.

In 1890, Leibl Toybsh began to publish a weekly in Yiddish under the name Yiddishes Wokhnblat [Yiddish Weekly] and he had a set purpose for it. The population in all of Austria then was about to undergo a census. At that time, Toybsh published an article in HaZamen that was printed in Krakow under the editorship of Asher Broydes whom he knew in Kolomea. In this article he proposed making the orthography of foreign words uniform in Hebrew. He had another proposal, that the Jews should give Yiddish as their national language in the census that was supposed to take place that year.

Wanting to wake the Jews to guard their nationality and to give Yiddish as their language, from the propagandistic stand-point, he began to simultaneously preach for the idea of settlement in Eretz-Yisroel. In his propaganda for the parliamentary elections in 1891, Toybsh supported the candidacy of Dr. Bloch against Dr. Bik. However one of the maskilim, Ephraim Laufer, who took part in the editorship, created difficulties for him and took money from the assimilated without his knowledge and against his wishes. This forced Toybsh to cease the publication of the Wokhnblat. In that year, 1891, an attempt was made to found a union for the settlement of Eretz-Yisroel, as a branch of the Vienna Union for the Society for Eretz-Yisroel, with the name, Zion. The writer, Ruwin Asher Broydes, spoke at the founding meeting [62] that took place on the 2nd of August, 1891. He demanded that the union work not only for the settlement of Eretz-Yisroel, but also on behalf of the idea of Jewish

[Page 72]

nationalism, in general. This union did not last long, despite the efforts of Leibl Toybsh and Yehoshua Fadenhecht.

In 1892, a weekly in Yiddish under the name Folk [people, nation] was published under the editorship of Zilberbush and Toybsh, as well as a weekly with the name Hem. Both organs were dedicated to national matters. Although there was a nationalist atmosphere, they did not succeed in supporting a national union. The founding of such a union again became real when Dr. Natan Birnbaum visited Kolomea in 1892. Dr. Birnbaum then stood at the head of the Zionist movement in Austria and he edited the weekly, Zelbstemancipacion [Self Emancipation]. At a meeting in which 60 people took part, a constitutional committee was elected to create a branch of Zion. But there was also no positive result then. Hem began a stronger propaganda effort for the founding of a Zionist society and it was successful in creating the atmosphere for it in 1894.

During that year, a National-Jewish Union, named Beis-Yisroel [House of Israel], was founded by Leibl Toybsh, Yehoshua Fadenhecht and Dr. Cypser, and its purpose was: 1) to support and to develop the national consciousness; 2) to spread the knowledge of history and Yiddish literature; 3) to look after the Hebrew language and to support Jewish colonization in Eretz-Yisroel.

At the general meeting that was held on the 16th June, 1894, the lawyer, Dr. Eliezar Cypser was elected chairman, vice chairman – Leibl Toybsh, secretary – Yehoshua Fadenhecht, treasurer – Yeshayahu Khius and as members of the committee – Yehuda Krebs, Ephraim Laufer, M. Shulbaum, Avraham Moshe Borten, Yitzhak Rozen, Mikhal Fiderer, Feywel Khonan, Euzer Engel and Markus Shafer.

A library and reading room was founded and the number of members reached 90.

On the 20th of December, 1894, the first Makabi celebration took place. [63]

Kolomea, just as other communities in Galicia was strongly influenced by a national sense in 1896. When a small brochure, Der Judenshtat [The Jewish State] by Dr. Theodor Herzl, arrived, it made a great impression among the young Zionist camp in

[Page 73]

Galicia. The exact expression of the aspirations that had a place in their hearts for so long was given for the first time. Among the first who registered for this brochure were the Kolomea Zionists who recognized that thanks to the program, "we now know what we have to do." "You have shown in a clear manner the high and true purpose and we need to do everything that is possible for its implementation," Leibl Toybsh wrote to Herzl on the 3rd of March, 1896. In Herzl they saw the leader who would raise "the flag of our people who are found in an inferior position.[64]

On the 7th of March, 1896, Toybsh wrote in the name of the editorship of Hem to Dr. Herzl about the terrific impression his brochure made on the Jews. The editorship placed its newspaper at his service and asked him to send material about how things stand with the matter and, particularly, about the development of the negotiations about the founding of the two societies that were proposed in the book. Secondly, Toybsh asked that he be given the right to publish the book in Yiddish. He obligated himself to selling it for 25-30 kreutzer a copy. Toybsh wanted to print 3,000 copies the first year. Herzl agreed to his proposal[65], but Toybsh asked that the right not be given to anyone else until the entire printing had been sold. The brochure was published in Yiddish during the month of September 1896, and after that, Toybsh requested that he be given the right to publish a translation in the Polish language. But nothing came of this.

Leibl Toybsh and the Galician Zionists wanted Der Judenshtat to be published in Hebrew, too.

The Kolomea Zionists concurred with Dr. Herzl and sent their representatives to the first Congress – Dr. Shlomo Rozenhek and Shlomo Zinger.

Kolomea occupied a visible place in the Zionist movement after the Congress, particularly during the rise of the matter of the union, Ahoves Zion [Lovers of Zion] in Torne which demanded that the Galician Jews should begin with practical work for Eretz-Yisroel. At the national conference that was held in Lemberg on the days of the 26th and 27th of December, 1897, Dr. Rozenhek, the representative from Kolomea, proposed the election of two national committees –

[Page 74]

one for practical work in Torne and one for organization and propaganda in Lemberg. His proposal was rejected. Leibl Toybsh and Dr. Rozenhek were elected from Kolomea to the Land Committee whose seat was in Lemberg. The business of Ahoves Zion in Torne which began with an activity to found a Galitzianer colony named Machanaim in Eretz Yisroel led to difficult conflicts among the Zionists in Galicia. A great war blazed on the canvas of this conflict that was actually a war between Hovevei Zion and the political Zionists. Kolomea and Stanislaw were fortresses of the political Zionists in this war and they blamed the Lemberg Zionists for their opposition to political Zionism. The Herzlistic movement found great resonance here. Dr. Rozenhek and Leibl Toybsh stood in strong opposition to the National Committee in Lemberg and they demanded of the limited Shareholders Committee in Vienna that it hand over all of the Zionist activity to the National Committee that would be elected at the new Congress.

At their initiative, a conference of the Zionists in Galicia and Bukowina took place on the 26th of June, 1898. The organizers of this conference did not connect with the higher authority that was elected by the Zionist movement in Galicia. The second half of this conference took place in Kolomea on the 29thof June. The conference was greeted by the head of the community and the vice mayor, Funkenshtein, in the name of the Jewish population. It was decided at this conference to support the existing organization with the Lemberg National Committee at the head.

Because of the conflicts among the 28 delegates to the Second Zionist Congress, conflicts that had a connection to the Practical Committee work in Eretz Yisroel, the representatives from the political direction were elected to the large Shareholders Committee as representatives from Galicia; among them were Dr. Rozenhek from Kolomea.

The peace and the compromise that was reached after difficult efforts at the conferences in Stanislaw and in Kolomea in the summer of 1898 quickly evaporated. The quarrels again broke out – between the predominant part of the Galitzianer Zionist organizations and at their head –

[Page 75]

the Lemberger National Committee on one side and the directors of the narrow Shareholders Committee in Vienna and its followers in Galicia on the other side. The Zionists from Stanislaw and Kolomea joined them.

Dr. Rozenhek received the support of the Zionist Shareholders Committee in Vienna to create a central office in Kolomea. The best people of the Galitzianer Zionists were brought to the Kolomea group and this excitement deepened the abyss between Lemberg and Vienna. There was no blessing brought to Zionism in Galicia as a result of Dr. Rozenhek, Sheinwaser, and Dr. Shor, the Galitzianer group from the Shareholders Committee, founding a central bureau for Galicia in Kolomea and choosing Leibl Toybsh as secretary of the bureau and, in this way, surrendering the National Committee.

Through the efforts of Dr. Broyde[26*], an agreement was finally reached to call together a conference of the Galitzianer Zionists in June 1899. Dr. Rozenhek agreed to this. But in a short time, he turned to the Shareholders Committee in Vienna with an inquiry as to whether it was necessary to call together the conference. The Shareholders Committee demanded the start of work for the conference in Galicia. But the disputes did not stop.

With the approval of Vienna, Dr. Rozenhek began to develop the organizational work. He worked out a plan to organize the Jewish workers in special Zionist unions that would also fulfill the assignment of the work bureaus and thus distance the workers from the social-democratic movement that had begun to strengthen itself in the ranks of the Jewish proletariat. His main activity was to arbitrate in workers' disputes between the bosses and the workers. Dr. Rozenhek dedicated much space in his organizational plan to the question of conquering the organized Jewish communities by the Zionists in order to eliminate the cliques that usurped the organized communities. He immediately proposed for this purpose to found a network of loan funds that would give loans for promissory notes.

A loan fund (Jewish National Bank Fund in Kolomea) was founded in Kolomea in the winter, 1898.

But in June, 1899, Dr. Rozenhek reported that the fund found itself in great difficulty because of the credit shortage. A pamphlet spread in Galicia against the fund.

[Page 76]

It was declared in the Welt [World] that the stories in the pamphlet had no substance.

Meanwhile, the Kolomea office began to propagandize that all Zionistic societies in Galicia should join the Viennese Association of Societies of Settlements in Eretz Yisroel as branches with the name Zion, which represented the organizational framework of the Zionist movement at that time in Austria. Leibl Toybsh, the secretary, traveled through the cities and shtetlekh and propagandized that they should join Zion. But his work was futile because it was impossible to achieve Dr. Rozenhek's plan to create Zionist groups as chapters of Zion in Vienna because the statutes of Zion did not permit the founding of any branches in Galicia. There was no great sympathy for Kolomea. The unions did not want to send Dr. Rozenhek the shekel-gelt.[27*]

An opposition, which turned with complaints to the Shareholders Committee in Vienna, also was created in Kolomea itself that was organized by Yehoshua Fadenhecht.

In March 1899 solicitations began for the Colonial Bank. And although extensive publicity was carried out in Kolomea, the results were very meager.

A compromise was reached because of the difficult situation in which the Kolomea office found itself. It was decided to call together a national conference at which Dr. Rozenhek's proposal would be made to leave the Zionist leadership in Galicia in the hands of the Kolomea office until after the Third Congress. It was decided to place at the head of the organization the organizing commission composed of representatives from every city that was elected by the conference. Dr. Shlomo Rozenhek and Moshe Haber were elected from Kolomea. From March, 1900, the bureau of the national committee was located not in Kolomea, but in Lemberg. Dr. Rozenhek still tried to renew the propaganda office for Galicia and Bukovina in Kolomea, but without success. Thus ended the chapter of Kolomea as a center of the Zionist movement in Galicia.

The union, Beis-Yisroel, was active in Kolomea itself and 119 members were organized in it. At the general meeting of the 15th January 1901, Dr. Shlomo Rozenhek was elected

[Page 77]

as chairman, Leibl Toybsh – vice chairman, Markus Berger – secretary, Nakhman Wider – treasurer, and as committee members: Yitzhak Meir, Zingl Ivanier, Alter Toybsh, Yakov Orenshtein, Josef Brecher and Moshe Frish.

In that year a union of Zionist women was also founded. Zionism particularly had an effect on the young students who in 1898 were organized in a secret Zionist Union of students in gymnazies [secondary schools] under the name Beitar [Translator's note: alternatively spelled Betar – the Revisionist Zionist youth movement founded by Ze'ev Jabotinsky]. The aspiration of this union was to educate the Jewish young in the national-Zionist spirit. Courses were arranged on the history of the Jewish people, courses on Hebrew, on the history of Zionism, geography of Eretz-Yisroel. The union also published a hectographic [printed on a gelatin-based duplicator] weekly named Nasze Myœli (Our Thoughts). Among the gymnazie youth activists were: Fishl Rotenshtreich, Dovid Toybsh, Yisroel Toybsh, Avraham Yitzhak Brawer, Ayzyk Sacher and, later, A. Sh. Yuris.

The activity of the Social-Democratic movement began in Kolomea at the same time. The student, Maks Ceterbaum, born in Kolomea, and Suzana Samuela, born in Kolomea in 1856, spread the socialist idea among the circle of the intelligentsia here [in Kolomea]. Meetings and the discussion of social problems took place in the home of Mrs. Samuela. She and Ceterbaum also took part in the national conference of the P.P.S. [Polish Socialist Party]. In 1893-1894 Maks Ceterbaum also took part in the publication of the P.P.S. that was published in Yiddish in Lemberg under the editorship of Karl Nached, Dr. Yaakov Frenkel and Dovid Salamander. (The newspaper was actually in German, but with Yiddish letters.) Ceterbaum would mainly sign his name with the initials M.C. He also wrote under his full name in the publication, Neue Zeit [New Times] of Karl Kautsky in Vienna. It is particularly necessary to mention his article: Di Klasen Bei Den Yuden [The Classes of the Jews] in which he dwelled upon the strike of the talisim workers in Kolomea.

The goal of the Jewish members was to create their

[Page 78]

own organization. They left the Polish Social-Democratic Union, P.P.S., in 1891 and founded their own union named Warheit [Truth], but within the framework of the P.P.S. The leaders of the union published their reports in the party organ, Der Arbeiter [The Worker], which was published in Lemberg "in the German language with Yiddish letters."

In the course of time the Jewish workers joined the Warheit. After 1905, the founding of a Jewish Social-Democratic Party was declared and they did not succeed in winning the majority of the Jewish workers and they remained a small minority.

With the crystallization of Zionism and the despair of their members based on their world view, the Zionists also struck deep roots in Kolomea, but with a religious hue. The already mentioned Yehoshua Fadenhecht (1846-1910) widened his activity for religious Zionism immediately after the first Zionist Congress in Basel. He published leaflets under the name Izrael in order to spread the idea of religious Zionism, "The mission of Izrael was, first of all, to speak to our brothers who were devoted to God's word and held his covenant, who, in Kolomea, had never thought of turning aside, God forbid, from their people and believed that this is the Torah that Moses gave to the House of Israel, and to awaken them so that they would know that they were Zionists, true Zionists, in the full sense of the word. Recognize your great love of your people and your strong desire for our land, to the land of Israel from generation to generation and you will know that you were Zionists even before the renewal of the name Zionism. You were Jews when your young, your sons, who have returned to our boundaries have said to themselves that they are French, German or British; and if our young have now returned to us with their whole heart and soul, to be Jews like us, we need to welcome them as sons who return to the homes of their parents and show them the road they should take."

Yehoshua Fadenhecht, who saw in the return of the Jewish intelligentsia a magnificent phenomenon, wanted the pious to understand this and also join the Zionist movement, which actually arose only with the help of

[Page 79]

the young who a short time ago were in the assimilated camp.

He believed that the religious circles were obliged to appear in the ranks of the Zionists and the rabbis also needed to help Zionism.[66] Fadenhecht endeavored to persuade the leaders of the pious Jews to take a positive position toward Zionism. Their publication, Mahazike ha-Dat [The Pillars of the Faith], stressed in an article published for the Congress that Zionism had no hope as long as the eminent righteous men were not the chief workers in this matter and "everything was done under their auspices and mission." Fadenhecht therefore made efforts to attract the righteous men for the Zionist movement. Yehoshua Fadenhecht was one of the first who paved a way in Galicia for Mizrakhi [religious Zionist movement] The Rabbi, Reb Gedalia Shmelkish, who occupied the rabbinical seat in Kolomea after the death of Rabbi, Reb Yakov ben Ephraim Taumim (1908-1914) helped him in his endeavors.

After the organization Mizrakhi was founded, in 1904, the leadership of Mizrakhi in Galicia was in the hands of Yehoshua Fadenhecht. He was the secretary in Galicia of the office of the Mizrakhi Central in Frankfurt am Main. After the death of Yehoshua Fadenhecht[67], the Mizrakhi Central in Galicia moved to Stanislaw.

One must also remember the preacher, Yitzhak Weber, one of the active Kolomea workers in the Zionist movement. He came to Kolomea from Poland with his brother, Moshe, and became a preacher. He received a very small salary from the kehile, but his friends supported him. He was a scholar and a radiant preacher. And he was persecuted by the Hasidim in Kolomea because of his Zionism, particularly by the Boyaner Hasidim, who were his deadly enemies because of his Zionist tendencies. However, he remained devoted to the Zionist idea and he campaigned for the Zionist idea in the surrounding cities and shtetlekh.

At the time of the election in 1907, he was among the best propagandists and the voting masses were very influenced by his speeches and sermons. But, once, after he returned from the Congress, he was transformed into a strong Zionist fighter because "None of the leaders of the Congress interested themselves in him."[68]

[Page 80]

Kolomea, the Jewish city, was also a Zionist city in the full sense of the word. The assimilated were not organized as a stable, organized administrative body. Individuals among them supported – in addition to political elections – the Union of Polish Students of Moses' Belief, Zjednoczenie [union] in Lemberg (founded in 1907) and Towarzystwo Szkoły Ludowej, the Society for the Folk School that was in Kolomea. Among the Kolomea Jews who were known as supporters of these institutions: Mikhal Bretler, Josef Funkenshtein, Wilhelm Grines, Gustav Libhart, Markus Shiler, Zigmund Weintraub, Mikhal Berlas and the medical doctor, Oswald Fleker.

8.

Several days after the outbreak of the First World War, the Russians conquered the city; then the Austrians came back for a short time. Later, the Russians again occupied the city and ruled there with a heavy hand. The Jews suffered greatly from the Russian occupation. In January, 1915, the Cossacks murdered the melamed [religious teacher], Shlomo Shechter. They entered his residence and wanted to rape his 16-year old daughter. When Shechter tried to protect her, a Cossack stabbed him. His body was thrown out in front of the threshold of his house. The Governor of Kolomea County, the Count Labonov Rostovski, savagely persecuted the Jewish population. He imposed heavy fines and war taxes on them and gave the soldiers a free hand to loot and to plunder.

Their rule in Kolomea lasted until the summer of 1915. The return to the city of the Austrian military and the second Russian invasion – this all placed its stamp on the kehile and on the Jewish population that for the most part escaped to Bohemia, Moravia and Hungary and, mainly, to Vienna.

With the end of the World War, in the autumn of 1918, a new storm arose over the Kolomea Jews, a storm accompanied by edicts and heavy persecution. The Kolomea Jews also suffered during the days of the Ukrainian Republic.

At the head of the national council, which was established

[Page 81]

in place of the kehile, stood the lawyer, Dr. Meir Laks. The district chief, Dr. Streiski, had a friendly relationship with the national council and endeavored to lead impartially, but he was helpless against the outbursts of the Ukrainian soldiers.

But the situation changed several days later. The newspaper, Sichow Holos[28*] [Voice of Sich] under the editorship of the radical leader, Dr. Trylovsky, published an article entitled: "The First Commandments of the Ukraine," in which the Jews are labeled as enemies of the Ukrainians and it is a good deed to hate them and to drive them out of the country. This article incited the Ukrainians against the Jews. The county commandant confiscated jewelry and money from the Jews of the city and of the locality with cruelty. Jews were arrested on the accusation that they were spies and contrabandists. Military divisions that went to the front looted Jewish businesses and beat Jews. Men – old and young – were dragged to forced labor.

On the 13th of January 1919, a policeman called out in the middle of the market at the time of a fair that people should not buy any horses and cattle from the Jews. Soon after, all Jews were driven from the market.

No intervention helped because the central regime was virtually helpless.

There were great difficulties in the educational-cultural realms, too. The Ukrainians assured autonomy but the central regime was the first not to make available the possibility of supporting Jewish folk-schools [public schools]. This negative attitude also hindered the founding of a folk-school in Kolomea. The Ukrainian policies severely undermined the economy of Jews in Kolomea. The Commissar, Professor Tsheikowsky, who was responsible for this, did everything to liquidate Jewish trade. He did permit any means of living to the Jewish population and in order to ruin the Jewish merchants, he organized the Ukrainian merchants with the purpose of removing trade, industry and crafts from the hands of the Jews. The Jews received an order to exchange their Austrian banknotes into Ukrainian [banknotes]. On the 3rd of May, 1919, military patrols entered apartments

[Page 82]

and Jewish businesses and forced them to turn in their Austrian banknotes for Ukrainian grivnas [or hryvni]. As a rule, the Jewish population was then forced to exchange 600,000 Austrian krones for grivnas.

Despite the difficult conditions, the organized Jewish society carried out its national-cultural activities. The elections to the local national council and to the national country council that were held in May 1919 were conducted very cautiously. The vigilant participation was accompanied by stormy party conflict.

At the end of 1919, the offensive by the Polish military began. The military of General Haler (the Halertshinkes had "acquired a reputation" for cutting beards and throwing Jews off trains) occupied all of Eastern Galicia and they began their march and ambushes of Jews, thievery; snatching from the Jews and arresting [them], were daily stories.

And the signs began of the era of an independent Poland.

[Page 83]

[Page 84]

Comments on the Proclamation of the
Kolomea Kehile Managing Committee of 1891*

On the 25th of March, 1883, the Krakower Rabbi, Reb Shimeon Sofer (a son of Chasam Sofer), who represented the election district of the three cities, Kolomea, Buczacz and Snyatyn, died.

As Dr. Joseph Samuel Bloch, the young 33 year-old rabbi from Florisdorf, near Vienna, was then famous as a result of his courageous struggle in the press against the anti-Semitic expert, Prof. August Rohling, the Kolomea kehile [organized Jewish community] asked him to become Rabbi Schreiber's successor in the Viennese Parliament and, several months later, Dr. Joseph Bloch was chosen with a majority of over two-thirds of the votes.

In the winter of 1885, Dr. Bloch was elected for the second time to the Viennese Parliament as the representative of the three cities. This time the opposing candidate was the Lemberg lawyer, Dr. Emil Bik, and the electoral battle was a stormy one. Jewish voters were literally ready to sacrifice their lives for Dr. Bloch because, "If Dr. Bik were elected, we would not dare circumcise the children."

In 1891 Dr. Joseph Samuel Bloch was elected for the third time in the Kolomea election battle for Parliament. This time Dr. Emil Bik withdrew and the candidate opposing Dr. Bloch was Leon Meisels, a grandson of the famous Warsaw Rabbi, Reb Berish Meisels. Leon Meisels was a wealthy Jew, an aristocrat, but a sensitive candidate.

The proclamation of the Kolomea community leaders that was written in a terrible Deitchmerish [Yiddish containing German vocabulary] interceded for the Rabbi, Dr. Bloch, and came out against Leon Meisels.

God be praised.

————————

* Supplement to page 54

[Page 85]

Footnotes and Bibliography:

1. Dr. Majer Balaban, Żydżi Lwowscy [Jews of Lwow]. Lwow, 1906, p. 386.
2. The first documentary information about the Kolomea Jews is from 1563 (see Eliezer Ferdman's article: "The oldest information about Jews in Polish cities in the 16th Century, Pages for History," Warsaw 1934).
3. Akta grodzki i ziemskie [City and land acts], t. [vol.] XII (Ziemia habicka [9*] [Halicz County, Halych in Ukrainian]), Nr. 3310, p. 314-314; Nr. 3412, p. 327, Nr. 3014, Nr. 4401, p. 450.
4. Dr. Ignacy Schipper: Studja nad stosunkami gospadarczymi żydow podczaz średniowiecza [Studies on the economic relations of Jews in Poland during the Middle Ages], Lwow, 191, p. 239, 242, 278.
5. Dr. Majer Balaban, Żydżi Lwowscy, p. 393, 399.
6. This cemetery was used from the first day of the kehile until 1783 when the old cemetery was closed and a second cemetery was established on the southern side of the city. This cemetery served until 1890 and was closed by an order of the state. A special committee headed by the rich man, Jakov Bretler, was involved in collecting money to buy a new bathhouse for the cemetery. It

was rededicated by the Rabbi Yakov Taumim and his rabbinical court. The ceremony celebrating the acquisition of the land for the cemetery was held in the large synagogue on erev Rosh Khodesh Khesvan [the eve of the new month of Khesvan] 5654 [1894] and in addition to the rabbi and his rabbinical court, the distinguished men from Kolomea and the rabbis of Sadigere, Kitev, Stanislav, Snytyn and almost all of the residents of the city participated in the dedication of the cemetery which took place the next day. (Haim Tzvi Teomim – Zikaron laRishonim, (In Memory of the Early Settlers), Kolomea, 1914) (?)

7. Tit Ha-Yaven, page 56... Chmiel [Chmielnicki] entered Russian history when he returned to the city of Kolomea and wiped out the Jewish population of 300 Jews.

8. Manuscript in Ossolineum [10*] (Lemberg), 94, 21a, reg. nr. 279.

[Page 86]

9. The Tax Collector Lease of Kolomea – arenda [lease of estates, right to collect taxes and tolls].

10. Israel Halpern: Pinkas Vaad Arba Aratzot [Register of the Council of Four Lands], Jerusalem, 5705 [1945], pp. 54, 60, 156.

11. And this is the description of his headstone on the Lemberg cemetery: "About this our hearts are anguished, about this our eyes are darkened, because God has magnified our suffering and took from us the crown of our heads and the jewel of our glory, the great scholar our teacher and rabbi Avraham the son of the master the great scholar our teacher and rabbi Yosef Katz, the head of the academy of the holy congregation of Kolomea, who perished because of our sins and was murdered in a gruesome manner by an accursed (person), and with awe sanctified God's holy and unified name, therefore may the Master of mercy shelter him in the shelter of His wings for eternity and may He quickly exact retribution for his spilled blood, because he spread the words of Torah throughout Israel and had taught many students. May his soul be bound in the Bond of Life." [Translator's note: The description of the headstone was translated by Rabbi Zev Silber of Binghamton, NY.]
    (Gabriel Naftali Hirsh Suchistov; Matseyvus Kodesh Lvov [Holy Headstones in Lwow]1864, Pamphlet B page 212)

12. Haim Tzvi Teomim – Zikaron laRishonim. Kolomea, 5677 [1917], page 31.

13. The version of the oath in the research work of Dr. Meir Balaban.

14. Shivhei Besh"t [In Praise of the Baal Shem Tov] (Sz. A. Horodetski Publishing House), Berlin 5682 [1922] pages 23-24.

15. He was called "Reb Hasid, the holy and devoted follower of the Besh"t" in the Hasidic literature. He was a great scholar and his new thoughts about the Torah are recalled in the book, Toledot Yakov Yosef [The Generations of Yakov Yosef] of Yakov Yosef haKohan of Poland (Hotzaot, Warsaw, 5645 [1885], page 173). He was also remembered by Reb Moshe Haim Efroim, chairman of the Sadikov kehile court in his book Degel Machanek Efraim [containing thoughts on the weekly Torah portion] (Shem hagadol hakhadash [The Great New Name] Warsaw 1870, page 86). Also see the book, haDorot [The Generations], page 13. About this – in the book, Dorot Khadash [New Generations] 2, Rodkinzohn: Ur Yisroel, 39.

16. His wife, Chaya, was a daughter of Zalman of Kolomea and a granddaughter of Reb Yakov Kopl Kamiel, who settled in Kolomea at the beginning of the 18th century. He was a rich man and gave very large sums for building the synagogue, house of prayer and mikvah [bathhouse]. His wife, Perl, was a sister of Yom Tov Lipman Heller (author of Tosafot [additions or supplements] Yom Tov [commentary on the Mishnah – a compilation of the oral traditions]). She was a granddaughter of Reb Dovid haLevi, the author of Turei Zahav [Rows of Gold, commentary on Shulkhan Arukh – written code of Jewish law and practices] on her mother's side, the esteemed Bluma, the daughter of the martyr, Reb Shlomo, who was murdered in Lemberg in 5424 [1664].
    Her sister Zisl was married to Reb Shaltial Aizik haLevi Sternhel of Kolomea, a rich merchant, a great, great grandson of Reb Adam Baal Shem, about whom Hasidic legend relates that he was a great Kabalist and left many manuscripts of Kabalistic wisdom. In his will he imposed upon his son that he search out the city named Okup where he would find a person named Israel ben Eliezer (Besh"t), 14 years old, and that he should give him the manuscripts because they belong to the core of his soul (Shivhei Besh"t. page 96). In his old age, Reb Shaltial Sternhal went to Eretz-Yisroel and died in Jerusalem.

[Page 87]

17. His father, Reb Josef, whom the people called "Safra vizlivi [11*]," was from Pystin. He was the son of Reb Moshe Swierczer who was murdered kiddush ha-Shem [in sanctification of God's name, as a martyr].

18. At that time there were no medical doctors in Kolomea, not Jewish and not Christian. It is interesting to note that at that time there were only seven doctors in all of Galicia (excluding Lemberg) (in Jaroslaw, Sokol, Rajcza, Zamosc, Radyn).

19. See my article: Dr. N. M Gelber: Statistics about Jews in Poland at the End of the 18th Century. The Writings on Economics and Statistics (YIVO), Berlin 1928, Volume 1, page 188.

20. Archive of the Interior Ministry, Galician Protocols, October 1784.

21. Protocols, August 1784.

22. [in German] Franz Kratter: Briefe ueber den ewigen Zustand von Galizien, Leipzig, 1796, Brief 38.

23. Protocols, September 1784.

24. Protocols, December 1784.

25. Protocols, May 1786.

[16*]

26. Protocols, March 1783.

27. [in German] Neueste phisikalisch-poltische Reise durch die Dacischen und Sarmatischen der nördlichen Karpaten.

28. Protocols, September 1795

29. In the remaining communities of the district, the rabbis also had the function of "religious leader." The rabbi in Snyatyn received a salary of 440 florin; in Horodenka – 110 fl.; in Kuty, the rabbi received only a free apartment in Yabluniv – 50 fl.; in Obertyn – 50 fl.; in Zabolotiv – 15- fl.; in Pystan – 78 fl.; the rabbi from Kosiv was compensated by exemption from paying the meat and candle taxes; in Pechenizhyn, the rabbi did not receive a regular salary; there were no rabbis in Chernelystsya, Gwozdziec and Khotimir. [16*]

30. Published in Zikharon Rishonim[In Memory of the Early Settlers] by Haim Tzvi Teomim, Kolomea, 5674 [1914] pages 60-68 .
    *[Translator's note: Footnote 30 is cited twice, once on page 33 and again on page 36.]

31. Michael Stöger: Darstellung der gesetzlichen Verfassung der Galizischen Judenschaft [Depiction of the Legal Constitution of Galician Jewish Community], Lemberg, 1833 B. 1 S 161.

32. In a correspondence from Kolomea, signed – M.K., in the Allgemeiner Zeitung dem Judentums [General Newspaper of Jewry] (German), 1845.

33. In a correspondence in Allgemeiner Zeitung dem Judentums, 1852, No. 22.

34. There were 15 Catholics (Poles), six Ukrainians and one German from the remaining places.

35. Allgemeiner Zeitung dem Judentums, 1872, No. 30.

36. Weiner Mitteilungen [Viennese Communications] (German), 1855, pp. 23 and 74.

37. Sefer [book] Irgot Soferim [Letters of the Scribes] 2 chapter 33 page 31 [20*]

38. Maskil el Dal [Contemplating the Needy] (Hungary [21*] 1867) Volume 3, detail 8, part 4.

39. Torat Hakana'ot [The Law of Jealousies], page 9, side 2.

40. Sefer [book] Tokhahat Megulah [Open Rebuke] of the rabbi Hillel Lichtenstein, Chairman of the Beis Din of the kehile of Kolomea, that was sent to the Holy City of Jerusalem in 5663 (1873) side 3. [16*]

41. Maskil el Dal

42. A. Y. Shahrai: Rabbi Akiva bar [son of] Josef Schlesinger, Jerusalem, 5702 [1942], sides 4-5.

43. A. Y. Shahrai, pages 20-27.

44. Chaim Yakov Lichtenstein; Toldot v'Zikhronus [History and Remembrances] of Rabbi Hillel Lichtenstein, Satu Mare, 5691 [1931] page 26.

[Page 88]

45. Der Israelit [The Israelite], Lemberg, 1883, No. 9.

46. Dr. Josef Block: Aus meinem Leben [From My Life], Vienna, 1922.

47. Letter from the estate to Dr. [Theodor] Herzl of September 8, 1900 in Herzl Archive, Jerusalem.

48. Dr. Ignacy Weinfeld: Ludność miejska Galicji i jej skład wyznaninowy [Urban Population of Galicia and its Denominational Composition], 1887-1910, Lwów, 1912.
    Dr. Stanislaw Grumski: Materjały do kwestji Żydowskie w Galicji [Material on the Question of Jewish Galicia], Lwów, 1910.

[Page 89]

49. For the living conditions of the talisim [prayer shawl] weavers, see Pinkus Galicia, Buenos Aires, pages 455-458; D.Y. Zilberbush, People and Events, Vienna, pages 49-56.
50. Article by Dr. Nathan Birnboim, in Self Emancipation.
51. Published in Historical Writings from YIVO, volume 3, pages 498-499.
52. Zionist Archive, Jerusalem.
53. As Gershom Bader describes it in his memoir-book, My Memories, Buenos Aires 1953, page 342. See the chapter about Khaskel Itzik Rozenshtok in Shlomo Bikel's A City with Jews, New York, 1943.
54. Songs of Shulamit (Kokhevei Yitzhak [Stars of Yitzhak – Hebrew periodical] volume 17 (1853), pages 50-51; volume 19 (1854), page 33; volume 25 (1860), pages 62-67, translated by "Nat Shots" of Yung. Unternomen [Young Undertaking] in In Spite of the Night, volume 18, pages 51-53; volume 24, pages 31-33; volume 27 (1861) pages 90-92; 27 (1862), pages 73-74; The Weasel's Dream in the Fall, volume 27 (1862), pages 74-75; Tavern Songs: Cups of Coffee, volume 29 (1863), pages 37-38; Enjoy Young Men Your Youth; Avoid Being Bitten By Deadly Snakes, volume 29, pages 39-44.
55. Kokhevei Yitzhak, volume 29, pages 65-71, volume 6 (1864), pages 58-59.
56. Kokhevei Yitzhak, volume 31 (1865), pages 130-131.
57. His son, who graduated from the university, converted.
58. It is interesting that in his memoirs Zilberbush does not describe his Kolomea era, except for the chapter about the strike of the talisim weavers.
59. Kokhevei Yitzhak, volume 27 (1862), pages 72-73.
60. In 1899 a teachers' conference took place in Kolomea under the chairmanship of W. Grynem; 230 teachers took part from the schools named for Baron Hirsch.
61. See the article of Yakov Khanini [Canaanite] in Leshonenu [Our Tongue] 5, page 992 about him as a pedagogue.

[Page 90]

62. See my article, Pre-Zionist Plans in Galicia in the book Mazkeret Levi [The Remembrance of Levi], Tel Aviv, 5704 [1944], pages 152-157.
63. "Letters from Galicia" by Yitzhak Abn, HaMagid 1891, number 29, page 231
64. Selbstemanzipation [Auto-Emancipation], 1891.
65. The correspondence in Herzl Archive in Central Zionist Archive, Jerusalem.
66. Dr. Avraham Yakov Brody: "Complete Memoirs" in the book Mazkeret Levi, Tel Aviv, 5704 [1944], pages 177-184.
67. Yehoshua Fadenhecht died in Kolomea on the 22nd of Tevet, 5670 [3 January 1910]. That year he was elected as a delegate to the 9th Zionist Congress, but because of his illness, several days before the meeting of the Congress, he could not take part in the Congress.
68. According to the words of his friend, Henoch Shechter in his book; Two Cities, Book of Memories of Two Destroyed Communities (Khorostkov and Kolomea), Tel Aviv, 5703 [1943], pages 172-173.

Translator's Footnotes:

1. The spelling of the name of the town used here is the Yiddish spelling. It is spelled Kolomyya in Ukrainian and Russian and Kolomyja in Polish.
2. Raysn, also spelled Reissen, is a geographic term describing the area of Eastern Galicia bordering on Russia, Romania and Poland.
3. Shabbetai Tzvi was a Jewish mystic born in Smyrna, Turkey in 1626, who claimed to be the Messiah and developed a large following. Threatened with death in Constantinople in 1666, he converted to Islam. He died in 1676.
4. Pokucie in Polish or Pokuttya in Ukrainian was a culturally separate area between Lwow and Halych inhabited by Ukrainians and Romanians.
5. Tisha b'Av, the 9th day of the month of Av, is a fast day and it is customary to refrain from eating meat for three weeks before Tisha b'Av
6. Yakov Frank was a messianic figure who attracted many former followers of Shabbetai Tzvi during the 18th Century.

7. dybbuk – singular form – disembodied spirit that takes over the body of a living person, often because the spirit is troubled or has sinned.
8. The Baal Shem Tov resided in Kosovo from which the small synagogue took its name.
9. "habicka" should be spelled "halicka."
10. The Ossolineum, a scientific library was established in Lwow in 1817 by Count Jozef Maksymilian Ossolinski. It is now located in Wroclaw, but a large part of its original collection remains in Ukraine.
11. A rabbi with vision and special powers.
12. July actually falls during the summer.
13. The scribe's name is spelled as "Wolter" above and as "Walter" below.
14. The collections of various taxes were leased to individuals, who received a percentage of the monies collected.
15. A gmiles khesid is a free loan institution. What is being described is the Khevre Kadishe, the burial society which took care of the preparation of a corpse for burial.
16. There is no number in the text corresponding to this footnote.
17. Israelitische Allianz – the name of an organization founded in 1872 in Vienna to promote Jewish interests.
18. Seal of the Scribe – Chasam Sofer is an acronym for the complete title – Chidushei Toras Moshe Sofer – the most important work by Moshe Schreiber, also known by the names Moshe Sofer and Chasam Sofer
19. Rabbi Uri Feywl Schreier is more commonly referred to as Uri Shraga Schreier. Shraga is the Aramaic equivalent of Feywl.
20. The chapter number in the footnote is given as "lamed-kuf." The number in the book is actually "lamed-gimel," that is 33.
21. The word 'Hungary' is misspelled.
22. August Rohling was the author of Der Talmudjude (The Talmud Jew), an anti-Semitic tract.
23. Although the Yiddish phrase is usually translated as unscrupulous or bad lawyer, in the context of this article, it appears to mean he did not have formal legal training.
24. See the enclosure: facsimile of the appeal.
25. They included 5,951 Catholics (Poles), 4,226 Greek Orthodox (Ukrainians), 930 others and 12,000 Jews.
26. The name is given as Broydes earlier in the text
27. Shekel was the name of the certificate of membership in the Zionist movement. Shekel-gelt was the membership money paid
28. The nationalist Sich Society was founded by Dr. Kyrylo Trylovsky

————

[Page 91]

Supplement

Jewish Factories, Businesses and Shops and their Owners

Kindling lights and various smearing oils – Fogel and sons.

Roof-shingles-cupolas – Yona Brettler and sons, and Hersh Ramler and Moshe Landau.

Beer breweries – Stefan Weiss, Jakov Brettler and sons.

Talisim [prayer shawls] factories – Shimshon Heller and son, Yona Zager and son, Pesakh Ringelblum, Asher Windshauer, Yisroel Grunberg and son.

Rugs and Embroidery [made on a frame] – Chaim Teitelbaum. Teitelbaum had factories and businesses across the country and employed over 250 people.

Artistic Embroidery [made on a frame] – Gussie and Motek Horowitz. This firm employed many workers who would take work to their homes. Many agents would also travel around outside the country for this same firm.

Silk cloth and rug weaving – Shlomo Grunberg. Grunberg employed only Hasidic, pious Jews with shtreimlekh [fur hats worn by Hasidim].

Large Mills – Jakov Brettler and sons. Water Mills – Nartenberg and Schiller.

Wet Mills for Grains – Lipshuts, Advokat, Dr. Goldberg and Waser.

Furniture Factories – Hersh Scheiner, Josef Pistyner, Moshe Kimel.

Soap and Soda Factories – Leibush Osterzecer and Leibush Horowitz, Shimkha Freilech and son.

Tanneries – Yehuda Grebler, Mendl Akselrad, the Avner Brothers and Yisroel Horowitz.

Riding Tools, Rope, Whips – The Menentsop Brothers

Paper Factory – Moshe Hammer.

[Page 92]

Carton and Copy Book Factory – Leib Chius and Leibish Herman.

Sweater Factory – The Reidts Brothers. Employed a large number of workers.

Bridge and Construction-Metal Works – Schiller and son.

Smaller Metal Works – Kornblit, Maks Nelber and son.

Bristle Brush Factory – Kalman Ber Hener. Smaller ones of the sort: Cyper and Dovid Leib Shechter.

Wax, Mead and Honey Factory – Yehuda Schmal, Noakh Schmal, Fishl Hener.

Liqueur Factory – Chaim Feldman, Gershon Thau.

Banks: Austrian-Hungarian Bank employed a large number of Jewish officials. The chief specialist in the sphere of the credit system was the trustworthy man, Yona Kizler.

City Savings Bank: Manager – H. Hules, Director – Josel Funkenstein, Syndicate – Dr. Shlomo Singer, Bookkeeper – Nusie Horowitz, Directors: Elihu Kriss, Yona Kizler, Inspectorate – Wilhelm Grines, Benyamin Hammer, Treasurer: Leib Tswecher, Yehuda-Borukh Feyerstein, Hesiu Bortn, Hershl Taycher, M. Rebhon.

Jiro-Bank (Brettler's): Director – Moshe Seidman, Mendl Brettler, Yona Brettler.

Galicia Trade Bank: Director – Aleksander Schorr, Aytsk Chius, Zelik Herman.

Export Bank: Directors – Yakov Beidof and son.

Credit, Trade and Industry Bank: Hercl Spindel, Note Welzer, Meir Welzer, Ayzik Wolf, Leibish Horowitz.

Credit and Savings Union (Factory Bank); Welwl Faktor, Yona Kisler, Note Welzer.

Baron Hirsch Bank: Directors – The Rabbi, Gedalihu Smelkes, Dovid Wieselberg, Yosye Marmorash, Maks Sharf, Yekutial Sensensich, Peysye Singer.

Cooperative Bank of Retailers and Artisans: Directors – Ruwin Osterzecer, Shlomo Scherr, Dr. Marek Laks, Dr. Moshe Faktor, Yona Aschenazy, Dovid Baumeil, Dovid Wieselberg, Mendl Grunwerg, Moshe Shneiberner.

Cooperative Bank Agudas Yisroel; Directors – Reb Leibish

[Page 93]

Kriss, Dovid Zaidman, Dr. Ben Tzion Felser, Dr. Isidor Bahr, Minye Kriss, Leibtsi Libman.

Cooperative Bank for Retailers and Industry: Directors – Meshulem Frenkl, Yakov Biter, Chief Bookkeepers – Chaim Ringelblum.

Interest-Free Loan Fund: Directors – Shlomo Scherr, Chaim Ringelblum, Dr. Moshe Faktor, Dr. Marek Laks, Moshe Schneiberner, Mendel Grunwerg, Yakov Shatsberg, Treasurer – Moshe Laks, Bookkeeper – Leon Reich.

Import and Export Businesses

Grocers and Delicacies – Schneider and Sharf, Hecht and Lunefeld, Fersher and son, Feywl Nagler, Leib Enre, Shtreifeld and son.

Grain and Beans – Jakov Brettler and son, Yakov Beiraf and son, Leibush Kriss and Zalman Czenirer, Meir Haker and son, Yisroel Eiferman, Leibtsie Eiferman, Shaul Breiter and son, Zisie Heilzenrot, Berish Heilzenrot, Ahron Leib Knopf and son, Jakov Haker, Avraham Haker, Kopl Marmorosh, Itsie Brettler, Avraham Aschenazy.

Flour (wholesale) – Jakov Brettler and son, Schiller and Gartenberg, Hersh Sechastower and Sheike Chius, Dovid Gliners and son, Itshe Dovid Nunik, Dovid Shprechman.

Retail Trade – Shmaye Ramler, Shaye Moshe Holker, Shaye Moshe and Motye Kelner, Moshe Wieselberg, Moshe Kreisberger, Itsik Sensensich, Moshe Smendig, Feywl Eizenrot and others.

Leather Trade (Wholesale) – Yisroel Horowitz, Yisroel and Mikhal Shmucher, Moshe Kanter, Shmay Kanter, Itsik Kanter, Alter Kanter and son, the Amzer brothers, Mikhal Sharf, Moshe Sak and others.

Haberdashery – Henrik Roznhek, Bortn and Helwig, Ramler and Nader, Shlomo Eltser, Liber Shaler, Moshe Wargan and son, Moshe Shaler, Borten and Elenberg, the Tseler brothers, Zysie Ziskind.

Wholesale Trade and Groceries and Delicacy Goods – Avraham Shmerts, Iser Herman, Berl Kupferman, Shaul Keish and Leizer Shtarer, Shuchner Mindl, Kamet and Baumgarten, Yehezkiel Shechter, the Salomon Brothers.

[Page 94]

Small Retail – Zelig Rish, Lipe Shuber, Rayzel Eiferman and Dovid Baumeil, Henech Shechter, Markus Nusbaum, Itsik Grunberg, Hersh Laks, Michal Zesler, Yisroel Lederfeind, Mendel Roizner, Yitzhak Shechter, Hersh Rechter, Chaya Ornstein, Chaim Brettler, Hersh Freier, Nisen Sternberg, Alter Finkl.

Manufacturing (Wholesale and Retail) – Motl Frish, Yehuda Ber Zeidman and son, Zeide Landman and son, Ben-Tzion Zulauf, Berman and Preminger, Shimeon Glazer, Iser and Bayle Horn, Malter and Burtman, Hersh Chius, Ayzik Herman, Sura Grunberg, Firsh and Bernal, Hersh Rein, Itsik Kenig, Shmuel Laden and son, Berl Lantshenr, Dovid Goldhaber, Brecher and Eizner, Emzig and Fridler.

Tailoring Requisites (Wholesale and Retail) – Shaul and Alter Kneper, Moshe Kuperman, Moshe Grunberg, Leibele Esnfeld, Naftali Bikl. Glonower, Gershon Henish, Robinzon and Heller.

Tailoring Accessories – Sh. Bank and son, Motye Bank, Josef Waks, Note Preminger, Shmuel Hausknecht, Josl Bank.

Dress Trade – Leibele Markus and son, Shmuel Deutsch, Moshe Fisz, Karal Bland, Yehuda Kutner.

Cloth and Peasant Goods – Shamai Feder, Yisroel Frenkel, Mordekhai Frenkel, Itsik Rubin, Shaul Weisman, Chaim Frenkel, Shaul Wizel, Zindl Neiman.

Paint Trade – the Feldman brothers, Fishl Fernbach, Masholem Welwl Eiferman, Hersh Fajerman, Moshe Shtreit.

Glass and China Crockery – Ephraim Rosenblatt, Shmuel Hirsch, Dovid Lindenberg, Avrahamtsie Heller, Moshe Einhorn.

Retail – Leizer Kreisler and Baron, Hershl Lindenberg, Josef Glazer.

Fur Trade – Itsie Schechter, Yona Hibner, Berl Distenfeld, Benyamin Stein, Yehoshaya Sensensich and son, Hersh Schechter.

Retail – Dovid Dandel (shtreimlekh – fur hats worn by Hasidic men), Gabriel Ziegellaub, Dovid Zenenreich, Hersh Kosten

Musical Instruments – Maks Blecher, Zalman Hodisch.

Mechanical Articles – Mikhal Schulman, Gershon Melzer, Lancener.

[Page 95]

Bookkeeping – Yakov Ornstein, Shmuel Royzenberg, Chaya Ornstein-Thau.

Paper and Writing Needs – Shimeon Sensensich, Gershon Gotlib, Zelig Schperber, A. Ginzburg, Moshe Lewkowitz, Leibish Chius, the brothers, M. and F. Scheierman, Berl Horner.

Dried Sea Fish (White) – Shmuel Hertsig, Yekutial Sensensich, Ruwin Oster, Feywl Herman.

Egg Export – Nusan and Dovid Bishel, Itsie Thau.

Wholesale Construction Materials – Aba Hammer, Avrahamtsie Kuswan and Meir Kuswan, Gershon Melzer and Lancener.

Retail – Yisroel Noakh Milstein and son, Fishl Kuswan and Meir Kuswan, Gershon Melzer and Lancener.

Wine Trade (Wholesale) – Lipe Schwager, Lipe Unger and Leibtsie Libman, Meshulam Shimkha Linder and Moshe Rauchwerger, A. Ditikschtein.

Weapons (Ammunition) Trade – Landsberg-Krasicki, Maks Blits.

Hotels _ "Grand" Hotel: Chana Bahr, Aleksander Blits, Hotel Sternberg, Hotel Speier, Hotel Friedman.

Restaurants – Chana Bahr, Ephraim Legjonow, Mendl Allweil, Mordekhai Leib Henzel, Moshe Weikselbaum, Ephraim Schnobl, Urtsie Scherl, the Rot brothers, Avraham Kremer, Dovid Schecberg, Menenbaum, Kopl Zlaczower (Meir Macele's son), Hersh Kalech, Shimeon Fuks, Mrs. Zenendish (Tutechia), Shlomo Krauthamer, Hersz Krauthamer.

Soda-Water Factories – Shimeon Munczek and son, Nisan Eizner and son, Shimeon Fuks, Moshe Dovid Fingerl.

Military Contractors – Albin, the Peczinik brothers, Meir Zacher and sons, Shimshon Grunberg, Sholem Grun.

Iron Trade (wholesale and individual sales) – Slopkowicer and Singer, Zelig Herman and Icyk Chius, Ruchel Bitman, Petrower and Fund, Zayde Zelber, Firma Wanenberg, Shmuel Hilzgrot, Leib Hirsh, Zisie Hochman.

Naphta, Candles and Soap (Wholesale) – Shlomo Scherr, Meir Steiner, Yosye Merner, Shmuel Rozenshtraus, Gershon Steiner, Berish Dankner and son.

[Page 96]

Kolomea – Capital of Pokutia

by Dr. Avraham Yakov Braver (Jerusalem)

Translated by Gloria Berkenstat Freund

Pokutia in Ukrainian (until the beginning of the 20th century, we would say Russian or Ruthenian [Ukrainian]) and Pokucie in Polish, designated a province in the form of a triangle in the southern part of Poland (from 1370 until 1772 and from 1919 to 1939) and – Galicia (1772-1918). The area is in large part hilly and stands like a pole between several borders. The Cheremosh River, a tributary of the Prut, which divided the former Poland from the Principality of Moldova and at the time when the area was Galicia – from Bukovina, flows on the southeastern side. The mountainous Czornahora (Black Mountain) begins on the southeastern side and to the east the mountainous Garnani which divided the former Poland, later Galicia, from Hungary and in a certain era – from Transylvania and in the time of the revived Poland, between the two World Wars – from Romanian-occupied Bukovina. The north side has no firm boundary, unless the intersection between the Prut and the Dniester, since many believe that Pokutia ends at the Dnieper.

Pokutia was a natural province with its own managing committee. The capital city, Kolomea, which had existed for years, already in the 16th century, later became the seat of the county court and the tax collector for all of Pokutia, or as Jews referred to it – the Kolomear area. The name Pokutia evidently had a connection to the city, Kuti (Kutev) and means: the environment, the region of Kuti. It is possible that Pokutia is called "corner region." The area of Pokutia is 5,000 kilometers, which includes the counties (Polish: Powiat) of the cities: Kolomea, Pechenizhyn, Kosev, Sniatyn, the western part of Horodenka county and on the west, part of Nadvirna county.

[Page 97]

Kolomea was the principal Jewish city of the Pokutia triangle; it was the administrative, military and cultural center; during Austrian times it was the fourth largest city in Galicia and the third largest Jewish kehile [organized Jewish community], after Lemberg and Krakow, at any rate, the third largest in the area of general cultural life.

The mountainous character (Carpathian Mountains) of Pokutia gave rise to its poverty and backwardness. In this respect, neither the Polish nor the Austrian rule changed anything. The Pokutia earth did not produce enough grain to feed its population. Wheat, rye for flour, barley for the cattle and for beer brewing had to be brought in from other places. Almost the entire wheat trade was found in Jewish hands. At the time of Austrian rule, the wheat trade was with Romania; during the Polish rule – with Podolia.

During the old times, rye was ground in the private watermills. Later, in the second half of the 19th century, rich Jews (Litman Brettler and Moshe Gartenberg) erected new, modern mills with turbines and provided first class packaged flour for Pokutia.

Thanks to the warm summer climate in the lower parts of the region, maize (corn), the bread of the poor in the cities and villages, which was widespread only in Romania, grew in Pokutia. But the maize did not cover the entire need of the dense population and in Austrian times, maize had to be brought from Romania. The maize was ground in small mills. Bread was baked from the maize that is called malai in Ukrainian and Yiddish. Kasha[1*] is also made of it (in Romanian – mamaliga and polenta in Italian). Potatoes that grow in the entire area, except on mountains higher than 800 meters, are just enough for the population, including for the manufacture of alcohol, as in other Polish areas.

The Ukrainians and the Jews here call the potatoes mandeburke. Studying the Yiddish dialect of Pokutia, we find the designation mandeburke for potatoes and mandeburtshenik for potato bread in the entire area; in Stanislav and farther on the western side, potatoes are called bulbe and potato bread – bulbovenik[2*] The harvest of various pod foods [such as beans] was, it appears,

[Page 98]

in a sufficient amount because it was even possible to export it. Some Kolomea Jews were exporters of beans.

The region also had its own oil [pressed] from the nuts (tshontshenik in Yiddish) and watermelon produced in primitive oil presses that were called olinitses. The Jews seldom used this oil. The forest was a source of livelihood in Pokutia. The Kolomea market was flooded with all kinds of forest fruits with the arrival of summer – wild raspberries, strawberries, blackberries and other fruits, particularly goguetzis [berry similar to a blueberry] – which were not available in the western Carpathian forests. Homemakers would make syrups and preserves from them for the entire year. The Carpathian forests also provided an abundance of mushrooms, so that they could even be exported from Pokutia.

There were no valuable fruit trees during the Austrian times, except for good plum trees in several villages, particularly in Klyuchov, south of Kolomea. Plum jam was made from them in autumn. Good housekeepers would cook the plum jam themselves.[2*] But it could be bought at the market. These goods were also exported.

Animal breeding was not very developed in Pokutia. Only the Hutsuls [residents of the Hutsul region in the Carpathian Mountains] in the mountains had good horses to ride and carry loads on the mountain roads. However, livestock was brought from Pokutia to the west, particularly to Vienna, mainly pigs. There was a pig market every day and one after the other the pigs were taken to the railroad. The odor and the shrieking of the pigs filled the entire city. Jews had some share in the export of pigs.

Jewish furriers sewed furs, vests and fur caps for the peasants out of the prepared sheep skins. The cow and horse hides were prepared in the Kolomea tanneries which were in Jewish hands.

The trees in the forest were an important source of income for the city. The bark of the spruce tree [which contained tannin] was used to tan the hides [to make leather.]

Salt served as the main source of trade for the necessary wheat – for bread – for hundreds of years. Sources of salt are found in several places at the foot of the Pokutia Carpathians. The richest of them are in Lanchyn and in Delatyn [Dilyatyn]. The water is cooked until it evaporates and the salt remains. The

[Page 99]

salt would be sent to Podolia on the other side of the Dniester. Wheat would be brought back from there in the same wagons. The connection between Kolomea and Podolia is mirrored in the life of the Baal Shem Tov,[4*] who lived for several years in Pokutia from where he returned to Podolia, before he was revealed in Tluste (Tovste).

Salt was a government monopoly during Austrian times and the sale in bulk and retail was in Jewish hands. During the last quarter of the 19th century kerosene began to be drawn from the sources in Sloboda-Rungurska in the southwest mountains of Kolomea. A railroad line was built that connected the city train station with the kerosene sources. The kerosene was refined in Petchinizhin [Pechenizhyn], the city nearest to Sloboda-Rungurska and also in Kolomea. In the village of Mishin, about eight kilometers south of Kolomea, a brown coal mine was discovered at the end of the 19th century. After it was exploited for a time, it was abandoned because of the small quantity of coal.

The Name Kolomea

The Polish designation for the city is Kolomyja and it is the same in Ukrainian[5*]. Evidently, according to old sources, the Russians write Kolomaya. In Hebrew sources from the Haskalah [Enlightenment] and under the influence of the new Yiddish alef-bet [alphabet], it was written: Kolymei, Kolomey, Kolymeia and later, as the letter ayin [e] began to be used for a vowel sound, it was written: Kolomye. Since the Haskalah era and onward, the new generation writes: Kolomye, as in German. There is a hypothesis about the source and meaning of the name, that the founder of the city was the Hungarian King Koloman, who came in 1099 to help the Russian duke. He suffered defeat in Przemysl and returned to his country. It is improbable that a foreign king would found a city in the time of war. But it is possible that he had his camp on the spot and the name remained for generations. Several locations in Poland carry names from the Turks and Tatars who only passed through, or camped there. A second hypothesis relates to the Roman name, "Kolonya." But no trace of the old Romans was found here. It could be the name is not The Polish designation for the city is Kolomyja and it is the same in Ukrainian[3*]. Evidently, according to old sources, the Russians write Kolomaya. In Hebrew sources from the Haskalah [Enlightenment] and under the influence of the new Yiddish alef-bet [alphabet], it was written: Kolymei, Kolomey, Kolymeia and later, as the letter ayin [e] began to be used for a vowel sound, it was written: Kolomye. Since the Haskalah era and onward, the new generation writes: Kolomye, as in German. There is a hypothesis about the source and meaning of the name, that the founder of the city was the Hungarian King Koloman, who came in 1099 to help the Russian duke. He suffered defeat in Przemysl and returned to his country. It is improbable that a foreign king would found a city in the time of war. But it is possible that he had his camp on the spot and the name remained for generations. Several locations in Poland carry names from the Turks and Tatars who only passed through, or camped there. A second hypothesis relates to the Roman name, "Kolonya." But no trace of the old Romans was found here. It could be the name is not

[Page 100]

Slavic and not Romanian, but comes from one of the nations that passed through here at the time of the wandering of populations. The name of the neighboring city, Pechenezhin [Pechenizhyn], without doubt recalls the Pecheninim, an Argo-Finnish tribe that fought a war with the Byzantines and Rusens in the 9-11 centuries. The name Prut also is not Slavic, just as the name Carpathian is not Slavic. In each case the names were fixed much before the Jews appeared in the area, so that the Jews took the names from the Slavs. The Jews did not have any meaning or spelling for Kolomea.

The Geographical Position of the City, its Terrain, Climate and [Bodies of] Water

Kolomea is one of the large number of cities that lie at the foot of the Carpathian Mountains, near the roads and valleys that lead out of the mountains. In the area of economic and municipal development, the Jews played the main role over the course of hundreds of years as trade intermediaries between the mountains and the southern lowlands.

The geographical position of Kolomea is: 48 degrees 31 minutes, north latitude and 25 degrees east longitude from Greenwich. It lies on a line of latitude that is 16 degrees and 45 minutes from Jerusalem and on the line of longitude 10 degrees and 45 minutes that is to the west. Noon in relation to Jerusalem is 45 minutes later. The altitude of the city is between 285 meters above sea level in the mountains of Prut, on the border between the city and the village of Verbizh and about 300 meters north of the railroad line.

The city was built on the eastern side of the Prut River which here flows in the southeastern direction. The city houses do not reach to the river itself, only to the Prut Canal which was built in order to drive the wheels of the large mill that for years belonged to Jews (Moshe Gartenberg and his heirs). The canal was named after the mill – Mill Canal. Jews, making noise and making a racket, would come to bathe on its shores on summer days, and on Rosh Hashanah they came here for tashlikh [casting of bread crumbs into a moving body of water as a symbol of casting off one's sins]. A wide area with small stones, covered here and there with shrubs and all kinds of swamp and river plants and grasses, spread out between the canal and the river. This area was called Zarinek – outside the city area and the swamp plants are called lengi in Polish.

[Page 101]

The place for military instruction, which drew onlookers, gangs of young boys and plain idlers, was on the Zarinek. Students would stroll along it. Discussions were also organized there, such as in the time of illegal organizations of Jewish students at the beginning of the 20th century.

Three small rivers flow in the city. The largest of them flows west from the city on the border of the village of Dyatkovtsy (Gyetkovits) and is named Kolomeyke. The second is named – Kyernitsa, that is, Brunem [well] River because if flows by the wells that have the best drinking water, which is used by the entire city. This is a low river, but after a summer downpour or in the spring when the snow melts, it grows, flows over the shores and rips away many houses. The Jews called the third river, east of the city, Klebanya, that is, the courtyard of the city priest because it flows by the Romanian Catholic church, to the east. The river was low and marshy and did not even grow much during the times of heavy rain.

The earth of the city is an accumulation from Prut and its rivers. Digging wells, one finds a yellow and blue-grey earth and under it, flint. This earth is used for the manufacture of earthenware pots and bricks. The blue earth is used for caulking or to mix with lime. The Jews called it "blue earth" and would sell it at the market. Water was found not too deeply all around the city, but the water contained coarse salt and other salts and it was not for drinking and it was not good for washing, either. Water carriers would provide the Jewish homes with water in barrels that they carried from the only good well that was located near the hill of the Greek church (during Austrian Poland, it was Catholic, later – Orthodox). According to a Ukrainian legend, the holy mother appeared and in her merit there was good water here. Once a year a pilgrimage was made to this church. The Jews knew of this holiday by the Ukrainian name: Bogoroditsa (God's mother). The holiday brought prosperity to the stores. Carrying water was a Jewish occupation There were also water carriers for the closest streets. Brick production lay in Jewish hands. But they did not take part in the manufacture of earthenware pots. A factory for good earthenware pots existed in the city. Jews

[Page 102]

were not employed in this trade, they only were involved with simple earthenware pots.

The climate of Kolomea is comparable to Krakow or even with Lemberg, a dry one. The contrast between winter and summer is greater here than there. The maize ripens during the second half of the summer thanks to the warmth and the moderation of the rains. During the growing season in places that are protected against strong winds, apricots turn out well. Tomatoes were known in the vegetables markets at the end of the 19th century, but only the landowners bought them then, that is, the well-to-do Christians.

The Veins of Communication of the City

Kolomea as a Jewish city was a city of commerce with great connections and important roads for contacts. The most important of them were the highway and the railroad line (from 1866?), which stretched from Chernowitz and Moldavia and from the Black Sea. They led to Stanislaw and Lemberg and from there to the west to Krakow and Vienna to the most western part of the European continent or from Lemberg to the north, to Warsaw and to the Baltic Sea. That is: Kolomea lay in the very center of the industrial communication veins. Pokutia was the gate to the larger world.

The Kolomea merchants actually had international contacts. And it was not only small town boasting when those from Kolomea told themselves that the events in Belgrade at the beginning of the 20th century – events of great economic and political significance – were known much earlier in the Kolomea trade circles, even before the Lemberg press. The connections with Romania and, even, with Turkey, which ruled in Romania until the middle of the 19th century, were apparent even in the Kolomea market. There were olives in Kolomea when not so often in the Balkans. Many had to become accustomed to the fruit after conquering their first nausea. Red watermelons were brought from Romania and they were sold in market booths. During the Austrian times, Galatser [town in Romania] fish would not leave the table during the winter Shabbosim [Sabbaths]. Cooling wagons were not then known in Galicia. A catch-all store, which existed at the end of the 19th century, was called by the eastern name, "Bazaar,"

[Page 103]

and those from Kolomea would go to shop in the bazaar as if in Constantinople (the name means market in Turkish). Those from Kolomea bought Turkish sweets in a shop from the "Turk," who wore a turban. Half Turk, half Sephardic Jew, he converted to Judaism and married a Kolomea Jewish girl. The Turk was very old at the end of the 19th century. He did not live to see the 20th century. The last trace of Turkishness, which was a tradition for generations when Bukovina was a Turkish province, disappeared with the Turk.

Limited trade and family connections were permitted between Kolomea and Yas [Iasi], the metropolis of Romanian Jewry, and, consequently, there was reciprocal spiritual influence. Reb Aryeh Leib Toybish, founder of the Hovevi Zion [Lovers of Zion] movement and one of the first followers of Herzl, was descended from Iasi rebbes. He was born in Bender, Bessarabia, and while still a child came to Pokutia with his parents. Without a doubt he was under the influence of the Romanian founder of Rosh Pina and Zichron Yaakov.

The Chernowitz-Lemberg line leaves Kolomea via the Prut Valley, through which it passes Bukovina and Galicia to Kolomea and turns and then goes northwest across the Dniester. A second old road goes in the Prut Valley near its sources. It also has an international significance, but a smaller one than mentioned above.

A highway was already built here at the end of the 18th century, but a train line was first built in the last years of the 19th century. Stanislav had a train line to Hungary before Kolomea, but earlier the traffic between Hungary and Pokutia went through Kolomea. Wandering tribes and merchants went through during the Middle Ages on the road from the Prut Valley to the Tisa Valley, across Delatyn [Dilyatyn]-Mikulichin [Mykulchyn]-Iasi-Sziget. The traditional trade in Hungarian wines began in Kolomea probably after the Middle Ages.

Kolomea on one side and Sziget on the other were the Jerusalems of Poland and Hungary in the matter of commerce and spiritual influence. Maramorsher [Maramues, Romania] Jews, dressed in shorter kaftans than the Galiciander kaftans and in flat velvet hats, would on the eve of the holidays after bathing, come in wagons or riding to Kolomea to their rebbes, the Galiciander and Bukoviner tzadekim [righteous men].

[Page 104]

Moldova and Hungary were richer than Galicia in general and, in particular, Pokutia. And many Kolomea Jews emigrated temporarily or forever to those countries. Ukrainian field and forest workers through the intervention of a Jewish broker left for work in Romania.[11])

In addition to the two international lines, Kolomea also served as a crossroads for roads of the second and third rank to the Pokutia mountain south and to Podolia north. Three rivers pour into Prut south of the city: 1) Sapuavka, 2) Pistinka, 3) Lutshke. A highway runs in the first river basin and a railroad to Petshinizshin and Slobokda Rungurska. The road goes uphill, but it does not go over the river crossing and the border to the Maramosh Province.

The second, small river, as its name says – comes from Pistyn (the city of Reb Leib Pistyner, the school friend of the Baal Shem Tov, who was brought for burial to Kolomea). The road to this shtetl lies more in the valley of Lutshka, because the valley of the Pistynke is narrow in the topmost part. The above-mentioned Mishin is located in the Lutshka Valley, and after Mishin – the town Stoptshet-Jablonow. From the Lutshka Valley we come over the mountain to Pistyn, which lies in a valley and carries the same name. From Pistyn the mountain divides there and leads to Kosow. This is the largest city in the heart of the mountain and is the county seat of the Hutsul Region. This mountain tribe speaks Ukrainian with a particular dialect. Rasish is differentiated from the Slavic and is closer to Romanian.

This city lived mainly by raising cattle and forest work. Kosow is a market place for these two economic branches. This was an important Jewish center and a residence for tzadekim from the dynasties of the Baal Shem Tov's bel-tefilah [prayer leader], Kopl Hasid. The road through

[Page 105]

the mountain connects Kosov with Kitev which lies in the Cheremosh Valley between Poland and Romania. On each side of the Cheremosh lies Vizshnits [Vyzhnytisa] (in Bukovina) that was also a real Jewish city, the residence of a rabbinical dynasty of the same Kopl Hasid's line. Kitev is known to Jews as the city of Rebbe Gershon, the brother-in-law of the Baal Shem Tov, who was the pioneer of Hasidic emigration to Eretz-Yisroel. In the autumn of 1939, Kitev was the witness to a great Jewish tragedy: here the Polish government crossed the border with a great mass of state workers, running from the Germans. But the Poles held back the Jews from saving themselves. With this began the deliverance of Jews into the hands of the Germans by the Poles, which lasted for almost six years.

There was heavy traffic of timber rafts on the Cheremosh; logs were lowered from the high mountain forests. The Jews took an active part in the wood industry and in the wood trade. They also were employed in the difficult work of connecting timber rafts and in their transport.

The most important roads are to the north: the highway to the Gvorzdets-Horodenka-Chortkiv railway line - and from there across the Dniester Bridge to Tluste [Tovste]-Jagielnica-Chortkiv. This is the main connection with Podolia. The railway line to Zalishchiki [Zalishchyky], which was built during the Austrian period, passes several kilometers in the Bukovina area. And when Bukovina was joined to Romania, the connection depended on the requirements of Romania.

Austria built a railway line for strategic reasons that connected Podolia with Pokutia and with Hungary.

Kolomea was an important strategic center during the Austrian era, from which the Jews drew their income both directly and indirectly. They were building contractors and military contractors. Soldiers and officers filled Jewish shops and restaurants and were an economic factor in the city.

Kolomea was, like other Polish cities, built according to the standard plan that was brought from Germany: in the center a four-corned ring-platz [circular place] with shops around it for a market. In each corner two roads lead out from the circle. Such a four-cornered [place] is also called a ring-platz in German, in Polish – rynek, and rynek in Ukrainian. In Kolomea, in the center of the ring-platz stands a group of houses on two streets. This group was called hintern rothoyz [behind the city hall] in Yiddish (in Polish: ratusz). In our generation, the city hall was located in a southwestern corner of the marketplace and also was called the ratusz in Polish. But the Jews for a not too clear reason called it the komune [Commune] as in Paris in 1871. In other cities in Galicia, the house of the city managing committee was called rothoyz and the communal council – magistrat [city hall], just as in Polish.

The "Commune" had a lookout tower with a balcony around it. A watchman walked around it day and night and blew a trumpet at the outbreak of a fire. The firemen's station was in the courtyard of the "Commune." The center for the city police was also there. New shops with shop windows were located on the third side of the ring-platz, among them three bookstores, one owned by a Pole who sold Polish belle-lettres; the second was owned by a Jew who dealt with textbooks. The Jew, Orenshtein, later became a publisher of Ukrainian books. The third was owned by a former servant at the Baron Hirsh School. He mostly sold textbooks for the folks-shul [public school]. South of the group of houses, hintern rothoyz on the ring-platz, during the Austrian era, there was a market with vegetables, poultry, eggs, which the peasants brought to Pokutia to sell. Potters displayed their goods here – earthen crockery.

The flour shops and shops with various foods were located on the eastern side. During the Austrian time, one-story houses also stood on this site; they were built of bricks like the other houses on the ring-platz.

On the northwestern side, mainly on the streets that go to the north, Jewish luft-mentschn [people of no specific occupation] were concentrated. Here stood brokers of wheat, of cattle, of field lessees and

[Page 107]

middlemen between lenders and loan takers. The loan middlemen were called hishtararim [mediators in financial matters].

There were esteemed, trustworthy men among them who would receive large sums from the lenders and have a free hand from the loan-brokers to give loans at their discretion to dependable people. One of the loan-brokers whom I knew was a former estate owner. He squandered his wealth on charity, descended from his higher status and became a hishtaran. Day and night he would sit in the beis-hamedrash [synagogue or house of prayer] and stuff the charity boxes with his last pennies. A second loan-broker was an esteemed man, a Jew, a clever man with an open hand for the needy. His conscience awoke in his old age that he had devoted himself to the business of interest, although he was always careful not to violate the trade document making the taking of interest possible, and he fell into melancholy.

For the Days of Awe, a market also stood in these surroundings for beli-tefilus [men who recite the prayers in the synagogue] for the villages.

On the eastern side stood new, beautifully finished businesses. The sidewalk on this side served as a corso – a place for strolling in Italy – for the city's "golden young" – students, officers, young office employees and, it should be understood – also the city's young girls of the best society, candidates for proper matches.

Between these sides in the garden in the center stood fiacres [small four-wheeled horse carriages] to rent, mostly to travel to the train station and for the doctors who went on visits to the sick. There was a rule in Kolomea: if you ordered a doctor, you also had to arrange for a fiacre, even when the residence was not farther than a several minute walk. A memorial for the Polish poet Franciszek Karpinski stood after the fiacres. The Jews thought little of this scene and would call it "Karpinski the goat."

The central area was a conglomeration of various wholesale and retail stores. Here the peasants and Hutsuls bought everything their hearts desired: fabrics, colorful ribbons, house utensils and work tools and horse implements for wagons and riding. Here on the market one could still a thirst with colorful lemonade and soda water and eat gigantic peppered knishes with onions, greased with oil. Noise was also not absent here

[Page 108]

from those hawking their goods, but the racket of the Arabian Yaffa or of another Arabian city did not reach hintern rothoys in Kolomea.

The main street led down from the "Commune" to the other side of the Prut. During the times of the Austrians and the Poles, the street was called Sobieski. At the beginning of the street stood the Greek Catholic (Ukrainian) church and, from there, down hill to the south, the road led to the city wells and to the large Jewish bathhouse, which was distinguished by its good water. On the other side of the wells flows the River Kierncia and behind it the neighborhood, the neye velt [new world]. Here lived the poorest population. Many of them emigrated to America at the end of the 19th century leaving their families on the Neye Velt in Kolomea. Many of their families left to join them in the new world on the other side of the ocean. A number of them returned to the Neye Velt in Kolomea.

The train line, which leads down to the southwestern shtetl Sloboda-Rungurska and to the northwestern village of Sheparavitz, runs along the length of Sobieski Street. In the lowest part of Sobieski Street and in its nearby alleys on the road to the villages, Gyetkevitz, Verbizh and farther to the shtetl Petchinizhin [Pechenizhyn] – also lived a poor population stratum. Here lived tanners, hat makers and other tradesmen who worked for [the patronage of] the peasants and Hutsuls who came to the city through the suburb that was named Nadvirna Forstot [suburb]. In Yiddish the road to Verbizh to the Prut Bridge, which was the boundary of the city – was called: "The Rogatke [city gate] Street." At the end of the city the money was collected for the city gate. At night, the city gate lessee, a Jew, it should be understood, locked the street for the complete width of the city gate. There was competition among many people interested in renting the gate and charging the fee. The income from the city gates was a difficult one. No Jew became rich from a city gate. But in the eyes of the non-Jews he was one of those who "sucked the blood from the Christians."

At the rear of Sobieski Street stood a small synagogue built of brick that was named "Dos Ellever Shulekhl" [the eleventh small synagogue]. If it really was the 11th small synagogue in number or if it was named that according to the number of its founders is not known. Located near the small synagogue was the bathhouse, built by Reb Yakov Brettler, the wealthy man, in

[Page 109]

which he had a separate room. He would come riding to his bathhouse in his fiacre every erev Shabbos [eve of Shabbos – Friday]. The water from this bath was red; it contained iron. No other millionaire in Kolomea had such a bathroom and bathtub in his house.

In the rear of the western side of the ring-platz was a street of warehouses. After this street was the "hey-platz" [hay square]. This was the center for the wagon-drivers before the era of the train and it also remained so later. Most of the houses here were one-story. In the middle of the square stood a low synagogue, built of wood, that was called royt-shulekhl [small red synagogue] – where the "ordinary Jews" prayed.

A small room in this synagogue for a separate minyan [10 men required for prayer] was called "di kelnye [the tiny synagogue or minyan]." Di kelnye was in relation to the synagogue in the same way as the synagogue was in relation to the city synagogue. Not far from here was a synagogue for the well-to-do businessmen. It was called – "the synagogue from Jerusalem." The majority of the synagogues in the city were concentrated around the "great synagogue." There was also a bathhouse from before the expansion of the city to the Neye Velt on the streets that lead out from the northeast of the ring-platz. According to Kolomea tradition, the Baal Shem Tov [founder of Hasidism] immersed himself in the mikvah [ritual bath] of this bathhouse.

A road to the north to the county office runs from the middle of the north side of the ring-platz. Therefore, the road was called the City Hall Road. This was one of the real streets in the city. From this street, a street, which was named after Kaiser Franz Josef during the Austrian times, divides the north and south. Here were the residences of the nobles and here lived several rich, educated Jews. The city garden was also here. There was an oil refinery, a mill and other small factories in the area.

The Roman Catholic church stands on the southeast corner of the ring-platz and is the most beautiful of all of the buildings on the ring-platz. On the top of the church shone the name of God in Hebrew letters. According to Jewish legend, the name of God was written by a Jewish convert. The building continually sank and the gentiles looked for a remedy so that the house would not sink farther. After the convert finished writing the name of God, he fell from the top of the church onto the ground and turned into a stone. And this is truly the most beautiful threshold at the gate of the church. It was also said that there was a Hebrew inscription on the bottom of the gate, not with such clear golden

[Page 110]

letters as on the top of the church, only with black writing which were erased over the years.

From the church, east of the street, passes Klebania Street on the road to Zablotov-Sniantyn-Chernovitz. The Polish and Ukrainian gymnasium [secondary school] is located near the church. The road to Koroluavka descends south of the church. The Jewish cemetery, which had been in use from the 16th century until 5545 (1785), is located on Kaminker Street, the street parallel to the "Commune." A second cemetery dating from the years 5545-5653 (1893) is located on the north side of the city, at the entrance to the German village of Baginsberg. The third and last cemetery is located north of the Klebania Street, between it and the train line.

The confines of Kolomea spread across a wide area and also encompass villages and half-agricultural sections. The boundaries of Kolomea were "scientifically" combined in what is called: "electoral geometry." In the last third of the 19th century until the year 1914, the actual city of Kolomea was 80 percent Jewish. In order to prevent the Jews from becoming a decisive power in the city government and in the elections to Parliament and to the Galician Sejm [parliament] – the city annexed two German villages as well as Polish and Ukrainian neighborhoods. The Jews were concentrated in a thickly populated area of the city and along the main highway. Ukrainians lived mainly in the southern suburbs, in the northern and northwestern – Poles and Germans, who in the Austrian and Polish times were servile and obedient to the orders of the regime and voted according to its will. The Germans all were more assimilated than the Poles, but when the Nazis entered, they instantly became Volks-Deutchn [ethnic Germans], followers of Hitler.

The Number of Jews in Kolomea and Kolomea County

Before 1914 there were 41,000 souls in Kolomea, half of them Jews. Three national minorities lived with them: Ukrainians, Poles and Germans. Since the census of 1890, a percentage of Jews had begun to leave Kolomea The reason was that in general, as in every Galician city, the influence of Poles and Ukrainians in the city had grown. Their

[Page 111]

striving to be free from Jewish power grew with their increasing and more widely spread education.. Private Christian businesses and cooperatives were created and the number of Christian artisans grew. Jews emigrated to the West, to America, Germany, to Vienna and even to Budapest. During the First World War many escaped to Austria, particularly to Vienna, and many did not return to Kolomea.

In August 1939 there were about 35,500 souls: 15,100 Jews, 11,000 Poles, 6,600 Ukrainians, 1,800 Germans (in the villages that were annexed to the city) and 1,500 half

Polish-half Ukrainians – Ukrainian speaking members of the Roman Catholic church. In the 25 years since 1914, 6,000 Jews left Kolomea, above and beyond the natural increase of at least one percent a year. There actually were much fewer of the old residents from 1914 remaining in the city. Of the 15,000, perhaps a third of those were from the villages and shtetlekh [towns] of Pokutia and beyond it, who during and after the First World War left their homes and flocked to the "big" city, to Kolomea.

Of the list of 84 settlements in Kolomea county that during Polish times again included Petchinizhin [Pechenizhyn], it is apparent that the number of Jews in the villages had diminished. In addition to Kolomea, there were Jewish communities in Petchinizhin, Nwozdziec and Jablonow. There was only an absolute Jewish majority in the last two communities. The Ukrainians had the absolute majority in Petchinizhin. In all, there were 19,500 Jew in the municipal communities.

Footnote:

1. Complements from Lou Grebler: The chief-broker for forest workers to Romania was Shimshon Konits, a brother-in-law of Peysi Zinger and of Avraham Ashkhenazi. Konits ran a large office with employees, among them his own daughter. He would receive blank passports from the county office and write the names in himself. Konits' house at the corner of Shevchenko and Mnichovska Street was besieged summer and winter by peasants from all over Pokutia who were looking for work in Romania.

Translator & Coordinator's footnotes:

1. Kasha is traditionally made from buckwheat. [Tr.]
2. In America, bulbovenik was often called "potatonik" [Co.]
3. My father once rode his bike south all the way over the Romanian border to buy plums for his mother to cook- the jam was called "podl." [Co.]
4. Rabbi Yisroel ben Eliezer, founder of Hasidism. [Tr.]
5. Kolomyya is the Ukrainian spelling. [Tr.] The more recent transliteraton of the Ukrainian spelling on their websites is Kolomyia. [Co.]

[Page 112]

Rabbis, Synagogues and Jewish Life in Kolomea

by Moshe Rat (Tel Aviv)

Translated by Gloria Berkenstat Freund

There are many indisputable sources about the Jewish kehile [organized Jewish community] in Kolomea. The old pinkasim [registration books] were burned during the second great fire in 5587 – 1827, when the large synagogue was burned, and in 5625 – 1865, when all of the Kolomea synagogues and houses of prayers were destroyed by the fire. Therefore, I must pilfer the subsequent sources:

The book, Zikhron Rishonim[1] [Memory of the Rishomim – leading sages of the 11th to 15th centuries] of the Rabbi, Reb Chaim-Tzvi Teomim, of blessed memory, religious judge and rabbi in Kolomea, 5674 [1914]; Anshei Shem [Notable Men] and Kiryah Nisgavah [Exalted City] of Reb Shlomo Buber and Shem haGedolim [The Names of the Great Ones] and Shem Hagedolim HeHadash [The Names of the New Great Ones] of Reb Chaim Azulai, Warsaw; Shivchei haBaal Shem Tov [a collection of stories of the Baal Shem Tov, the founder of Hasidism]; manuscript and family tree and mainly a manuscript of my great grandfather, the Rabbi Pinkhas Epshtein, of blessed memory, chairman of the rabbinical court in Kitev [Kuty], of blessed memory, and which is now with my brother, the Rabbi Reb Meshulam Rath, previously chairman of the rabbinical court in Chernovitz [Chernivitsi] and today a member of the Chief Rabbinate in Jerusalem. I also am making use of facts that were given as word of mouth and of my own memories of that which I heard and saw in my childhood and early years at the time when I was studying in a small synagogue and I was a student of rabbis and sages.

The rabbis who sat on the rabbinical throne of our kehile during the course of 300 years as chairmen of the religious court, rabbis and heads of the religious court, judges and heads of yeshivus:

1. The first of the rabbis who was known to us as the chairman of the rabbinical court and head of the rabbinical college in Kolomea was one of the sons or sons-in-law

[Page 113]

of the gaon [sage], the author of Mas'at Benyamin [The Aim of Benyamin], of blessed memory from before the year 5400 [1640] as is mentioned in the book, Shevile Olam [Pathways of the World]. Many years ago his headstone was found sunken into the earth. But the entire inscription on it could not be deciphered.

2. The Rabbi, Reb Avraham Zav (Avraham son of Wolf) of blessed memory, of Kolomea, is remembered in the pinkas of the kehile of the holy community of Zsholkowa (Zsholkev) in connection with the acknowledgement of the kehile rules that were set in the year 5424 – 1664, and signed by: the Reb Shimeon Ginzburg of Przemysl, the Rabbi Josef Ayzyk of Javoriv, the Reb Shmuel Zaynvl Segal of Lemberg, the Reb Dovid Preger of Buczacz, as well as the Gaon, author of Turei Zahav [Rows of Gold, authored by David HaLevi Segal] signed there (see: Kiryah Nisgavah [History of the Jews of Zolkiew]).

3. The Rabbi Reb Avraham bar [son of] Josef Kohen Tzedek [priest of righteousness], of blessed memory, was the head of the rabbinical panel in Kolomea. There were pogroms in Lemberg in 5424 [1664]. This was on the day of the holy Shabbos [Sabbath], the 2nd of Iyyar, where more than 120 souls were murdered, including distinguished rabbis and religious judges. Among the hundreds was also the above-mentioned Gaon, Reb Avraham K"Tz [abbreviation for Kohen Tzedek that means "righteous Kohen" and is the origin of the surname "Katz."], who was in Lemberg by chance (according to his headstone at the Lemberg cemetery). The inscription of the headstone of the Rabbi Avraham K"Tz, of blessed memory appears in the book, Notable Men, and, incidentally, it says: The great scholar, our teacher and rabbi, Reb Avraham, son of our teacher and rabbi, Yosef K"Tz, head of the yeshiva in the holy community of Kolomea.

4. Reb Chaim ben [son of] Reb Yehoshaya (chairman of the rabbinical court in the community of Krakow) was the chairman of the rabbinical court in the community of Kolomea; later he was head of the rabbinical panel in Lemberg and he died there on the 9th of Adar 5433 [1673]; he was the son of the Gaon, the author of Maginei Shlomo [Shlomo's Sorrow], of blessed memory and a son-in-law of the Gaon, Reb Tzvi Hirsh, of blessed memory, the chairman of the rabbinical panel of the Mezrich kehile (see Responsa in Emunat Shmuel [Faith of Samuel] of the Gaon, Reb Ahron Shmuel bar Yisroel Keidanover, Frankfurt-on-Main, 5443 [1683]). On his headstone is etched the words: On 9 Adar 5433 [25 February 1673], passed away the holy man of life, who is buried here. He was a teacher in yeshivas in several places, in particular, in the great and important old Jewish community of Kolomea; he was the rabbi and great scholar, our teacher, Rabbi Chaim, son of the great scholar, our teacher and rabbi, Reb Yehoshua, head of the religious court in Krakow. In his merit, may his soul be bound in the bond of the living.[2]

5. The Rabbi, Reb Efraim Fishel ber Chaim, of blessed memory, the son of the above mentioned. He also was the chairman of the rabbinical court in Kolomea. He was the brother of the Gaon, Reb Tzvi Hirsh, of blessed memory, chairman of the rabbinical court in Berezhany, Drohobych, Brod, Lisk (see Anshei Shem).

[Page 114]

6. It is mentioned in a manuscript that is located in the library at Oxford that the Rabbi, Reb Dovid Kohen, of blessed memory, of Kolomea, was chairman of the rabbinical court in Kolomea in 5470 [1710] (see Zikhron Rishonim under the name of the Rabbi, the sage, Reb Yekutiel Yuda Grinwald).

7. Reb Yisroel Baal Shem Tov,[3] may the memory of a righteous man be blessed, came to Kolomea from the village of Kshilovic and was revealed here. His apartment was – as is accepted – in the house, which later became a synagogue, "the small Kosever synagogue."

The old bathhouse was called the Mikhvah funem Besh't [the Baal Shem Tov's ritual bath – Besh't is an acronym for the Baal Shem Tov], because according to tradition, he immersed himself there. From here, the Besh't went to Tlost (Tioust) and from there in 5500 [1740] to Medzhybizh and died on the 7th of Sivan 5514 [28 May 1754].

8. The Rabbi Dovid Shlomo, of blessed memory, one of the students of the Besh't, was Magid Meisharim [one who gives sermons in the synagogue] in our city; he died in the community of Skolye, near the city of Stry. On his headstone is engraved: Died Tuesday, 16 Shevat 5492 [12 February 1732]; here is buried the pure and holy man, our teacher and Rabbi David[4], son of

our teacher Shlomo, of blessed memory, the preacher in the Holy Community Kolomea (see: Shem Hagedolim HeHadash).

9. The Rabbi, Reb Leib Pistener, of blessed memory, rabbi, Hasid and holy man, one of the students of the Baal Shem Tov, is mentioned several times in the book Toldos Yakob Yosef [History of Jakob Josef], as well as in the book, Degel Makhneh Ephraim [Banner of the Camp of Ephraim]. He lived in Kolomea and spread Torah in our city and he died here on the 3rd of Iyyar 5505 [May 5, 1745]. On his headstone in the very old cemetery in Kamionka Street – which was damaged and was restored in 5633 [1873] – is carved his name and the date of his death.

10. The Rabbi Menakhem Mendl, of blessed memory, of Kolomea, rabbi, gaon and holy man, a friend and a student of the Besh't. According to the hypothesis of the author of Zikhron

Rishonim, he was a brother-in-law of the Rabbi, the pious man, Reb Moshe of Kitev, of blessed memory.

11. The Rabbi, Reb Meshulam bar Yeshayahu, of blessed memory, is remembered in the book of the kehile of the holy community of Lemberg, page 100, in a judgment of Rosh Kodesh [start of the month] Iyyar 5487 [22 April 1727]. He was the head of the rabbinical court in Kolomea He was the son-in-law of the Gaon, Reb Efraim Fishl bar Chaim, of blessed memory, head of the rabbinical court and kehile in Kolomea (see above number 5) and his successor on the rabbinical seat in our city. His son-in-law was the Rabbi, Reb Shimshon of Buczacz, of blessed memory, the father of the Gaon, Reb Meshulam Freshburger, of blessed memory (according to the pedigree of my great grandfather, the rabbi and pious man, Reb Pinkhas Epshtein), who was the father-in-law of my grandfather, Reb Josi Rath, of blessed memory; his second son-in-law was the Gaon Reb, Noakh Efraim Fishl bar Moshe,

[Page 115]

of blessed memory, who was his successor on the rabbinical seat as leader of the religious court and head of the rabbinical academy in Kolomea; his third son-in-law was the Gaon , my great grandfather, Reb Yitzhak, of blessed memory, the father of the Gaon, Reb Nakhman Epshtein, of blessed memory, both heads of the rabbinical court in Kolomea. The father of the Rabbi, Reb Meshulam, the Gaon Reb Yeshayahu, was the head of the rabbinical court in Lemberg. The Rabbi, Reb Meshulam bar Yeshayahu died on the Monday of Khol HaMoed [intermediary days of a religious holiday] in 5506 [1746] according to what is inscribed on his headstone at the very old cemetery on Kamionka Street.

12. The Rabbi Noakh Efraim Fishl bar Moshe, of blessed memory, head of the religious court and head of the yeshiva in Kolomea, was the successor to his father-in-law, the Gaon Reb Meshulam, of blessed memory who is mentioned above. He died on Shabbos, the 13th of Tishrei 5542 [1782], and lies in the very old cemetery on Kamionka Street.

13. The Rabbi, Reb Yakov Kopl bar Nekhemiah Feyvl, of blessed memory, rabbi, Hasid and holy man of the members of the holy temple of our teacher, the Besh't, may the memory of a righteous man be blessed, who was called Reb Kopl Hasid and he was the father of the holy man, our leader, teacher and master, Reb Menakhem Mendl of Kosov, may the memory of a righteous man be blessed, author of the book, Ahavat Shalom [Lover of Peace], the father of Kosover and Vizhnitzer dynasties. The Rabbi, Reb Yakov Kopl lived in our city for many years. He later moved to Mismenic, where he died on the 16th Elul 5547 [1787], as is inscribed on his headstone.

His wife, haRabnit [the rabbi's wife], Chaya bas [daughter of] Reb Zalman, of blessed memory, of Kolomea, was a granddaughter of the Rabbi, Reb Yakov Kopl Kamiel, of blessed memory, born of the Schnaittach [family] in Germany, a granddaughter of the rabbi Ovadia of Bartenura. A very rich man, he came to Kolomea from the city of Chechnovtse [Ciechanowiec] and used his money to build a synagogue, a house of study and a bathhouse; he took the sister of the Gaon, the author of Tosfos Yom Tov, Madam Perl, may she rest in peace, as a wife. His son, the Rabbi, Reb Zalman, who was also the uncle and father-in-law of the above mentioned Rabbi, Reb Kopl Hasid, married the Rebbitzin [wife of rabbi] Bluma bas [daughter of] Reb Shlomo, of blessed memory, the son of the Gaon, the author of Turei Zahav [Rows of Gold], of blessed memory. Reb Shlomo, of blessed memory, was murdered in Lemberg in 5424 [1664]. The above-mentioned Rebbitzen Chaya died in Kolomea on 13 Iyyar 5535 [13 May 1775] and she lies in the very old cemetery on Kamionka Street.

14. The Rabbi, Reb Shaltial Eyzyk haLevi Shternhel, of blessed memory, of Kolomea, a giant of Torah, a righteous man, a very rich man, the brother-in-law of the above-mentioned, the Rabbi, Reb Kopl Hasid, a grandson of the Rabbi, Reb Adam the baal hashem [miracle worker], of blessed memory. He was also a merchant and a liberal donor. He emigrated to Eretz-Yisroel in his old age and died in Jerusalem.

[Page 116]

15. My great grandfather, the Rabbi, Reb Yitzhak bar Nakhman Tzvi haLevi Epshtein, of blessed memory, head of the rabbinical court in Bar, known by the name, Reb Nakhman Barer, was the chairman of the rabbinical court in our city. The Rabbi, Reb Nakhman Tzvi Epshtein of Bar, Podolia, belonged to the followers of the Magid [preacher], Reb Dov Ber of Mezritch; he was considered a miracle worker and as a holy man. He died in the year 5495 [1735]. His father, Reb Avraham Segal Epshtein, was the rabbi in Rowna and later in Recnitz [Rahonc], Hungary. He was one of the three rabbis who chose Reb Shimshon Wertheimer as a teacher in his House of Study in Vienna. This Reb Avraham was a grandson of Reb Avraham bar Meir haLevi Epshtein; he was descended from the Rabbi Nusan Epshtein, of blessed memory, of Frankfurt on Main, who was rabbi in Horodna, later rabbi in Brisk, Lithuania and in Lublin.

Some of his answers on Halakhah [Jewish religious law] are found in Shalus vaTeshuvas [Reponsa] as well as in a book of responsa, Penei Yehoshua, Even Ha'ezer [a section of Rabbi Jakob Asher's compilation of Jewish Law], Arba'ah Turim], chapter 9 and in Responses of the Latter Geonim [spiritual leaders of Jewish community], paragraph 23. Another grandson was Reb Arieh Leib, Rabbi in Konigsberg during the years 5505-5535 [1745-1775]. There he spread the Torah, improved on precepts and wrote 10 books about the mitzvahs [commandments] in Halakhah, Kabbalah and Muser. The most important of them: Sefer haPardes [Book of the Orchard] which takes in commentaries to the commandments of the Krias Shema [Shema Yisroel prayer – Hear O Israel – opening words of the central prayer in Judaism] and of Shemiras Shabbos [guarding or keeping the Shabbat], sermons, innovations in Halakhah, the majority about annotated order, eulogies, commentaries to Moed Kattan [Little Festival – tractate of the Talmud], Taanis [Fasting – tractate of the Talmud] and others, published in Konigsberg 5519 [1759]; Or Hashanim – Kavanot LeTaryag Mitzvot [Light of the Years – Meaning and Intention of the 613 Commandments], published in Frankfurt on the Oder, 5514 [1754]; Mishnat Gur-Arie [The Study of Gur Arie] – a commentary on the order of the prayers according to the Kabbalah, published only in part in Konigsberg in 5525 [1765]; Teshuvot Mahal [Answers of Mahal], a collection of his answers in Halakhah, there, 5529 [1769]; Shulkhan Orekh chapter 10 and innovations to the Talmud and Shulkhan Orekh, chapter 10 with the innovations of his son Reb Avraham Meir, of blessed memory, was published in Vilna in 5643 [1883].

The Rabbi Reb Yitzhak Epshtein was the son-in-law of the above-mentioned Gaon Reb Mesholem, chairman of the religious court of our kehile and after the death of his brother-in-law, the above-mentioned gaon Reb Noakh Efraim Fishl, of blessed memory, he took his place on the rabbinical seat in Kolomea. He died on the 3rd of Adar 5555 [22 February, 1795] and was buried in the very old cemetery on Kamionka Street.

16. My great grandfather, the Rabbi, Reb Nakhman Tzvi Epshtein, of blessed memory, the son of the above-mentioned Rabbi, Reb Yitzhak haLevi Epshtein, of blessed memory, was taken as rabbi and chairman of the rabbinical court in our city after the death of his father, of blessed memory.

[Page 117]

He was the friend of the gaon, the author of Ketsot haKhoshen [Ends of the Breastplate], of blessed memory, and he studied with him in the yeshiva. He died at a very old age, 28 Tishrei 5590 [25 October 1829] and was buried at the old cemetery (not at the very old cemetery of Kamionka Street). His son, the Rabbi, Reb Meshulam, of blessed memory was raised in Kolomea and later he was the rabbi and chairman of the rabbinical court in Pistyn. He died when young in Kolomea, 7 Tevet 5580 [25 December 1819] and was buried in the old cemetery near the grave of his father, the above-mentioned gaon, Reb Nakhman Tzvi, of blessed memory.

17. My great grandfather, the Rabbi, Reb Yitzhak Zev bar Nakhman Tzvi haLevi Epshtein, of blessed memory, was the successor to his father, the chairman of the rabbinical court in Kolomea. He died on the 15 Heshvan 5609 [11 November 1848] and was buried in the old cemetery near the grave of his father, the gaon, Reb Nakhman Tzvi, of blessed memory. His son, the Rabbi, Reb Meir Shimkha haLevi Epshtein, of blessed memory, Rabbi, giant of the Torah (see the eulogy about him the book Revid haZahav [The Golden Necklace] of the rabbi and righteous man, Reb Yisroel Dov Gelernter, of blessed memory, chairman of the rabbinical court in Jablonov, near Kolomea), died in our city, 24 Elul 5605 [26 September 1845] and was buried in the old cemetery.

18. The Rabbi, Reb Khiskie Nukhem bar Yitzhak Toybish, of blessed memory, was taken on as the head of the rabbinical court in Kolomea and the province after the death of the above-mentioned Gaon, Rabbi Yitzhak Zev, of blessed memory. He was a giant of Torah and also educated in worldly subjects. Previously he was a religious judge and Moyre-Tzedek [one who knows justice, rabbinical title] with the gaon, the author of Yeshuot Yakob [The Salvation of Jakob], of blessed memory, in Lemberg.

19. The Rabbi, Reb Mordekhai Ziskind bar Yehuda Leibush, of blessed memory: his father was the chairman of the rabbinical court in Levertov, and he, himself, sat on the rabbinical seat of the community of Burshtyn. He settled in Kolomea in his older years and spread Torah. He died in our city on 27 Shevat 5620 [20 February 1860] and was buried in the old cemetery.

20. My great grandfather the Rabbi Reb Pinkhas bar Josef Epshtein, of blessed memory, chairman of the rabbinical court of Kitev, the father-in-law of my grandfather, Reb Josef Rat, of blessed memory. His father, the gaon Reb Josef Epshtein, of blessed memory, also the chairman of the rabbinical court in Kitev, was the son-in-law of the above-mentioned gaon Reb Nakhman Epshtein, of blessed memory, chairman of the rabbinical court in Kolomea. Reb Pinkhas, the father of my grandmother, Dvora Rath, may she rest in peace, died in Kolomea on the 21 Iyyar 5621 [1 May 1861] and was buried in the old cemetery near the grave of the Rabbi, Reb Tzvi, of blessed memory, the chairman of the rabbinical court of Delatyn. My above-mentioned grandfather, Reb Josye Rath [diminutive of Josef], of blessed memory, of Kolomea, was one of the most important Hasidim of

[Page 118]

our teacher, our rabbi from Rizhin [town in Ukraine]. He was the author of the book, Yeshuat Yisroel [Salvation of Israel], which contains religious laws from the Rizhiner and short stories about the righteous man, Reb Yisroel (Fridman) from Rizhin. My grandfather, Reb Josye Rath, left for Eretz-Yisroel in his old age, lived there in Tsfat for several years, died and was buried there. The second son-in-law of Rabbi, Reb Pinkhas Epshtein, of blessed memory, was Reb Dovid Melzer, of blessed memory, the father of Reb Josl Melzer of Kolomea, who died

in 5710 [1950] in Tel Aviv and of Reb Sholem Melzer of Rohatyn, one of the first Zionists and intimates of Dr. Herzl, the father of Dr. Nusan Melzer, of blessed memory – one of the first [members] of Poalei Zion [Workers of Zion – Marxist Zionists].

21. The Rabbi, Reb Eliezer bar Shlomo of Doline, of blessed memory, know by the name, Reb Eliezer haGodel [the great one], a student and Hasid of the Rabbi, the Khozeh [Seer] of Lublin [Jakob Yitzhak Horowitz], may the name of a righteous man be blessed, and of the righteous man, Reb Tzvi of Zirimshov, may the name of a righteous man be blessed. He lived in Kolomea where he died on the 13th of Shevat 5622 [14 January 1862] and was buried in the old cemetery.

22. The Rabbi, Reb Gershon bar Yehuda, of blessed memory, author of the book, Avodat haGershoni [Gershon's Service], chairman of the rabbinical court in Kolomea, a grandson of the righteous man, Reb Gershon, may the memory of a righteous man be blessed, chairman of the rabbinical court in Rozli, a son of the gaon and righteous man, Reb Menakhem Mendl, may the name of a righteous man be blessed, of Kolomea and the brother-in-law of the righteous man, Reb Chaim, may the memory of a righteous man be blessed, of Kosev. At first he was the rabbi and chairman of the rabbinical court in Rozli, from 5581 [1821] to 5589 [1829]; later he was chosen as the chairman of the rabbinical court in Tolmitsh (Tlumotsh); from there he moved to Horodenke, later he was received as the chairman of the rabbinical court in Kolomea.

The Rabbi, Reb Gershon, created many useful precepts and founded institutions of learning, charity and mercy that existed there until right up to the Holocaust. This great rabbi died in our city on the eve of Shavous [the holiday celebrating the giving of the Torah], 5623 [1863], after he had been the rabbi in several communities for 46 years. He was buried in the old cemetery.

23. The Rabbi, Reb Zev Wolf bar Efraim, of blessed memory, a student of the gaon, Jakob Teomim of Lita [Lithuania], of blessed memory, was a judge in the religious court of the mentioned Rabbi, Reb Gershon; he died on erev Shabbos [on the eve of the holy Shabbos] 28 Sivan 5625 [22 June 1865] and was buried in the old cemetery near the grave of the Rabbi, chairman of the rabbinical court, Reb Gershon, of blessed memory.

24. The Rabbi, Reb Eliezer bar Meir, of blessed memory. He also was a rabbinical judge in Reb Gershon's rabbinical court; he died on the 21st of Shvat 5627 [27 January 1867] and he is also buried near the grave of the Rabbi, Reb Gershon in the old cemetery.

[Page 119]

25. The Rabbi, Reb Hillel bar Borukh Bendit Lichtenshtein (Lash), of blessed memory, chairman of the religious court in Kolomea. He was born in Veca, Hungary (Slovakia) in 5574 [1814], a student of the gaon, Reb Moshe Sofer, of blessed memory, author of the

book, Khasam Sofer [Seal of the Scribe]. He was the rabbi and chairman of the rabbinical court in the Hungarian communities: Marghita (Margaretin), Klozenburg, Szikszo (Siks). Later, he became chairman of the rabbinical court in the community of Kolomea in 5627 [1867] and he was the rabbi of our city during the course of 24 years. The religious judges serving in his religious court were: the Rabbi Reb Zechariah Mendl Zilber bar Avraham Pesakh, of blessed memory, and the Rabbi, Reb Moshe Yehoshua bar Avraham Yehuda, the above-mentioned head of the yeshiva.

The Rabbi Hillel L"Sh was famous as a righteous man and a Torah giant. He was a fanatical opponent of every religious reform, particularly against Rabbi Ezriel Hildesheimer, chairman of the rabbinical court in Eizenshtat (who later was the founder and leader of the Rabbinical Seminar in Berlin) for his endeavors to bring education into the circles of Talmud sages. He took part in the rabbinical conference in Nyíregyháza, in 1864 that sent a delegation to the Austro-Hungarian Kaizer Franz-Joseph I to intercede against the founders of the Rabbinical Seminar in Budapest. He was also one of the main speakers at the Rabbinical Conference in Michalovce in 5624 (1864) that banned the giving of German sermons in the synagogues.

The Rabbi Hillel L"Sh was a strong person in his convictions and would give in to no one. He would publicly berate the transgressors. My father, of blessed memory, told me: When the Rabbi, Reb Hillel learned that a grandson of Reb Itsikl Sheykes (Fridfertig), of blessed memory, a Hasid and fiery bel-tefilah [reader of prayers on holidays] in the synagogue named for Reb Itsikl Rozshivilner, studied dancing in the Young Men's Society – he came to the mentioned synagogue on Shabbos, interrupted the prayers and protested against this "dreadful sin" with flaming-fiery words.

He was not a misnagid [opponent of the Hasidim]. He himself would even travel to the tzadek [righteous man], the gaon, Reb Chaim Halbershtam, the head of the rabbinical court in Tsanz (Sandz). But he did not agree that the rebbes should mix in matters such as hiring shoykhetim [religious slaughterers] and religious judges. The quarrels that broke out between him and Vizhnitz [Vyzhnytsia, Ukraine] at the time of the Admor [our teacher and our rabbi - rebbe], Reb Menakhem Mendl (Hager), the son of the tzadek, Reb Chaim Kosever, come from this because a shoykhet, who received ordination from the Rebbe, Reb Mendl of Vizhnitz, was later prohibited by the Rabbi, Reb Hillel.

[Page 120]

In his Shabbos sermons during the third and final meal he said about the Vizhnitzer tzadek that he behaves like Jeraboam the son of Nebat: he sinned and caused others to sin – he sinned and caused the community to sin. Reb Itsi Brettler, one of the first Vizhnitz Hasidim, who was present at this sermon, stood and with anger left the house of the rabbi. The fanatical Vizhnitzer Hasidim took revenge on the old rabbi; they attacked him in the street.

The Rabbi, Reb Hillel was a distinguished speaker and sermonizer. He would travel from place to place with his moralizing sermons. His strength was great in Mile da-agadeta [Words of Legends]. He delivered his sermons in a popular manner.

On Yom Kippur in the year 5641 (1880), the Austro-Hungarian Kaiser, Franz Josef the First, came to Kolomea for a visit. The Jews prayed the morning prayers very early and with the Rabbi, Reb Hillel, of blessed memory, at the head, went to welcome the Kaiser. The Rabbi blessed the Kaiser according to religious law.

The treatises by the Rabbi, Reb Hillel are: Maskil el Dal [Considers the Poor] – sermons in four volumes; Avkat Rokhel [Powers of a Peddler] – talks on moral conduct in two volumes; Et

La'asot [It Is Time to Act] - in Yiddish – in two volumes; Mikrei Dardeki [Examples for Small Children] - a commentary in the manner of sermons on Khumish [the Torah]; in letters.

The Rabbi, Reb Hillel Lichtenshtein (L'Sh) died at the age of 77 on the 10th Iyyar 5651 [15 May 1856] and was buried in the old cemetery.

His sons, Reb Borukh Bendit and Reb Zalman lived in Kolomea and Reb Zalman occupied the office of the secretary of the kehile. His youngest son (from his second wife), Reb Ben-Tzion,

lives today in Jerusalem. His son-in-law, the Rabbi, Reb Anshl was a distinguished scholar, spread Torah and had a synagogue in the suburb of Kolomea, in Werbiaze.

26. The Rabbi, Reb Zechariah Mendel Zilber, of blessed memory, bar Avraham Pesakh, of blessed memory, was the chief religious judge in our city for many years. He was a Torah giant, a distinguished master of religious practices and people would come to him from afar for religious cases; he died on the 14th of Iyyar 5652 ([11 May] 1892) and his son, our master, our teacher, Reb Yehoshaya Heshl, of blessed memory became his successor as the religious judge on the high court.

27. The Rabbi, Reb Moshe Yehoshaya, of blesses memory, bar Avraham Yehuda, of blessed memory, the so called Rosh haYeshiva [head of the yeshiva], came to our kehile from Hungary. He was the Rosh haYeshiva there. As an ordained rabbi, he occupied the office of religious judge in Kolomea for many years along with the above-mentioned Rabbi, Reb Zechariah

[Page 121]

Mendl in the Beis-Din of Rabbi, Reb Hillel Lash, of blessed memory, of the Rabbi Reb Jakob Teomim, of blessed memory, and also of the Rabbi, Reb Gedalia Shmelkis, of blessed memory. He was a holy man and his admirers were drawn to him as to a Hasidic rebbe although he did not belong to the Hasidic world. He died on the eve of Rosh Khodesh [the new month] of Adar in the year 5664 [14 February 1904]. In my youth I was at his agonizing death, which lasted an entire day, while around his bed stood his students and Hasidim and the worshippers from the old synagogue, among them Reb Shaul Knepfer, of blessed memory. His son, the Rabbi, Reb Alter was his successor as an ordained rabbi and religious judge.

28. The Rabbi, Reb Yehoshaya Eliezer, of blessed memory, bar Moshe Josef Chodorov, a holy man and a Torah giant and sage, a son-in-law of the Rabbi and righteous man, Reb Chaim of Kosov, our rabbi, our teacher, may the memory of a righteous man be blessed, lived in Kolomea for many years. He died on the first day of Khol Hamoed Sukkos [intermediate days of Feast of Tabernacles] 5655 [18 October 1894] and was buried in the new cemetery. His wife, the rebbitzin [rabbi's wife], Sheyndl, may she rest in peace, the daughter of the rabbi and teacher, Reb Chaim of Kosov, of blessed memory, who died on the seventh day of Passover 5664 [30 March 1904], is also buried there.

29. The Rabbi, Reb Uri Feyvl Schreier, of blessed memory, bar Moshe haLevi, of blessed memory. He was considered as one of the gaonim among the Galicianer rabbis of his time. He was the author of the sforim: Aseifet Zekenim [Assembly of Elders], Mikdash Me'at [A Small Temple] and Da'at Kedoshim [Wisdom of the Holy Man] of his Rabbi, the Gaon, Reb Avraham Dovid, may the memory of a righteous man be blessed, the chairman of the community court of Buczacz. The Rabbi, Reb Feyvl Schreier was chairman of the community court of Brodshyn; he was later taken on as the head of the rabbinical court in Kolomea. In old age he returned to the

rabbinical seat of the holy community of Brodshyn and he died there on the 5th of Kislev 5689 [18 November 1928,]. The Rabbi and Gaon, Reb Nakhum Burshtein, the chairman of the community of Nadverne and Dr. Shmuel Schur, the president of the Eretz-Yisroel society in Stanislav eulogized him. His son, the Rabbi Reb Ahron, of blessed memory, became chairman of the community of Botoshan [Botosani], Romania. He died prematurely.

The Rabbi, Reb Feyvl Scheier, of blessed memory, was an enthusiastic Zionist even before Dr. Herzl. He was active in the Hovevei Zion [Lovers of Zion] movement in the 1890's and, later, also in the Zionist political movement. He tested me in the Gemara when I was a small boy during his visit to Kolomea. I still remember his stately appearance and the high fur hat that he wore. My friend, Reb Yehoshaya Horovitz, a grandson of the Rabbi and Gaon, Reb Mesholam, the chairman of the community of Stanislav, wrote about Rabbi, Reb Feyvl of Brodshyn in the monthly journal Hahed [The Echo], Jerusalem, Notebook B, year of publication 28 Cheshvan 5710 [20 November 1949].

[Page 122]

Reb Shraga Feyvl Scheier, of blessed memory, was famous in his generation as a Torah giant and those from near and far turned to him for answers to their questions because of his sharpness in the discussions on the commentaries of the Torah as well as an authority on the right to make decisions concerning Halacha [Jewish law]. He distinguished himself with his beautiful Hebrew style and he was also considered a great scholar and wonderful orator and interpreter among the greatest rabbis. As the idea of the community of Eretz-Yisroel and of Hovevei Zion began to spread, Reb Shraga Feyvl, of blessed memory, was one of the first who supported it and when Dr. Herzl also appeared and the rise of political Zionism began, the Rabbi Reb Shraga Feyvl was among the first followers of this movement and even was a courageous fighter for the Zionist idea. A public polemic developed between Reb Shraga Fewyl, of blessed memory, and the rabbi and teacher, Reb Yehezkiel Halbershtam of Shineva (Sieniawa, Poland), over the split between the Lemberg newspaper, Makhzikei Hadat [The Upholders of Religion] on the side of the Shinever, and the Krakower HaMagid taking the side of the rabbi from Brodszyn on the question of esrogim [citron, a fruit used in the celebration of Sukkos – the Feast of Tabernacles] in Eretz-Yisroel. Until his deep old age, already an octegenarian, he still bravely fought for his convictions and for Hovevei Zion.

H. Sekler[5], a grandchild of Reb Shraga Feyvl Scheier is the well-known Hebrew-Yiddish-English dramaturge and storyteller in New York.

Reb Yeshaya Horovitz tells in the earlier mentioned tract about Rabbi, Reb Shraga Feyvl taking part in the Zionist national conference of Stanislav, Galicia in the spring of 5658 [1898]. His appearance was the sensation of the conference. The Zionists of that time were almost all young people, students and doctors and here appeared a worthy old man of 81, a well-known rabbi and gaon, famous as an authoritative personality among the rabbis of the country. He listened attentively to the discussions and before the end of the conference he was asked to speak to the gathering. After he praised the holy idea of Zionism and encouraged its activists, he clarified the motivation that had pushed him to join the movement, that is, because of the sanctity of the idea and because he saw in it the beginning of the redemption and the beginning of the rebirth of Israel and the survival of his land.

30. The Rabbi, Reb Asher Anshel, of blessed memory, bar Mordekhai Aszkenazi, of blessed memory, the author of Shalus vaTeshuvas Shemen Rosh [Anointing Oil]. His father, the Gaon, Reb Mordekhai, of blessed memory,

[Page 123]

was chairman of the religious court in Pistyn, a grandson of the Gaon, Reb Moshe Dovid, of blessed memory, chairman of the religious court in Molgshowa and also in old age in the holy community of Sfat. In Kolomea, the Rabbi Anshel married the daughter of a rich man, Reb Litman Brettler, the father of the millionaire, Reb Jekl Brettler and lived for several years in our city and spread Torah. He was then the leader of the holy community of Stanislav and died there on the 3rd of Shvat 5662. [1902] His son-in-law was Reb Ahron Kohen, of blessed memory, parnes [elected leader of the religious community] of the kehile in Kolomea, a Vizhnitzer Hasid.

31. Our venerable teacher, Jakob bar Efraim Teomim, of blessed memory, the chief judge of the rabbinical court of our kehile, a grandson of the Gaon, Reb Jakob of Lisa, the author of Khavat Da'at, of blessed memory and a great grandson of the Gaon and author of Hakham Tzvi [Rabbi Tzvi – Rabbi Tzvi Hirsch Ashkenazi – it is customary to refer to an author by the name of his book], of blessed memory. His father, the Rabbi, Reb Efraim Teomim, of blessed memory, was the chief judge of the rabbinical court in Krasnipolle [Belarus]; all of his brothers and brothers-in-law were great rabbis: the Rabbi, Reb Moshe Teomim, of blessed memory, chief rabbi of the rabbinical court in Horodenka, the Rabbi, Reb Yitzhak Teomim, of blessed memory, chief rabbi of the rabbinical court in Krasnipolle, his brother-in-law was the Rabbi, Reb Yitzhak Horovitz, of blessed memory, the chief rabbi of the rabbinical court in Stanislav, his uncle was the Gaon author of Khesed le Avraham [Mercy of Abraham], the chief rabbi of Buczacz.

The Rabbi, Reb Jakob Teomim first was the rabbi in Wilkocz, then he was received as the chief judge of the rabbinical court in Tarnogrod, Russian Poland, and from there he was received in our kehile as chairman of the rabbinical court and he remained in this office for 18 years. In my youth I was a student of this esteemed rabbi and respected him as a distinguished rebbe. The judges of the religious court were Reb Moshe Yehoshaya, of blessed memory (the so-called Rosh Yeshiva [head of the religious school]), and Reb Yehoshaya Heshl Zilber, of blessed memory, as well as Reb Alter, of blessed memory, the son of the Rosh Yeshiva, who was the successor to his father. His son-in-law was the Rabbi, Reb Dovid'l Teomim, of blessed memory, the son of Rabbi, Reb Moshe Teomim, of blessed memory, chairman of the rabbinical court in Horodenka who was also my teacher and rebbe.

The Rabbi, Reb Jakob Teomim, of blessed memory, died on the 1st of Iyyar 5668 [2 May 1908] in old age and was buried in the new cemetery. He left several works in manuscript form that were not published.

32. His son, the Rabbi Reb Chaim Tzvi Teomim, of blessed memory, author of the book, Zikaron LaRishonim [A Memorial for the Early Scholars] (in which I found many facts about rabbis in our city and I have used them in my treatise), was a scholar and a follower of the Enlightenment; his wife was a granddaughter of the Rabbi and Gaon, Reb Berish Meizlish, of blessed memory, chief judge of the rabbinical court in Warsaw. After the death of

[Page 124]

his father, Reb Chaim Tzvi was chosen as the judge and rabbi in our kehile.

33. Our venerable teacher, the Rabbi, Reb Yehoshua Heshl Zilber, of blessed memory, was the religious judge of the high court in our kehile for many years, as a successor to his father, the religious judge, Reb Zechariah Mendl, of blessed memory. He was a superlative teacher, a sharp intellect in the most complicated matters, taken into commercial circles as a religious

judge and arbitrator in monetary cases; he was a Chortkower [Czortkow] Hasid; he prayed in the small Chortkower synagogue, where he would study a page of gemara with the young boys in the wintertime – "and I was among them."

34. Teacher and Rabbi, Reb Yitzhak Weber, of blessed memory, was during the course of 50 years preacher in our community. He came from Russia, was a Czortkover Hasid, with a stately appearance, a scholar and wonderful preacher; he recited the prayers well, could sing and was the author of nigunim [religious melodies]; he was a communal and sympathetic man with lively humor. He was very beloved.

The number of his followers and those who listened to his sermons was large and his house over-flowed with people on Friday nights and on holidays. He was a man of liberal beliefs and, therefore, he had opponents among the Vizhnitzer and Boyaner Hasidim. He was a nationalist and a Zionist for many years and did not hold back from publicly disclosing his beliefs in his sermons, speeches and in his actions. However, in the 1920's, after he returned from the Zionist Congress in Switzerland, his beliefs changed and he was an extreme opponent of nationalism and Zionism and he moved entirely towards the assimilated at the time of the parliamentary elections. Many of his intimates saw in this a deviation and even a betrayal and were entirely estranged from him. In my youth I studied with him, was a visitor in his house and truly loved him.

35. The Rabbi, Reb Gedalia Shmelkish, of blessed memory, head of the religious court in Kolomea, a nephew and shining student of the Gaon, the Rabbi of all the Jews in the Diaspora, Reb Yitzhak Shmelkish, of blessed memory, head of the rabbinical court of Lemberg, the author of Beit Yitzhak [House of Isaac]. He was a child prodigy in his youth and also took the baccalaureate exam in the Humanistic Gymnazie [secondary school]. First he became the rabbi and head of the religious court of Premishla (Przemysl), then after his father left [Kolomea] in order to take on

[Page 125]

the rabbinical seat as the head of the religious court in Lemberg, in 5658 [1897], he became the head of the religious court in Kolomea and after six years he was called back as the head of the religious court in Przemysl.

As a child, the superb and solemn welcome by the city at his arrival in our kehile made a strong impression on me. Thousands of people stood on the sidewalks, from the main street to the train station. All businesses were closed; all of the elected members of the kehile and representatives of the city and state officials waited for him at the train station. Several came to the meeting from Stanislav and arrived together with him. Thousands of people greeted him with an enthusiastic "Barukh haba" [welcome] as he passed in the carriage with the kehile representative, Josef Funkenshtein. He immediately traveled to the Great Synagogue and gave a sermon on halakhah [Jewish law] and agadah [legends] and ended his speech in German.

On the first day, the Otynier Hasidim came nearer to him, wanting to receive his approval for the hiring of a shoykhet [ritual slaughterer] the one that they desired. Every Friday night they would come to the rabbi, where they sang and danced in the Hasidic manner, although the rabbi was not a "Hasid" and he was not accustomed to this.

But when the Otynier Rebbe came to Kolomea for a visit as he would habitually every year, the Hasidim asked of the Rabbi, Reb Gedalia Shmelkish that he come to receive greetings from the Otynier Rebbe, the Rabbi, Reb Jakob Teomim, of blessed memory, as was done. The Rabbi,

Reb Gedalia Shmelkish refused with the contention that he is the rabbi in the town and the rebbe first should visit him because if he acted otherwise, he would have to do this week after week because another rebbe came to Kolomea almost every Shabbos and there was no distinction as to whether he was a "great" rebbe or a minor one. And from then on the Otynier Hasidim left. The intimates were the Hasidim of the Rabbi, Reb Hillel Lichtenshtein, of blessed memory, and, mainly, Reb Isser Kirs, Shaul Knepfer, Mekhl Hammer and others. In 1899 elections to the Austrian parliament took place in Kolomea. The socialists placed Dr. Shor against the official candidate of the Poles and the assimilated Jews – who also was a Jew – Dr. Zeinfeld, railroad director

[Page 126]

in Stanislav (a son-in-law of the millionaire Gartenberg of Drohobych) and scheduled a public gathering for Shabbos in the Great Synagogue where Dr. Shor was to speak. However, one of the chief gabbaim [singular gabbai – synagogue sexton], Yosye Marmorosh, disrupted the plan; immediately after the end of prayer, gentiles, on Shabbos! – set a fire in the woman's section. A thick smoke filled the synagogue and the meeting could not take place. This happened on Shabbos Meworkhim [the Sabbath on which the new moon is blessed] in the month of Adar. The Rabbi Shmelkish, as was his wont, would pray at home on Shabbos, where he had a customary minyon, but on Shabbos Meworkhim and during the Days of Awe he would come to the Great Synagogue. And just on this Shabbos Meworkhim the rabbi did not come to the Great Synagogue. The gabbaim probably reported to him earlier about the scandal that awaited him because of the socialistic assembly that was scheduled in the synagogue against the will of the gabbaim. However, the socialists blamed the rabbi that he knew about the plan of Yosye Marmorosh to desecrate the Shabbos and, therefore, he did not come to pray. And as they understood it, the rabbi certainly needed to come in order to avoid such an act of sabotage. The party, for which one of the main spokesmen was Naftali Kesten, a worker in the talis [prayer shawl] factory owned by the Heller family, a religious Jew and a learned man, a frequent visitor to the Rabbi, Reb Jakob Teomim, of blessed memory, but a fervid socialist who also organized large strikes in the above-mentioned talis factory – a rare phenomenon at that time – decided to take revenge on the rabbi during his sermon on Shabbos haGadol [the Shabbos before Passover]. Hundreds of workers did assemble in the afternoon in the Great Synagogue on Shabbos haGadol and when the rabbi went up to the Torah during Minkhah [the afternoon prayer] for his sermon, they all began to "cough" and disturbed him when he recited the blessing.

Nevertheless, the rabbi wrapped himself in his talis and began his sermon. At first, there were no disturbances, but a quarter of an hour later, in the middle of his speaking, insulting calls began and the rabbi could not continue. He descended after the priestly benediction and angry and embittered, he left the synagogue. On the way home he was accompanied by his friends and the workers chased after him along with the street urchins and idlers and the rabbi was attacked with insults. There was excitement in the city for several days. The representatives of the kehile and the government officials met and searched

[Page 127]

for ways with which to punish the demonstrators without success. Street people ran after Yosye Marmorosh for an entire year with insulting calls and the police had to protect him against the demonstrators. He would not leave his house without the accompaniment of the police.

At first, the Rabbi, Reb Gedalia Shmelkish, did not reveal any connection to Zionism and to the national movement. And then the Poles celebrated the 100th birthday of the great Polish poet, Adam Mickiewicz, in December 1898, and organized a solemn meeting in Lemberg, where the new Mickiewicz monument was unveiled. The representatives of the assimilated [Jews] took part in this celebration and the Rabbi, Reb Gedelia Shmelkish, was the only rabbi from the large cities who officially appeared there, dressed in a high, sable hat and with a red-white badge (the national colors of the Poles). The Zionists and national Jews behaved neutrally then in the struggle between the Poles and the Ukrainians (Rutener), but only fought against the assimilated who then had power in most of the kehilus. When the photograph of the respected Kolomea rabbi was published in the Polish newspapers among the elite taking part in the Mickiewicz celebration, the Zionists at first appeared in the Lemberg Yiddish Tagblat [Daily

Newspaper] against this action. There were many complaints against him in our city and after that the relations between the Zionists and the rabbi were strained. Many of the learned men and followers of the Enlightenment from our city also were disappointed in him because of the lack of activity in the area of education and the spreading of Torah.

However, later, the rabbi grew closer to the Zionist movement, particularly to the Mizrakhi [religious Zionists] and returning to Przemysl in 1904, he publicly joined Mizrakhi and was one of its leaders. And in 1906, Adolf Shtand was a candidate to the Austrian parliament in the city of Brod and the Rabbi, Reb Gedelia Shmelkish came to Brod and spoke in the Great Synagogue on Shtand's behalf and against the assimilated. This step made a great impression on all of Galicianer Jewry. In 1907 the Rabbi Shmelkish was the Zionist candidate to the Austrian Parliament in Tarnobrzeg County and his opponent was the Minister Bobczinsky, was governor for many years

[Page 128]

in Galicia. The Rabbi Shmelkish spoke mainly in the meetings of Mizrakhi as one of the main leaders of the movement. At the time of the First World War, the rabbi lived in Vienna (in 1915-1917) and there he was active in the national movement. We met at several gatherings and meetings as well as at the Zionist Congress in Carlsbad in 1921. He was not active in his old age because of illness.

His oldest son, my dear friend, the Rabbi, Reb Shmuel Shmelkish, of blessed memory, was the son-in-law of Reb Alter Knepfer of Kolomea and was religion teacher in the state gymnazie [secondary school] in Krakow from 1906 to 1940 and from 1921 to 1940 also as the second rabbi in the temple, in the time of the chief-rabbi, Dr. Yehoshaya Ton, of blessed memory and, also after the death of Rabbi Ton. He and his wife Janete, the woman of valor, born a Knepfer, their two sons and daughters and their families all perished in the Holocaust.

36. The Rabbi, Reb Dovid Reis, of blessed memory, rabbi and head of the religious court in Kolomea. After the death of the Rabbi, Reb Teomim, of blessed memory, the Rabbi, Reb Dovid Reis, of blessed memory (until then he was the head of the religious court in Sahl) was taken as rabbi and head of the religious court in our kehile. He was not descended from a rabbinical line, but he reached the high position of a respected rabbi, Torah giant and was loved by the people through his great ability and diligence.

He headed the yeshiva in Kolomea in his house, where he taught only a small number of students. He was a Chortkower [Czortkow] Hasid. He perished in the Holocaust, 5701 [1941].

37. The last rabbi and head of the rabbinical court in Kolomea was the Rabbi, Reb Josef Lau, of blessed memory, a son-in-law of Reb Jakob Baidaf, of blessed memory. Rabbi Lau studied with rabbis and received ordination, but he did not dress as a rabbi, but spent many years in commerce and was the representative of Agudas Yisroel [religious political organization] in Kolomea. In 1930 the Vaad haKehile [Council of the Organized Communities],

of which the majority consisted of members of Agudas Yisroel, nominated him as head of the rabbinical court in the community and this caused a sensation in rabbinical and scholarly circles in Galicia. But, when he appeared in his office as Rabbi and head of the rabbinical court, he interrupted his political activities and dedicated himself to the remaining circles in the city and nearly won their trust.

His younger brother, the Rabbi Moshe Lau, of blessed memory, was the rabbi and head of the rabbinical court in

[Page 129]

The tall synagogue

Boyaner synagogue

Azipolier Synagogue

[Page 130]

Piotrkow [Trybunalski]. Both perished in the Holocaust in the years 5701-5702 [1941-1942].

These are the 37 rabbis and righteous men who sat on the rabbinical throne in our community and spread Torah. Several of them were giants of their generation.

————

Translator & Coordinator's footnotes:

1. Zichron Rishonim, a Hebrew book used as a reference was published in Kolomea in 1913 and reprinted in Israel in 1968. It can be found in major libraries catalogued as Zikaron Larishonim or Zikhron Larishonim. The original 1912 edition transliterates the Hebrew title into the Germanic Sichron Larischonim and the author name as Chaim H. Thumim. [Co.]
2. "the holy man of life" is a word play on his name Chaim, which means "life" in Hebrew.] [Tr.]
3. Yisroel Baal Shem Tov is the founder of Hasidism [Tr.]
4. See pp. 22-23 of this Pinkas Kolomea translation for a story of Rabbi David's experience at the home of the Baal Shem Tov [Co.]
5. H. Sekler, who came to America in 1902, was known as Harry Sackler (1883-1974) and wrote many plays performed in the Yiddish Theater. A brief biography, Harry (Tsvi Hersh) Sackler, which mentions his great-grandfather, can be found at www.museumoffamilyhistory.com/yt/lex/S/sackler-harry.htm [Co.]

[Page 130]

Shuln un bote-medroshim in Kolomey

Synagogues and study-houses in Kolomey

Pages 130-142 translated by Tina Lunson
and Pages 143-156 translated by Gloria Berkenstat Freund

In my youth, before the First World War, Kolomey had – besides the great shul – another thirty shuln [synagogues] and kloyzn [small, often trade-specific synagogues] and two bote-medroshim [study houses]. In addition to those there were many minyonim [prayer quorums] in shtiblekh [prayer rooms, often Hasidic]. The majority of them were built after the year tav-khof (1660); the great shul was completely rebuilt after the conflagration of tav-kuf-pey-zayn (1827) and remodeled in the year tav-reysh-khof (1860) during the time of Rebi Tsvi zts"l [may his holy memory be for a blessing] of Rimanov. In tav-reysh-khof-hey (1865) most of the shuln and bote-medroshim burned down, along with the old pinkusim [community record books].

In the year tav-reysh-yud-giml (1853) there was a misfortune on yonkiper [Yom Kippur, the day of atonement]: during nile [the closing prayers of the day] some scoundrels spread the rumor that a fire had broken out in order to create a panic among the women in the women's section of the great synagogue, thus enabling the scoundrels to rob them of their jewelry. The women began to run in great disorder, and in the chaos 33 women and 2 children were killed. From then on there was a law against women wearing jewelry on yonkiper. In the old pinkes of the khevre kadishe [burial society] "gemiles khsodim"[loving kindnesses] is printed the lament that was composed for those very victims with the words (as it was recorded in the book zikron lroshonim [in memory of the forefathers] by Judge Khaym Tsvi Taumim z"l [of blessed memory]:

"Sun and moon darken, and the stars of the heavens do not shed light either. O, one must cry out in witness to the tremendous distress. The stern decree of utter destruction came down upon tranquil women, faithful daughters tender and delightful, and also precious and playful children on yonkiperduring the time of the nile [when] suddenly a ripping voice caused the doorposts to tremble and a loud noise filled the house of God and the beseechers urgently left. Then You will ask to return their souls to the heavens; therefore Master of Mercy shelter them in the shelter of your wings forever, among the residents of the Garden of Eden in the highest heavens – there will be their proper resting place. Omeyn."

The representatives and trustees of the great synagogue in my day were: Yomye Marmorosh, Yoyne Kizler, Itskhok Zaydman, Mendl Fridman, Shimen Zenenzib and others. Among those who prayed there

[Page 131]

I remember Shmuel Herman, Yekheskel Holes, Moyshe Hamer, Avrom Neyder, Aleksander Shor, Shloyme Fridman, Antshl Bishel, Zalman Grinberg, and many others of the residents who did observe the mitsvos [Jewish laws] but who were for the most part not Hasidim and even were considered "modern."

Off the corridor of the main entrance on the right and the left were another two large rooms that served as a study-house for prayer and study.

The Hasidic kloyzn were: Boyan, a handsome building built in 1893, most of the money for its construction coming from the family Heler; Vizshnits, at first together with the Atinye Hasidim; Atinye, after the split; Zshiditshov; Tshortkov, the main funds for construction given by the Tshortkov Hasidim Ayzik Sharf and my father Meshulem Fried; Kosov (in whose house, according to legend, the Bal Shem-tov zts"l stayed when he lived in Kolomey). Various Hasidim and eminent householders prayed in "Reb Itsikl's shul", named after the Radzivil saint; regular observant Jews prayed at the Azipol and Sharigrad shuln, along with various Hasidim.

Hundreds of men and women prayed in the large and spacious "yerushalayim" [Jerusalem] shul; the old besmedresh; the new besmedresh; the shul "Kamionke" near the very old cemetery; the shul Siks named after the town of Siks where Rov ["rabbi"] Hilel Likhtenshteyn was rov before he came to Kolomey, where there prayed the very observant and God-fearing, Hasidim of Rov Hilel Likhtenshteyn headed by Iser Kris; they generally prayed before dawn, very early in the morning, even on shabes [sabbath] and holidays, and then studied a page of Talmud; they were almost like ascetics, puritans, and the fanatic Hasidim called them "di trukene kroym" [those dry Karaites] or Karaites; Klebanye shuln; train shuln; Verbish shul; Dietkovits shuln; shuln for craftsmen: tailor's shul, shoemaker's shul; the shul in the Zionist club "beys yisroel" [house of Israel]; the minyonim in the homes of rabonim ["rabbis"]; khab'ad[Khabad Hasidism, based on the tenets khokhma, bine, khesed or knowledge, wisdom, loving kindness], harav'd, the magid [preacher], the Sohole Rebi [Hasidic charismatic rov], the Yase rebi, the Rebi "Bakhor", the Rov Antshl (the son-in-law of Rov Hilel) and other small minyonim on other streets.

In the Hasidic kloyzn, as also in the two bote-medroshim and in the Siks shul, young men studied by day and by night in Talmud and in the shulkhn orekh [laws for Jewish life as compiled for Ashkenazi Jews by J. Karo in the 16th century], and many of their fathers – sons of the Torah and observers of the mitsves – also sat after morning prayers and in the evening over a page of Talmud or looked up a commentary in ayn yankev [ethical and inspirational teachings of the Talmud by Rov Yankev ibn Khaviv, 15th century] or another book. On shabes and holidays there were two minyonim in almost all these houses of prayer: in the morning from 7 until 9 and from 9 until 11 or 12. During the week there were several minyonim, from before dawn until 10 o'clock.

In the kloyz of the Boyan Hasidim the family Heler held sway, the sons and the sons-in-law and grandsons of the wealthy and saintly Rov Shloyme Haleyvi Heler, who was a great-grandson of the fifth generation of the genius Rov Yomtov Lipe Heler, author of tosafos yomtov [commentaries by Yomtov]. His oldest son, the wealthy Shimshon, was a fiery Boyan Hasid. His three sons – Avrom Shmuel, Yosl and Lipe – were very dignified, Talmud scholars, prayer leaders and leaders of minyonim, and together they operated the big talis [prayer-shawl] factory that became famous all over the world.

During the First World War, in 1915, Yosl, the second son, was taken back by the Russians as a "hostage", and perished there. The third son, Lipe, was a Talmud scholar and became the son-in-law of his uncle Sholem Robinzon, who was a son-in-law of Shloyme Heler. The younger brother of Shimshon, Mayer Heler, was also a great Hasid full of religious enthusiasm, an outstanding prayer leader and composer of nigunim [melodies without words]. He became a partner with his father-in-law Sholem Robinzon in the great enterprise "Robinzon and Heler". His son, my boyhood friend Yekl Heler, lives in Tel Aviv. And Azriel Heler, the son-in-law of Shloyme and his five sons, prayed and studied in that same kloyz. The members of that family – according to the example of their rebi – conducted themselves aristocratically, in the elegance of their clothing and in giving charity. Thanks to that and due to their good breeding, which included great Torah scholars from many generations, they were highly esteemed and they left their mark on that very beautiful kloyz. The other Boyan Hasidim and other pious Jews who were not Hasidim attached themselves to that family, because they strove to have their children educated in that Hasidic-scholarly-wealthy atmosphere. So, for example, joined Leybush Osterzetser and his sons, who was a grandson of the genius Meshulem Halevi Ish Horovits, head of the beys din [Jewish court of law] of Stanislav, a great Talmud scholar, a fearer of heaven, although far from being Hasidic. In the end he left the kloyz because of a dispute and

[Page 133]

went over to Rov Itsikl's shul.

People sat in that Boyan shul studying throughout the whole day, and especially in the evenings. On Friday nights in the winter everyone went to the shul after dinner and spent a pleasant time dancing, singing and hearing words of Torah until late at night. I remember that once when Avrom Shmuel Heler was a half-hour late – and he was in his middle age by then – his father Shimshon shouted at him in front of all the onlookers, "You sit with the women and you chatter about nothing, and that is why you are late." Another of the members of the Boyan kloyz was Nisn Ayzner. They called him Nisn Cabinet-maker because he was a wonderful artisan of house furniture, who was also called to the Boyan rebi's. Once, on his way back from Boyan, he met Motye Herman who was a joker, who asked him, "So, Nisn, how was the rebi's table? You are such an expert with tables..."

When there arrived a rebi who was a grandson or great-grandson of Rizshin, like, for example, the Gvozdiets rebi, the son-in-law of the Sadiger rebi who was a brother of the Boyan rebi, he would pray shabes at the Boyan kloyz.

During the time of the elections to the Austrian parliament I made a special trip from Krakow to Kolomey and spoke in several shuln in favor of the national candidate, and in the Boyan kloyz I had permission to speak from the bime on shabes, although they were opposed to Zionism. I was not allowed to set foot in the Vizshnits kloyz. One could say that the Boyan Hasidim were the aristocrats among the Kolomey Hasidim.

The Vizshnits kloyz was completely Hasidic. Frequent disputes would erupt between the Vizshnits and Atenye Hasidim even though the two rebis were brothers. Finally they split in tav resh samekh zayn [1907] and the Atenyes built their own beautiful kloyz.

People studied day and night in that kloyz as well. Among the worshipers there I remember: Aron Koen and his sons, Itsye Bretler and his sons and grandsons, Alter Finkl, Moyshe Kopler, Yehuda Ber Zaydman, a son-in-law of Iser Kris who came over from the "Siks" shul, an intellectual Atenye Hasid (his son is

[Page 134]

the writer and teacher I. A. Zaydman in Jerusalem), Mendl Shayerman, Dovid Kasvan, one of the leading Atenye Hasidim, Mendl Dikman, a son-in-law of Hirsh Ramler, Yoysef Shpits and Avrom Mayer Berish's, Liber Shaler, Zelik Sharf, Itsik Khasid, the "flogger" of the Atenye Hasidim, Efraym Mayer Menashe's, Moyshe Drimer and his son-in-law Yekhiel Rozenberg, Moyshe Mendl Zaydman, Meshulem Eyferman, his son Leybele and his son-in-law Itsye Grinberg, Hersh Kats and his sons, Vovik Rozenkrants, Moyshe Pidvisoker, Moyshe Sharf and his son Lipe, a loyal Zionist and collector for "keren kayemet" [Jewish National Fund for purchasing land in Palestine] who now lives in Jerusalem, and others.

The site for building the Zshiditshov kloyz was the gift of Elye Heger, who was also called Elye Honeymaker. His house was closely connected to the kloyz. He was also the main gabay [warden] and very strong-minded. I recall that one shabes there arrived a grandson of the Zshiditshov rebi, the son of the sainted Mendele of blessed memory, and Elye would not allow him to pray in the kloyz because he – Elye – only recognized one Zshiditshov rebi, the one who was then the head of the beys din in Zshiditshov and he was necessarily the younger one, who came every year to Kolomey, and therefore the son of the sainted Mendl Getsvongen had to go to pray in Rebi Itsikl's shul. And the saint of Doline, who stemmed from the Zshiditshov line, used to come to our town for shabes and pray at the Zshiditshov kloyz. Also a second grandson, Moyshe Aykhenshteyn, who lived in Kolomey, used to pray in Rebi Itsikl's shul because Elye Honeymaker did not recognize him either.

Pious, respectable Jews who were not Zshiditshov Hasidim also prayed in that kloyz, such as: Shmuel Horovits and his sons and sons-in-law, Fishl Etinger (his father Gershon and his brother Hirshe Volf were Zshiditshov Hasidim), Zelig Khayes and his sons Zeyde and Leybush, Fishl Heger, Itsik Herman and his son-in-law Yekl Helitsher, and others.

And still many other Zshiditshov Hasidim prayed in other shuln, in particular the shul named for Rebi Itsikl of Radzivil. Outstanding prayer leaders in the Zshiditshov kloyz were Mayer Frantsoyz [a] and Hirsh Volf Etinger.

[Page 135]

The Tshortkov kloyz was small and the number of attendees was not large. A lot of Tshortkov and Sadiger Hasidim also prayed at other shuln. The kloyz was completely destroyed by canon during World War I.

During my childhood I prayed and studied in that kloyz and my father often led from the cantor's stand on shabes, holidays and high holidays, but even before my barmitsve he had gone from the Tshortkov kloyz over to Rebi Itsikl's shul.

Of the people at the Tshortkov kloyz I remember: Ayzik Sharf, Meshulem Fried, Efraym Kopl's, Berl Dinstfeld, Hirsh Rekhter, Berl Sekhestover and his son Hershl, Leyb Esnfeld, Fayvish Mentshl, Motl Sher, the orator Rov Itskhak Veber, his brother Moyshe Veber, Henekh Shekhter, Mordkhe Nusboym, Binyumin Shekhter, Yosye Kreyttser, Gavriel Grinberg, Shloyme Grosbakh, Moyshe Sadigurski, Berl Bortn, Aron Peysakh (a son-in-law of Mayer Frantsoyz.)

I did not go to the Kosov kloyz and so I do not know who did go there. I only remember that Dovid (Dudye) Kramer, a wonderful prayer leader, was the cantor.

In that shul named for Rebi Itsikl the Radzivil Saint, there were many very respectable Jews, pious Talmud scholars, various Hasidim and proprietors. It was reckoned among the most distinguished shuln in our community. The [Jewish] judge Rov Yehoshe Heshl Zilber of blessed memory who prayed there, used to study a lesson from Talmud for children, myself included, on the winter nights. And Mordkhe Itsye – a Talmud expert and very pious, a Hasid after the brilliant and saintly Rov Avrom Dovid Butshatsher may his holy memory be for a blessing – used to teach an open commentary session every evening and on shabes before the late-afternoon prayers.

As in all the kloyzn, here too all the pious Jews sat at the third feast of shabes and sang long after the first stars had been sighted [indicating the end of the Sabbath]. Itsikl Shayke's (Fridfertig) sat at the head of the table and sang the shabes songs. Among the attendees were: Yom Tov Lipa (Lipman), Haleyvi Herman, the head of the shul, his son Motye Herman, who would inherit being head of the shul, vice-president of the community council; Shloyme Bikl-Khalfn, an anti-Hasid, a Talmud scholar, a banker; Zerakh Erlikh, his son Yeshaye, Shloyme Heler, a Boyan Hasid, Aron Shoykhet, Sender Yoel, an in-law of the Zshiditshov rebi; Itskhak Leyb Goldshteyn, Yosl Meltzer, a Tshortkov Hasid, Meshulem Simkhe Linder (Vizshnits Hasid), Hirsh

[Page 136]

Ramler, a very rich man, with his sons-in-law: Moyshe Landoy (a Sadiger Hasid and a Talmud scholar), Efroym Klarman, from Krakow, a Talmud scholar and an enlightener, very pious, a fervent Zionist; the judge Rov Yehoshe Heshl Zilber, Tshortkov Hasid, Menashe Roykhverger and his son, my friend Dr. Zerakh, attorney, Talmud scholar and pious Jew, Moyshe Aykhenshteyn, a grandson of the Saint of Zshiditshov; Moyshe Brandes, the son of a rov, Talmud scholar, enlightener, Stretin Hasid; Sholem Veber and his sons Yekhezkl (Khaskl) and Mordkhe and his son-in-lawYudl Nagelberg, Leybush Osterzetser, Talmud scholar, a grandson of the genius Rov Meshulem Horovits head of the beys din of the community of Stanislav and his sons Ruveyn, Shloyme and Nosn; Mordkhe Bikl (son of Shloyme Bikl) and his father-in-law Motl Kahana with the nickname "Ponia", a Russian Jew, his father-in-law Simkhe Tsimels, from Brod, a Talmud scholar, and expert in Torah, Prophets and Writings, and his son-in-law Hershl Tsimels, also from Brod, Talmud scholar and enlightener; Yosl Gotlib, Atenye Hasid and his son Gershon, Yosele Brotshiner-Vahl, a distinguished scholar (who also arranged for guests to have Friday night dinner in the homes of local householders). Mordkhe Itsye's, scholar of spreader of Torah, Dovid Leyb Hofman, a scholar, a friend and the right-hand man to the preacher Itskhak Veber, Sholem Robinzon, Shmuel Fried, Zalman Shperber, Sh. Grayf and his sons Aron and Zerekh, a son of Torah and a brilliant prayer leader, Berl Vinkler, Hershl Bernshteyn from Tarnov, Gedalye Fayr a son-in-law of Aron Shoykhet, Shloyme Shrayer, Fayvish Hanoman with the nickname "Holopietnik", a passionate Zshiditshov Hasid, a fiery prayer leader [a]; Yoel Mayer Prays, the Toah reader at the shul for decades; his son Dovid Shloyme, Efraym Hibner, Gershen Tahau and his son Itsye and others.

Motye Herman led the shul with a strong hand. I remember that one simkhes toyre [rejoicing in the Torah] at night, quite a few Jews who on holidays studied with Judge

Yehoshua Hershl Zilber arrived along with the Judge, with torches and song as was the custom, late for the evening service and late for the hakofes [circuits, in which the Torah scrolls are carried around the shul]. Motye Herman was leading the service. The Jews with the Judge came in during the evening shimenesre [Eighteen Benedictions, recited standing] and were angry that they had not delayed the prayers on account of the Judge and of them. And one of them – Dovid Leyb Hofman – began to loudly sing the borekhu [introductory prayer], and broke into the shimenesre. After finishing the prayer, Motye got up on a lectern and shouted like a commandant, "Have respect!"

[Page 137]

Another episode from my youth is etched in my memory: On simkhes toyre the title of "bridegroom of the Torah" belonged to Rebi Moyshe Aykhenshteyn, a grandson of Zshiditshov rebis; and the honor of the first reading in Genesis belonged to Motye Herman. One time Rebi Moyshe was ill and his title "bridegroom of the Torah" was sold for 200 gulden to the wealthy Hirsh Ramler, who was a pious and genial Jew but really quite simple, not a student of Torah and not even a reader of holy books. He was busy day and night with his businesses. I was very chagrined at this insult to the honor of the Torah and I told the shul wardens a joke that was repeated about the genius Rov Shemen Soyfer head of the beys din of Krakow. When a similar thing had happened in his community in his time, he had remarked to his wardens, "We see today a match made in the style of the Polish Hasidim." When asked the meaning of his remark, he translated it "The groom has not met the bride before the wedding."

I remember another event that well illustrates the morals of those who prayed at that shul. A Jew by the name of Berl Vinkler, who loaned money for interest, made a complaint in court against the debtor Zalman Shperber, who also prayed there, because he had not repaid his loan within the terms set. One weekday he came into the shlul full of righteousness and occupied the debtor Zalman Shperber's special assigned chair. The wardens and the congregants were enraged at this ignominious act, and they made a decision: accordingly, on shabes they interrupted the service in the middle when Berl Vinkler showed up, saying that they would not pray with such a person. Since Berl Vinkler would not leave the shul, they all – led by Motye Herman – went to the besmedresh next door and continued their service there.

Most of the people who prayed at the Azipol kloyz were those who lived in that area (behind the town hall). I remember some of them. Moyshe Aynhorn, a distinguished householder and father of 14 sons and daughters, all by one mother; Yehuda Leyb Grin, a son-in-law of Yehuda Hirsh Glinert, a Talmud expert and Enlightener, an extreme anti-Hasid; Moyshe Bokhnier, a Zshiditshov Hasid, an exquisite prayer leader, Khaym Dovidl's Halbershtam, a Talmud expert and a very pious Jew, my father-in-law Moyshe Zinger may he rest in peace, Berish Hilzenrat, Moyshe Tsukerman, a scholar and a passionate prayer leader, a faithful follower and the right hand of the preacher Rov Itskhak Veber,

[Page 138]

Alter Toybish, a son-in-law of Shaul Vaysman, a scholar and enthusiastic Zionist; Shmuel Laden, Mendl Shayerman.

The Sharigrad kloyz comprised mixed Jews of every type. It was well known that every simkhes toyre disputes broke out there about the honors for leading certain prayers, for carrying the Torah in the circuits and for the Torah blessings, and the ardor for honors often led even to fisticuffs.

Of those who went there I remember Khaym (Finies) Frenkl, a Zshiditshov Hasid and fine prayer leader; Motye Bretler, the eldest son of the millionaire Yankev Bretler; Motye Peye Malke's, Hasid, Torah expert and prayer leader, Yisroel Eyferman, the father-in-law of Dr. Fishl Rotenshtraykh, the former member of the Sokhnut management in Jerusalem; Khaym Zizkind, Hirsh Kris, his son-in-law Leyb Post, Zisye Hofman and his son Dovid, Yekl Sokal, a scholar and Enlightener, Dovid Glinert, Yisroel Kantor and others.

In the "Yerushalyim" [Jerusalem] shul there worshiped various sorts of Hasidim and regular, observant, prominent householders and many who lived in that area. On weekdays six or eight minyonim prayed there, from before dawn until noon. And flocks of orphans came to say kadish [a praise to God that is recited by mourners] at the combined afternoon-evening service. On shabes afternoons they studied a page of Talmud or commentary, and often preachers and orators spoke, visitors from other places; and the Zionists held their meetings there, where there were often religious speakers who clarified the Zionist and nationalist thinking and who spiced their speeches with many kinds of examples, commentaries from holy sources, and sayings of the sages. Of those who prayed there I remember: Yankl Beydaf, the head of the Jewish community and the town council, a passionate Vizshnits Hasid who also used to travel to Zshiditshov, exceptionally wealthy, the father-in-law of Rov Yosl Lau; the Vizshnits Rebi and the Zshiditshov Rebi, who used to come to Kolomey for shabes stayed with him.

He was a clever Jew, nimble and ebullient, a social person. But the same Hasid who on Friday night danced on the table before the rebi, as was the Vizshnits custom, was one of the most assimilated, one who danced to the humiliating tune of the Polish princes, who spoke in the name of the Hasidim against the nationalist Jews and Zionists and for those assimilated to Polish culture, in particular during the time of the elections to the Austrian parliament, to the parliament of Galicia and the council. (Aron Koen, the head of the Jewish community, a Vizshnits Hasid, wealthy,

[Page 139]

well-dressed, behaved in just the same way, although neither of them could speak a word of Polish...) His two sons, Itsye Beydaf and Leybush (a son-in-law of Shmuel Horovits); Yankl Bretler, a multi-millionaire, religious but not a Hasid, his two sons Yoyne and Mendl; his three sons-in-law Moyshe Zaydman, Moshe Breyer and Nosn Baron; Motl Breyer, Meylekh Tsvibl, Shimshen Koynits, Motl Kramer, Shaul Vaysman and his son-in-law Motl Frish, Aba Hamer, A. Slopkovitser, a son-in-law of Moyshe Zaydman, a Talmud expert and Enlightener and very pious, who dressed in modern clothes, a Zionist; A. Kristiampolier, a son-in-law of Moyshe Breyer, from Brod, a Talmud expert and an Enlightener, from a good family, very pious, dressed in modern clothes; Moyshe Rohatin, a son of the head of the beys din of Zlotshev and a son-in-law of Moyshe Breyer, a Torah scholar and champion of Enlightenment, an active Zionist and a good speaker; Yisroel Khaym Henish, a teacher of Torah, Prophets and Writings [the "old testament"] and Hebrew grammar on a high level (an uncle of the writer and journalist Mayer Henish in Tel Aviv); Moyshe Feldman and his sons Khaym and Leybush; Khaym Laks, Gedalye Biter and his sons, Itsye Hekht and his son Shmuel, Shloyme Ashkenazi, Alter Rat, Volf Faktor, Yehuda Hersh Gliner and his sons, Avrom Itsye Soykher, Itsye Heger, Avrom Elye Ramler, and others.

Rov Yankev Taumim and Rov Gedalye Shmelkish used to pray there during the week on the days when Torah is read and on the new moon.

There were a lot of people at the old besmedresh, mostly regular observant Jews and no Hasidim, and on shabes afternoons the orator Itskhak Veber of blessed memory used to preach to a large audience.

That was where the judge Rov Moyshe Yehoshue of blessed memory, the so-called "head of the yeshiva" prayed, and also his sons Alter and Khaym. Of the others I remember: Yudl Krebs, the chief warden, the wealthy Shaol Kneper, his son Alter Kneper, an in-law of Rov Gedalye Shmelkish of blessed memory, his son-in-law L. Mandel, a Talmud expert and very pious, Dovid Vayzelberg, Kopl Bekher and his sons, Yonatan Vielitshker and his son, Shloyme Vaysbakh, Moyshe Ivanier and his son Zindl and others.

On shabes parshas yitro of tav-reysh-samekh"khes [the Sabbath on which the Torah portion called Jethro is read (sometime in February) in 1908] a terrible fire broke out in the old besmedresh and 11 Torah scrolls were burned. The whole town was greatly saddened and the rabonim called for a community fast and buried the remains in the Jewish cemetery.

Many proprietors prayed at the new besmedresh. It is possible I am mistaken about the place where the preacher Itskhak Veber sermonized, and that he preached at the new besmedresh, which was near the building of the old one.

[Page 140]

In both of them, many people studied Talmud, commentaries, ayn yankev and even Torah with RaShI's commentary [acronym for Rov Shloyme Itskhaki, 11th century].

The main people at the Siks shul were: Iser Kris, vice president of the Jewish community, very pious, wealthy, a follower of Rov Hilel Likhtenshteyn and later also of Rov Gedalye Shmelkish (I recall that in the memorial speech at his funeral, Rov Gedalye Shmelkish said of the deceased, with a bitter cry, that he was a "holy Jew") ; his son Leybush Kris, his son-in-law I. Zshenirer, his son-in-law Yehude Ber Zaydman, of the main Atenye Hasidim that later went over to the Atenye kloyz; Shmuel Shupt, A. Shoym, Mikhal Hamer, the children of Rov Hilel Likhtenshteyn, Borekh Bendit, Zalman and his sons. For many years after Rov Hilel passed on his spirit still hovered over that besmedresh, though the Hasidim and especially the Vizshnits Hasidim disparaged it.

Various people prayed at the "Talmud-Torah" shul, members of the "Talmud-Torah" (see further on) and those who lived in that neighborhood, and headed by Tomed Shoykhet, a son of Aron Shoykhet. He was a kind of recluse and holy man who rarely spoke, and on shabes he would speak only Hebrew. (It is said that he would say to his wife [in Hebrew] "Tnay li khalav yoyshev" which means "milk that has sat" [in a glass together with sour cream]; and every Friday he would go from shop to shop and collect donations for little-known poor people.

His father Aron Shoykhet was the founder and agent of the "Talmud-Torah", a large religious school for poor students, and devoted himself to it well into his advanced years.

The Kamionk shul, on Kamionk Street near the very old cemetery, held mostly people who lived in that vicinity, among them some Hasidim. I only remember a few of them: Alter Taykher and his son Shimen Taykher, owner of a famous Hebrew press, Hirsh Rat, the eminent teacher (see further on), Moyshe Tindl, Yekl Tindl, Hirsh Leyb Rat, his sons Shimen and Moyshe, Yoyne Zager, owner of a talis factory, Yoyne Hibner. Housed in that building was the best school of that time, with the teacher Hirsh Rat.

In the Zionists' shul, "beys yisroel", were the leaders of that movement and many of its members. I can recall a few of them: Yehoshue Fadenhekht, the president of the shul and of the club "beys yisroel", the headmaster, a Talmud scholar, Enlightener, pious, a passionate Zionist; Leybl Toybish, the son of the head of the beys din of Atenye, a Talmud scholar, Enlightener

[Page 141]

The wooden shul in Petshinizshin

The wooden shul in Yablonov

The Talmud Torah

[Page 142]

a popular speaker and a wonderful interpreter of Zionist thought, Leybush Yeger, Talmud expert, Enlightener, I. Mayer, the grandfather of a professor of archeology at Jerusalem University; A. Slopkovitser, Motl Berger (a freethinker and yet he never missed coming to pray on shabes and holidays), Mayer Henish, Avigdor Khaym Shternberg, well-known prayer leader, Moyshe Laks, a son of Khaym Laks, a Talmud expert and good speaker, editor of a Zionist weekly newspaper in Yiddish in which I published articles during the time of the elections to parliament.

The other shuln and minyonim in the streets that were farther from the center of town and in the suburbs were filled with the people who lived in those areas, mostly craftsmen and small merchants and a few Hasidim and Talmud scholars. The locals of the suburb of Verbish prayed at the minyon at Rov Antshl's (a son-in-law of Rov Hilel Likhtenshteyn); and among them was my wife's grandfather Hirsh Vagenberg, a Vizshnits Hasid, a Torah scholar and giver of charity, his wife Bobole was active in the community with aid and charity.

During the time of my youth the community numbered three thousand families, about twenty thousand souls. Upwards of eighty percent of the Kolomey Jews were religious, observers of all the mitsvos [the Ten Commandments plus 613 other laws and rules of Jewish life], half of these Hasidim of various rebeyim. Among them were Talmud scholars, completely reverent Jews, and also Enlighteners and many pious householders. Of those about ten percent were "modern", having given up shtraymlekh [wide-brimmed fur hats] to wear top hats on shabes and holidays, and sending their children to modern, non-religious schools and marrying their daughters to doctors who were freethinkers, far from Jewish tradition, although they themselves were still religious. And less than ten percent, some trade-intellectuals, attorneys, doctors, state agents, teachers and a few rich people, desecrated the shabes and only came to shul on the Jewish new year and yonkiper.

And yet they stood at the top of the community and they represented the Jewish interest in the town hall, as was usual in Galicia at the time, and the majority of the religious Jews had to be satisfied with providing for their own needs in matters of ritual slaughter, mikve [ritual baths] and so on.

All the businesses were in Jewish hands, and on shabosim un yontoyvim not one business was open except for the three apothecaries, two of which were Christian-owned. Even among the non-religious merchants no one would dare to open on shabes, and it was not worthwhile because there would not be any customers because even the non-Jews knew that everything was closed on shabes. When Maks Feldman, the youngest son of Moyshe Feldman, opened his drugstore on shabes with the explanation that it was under the regulations of an apothecary, the town went off its wheels.

The character of the community was pious. I do not know how Kolomey seemed in the nineteen-twenties and -thirties because I lived in Vienna in those years, and the ties that bound me to my hometown were broken.

[Page 143]

The Best Bale-tfile [1] Tof Our Kehile

The synagogues, kloyzn [houses of prayer, often specific to an occupation or Hasidic sect], Boti Medroshim [houses of study], shulekhn [prayer houses] and the many minyonim [quorum of 10 men necessary for prayer] were always full of worshippers and on the Shabbosim [Sabbaths] and yontovim [holidays] bale-tfile, bale-menagnim [those who are talented musicians], Hasidim and folksy sheliekhi-tsiber [leaders of communal prayer] would [lead the] prayers without pay.

The khazonim [cantors] were paid in the large synagogue, but they were never the best because the wages were small. But well-known khazonim often came from outside on one or two Shabbosim and appeared at the large synagogue.

Of the bale-tfile I remember the best known of them: Zhiditshov [Zhydachiv] liturgical tradition: Reb Meir Francoiz, who was the best of them; Reb Hirsh Volf Etinger; Reb Chaim Frenkel; Reb Moshe Bochnier; Reb Itzikl Sheikes-Fridfertig; Reb Dovid Haker; Feyvish Khanaman. There surely were others whom I did not know or whom I can no longer remember. In the Sadigurer liturgical tradition: my father, Reb Shimeon Rat, of blessed memory, a Chartkover Hasid, was a talented musician, had a very pleasant voice, was a good leader. Over the course of 45 years, he prayed on Shabbosim and holidays and on the Days of Awe as the bal-musaf [leader of the recitation of the additional prayers] and Neilah [concluding Yom Kippur prayer] at the Chartkover Hasidim's kloyz and then at the synagogue named Di Itzikl [the Itzikl] and he would evoke pleasure and delight

[Page 144]

in his listeners. Motzei Yom Kippur [evening right after Yom Kippur] the representatives of the synagogue came home to my father to express their thanks and respect to him and then to spend time singing and dancing. The magid [preacher], Reb Yitzhak Weber, of blessed memory, was a wonderful prayer leader; he composed melodies that were also sung by other bale-tfile: his student and admirer, Reb Moshe Cukerman; Reb Motel Szer; Reb Meir Heler; Reb Avraham Shmuel Heler; Reb Zorekh Grajf; Reb Dovid Kramer; Reb Ruvin Osterzetser.

Those of the Vizhnitz-Otinya [Otyniya] liturgical tradition: Reb Menashe's Efroim Meir (Sucher); Reb Vovik Rozenkranc; Reb Liber Szaler; Reb Moshe Pirvisoker. All sang their prayers with Hasidic melodies that they took from the well-known khazonim at the rabbinical courts. In this area no one was isolated and superior; everyone benefited from all Hasidic melodies and spread all of their melodies. In the kloyzn were singers who would travel to rebbes and there learn melodies by ear; among them also were those who transcribed the notes and brought the new melodies to the city, where they spread immediately to all kloyzn through the prayer leaders. I remember that at the Vizhnitz-Otinya kloyz there was a fervid Hasid, very musical, although he had a weak voice. He was named Reb Berish's Avraham Meir and he would go to the Otinyer Rebbe twice a month for Shabbosim. There was a famous khazanthere who would compose Hasidic songs sung at the Shabbos table. He was named Reb Yisroel Sztajnfert. Reb Yisroel was born in 5612-1852 in Berdichev. He was a choirboy with Avraham Goldfaden with Reb Yeruham ha-Koton [the little one] at the Berdichev Choral Synagogue. He was khazan in the court of the Sadigurer Rebbe, then at the court of the Rebbe, Reb Shmuel Aba Haner from Horodenka, may the memory of a righteous man be blessed, and finally in Otinya for many years. From 1914 until 1930 he was in America and then returned to Stanislav, where the Otinyer Rebbe lived after the First World War.

His melodies and Shabbos songs were sung by thousands of Hasidim in all of eastern Galicia. Reb Berish's Avraham Meir would always bring new melodies and sing them for other prayer leaders and thus they spread to all of the kloyzn and synagogues, not only during the prayers, but also in the mornings and nights; they would sing the various Hasidic melodies at the holidays and at every celebration.

[Page 145]

Scholars, Learned Men and Followers of the Enlightenment in Kolomea

In general, we cannot say that Kolomea was a city of pure learned men and followers of the Enlightenment as, for example, Brod, Tarnopol or Buczacz [Buchach]. The majority of its residents were businessmen who barely knew Khumish [Five Books of Moses] with Rashi [commentary], a chapter of Mishnayos [Oral Torah], Ein-Yakov [inspirational and ethical teachings of the Talmud], and such people were not considered as "scholars" at that time. Among the Hasidim, too, were simple men of the people, honest but not learned men. In contrast, I in my youth knew artisans, tailors, cabinetmakers, locksmiths, bakers, typesetters, who were scholars, philanthropists, hospitable men and they were respected in the city. However, there also were a number of scholars and learned men and even more scholars who had a knowledge acquired in childhood and as adults studied a page of Gemora [commentaries] in the evening and on Shabbosim. Understand that I remember only a few names from my youth, but in that era there were scholars, learned men and followers of the Enlightenment.

And these are the scholars who I knew in my youth: mentor and teacher, Reb Dovidl Taumim, of blessed memory, the son-in-law of the Rabbi Reb Yakov Taumim, of blessed memory, the head of the Beis Din [religious court] of our community, of blessed memory, and the son of the Rabbi, Reb Moshe Taumim, and the president of the Beis Din of our community; Reb Fishl Etinger, the son of Reb Gershon, to whom the religious teachers would bring the children [they taught] on Shabbosim to be quizzed; Reb Alter Finkel, Reb Josele Brodtshiner (Vahl); Reb Avrahamle Sohler; Reb Khaskl Icik, who also was a follower of the Enlightenment and philosopher, Reb Chaim Dovidl's Halbershtam. I also heard about the learning of Reb Shlomo Bikel (Khalfan [money changer]), but he belonged to a previous generation and I did not know him.

And these were the learned men who I knew in my youth: Reb Moshele Eichensztajn, a grandson of the Zhiditshover Rebbe; Reb Itmar Shoykhet [ritual slaughterer]; Reb Meshulem Frier; Reb Mikhl Braver, a Zhiditshover Hasid who authored books about the Zhiditshover righteous men, a follower of the Enlightenment, the father of an educated geographer and well-known writer, Dr. A. Y. Braver in Jerusalem and of his brother, the teacher in Haifa; Reb Moshe Brandes, a son of a rabbi; Reb Moshe Shternhel (a son of Rosi Shternhel); Reb Efroim Klarman; Reb Feywl Francoz (a son of Reb Meir), Reb Leibush Osterzetser; Reb Leibush Horovitz (also secularly educated); Reb Moshe Landau; Reb Fishl Shorf; Reb Avraham Sofer; his son Berl Sofer (an exceptional student and the right hand of the Rabbi, Reb

[Page 146]

Yakov Taumim, of blessed memory); Reb Lipa Heler; Reb Leibl Mandel (a son-in-law of Reb Shaul Kneper); Reb Leibl Eiferman; Reb Mordka Nusbaum; Reb Henekh Shechter; Reb Itsie Grinberg; Reb Mendl Dikman; Reb Hirsh Rechter; Reb Berl Distenfeld; Reb Tsimel's Shimkha; Reb Tsimel's Hershl; Reb Dovid Leib Hofman, Reb Menashe's Efroim Meir; Reb Mordka Itsie, and, understand, the religious teachers about whom I will particularly dwell in the next chapter.

To the learned men also belonged: Yehuda Ber Zajdman; Reb Avraham Shmuel Heler; Reb Yehosha Fadenhecht (also a follower of the Enlightenment); Reb Leibl Taubish (also a follower of the Enlightenment); Reb Leibush Jener (also a follower of the Enlightenment); Reb Berl Borten; Reb Y. Slopkowicer (also a follower of the Enlightenment); Reb. A. Kristiampoler (also a follower of the Enlightenment); Reb Moshe Cukerman; Reb Feyvish Mentshl (emigrated to America), Reb Moshe Rohatin (also a follower of the Enlightenment), Reb Ruvin Osterzetser, a son of Leibush and a son-in-law of Reb Alter Finkel; his son was the educated Dr. Yisroel Osterzetser, who was a lecturer at the Institute for Jewish Scholarship in Warsaw; Reb Shlomo Osterzetser; Reb Hershl Rozenbaum (the father of Dr. Elihu Rozenbaum-Mruz, of blessed memory, leader of the Department of Education in the municipality of Tel Aviv); Reb Itsie Zajdman, a dear student and admirer of the above-mentioned Reb Khaskl Itsik; Reb Dovidl Khahn (also secularly educated), a son of Reb Ahron Khahn, his brother Eliezer; Reb Zelig Szarf; Reb Shmuel Bretler; my father, Reb Shimeon Rat, of blessed memory; Reb Yehosha Leib Grin; Peya Malka's Reb Motie; Reb Kopl's Efroim; Reb Yosl Melcer; the sons of Reb Itsik Lieb Goldsztajn: Motele, Berele, Yisroel, all followers of the Enlightenment; Reb Itsie Bikel (a grandson of Reb Shlomo Bikel); Reb Antshl Wanenberg; Reb Leibush Kris, Dr. Zorech Rojchwerner; Reb Kalman Wajc (also a follower of the Enlightment).

Characteristic of the relationship of the city population to the rabbis and learned men is the fact that the two first deputies to the Austrian parliament who were elected in Kolomea were not only Jews, but also rabbis: the Rabbi and Gaon [genius] Reb Shimeon Sofer, of blessed memory, head of the Beis Din of Krakow (the son of the Gaon, the Mikhtav Sofer [book of responsa – as is customary, he is known by the name of his most famous book], of blessed memory), the Rabbi, Dr. Josef Bloch, of blessed memory, rabbi in Vienna and editor of the Viennese newspaper, Estreikhishe Vokhenshrift [Austrian Weekly]. In 1907, the Zionists also entered the candidacy of Dr. Yehosha Thon, rabbi in Krakow.

Even the Hasidim, who were more drawn to Hasidic religious ecstasy than to learning, which in their eyes was the status of the rebbe, the righteous man was a thousand times higher than a rabbi and head of a rabbinical court, even when he was a rabbi of all of the members of the diaspora, they were proud that their rebbe was a Torah giant and

[Page 147]

the rebbes were: Reb Yisroel from Chartkov; Reb Yisroel from Vizhnitz and his brother the rebbe from Otinya; the rabbi-rebbe from Zhiditshov Reb Meshulem of Zolynia-Nadvorna – was a great scholar in open and in secret and also one of the rabbis considered as a Torah giant.

Great respect was given in the synagogues and kloyzn to the learned men because there was great respect for learning in our community.

Melamdim [religious school teachers] and Khedorim [religious primary schools] in Kolomea

During my childhood and youth, at least 90 percent of the Jewish children in the city studied in a kheder and the majority of them studied for the entire day, particularly during the winter evenings. Only a third of them studied in the state public school in the morning and in the kheder in the afternoon. Approximately 20 percent of the young people, aged from 10 to 18, studied at the gymnazie [secondary school] and a few percent continued to study until age 14 in the burger-schule [modern secondary school]. The rest studied in kheder and the young men at the kloyzn.

The melamdim whom I remember from childhood and my young years were: for the youngest children: Reb Leibush, Reb Khaskl, Reb Yekl Kreps. In these khederim, the youngest children studied Hebrew, prayers and Khumush [the Torah] from three to six years of age. Reaching the age of six or seven, they would move to the Gemore-Melamid [teacher of commentaries]. And these were the best teachers of that time:

Reb Hirsh Rat, whose kheder at Kamionker Street near the synagogue with the same name was the best in prayer books and teaching methods; Reb Moshe Altshteter; Reb Shmuel Hirsh; Reb Vovik Rozenkranc; Reb Shlomo Mordekhai; Reb Yosi Kopler, the so-called Buczaczer [Buchacher] Melamid; Reb Leibush Horodenker; Reb Chaim Flach; Reb Yosele Brotshiner-Vahl; Reb Avrahamel Sohler; Reb M. Kohn, called the Kalisher Melamid, was considered a "modern one," and he mainly taught the last two parts of Tanakh [the Torah, Prophets and Writings] and Hebrew grammar; as well as Reb Yisroel Chaim Henish (the father and teacher of Reb Meir Henish, the writer and journalist in Tel Aviv).

The teacher Z. Fiszbach, the Chartkover Melamid, was the teacher of Hebrew and Tanakh at the Baron Hirsh School and taught a "modern" Hebrew in courses for adults. The well-rounded scholar and philosopher, the teacher, Reb Khaskl Itsik, only taught a few adult young men. The pious suspected him of an apikorses [heresy] and the Vizhnitzer and Boyaner Hasidim

[Page 148]

bitterly persecuted him. I remember: he died during Shavous and the preacher, Reb Yitzhak Weber, took part in the funeral, and returning, Reb Leibush Osterzetser (who was not a Hasid) opposed him and reproached him bitterly for giving respect to an apikoyres [heretic] who had, ostensibly, caused many people to sin.

I studied with six of the teachers mentioned from my first year to my Bar Mitzvah. And then I began to study - only in the evening – with Reb Dovidl Taumim, with the preacher, Reb Yitzhak Weber, the Rabbi, Reb Yakov Taumim and with the religious judge, Reb Heshl Zilber.

There were other good religious teachers at the Talmud Torah [primary religious school for the children of the poor] where approximately 300 poor children and boys studied. But there also were several khedorim – on a mediocre level – where there was a lack of methods [of teaching], equipment, assistant teachers, and the fathers would often transfer [their children] to another kheder.

Hasidus in Kolomea

There was no Hasidic rebbe in our city whose followers would flock to him from other communities. But over the course of time, three rebbes whose influence in the city was negligible settled there. No one came to join them from outside [the city] to add to their small number of followers.

One was the Sohler Rebbe, who moved to Kolomea from Sohel. He was a scholar and Kabbalist, a prominent man with a distinct liturgical tradition in the prayers and a singer of Shabbos melodies; he was beloved by everyone. He was more devoted to learning than to ritual bathhouses and religious ecstasy. He did not talk at excessive length during prayers and did not host tishn [gatherings held by a rebbe for his followers at which he presents his teachings].

His few friends and the Hasidim who prayed with him provided his meager income. Women would also come to him with gifts. We lived as his neighbor and I would often go to him to pray on Friday nights. Twice I was at Seders in [his house] that would last until the middle of the night, singing Shabbosmelodies. Many like me came to witness his Seder after the Seder at home had ended. His older brother was the rebbe in Tysmenic [Tysmenytsya] and they arranged a marriage between them: the daughter of the Sohler married the son of the Tysmenicer.

[Page 149]

The second one was the Jaser [Iasi] Rebbe, old and weak, almost blind. He moved from Romania to Kolomea in his old age. A small number prayed with him and it was difficult for him to support his family. The third was the Rebbe-Bukher [young man]. He was a grandson of the righteous man, Reb Mordkale Nodverner. While still a young man, an orphan of 17, he would come to our city for Shabbos and stay here with Reb Leib Zegenreich, a Hasid of the righteous man, Reb Mordkale, and he would host a tish in the rabbinical manner. During my childhood, I attended such a tish twice and I smiled. After a certain time, when he got married, he settled in our town and followers from the "common people" concentrated around him. But his behavior, his speech and his appearances in public created little respect for his rabbinical authority. The avowed Hasidim of all sorts in other cities opposed him and even scorned him. I learned later when he was living on Klebania Street that he was not engaged in Torah [study] and not in devekut [dedication to a goal] – except for the 310 ritual immersions in the mikvah [ritual bath], about which he was a great expert... And he was also involved in gossip and cheap jokes with idlers. And I was little impressed by his "wisdom" and I could not be a partner to the admiration with which our landsman [person from the same town], the writer Dr. Shlomo Bikel, in his book, A Shtot mit Yidn [A City of Jews] related to Rebbe-Bukher. Although I also heard about the readiness of the Rebbe-Bukher to help the needy.

However, of the unique qualities of the other rebbes, among them his grandfather, Reb Mordkale, and his father, the righteous man, Reb Meshulem Cziliner, I did not see even a trace of those in him.

Consequently, there was no proper rebbe's "court" in Kolomea. However, Kolomea was a city of Hasidim who were connected to great rabbinical courts with their Admoyrim [acronym of our leader, teacher and master], sons of historical dynasties in the Hasidic world, and chiefly: Boyan, Chartkhov, Viznitz, Otinya, Sadigure, Kosov, Zhiditshov. There also were individual Hasidim who would travel to Nodverne, to Belz, Husiatyn, Stratyn, Kopyczynce. The tzadikim [righteous men] of the Riziszner Dynasty, of the Frydman family, of Chartkhov, Sadigure, Boyan, Husiatyn, Bohush [Buhu?i, Romania] would not travel anywhere and the Hasidim would go to their rebbes for Shabbosim, holidays and the Days of Awe.

[Page 150]

They would remain alone with their rebbe in prayer, at the tishn [literally "tables" – meals eaten with the rebbe] and in giving gifts and kvitlekh [notes to a rebbe requesting a blessing].

In contrast, the other righteous men came to Kolomea once a year for a Shabbos and stayed a week, several for even two weeks. And then the Hasidim from Kolomea and from the surrounding area came to seek support under the sacred wing of their rebbe. Hundreds of people would push into the large synagogue or into the kloyz during the rebbe's praying, where the rebbe himself would pray at the pulpit and talk at length until two or three o'clock in the afternoon, as well as at the tishn Friday night and Shabbos, and during the weekdays they streamed to him to see him and have the merit of receiving his blessing that the requests that were in the kvitl would come true.

The tzadik [righteous man] of Kopitshinits [Kopychyntsi], who did not have a kloyz in our city and also not a lot of Hasidim, but did have a reputation for performing "miracles," had visits from literally thousands of Jews who ran to him with gifts of money and kvitlekh. I remember that in his inn in the house of his Hasid, Reb Hirsch Bloch, all of the windowpanes and furniture were broken and the police had to restore order at the entrance [because] the crush was so great. A year later, his Hasidim rented a large apartment with a large room and the rebbe then spent two weeks in our city, but the thousands had decreased then to only hundreds.

When the tzadik of Vizhnitz, Reb Yisroel Hager, would come, his principal Hasid, the rich man and landowner, Reb Itsia Bremler, would bring the rebbe in his carriage hitched with eight horses and he, Reb Itsia Bremler, personally was the "coachman."

There were two tishn on Friday nights. At the first, the rebbe sang Sholem Aleikhem [Peace upon You], Kidush [blessing over wine] and words of Torah, seasoned with incomprehensible talk about Kabbalah and gematria [assigning numerical value to letters of the alphabet, words, etc.] and the Hasidim would present or offer wine and the gabbai [manager of synagogue affairs], if I am not mistaken, even the rebbe himself would call out everyone by name. At the second tish, they would sing and dance together, the rebbe with the

[Page 151]

Hasidim, because the Vizhnitzer Rebbe was very folksy and the Hasidim called him Baal Ahavas Yisroel [devoted to the Jewish people].

His brother, the Otiner Rebbe, a son-in-law of the Buhusher [Buhu?i, Romania] Tzadik, from the [Ruzhiner court, was influenced by the Ruzhiner "royal" custom. He was measured, withdrawn from the people. And the tradition, that is, the particular motif in the prayer was more lyrical, quieter and restrained than the quick, hurrying and shouting tradition of his Vizhnitzer brother.

Both were great scholars. Their younger brothers – the rebbes from Horodenka, Zalishchyky, Seret, Storozhynets – would also come to our city and although they did not have their own designated Hasidim, the Vizhnitzer and Otiner Hasidim would also come to them because all of them were the sons of the previous Vizhnitzer Tzadik, Reb Borukh, may the memory of the righteous man be blessed. The son of the founder of the dynasty, Reb Mendele, may the memory of the righteous man be blessed, author of the book, Tzemakh Tzadik [Religious Scion], was the son of the tzadik, Reb Chaim, may the memory of the righteous man be blessed, the author of the book, Toras Chaim [Theory of Life]. The Kosover Rebbe also would come to us. He would behave modestly, did not talk excessively during his praying and at his tishn. His Hasidim were not many and they did not react to their rebbe with the same enthusiasm and religious ecstasy as the Vizhnitzer, Boyaner and Otiner Hasidim.

There were conflicts among the Vizhnitzer and Kosover Hasidim over the course of years. When one of the two rebbes designated a shoykhet [ritual slaughterer] or intervened for him, the other rejected him and the conflicts in the city grew and this despite the fact that both, as already mentioned above, were grandsons of the Tzadik Reb Chaim Kosover, may the memory of the righteous man be blessed.

The Vizhnitzer and Otiner Hasidim made fun of the Kosover Rebbe, who would start praying early and finish the Shabbos praying by 10 or 11 o'clock.

The watchword: "In Zhiditshov a hellish fire burns" in the time of the righteous men, Reb Tzvi (a grandson of the Baal Tosefet Yom-Tov [Yom-Tov Lipmann Heller], father-in-law of Arteres Tzvi [the crown of Tzvi – Tzvi Hirsch of Zhiditshov], [author of] Beis Yisroel [House of Israel] and Sur Mei'ra Ve'Asei Tov [Refrain from Evil and Do Good] and Pri Kodesh

Hilulim [Holy Praises] and his brother's son, Reb Ayzykl, may the memory of the righteous man be blessed – [only] flickered in the time of their grandsons, who were only epigones [less distinguished imitators] of their grandfathers.

The liturgical tradition, the motifs of the prayers of the young rebbes and, even more, of the proclaimed bale-tefile, as for example: Reb Meir Francaz, Reb Chaim Frenkel, Reb Hirsh Wolf Eminger, Reb Feywish Hanam, Reb Itsikl

[Page 152]

Shajkes, Reb Moshe Bochner and others – were really ardent, fascinating and distinguished as in the time of the first Zhiditshover Tzadikim, but the "grandsons" as rebbes did not reach the ankles of their ancient grandfathers in their influence over the Hasidim and they did not have the same appeal or respect and reverence on the part of the Hasidim as the former did. When the rabbi from Zhiditshov or the rebbe from Dolyna arrived in Kolomea for a Shabbos, only tens of the devoted Hasidim sat at the tishn and the impression in the city was not the same as during a visit from the Vizhnitzer, Otiner, Kopitshinitser or even of the Kosover.

The Nadvorner Hasidim did not have their own kloyz because their number was not large and especially after the death of their rebbe, the holy Reb Mordkale, may the memory of the righteous man be blessed. But several of them who were devoted to the rebbe remained devoted to their grandsons. Reb Leib Zenenreich, a respected Jew, a learned man and communal man, stood at their head. During my childhood, we lived as neighbors with him and every time a grandson of the Rebbe, Reb Mordkale Nodverner stayed with him, I would go there to pray and to the tish.

The Tzadik Reb Mordkale had a son-in-law who was named Reb Meshulem. He was not from a branch of a rabbinical line nor from any "dynasty," but was only descended from a rabbinical family. In his youth he was a child prodigy and an exceptional student of the gaon [genius] Reb Meshulem Horovitz, head of the beis-din in Stanislav. After he married the daughter of Reb Mordkale, the Nodverner Rebbe and spent several years in his house, he devoted himself completely to being a nister [hidden holy man or hermit] and to religious ecstasy and prayers and ritual immersion and went so far that his faither-in-law, the Tzadik, who was known as being excessive in prayers until the afternoon and whose voice of supplication every day reached the distant land, once said of him – as his Hasidim said – "He exceeds me in his obsession..."

Reb Meshulem would travel to the old Chartkover Rebbe, Reb Dovid Moshe, may the memory of the righteous man be blessed, the son of the Riziszner Rebbe. When he felt that he had reached the level of a tzadik, he asked the Chartkover Rebbe if he was suitable and worthy to take kvitlekh from his followers and the Chartkover Rebbe gave him ordination to do so. He settled in Chrzanów near Krakow and then in Zielin and then in another place and was well-known under the name the Zeliner

[Page 153]

Rebbe and by the masses with the name Der Rebbe Kvitsher [the shouting rebbe] because despite the mortifications and fasts of this thin and short man, his noise and shouting while praying literally deafened and upset the listener.

In my childhood I was present at his praying in the house of Reb Leib Zegenreich. He prayed alone in a secluded room and only came to the worshippers for Kdushe [the exaltation of God's holiness during group prayer] and when the Torah scrolls were taken out. His noise and force and his unnatural gestures are indescribable. When reciting Barukh Shamiya [Blessed is the Name], he climbed onto a chair and from there, he – literally – jumped onto a bench and then back and forth with a heartrending cry and then he fell with his face to the ground (on Shabbos!!!) and cried for several minutes. Then, when his Hasidim finished praying in the afternoon, alone in a room he began with Borekh Sheomer [beginning of a morning prayer] and continued until six o'clock at night. Many passersby remained standing outside and shuddered at his high shouting. At a time when the entire city was celebrating the third Shabbosmeal, the rebbe made Kiddush [prayer over wine] for the second Shabbos meal and sang Asader l'Sudoso b'Tzafra d'Shabata [I shall offer praise at the Sabbath morning meal]. Then he said the Minkhah [afternoon] prayers, celebrated the third meal and then very late he recited the Maariv [evening] prayers and made Havdalah [the concluding Sabbath prayers].

As was the custom of the Noverdner, he would also remain for another Shabbos. And chance provided that this second Shabbos fell on erev-Tish b'Av [the eve of the fast day commemorating the destruction of the temples in Jerusalem], a nitkhe [a fast that is postponed because it occurs on a Friday or Saturday]. We all were curious as to how the rebbe would conduct himself when he had to fast and had to prepare to be a mourner on Tish b'Av. To our wonder, he then ended his praying at three o'clock and at around six o'clock he celebrated the last meal before fasting. I was with him a second time after a number of years and, even then, already old and weak, his shouting and enthusiasm had not weakened.

As I asked Reb Leib Zegenreich in my childish naivete why the rebbe jumped and shouted so, the Hasid answered me: "Go on, try and take a burning coal in your hand, you will see that you will also shout, cry and jump like he does. When the rebbe prays, his body and soul is wrapped in burning fire, a flame, a holy fire, and therefore, he acts like this." I

[Page 154]

will never forget this sublime explanation from the Hasid, Reb Leib. On balance we can say that Kolomea was more Hasidic than other nearby cities, as for example, Stanislav or Czernowitz [Chernivtsi]. And yet the city was not ruled by any religious-Hasidic fanaticism in regard to the non-religious and even in regard to the non-observant. And regarding the national-Zionist movement, many of the pious who were infected by the ideas of the Enlightenment were simply Zionists or members of the Mizrakhi [religious Zionists] and only individual fanatics from the Vizhnitzer or Boyaner Hasidim would sometimes appear against the Zionists. Patience, mutual tolerance reigned between both sides, the pious and the intelligentsia. No sharp opposition arose as in western Galicia.

This all was in Austrian Kolomea before the First World War. But in Polish Kolomea after the war and until its destruction, the situation changed. As soon as Agudas Yisroel [Union of Israel – Orthodox opponents of Zionism] was founded, its leaders and spokesmen, with Reb Yosl Lau at the head, immediately began a vigorous campaign against the nationalists and Zionists. On one side, the Agudah [Agudas Yisroel] movement grew in all areas of politics and not only in religious life. And on the other side, a new generation grew up of hundreds of young people who studied in the state elementary and middle schools in place of in the kheder [religious school], students and intellectuals, enlightened in their thinking and in their conduct, the majority enthusiastic Zionists, some socialists, and thus the population split into two opposing directions, into two opposing camps. The idyll that had reigned in the kehile at the time of my childhood and youth disappeared, not for the benefit of religion and not for the benefit of the people.

And then came the horrible catastrophe of the genocide by the Germans and their local helpers from among the Poles and the Ukrainians who did not make a distinction between the two camps. All of the Jews in the city met the same fate. And our dear community, the large and important Jewish city, was erased from the earth. Almost all of its dear sons were slaughtered by the Nazi Satans. The few survivors were widely scattered to all the corners of the earth. An end came to

[Page 155]

to this dear community. Only earth and dust saturated with blood and ash remained of it.

The Talmud Torah named Tamkhim d'Oiraisoh [Supporters of Torah] in Kolomea

Founded in 5620-1860 at the initiative of the brilliant rabbi, Reb Tzvi Elimelikh of Dynow: at the time of my childhood Reb Ahron Shoykhet, of blessed memory stood at its head and at the time its situation was humble. The teachers received a small wage and it was not punctually paid. The supervision was inadequate. However, in the years 5664-5674 [1914-1924] it was reorganized and 300 children learned there with good teachers and a number of the subjects were dedicated to worldly education. Committee members of the leadership were: Messrs. Alter Kneper, Avraham Shmuel Heler, Mikhl Hamer, Hirsh Bolch, Chaim Sholem Shoykhet, Yehuda Ber Zaydman. They restored the building and brought in a regimen as in one of the standard schools. There also was a synagogue in the same building, as already mentioned in an earlier chapter.

Jewish Printing Shops in Kolomea

For 200 years, there were Jewish printing shop in Kolomea, where not only sidurmim [prayer books] and makhzorim [holiday prayer books were printed], but also books of Tanakh [Torah, Prophets and Writings], gemores [commentaries], books of interpretations and scholarship. At the time of my youth, the owner of the large Jewish printing shop was Reb. Alter Teycher and his son, Shmuel.

Beis-haKhoylem [hospital], Bikur Khoylem [Society to Visit the Sick], and an Old Age Home

In 5614-1854 two philanthropic institutions were founded from contributions: the hospital and the Society to Visit the Sick and in 5658-1898, at the 50th anniversary of the reign of the Austrian Kaiser, Franz Josef I, the old age home was founded and in it also a synagogue. The rich man, Reb Yakov Bretler, donated 20,000 crowns for the building and the kehile [organized Jewish community] supported the mentioned institution from the communal treasury. The Kolomea kehile also supported important philanthropic institutions this way.

[Page 156]

Cemeteries

The cemetery at Kaminker Street is the oldest, from 300 years ago, and there lie rabbis, great scholars and tzadikim, not only Kolomea residents, but also those from other places. In 5543-1783, this cemetery was closed and another field was designated as a cemetery, in the south of the city and it served as a cemetery for more than 100 years and rabbis and tzadikim are also buried there.

In 5650-1890, a new cemetery was [consecrated] in Vincentovka. Great rabbis from eastern Galicia were present at the ceremony at that time: the brilliant rabbi, Reb Arya Leibush Ish Hurvits, of blessed memory, the head of the religious court in Stryi and then Stanislav, author of responsa, Hare Besamim[Mountain of Spices]; the brilliant rabbi, Reb Avrahm Manakhem Shteinberg, of blessed memory, the head of the religious court in Sniatyn and later Brod; the brilliant rabbi, Reb Yehuda Leibush Landau, of blessed memory, the head of the religious court in Sadigura, author of Yad Yehuda [Hand of Yehuda]; the brilliant rabbi, Reb Yosef Shmuel Gelernter, of blessed memory, the head of the religious court in Kitev; the brilliant rabbi, Reb Yakov Taumim, of blessed memory, the head of the religious court in Kolomea.

Afterword

My task was to bring to life the kehile in memorium only from one standpoint: the Jewish-religious Kolomea. However, it was difficult for me to fulfill all that I had undertaken because in the half-jubilee anniversary of the [25] years that I had lived in Vienna – from 1914 to 1939 – I had no contact with my birth city after my parents left the city at the outbreak of the war in 1914 and settled in Grosswardein (Oradea Mare). Therefore, I could only speak of and describe religious Kolomea until the end of the era before the First World War.

May my modest contribution in this memorial book be a kaddish yatom [memorial prayer recited at a parent's grave] for the neshama aliyah [may the soul go to a higher place in paradise] of the mother kehile in which I was raised, where the bones of my grandfathers of generations rest, a mourner and alone with sadness and grief for the dear ones who perished, who died el kiddush haShem ha-ummah [in sanctification of the Name and the nation].

Yitgadal v'yitkadash sh'mei raba [Glorified and sanctified be God's great name; the beginning of the mourner's prayer].

Translator's footnote:

1. Bale-tfile are those who lead communal prayers. A kehile is an organized Jewish community.

Original Footnotes:

a. See Shloyme Bikl's chapters about Mayer Frantsoyz in A shtot fun yidn [A town of Jews], New York, 1943

b.   See about him in Shloyme Bikl's A shtot mit yidn [A town of Jews], New York 1943

[Page 157]

A List of Books

Books that were published in Kolomyya between the years 1880-1930
Assembled from the Bibliographer A. Yaari (Jerusalem)

Translated by Jerrold Landau

1.   Imrei Shoham by Rabbi Moshe the son of Dan Shoham, 5640, 1880.
2.   Maskil El Dal by Rabbi Hillel Lichtenstein, Volume I, third printing, 5640, 1880.
3.   Zichron Sheerit Yosef by Rabbi Yosef of Pozna, 5682, 1882.
4.   Passover Haggadah with the commentary of Damesek Eliezer by Rabbi Eliezer Schwerdscharf, 5683, 1993.
5.   Maase Nisim, about the ten tribes, by Rabbi Moshe Edrei, 5643, 1993.
6.   Avodat Hagershuni by Rabbi Yehuda Gershon Pikholtz, 5683, 1883.
7.   Teivat Gomeh by Rabbi Yosef Teomim, the author of Pri Megadim, 5683, 1883.
8.   Avkat Rochel by Rabbi Hillel Lichtenstein, 5645, 1885.
9.   Or Tzadikim by Rabbi Alter Teicher, 5646, 1886.
10. Yetziv Pitgam by Rabbi Yaakov Emden, 5646, 1886.
11. Shem Olam, the book on Moses Montefoire, by Rabbi Yehuda Tzvi Gelbard, 5646, 1886.
12. Maskil el Dal by Rabbi Hillel Lichtenstein, part I, third edition, 5647, 1887.
13. Shemesh Umagen, a book on the death of Yehoshua Meir Shapira the head of the rabbinical court of Czortkow, by Rabbi Yehuda Tzvi Gelbard, 5647, 1887.
14. Koach Shor, Responsa of Rabbi Yitzchak Schorr, 5648, 1888.
15. Shulchan Hatahor Hamezukak by Rabbi Yosef Pardo, 5648, 1888.
16. Mili Dechasiduta by Rabbi Avraham Dov, head of the rabbinical court of Buczacz, 5650, 1890.
17. Chidushei Hagershuni by Rabbi Yehuda Gershon Pikholtz, 5651, 1891.
18. Divrei David by Rabbi Avraham David, head of the rabbinical court of Buczacz, 5652, 1892.
19. Kol Yehuda by Rabbi Yehuda Tzvi Gelbard, 5652, 1892.
20. Kuntrus 5630 by Rabbi Avraham David, head of the rabbinical court of Buczacz, 5653, 1893.
21. Zichron Zion or Even Bochen, clarifications of the holy idea of the settlement of the Land of Israel, by Ish Yehudi, 5657, 1897.[1]

[Page 158]

22. Documents of the Jews of the Four Land of the Kingdom of Poland, by Rabbi Moshe Yaakov Schwerdscharf, 5659, 1899.
23. Torah Haamim, to bring the nations into the covenant of "fear of G-d", by Rabbi Moshe Yaakov Schwrdscharf, 5660, 1900.
24. Proceedings of the Zionist Annotation Office of Galicia and Bukovina in Kolomyya, 5661, 1901.
25. Tikkun Olam... Anthology of rabbinic enactments in the Four Lands of the Kingdom of Poland by Rabbi Moshe Yaakov Schwerdscharf, 5661, 1901.
26. Matnat Yehuda by Rabbi Yehuda Gershon Pikholtz, 5662, 1902.

27. Geulat Yaakov on the commandment of honoring parents by Rabi Yaakov Sofer of Staraginets, 5666, 1906.
28. Horaat Deah, 5672, 1912
29. Zichron Larishonim, enactments and customs of the Gemilut Chasadim [charitable organization] of Kolomyya by Rabbi Chaim Tzvi Teomim, 5674, 1914.
30. The Education of the Jewish Child in the Past and Today, Tarbut School, 5690, 1930.
31. The "Lulav", Iton Hatalui, 5691, 1931.

———————

Translator's Footnote:

1.   Ish Yehudi [A Jewish Man] is evidently a pseudonym.

———————

[Page 159]

Three Eras

(A little history and memories about Kolomea, my city)

by Yisroel Isser Zeidman (Tel Aviv)

Translated by Gloria Berkenstat Freund

Now, when I describe my home city, my heart fills with longing and my soul becomes full of memories, experiences from my earliest childhood years, of khederim [religious primary schools] and melamdim [teachers in religious schools], dayanim [judges in religious courts] rabbis and rebbes [Hasidic rabbis], of holy Shabbosim [Sabbaths], holidays and the Days of Awe. I spent my best young years in Kolomea, until the year 5674 [1914]. I left the city with our entire household during the bitter month of Av [August], when the First World War broke out and we wandered from place to place and from one country to another. At the end of the war, we returned to Kolomea – and I spent a few beautiful, interesting years there, until 5683 [1923]. That year I left for Eretz-Yisroel. Later, I visited and spent time in my first home twice – in 5689 [1929] and in 5694 [1937].

And today, after a few dozen years, when I want to erect a matzeyvah [headstone] for our dear, beloved city, I must divide its history of the last sixty years before the destruction into three eras, which are in large part characteristic of other cities and shtetlekh [towns] in eastern Galicia: a. the first era before the war – a time of strength and stability; b. the second era begins with the end of the [First] World War; and it extends until the year 5690 (1930) – an era of awakening, of sturmm und drang [storm and distress] in the Jewish neighborhood; an era of great national hope and for a drive for Zion and Eretz-Yisroel; c. and the third era – an era of internal dejection and external heavy stress. In this era we see an evident hint of great misfortune,

[Page 160]

of the catastrophe that would meet the House of Israel in East Europe. In truth, we received signs from above, but we closed our eyes and it was as if we did not notice anything.

A.

During the first era, Kolomea was a quiet, Jewish city. The majority of Jews were Hasidim and only a minority were Zionists and followers of Mizrakhi [religious Zionists]. But during elections or with other communal matters – the Zionists were active and they were the most active element in the life of the city. They were taken into account and discussed. There was also a small minority of assimilated Jews who represented the Jews before the local Polish government. It can be said that the various Hasidic groups were visible in communal life; on the contrary, in important matters the Zionists always emerged on the public level.

The Hasidim prayed in small synagogues that were named after famous rebbes: there was a small synagogue of Kosover Hasidim, Vizhnitzer Hasidim, of Otynier, Ziditshover, Boyaner and Chortkower. And the Hasidic followers would travel to their rebbes, who lived in small shtetlekh [towns], for the Days of Awe and for holidays. It is certainly no coincidence that the great rebbes nonetheless, lived in small shtetlekh. There, their organization was not insignificant as it would be in the bustle of the large city. But in the interwar years, between the two world wars, when Hasidism began to sink, the famous rebbes began to move to the large cities, such as Lemberg and Stanislaw.

And how beautiful and enchanting our Jewish city looked on the eve of a holiday or on the eve of the Days of Awe when the Hasidim and their children – some on foot and others in wagons – with their packs in their hands, went to the train station, to travel to their rebbes, to absorb the holiness, be blessed. Some small synagogues were almost empty during the holidays because only the very simple businessmen remained in the city.

As in the majority of all cities of exile, the Jews of Kolomea also were occupied with commerce and craft, but Kolomea was renowned for the manufacturing of taleysim [prayer shawls]: two large factories produced taleysim – the factories of Yona Zager and of the Hellers. The Heller family

[Page 161]

was an illustrious family. The Hellers were descended from the author of Tosafot Yom-Tov [commentary on the compilation of the oral law named after its author Yom-Tov Lipman Heller] and they were a little haughty. They were Boyaner Hasidim. And after Reb Shimshon Heller died, the business went to his three sons, who were famous scholars, men of good appearance and also versed in worldly matters. Their taleysim were well known in Europe and even in Asia. A traveling, smart and shrewd Jew would travel through all of the Jewish cities and shtetlekh in the old home and would there sell Heller's taleysim, which made famous the Heller firm as well as the city of Kolomea. There were also families that were involved with world trade. They had connections to Germany, Romania and other lands. They were especially involved with the wheat trade. The majority of Jews of the city lived frugally. They were employed in the clothing trade; many were shopkeepers and brokers. Others were artisans and workers. Therefore, even without political pressure, still in the time of the Austro-Hungarians, thousands of Jews from our city took their walking sticks and went west to earn a living. Some of them went as far as Vienna, the capital of Austria; others crossed the border and settled in Germany. (When I was in Leipzig in 1930, I found a small Kolomea synagogue. Our landsleit were employed there mainly with the fur trade.) And many of those from Kolomea immigrated to America to seek employment.

At that time, education in our city was in a rigid and set form: the Hasidim sent their children to khederim of many kinds according to each group's beliefs. In many small synagogues, finding a student of a gymnazie [secular secondary school] was like searching for a bread crumb right before Passover, not to be found. The children received their general education from private teachers – in the afternoon hours or at night. The great mass of people – some of them sent their children to the Jewish school named for Baron Hirsch, and some – to the Polish public school. Only the middle class, assimilated and general Zionists sent their children to the gymnazie. Yet, there were a few families, select ones, whose sons were educated simultaneously in Torah and in general, worldly education. And the sons did not abandon the old way of life. And this was a surprise and a great wonder.

[Page 162]

In spite of the folks-shuln [public school] law, the Hasidic Jews knew how to find a solution: dozens of khederim were overfilled with students of all ages. It was characteristic; the teacher of the youngest children and the teachers of Khumish and Rashi, as well as the teachers who taught the start of the Gemara, were mostly born in Kolomea and they were referred to with their name and occupation: Zalman Melamed and Zayde Melamed. There was also one who was well-known as a pedagogue and he would also teach writing. He also was referred to by his family name: Hersh Rat. However, the well-know Gemara teacher, all the more, the melamdim who taught Gemara and the Rashi commentaries, the melamdim who taught Gemara, commentaries and Tosafos [Talmudic commentaries] were, in general, from other cities and they were called according to their places of origin: Leibish Horodenker, Yosya Buczaczer, Josele Berezaner and Reb Chaim of Rzeszow (he also was a melamed only for adults and even bridegrooms studied with him).

My first teacher, Reb Leibush, lived outside the city, in the fresh air. His house was a poor house, like the poor houses of the poor people and the laborers: a dirt floor and a shingle roof. But, because this was his own house, he was careful with it and gave it his attention. He had a small garden near his house where he planted vegetables: corn, carrots, beans and other vegetables. In general, he had a strong inclination toward trade and employment; he would repair his roof and household objects himself.

Reb Leibush was good at explanations and the students had respect for him. In the afternoon, the kheder was full of children. More students, who in the morning studied at the public school, joined the Hasidic children who studied [in the kheder] in the morning. His son, Shimshon, helped him on Thursdays.

His daughters emigrated to America and he would receive support from his children across the sea during the time between the two World Wars and he lived in comfort.

I started to study Gemara with him. We studied the first chapter of Bava Metzia [Talmudic tractate – The Middle Gate], the chapter, "Shnayim adukin be-tallit' [if two people are holding on to a garment]. And in studying the Mishnah [compilation of Oral Torah] we learned the law: "One shall swear that his share in it is not less than half, and the other shall swear that his share in it is not less than half." Emphasizing his interpretation and repeating many times – a matter that was written on another side of the Gemara – that it could be that both were swearing the truth: because it was possible, that both

[Page 163]

had lifted the object equally and one did not see the other one. Therefore, each is entitled to half of the bargain. I remember that he would lecture the students that they should live in peace, in friendship and brotherhood. In addition he would bring an example from the animals and birds that live quietly and calmly and help one another. A student once asked him a question:

– Rebbe [teacher]! We still see that the flies – they were a heavy scourge in kheder – attack one another and fight each other.

The rebbe answered authoritatively, "They do not fight with each other, that is how they multiply."

I moved from Reb Leibush's kheder to Reb Josye Buczaczer. He came to the teaching profession after several transformations: first, he was a merchant in his city of Buczacz [Buchach, Ukraine]. But as he was not successful, his relatives advised him to try his luck in teaching. He then moved to Kolomea and opened a kheder for young men studying Gemara. He was an Otynier Hasid. He was a mixture of a teacher and a pedant. He would explain the vowels of le ekohl-lekhem ["to eat bread."] (in the Torah portion, Yitro [fifth portion of the Book of Exodus, 18:12], with lots of rules, according to the well-known book, haMaslul [The Path]. His explanation was a good one, but his discipline of the students was weak. He would sometimes permit the good students to spend time outside in the street, as long as they knew the page of Gemara and the Torah portion by the end of the week. When I studied with him, his kheder was near the hill on which we slid during the winter.

Once, I remember I went to talk to my friends and on a winter night I went out with them to slide down the hill. My father, of blessed memory, learned of this. He came to the hill, took me under his arm and led me back into the kheder.

Reb Josele Brotshiner, my teacher for commentary on the Mishnah, commentary on Jewish law and Tosafos, was a melamed of another style (Dr. Shlomo Bikel dedicated beautiful pages to him in his book, A City with Jews). Reb Josele was a remarkable type. He was a great and deep scholar, a distinguished Hasid. He had a strong love for Eretz-Yisroel and tended to reflect on Jewish philosophy. The first term in which I studied with him left a strong impression [that has lasted] until today. We studied the tractate, Nederim [Vows] with Perush haRan [commentary by the RaN, an acronym derived from his name Nissim ben Reuven] (Reb Nissim). While studying we would

[Page 164]

become engrossed in the sugye [Talmud question being studied]. Between the school sessions, he would teach us the eight chapters of Rambam. And thus was the order of instruction in this kheder: from six until eight in the morning – commentary, that is: Yoyre-Deye [second part of the Shulchan Aruch – Code of Jewish Law] or Khoyshn Mishpes [fourth part of the Code of Jewish Law], which we would also refer to as Shach, the [abbreviation of the] name of the commentary Siftei Kohen [Lips of the Kohen written by Rabbi Shabbetai Kohen – referred to as the Shach]. From eight to eight-thirty we would pray together with the rabbi in the small Kaminker synagogue. After praying until 10 o'clock – the students spent time at home for breakfast. From 10 to one – a reading; each would study a page of Gemara alone. And then he repeated it for the rabbi. In the afternoon and during the long winter nights, the teacher would recite a page from the Gemara with Talmudic commentaries and commentaries from rabbinic literature in a very profound manner. On summer nights we would study "posek" [verse of scripture] – Joshua or Job, with commentaries from Meir Leib Weiser. Sometimes he would dictate letters in Hebrew – in the style of flowery language. Thursday in the afternoon we would study the weekly Torah portion and his custom was that he auctioned the sections (Kohan, Levi, shlishi [third] and the like) of the portions among the students – for the benefit of the fund of Reb Meir the miracle worker.

Reb Josele knew to enliven the instruction in that he would let be heard wonderful stories and subjects: once he asked a question: "Who is bigger than the other – The sea or the person?"

– Certainly the sea – the students answered.

– No! – the teacher answered and he explained:

– The size of the sea and its depth has a limit and a foundation: its territory is so much and so much; its depth is so much and so much; however, a person and his soul – who can explore it and fathom it?

He also told us a strange and frightening story: Thus a man was born, grew up, became educated, married and brought children into the world; engaged in business, ran away, was chased and escaped and saw a wonder; in all of his deeds and matters to which a man turns, goes and runs away – an old one runs after him. He sits on the train – the old one with him; he runs away from him across the sea – the old man chases after him; he runs away – and the other one after him; he runs – the old one with him. In short: chasing, running and overtaking until the man fall down exhausted and dead tired and digs him a grave and winks at him: come brother, lie down here, here is your place of rest And Reb Josele Brotshiner, with a luminous smile on his lips, ends

[Page 165]

the story and solves the riddle about the old man: old age – the old one runs after the people.

He would say and repeat for his students: we recognize the man from his walk, from his manner of speaking and from deeds and even from the tip of his pencil.

Of the students who studied with me, Meirtsie Etinger, of blessed memory, should be remembered here. He was a great assiduous student. During the wartime he turned up in Bohemia with his family. He acquired a general education and he passed his exams to enter university. Then he studied oriental scholarship in the University of Prague and received the title of doctor there. He dedicated his few years of life to Hebraic education and was a teacher in the famous Hebrew gymnazie in Muncasz. He remained firm and devoted to Torah and tradition. He visited Eretz-Yisroel twice – with the hope of working in the Hebrew University in Jerusalem. But, in Israel, he suddenly was stricken with severe typhus and he found his last rest on the Mount of Olives (alas, today outside the borders of the Land of Israel).

B.

The day of the outbreak of the First World War, Tisha b'Av [the 9th of Av - a fast day commemorating the destruction of the first and second Temples in Jerusalem] of the year 5674 [1914], left a strong impression on the Jews of our city. I remember when the military was sworn in at the market, an immense group of soldiers stood organized with discipline with the flags and officers and all ready to go to war. On the first day of the war – and an event chases an event: masses of the military were taken – on foot and by train – to the eastern front. And the Jewish population provided large tables with food and drink – on both sides of the highway and near the train – and food and packages were divided generously for all of the soldiers. (It is worth remembering this self-sacrifice of our Jews for the military – which was warmly honored in a collection of letters from Jewish soldiers that was published after war in the capital city of Vienna.)

The first stage of the war turned out bad for

[Page 166]

Austria-Hungary. The Russians crossed the border of Galicia immediately. A storm of Jewish refugees began to move from the border cities, from Czortkow, from Buczacz and from other cities and they came to Stanislaw and Kolomea. But before they could rest, they had to run further. On a Sunday of the first weeks of the war, they began to run from our city, too. But the trains were taken and there were no horses and wagons to be gotten. The rich and wealthy men obtained wagons with great difficulty and for large mounts of money. And thus our family left the city, crowded and pressed together on a simple peasant's wagon and four generations in it: my grandmother Hentsha from Buczacz, who spent the summer months with us, my parents and their children and grandchildren. We dragged ourselves this way to Delatyn and, from there, after we had eaten lunch, we traveled further until we arrived at night in Kereshmeze [Jasina], a small shtetl near the Hungarian border. There, for the first time, we saw the mountain-Jew type who, with his appearance and characteristics, was a product of the Carpathian Mountains.

On a beautiful Friday, my brother and I and several cousin children went out for a stroll in the mountains. We climbed to the mountain top with a hidden feeling of fear and a simultaneous sense of boldness. After we came home, we tasted the kapuste (the cabbage) and the potatoes – really delicious. It was possibly the first time in our lives that we ate with hunger and appetite.

Meanwhile, the Russian occupation expanded. We had to travel further through Hungary – with one stop in the city of Krail – we arrived in Vienna, where we remained until May 1917. From there we traveled to Galanta [Slovakia] in order to be able to study in the famous yeshiva where the Rabbi [Yosef Tzvi] Dushinsky stood at its head. We spent an entire year there. In May 1918 we returned to our city of birth, Kolomea.

C.

That year the Germans as well as Austria-Hungary suffered great military defeats on all fronts; and after, there was a period of political upheaval. The famous 14 Points of the American President Wilson hovered in the air of the wider world. And in the Jewish neighborhood – it was the sweet year of the famous Balfour Declaration. While still in Hungary we heard that a well-known rabbi, a head of a yeshiva had incited and encouraged one of his students, who was a Kohen [priest – descendant of Aaron, the brother of Moses] to learn the Seder Kodashim [the section of the Mishnah – the Oral Law – containing the rules of sacrifice in the Temple in Jerusalem] "because immediately, speedily in our days the Temple would be rebuilt." Therefore, he had to be ready for his appointment.

There was a great awakening among the Ukrainians for political independence in our area. The Kaiser Karl [Charles I] wanted to bring a remedy for the plague and he proclaimed the liberation of all the people who occupied his land, with the proviso that the Kaiser of the state would be considered as the central figure, who connected all the people of his state, as a unified common political entity. However, it was already too late. After the military suffered defeat on the front, the state crumbled from the inside. And suddenly, over night, a group of small independent nations arose on the ruins of imperial Austria-Hungary, which immediately began to argue and even to fight with one another.

The days of the Ukrainian government in east Galicia were considered as "when a slave reigns." It was a government of terror for the Jews. Jewish corpses were often brought into the city from the surrounding villages. If one wanted to travel from one place to another, one had to be furnished with official papers and with a particular certificate, with a prepustka [pass] as was said in Ukrainian. And after all of this, one traveled in freight cars. There was a state of war and one was not permitted to go out in the street.

During this terrible time my father, may he rest in peace, came home from Budapest at night. He did not know about the edicts in the city and left for home alone on foot. A Ukrainian patrol detained him on the way. And one said to the other: "Shoot

[Page 168]

him!" My father, may he rest in peace, grabbed him by the arm. He did not lose his courage and said to him: "Come with me to the police. I am an old citizen of the city. They will clarify the matter there." And thus a miracle happened for him. The Ukrainian patrol obeyed him and went with him. Thus he survived.

During this time, earning a living was more difficult, it was very austere. No commerce could be carried out from one city to another. The Jews began to manufacture things at home. For example: Ersatz coffee was created from certain plants; they fabricated shoe paste [shoe polish], various soaps and similar articles.

The Jewish street was very lively then. Communal life had blossomed during that time. The Balfour Declaration was interpreted as having a literal meaning: a Jewish state. Each group of people organized according to their political faction and leanings. The haHalutz [the pioneer – Jewish youth movement] was founded in Kolomea and various hakshorus [preparatory training for prospective agricultural emigrants to Eretz-Yisroel] in the area of the city. HaShomer [the watchman – Zionist youth group] then developed robust cultural and educational activities. Poale-Zion [workers of Zion – Marxist-Zionist workers movement], Tzeiri Zion [young Zionists], as well as Shomri Tzion [guardians of Zion] (these were the orthodox Jews and the religious young people who yearned for redemption and renewal), also were active and vigorous. And the Bund was very active and the Zionists and the Mizrakhists [religious Zionists] carried out varied activities.

In short, at that time, there was a very stimulating communal spiritual life in all circles: local newspapers were published in Yiddish, many studied Hebrew and there were even groups – particularly from HaShomer – who spoke Hebrew. The assimilated disappeared from view. Many of them became "Jews," that is, they began to speak Yiddish.

As was said earlier, income was inadequate. We learned an aphorism then: "Income is lacking, let us go study."

Every night the halls of the parties were full of people who came to various readings and lessons. They studied Khumish [Five Book of Moses – the Torah], Mishnius [commentaries on the Torah], Ein Yakov [Jacob's Well, title of a 16Wednesday, December 18, 2013sacherth century book of rabbinical commentary] and a page of Gemara [Talmudic commentaries]. Every day another party arranged public lectures, gatherings with discussions, literary evenings and even performances.

[Page 169]

ליטעראַרישער אָוונד

לכבוד דעם ייִדען מ. מ. ספרים.

שבת, דעם 22 פעברואר 1919 (כ״ב אדר א׳)

אין ם נאואדא־זאל

פֿון דער ציוניסט. אקאדעמישער פֿעראיייניגונג ״עבריה״

פּ ר אָ ג ר אַ ם :

I. טייל :

1) ערעפֿנונג: מנדלי ־ דער נעטאָמאָהיקאַנער . . .
ה׳ ביטער.

2) קלאַוויר־סאָלאָ: בעטהאָוען סאָנאַטע „C mol"
פֿרל. חנה בראָגדעם

3) רעציטאַציע: מ. מ. ספֿרים־שפֿיל סאָלאָוויטשיק...
(מיט קלאַוויר בענלייטונג) . ה׳ קרייזעל
ביים קלאַוויר . . . . פֿרל. בראָגדעם.

4) טענדענצרעדע: דער ייִדע און זיין בערייטונג אין
דער יודישער ליטעראַטור ה׳ הוטשנעקער.
15 מינוטען פּויזע.

II. טייל :

די קדושים

דרעם... [illegible small text]
זי.. [illegible]
די נפשות :

	די נפשות
ה׳ נאטטאָריד	1) דער אַלטער שמש .
ה׳ סאַפֿער	2) דער סוחר
ה׳ פֿישאַר	3) דער מלמד .
ת׳ שטאָמפֿלעד	4) דער קצב .
ה׳ קרייזער	5) דער סטודענט.
פֿ־ל. קדם	6) דאָם מיידיל .
פֿרל. זאָבער	7) רחל אמנו .

Literary Evening

In honor of the grandfather [of Yiddish literature] M[endele] M[Mocher] Sforim [pen name of Sholem Yankev Abramovich]

[illegible, blurred type]

Shabbos, the 22nd February 1919 (22 Adar 1 [5679])
In the Nuoyzda Hall
Of the Zionist Academic Unions, *Avoda* [an organization]

Program:

Part I:

1) Opening: Mendele - *Der Getomohikaner* [*The Ghetto Mohican* – an allusion to *The Last of the Mohicans* – in this case the last ghetto Jew]

H. Biter

2) Piano solo: Beethoven Sonata in C minor

Miss Chana Brandes

3) Recitation: Mendele Mocher Sforim play Soloveitchik...
(with piano accompaniment) . . .   H. Kreizler
At the piano . . . .   Miss Brandes

4) [Talk about trends]: the grandfather and his significance in Yiddish literature

Mr. Hutshneker

15-minute pause

Part II:

The Martyrs

A dramatic symphony in three acts by Yakov Gordin translated from Hebrew by Yisroel Biber

The Souls

1. The old *Shamas* [synagogue sexton]	Mr. Gotfrid
2. The merchant	Mr. Shafer
3. The *melamed* [teacher in a religious school]	Mr. Paysakh
4. The butcher	Mr. Shtampler
5. The student	Mr. Kreizler
6. The Girl	Miss Krys
7. Ruchl Amnu	Miss Sacher

[Page 170]

Yiddish community representation crystallized at the time under the name "Jewish National Council," in which both active and passive voting rights were given to women. The idea of Eretz-Yisroel and national independence fused. The famous Zionist communal worker, Reb Moshe Laks, of blessed memory, once began to speak in the large synagogue with great inspiration, as if drunk from victories. He began with the famous words from Psalms: "When God will return the captivity of Zion, we will be like dreamers" [Psalm 126:2]. From one thing to the other, he came to the actual question of voting rights for the women. He argued with the audience in the following manner: "It says in the Torah (in the chapter of Berashis ["In the beginning..."]), "v'hu yimshal bakh," which is usually translated as, "And he will rule over you." However, we can also translate from fhe word "yimshal," a moshal [an example], a parallel, and then the translation – v'hu yimshal - "And he will be equal to you."

At that time, many Jews from the villages and from the smaller cities came to Kolomea and began to occupy a respected place. This development ended with the collapse of the Ukrainian government when the area was occupied first by the Romanians and then by the Poles. The provincial Jew, the agile one, who could climb the stairs of the economic ladder began to push out the old merchant, both in retail [trade] and in wholesale [trade], and even in industry. The Kosower Jews excelled particularly in this regard.

The newly-arrived also had an influence on the communal and cultural life and thus Kolomea became a mother city to the daughters [the shtetlekh]. These sincere young men from the shtetlekh brought fresh blood to the city and provided it with a particular hue. And on the other hand, many from Kolomea traveled to the larger cities and cultural centers of the Jewish world and there they were teachers of Hebrew and other subjects. There were many teachers from our city in Krakow, Munkacs (Czechoslovakia), Lodz and Warsaw. And Dr. Israel Osterzecer had the privilege of being a teacher in the famous Institute of Jewish Studies in Warsaw.

[Page 171]

The enthusiasm of the young faded over the course of years. As long as the political situation in Kolomea district was still not clear, the Jewish population developed educational establishments and cultural institutions that were dedicated to Yiddish and Hebrew. Only after the western states recognized the annexation of east Galicia to Poland did strong assimilation in Poland begin – not as a world view, but as a result of the Jewish life in exile where economic independence did not leave a place for a separate cultural-linguistic existence. Without doubt thousands wanted and strove to go to Eretz-Yisroel, but on one hand there were the bloody events in the country that were repeated often and, on the other hand, there were emigration restrictions; both factors prevented the accomplishment of the aspirations of the masses. This Zionism was a local matter in the kehile [the organized religious community] elections in the lands of exile, representation in the Sejm [Polish parliament], selling Shekels [membership in the Zionist party] and sending delegates to Zionist congresses. Only a small minority of the young chose the long, difficult road of halutszim [Zionist pioneer movement] and hakhshara [agricultural settlements where young Zionists prepared for emigration to Eretz-Yisroel].

D.

The third era stood as a mark of impoverishment and even decline. The Polish government published new edicts every day. True, Eretz-Yisroel was an actual reality; almost every family had relatives in Eretz-Yisroel. But, on the other hand, while they lacked power, there was a great awakening yearning for revolutionary actions, for a mass "clandestine immigration" movement in order to achieve the drive for liberation. And as true idealism was lacking and a certain weakness and indifference ruled on the Jewish streets, an interest began in the ephemeral life and "catch as catch can"– grab and eat. The physical discipline fit like a glove. During my last visit – in 1937 I could see for myself that many synagogues

[Page 172]

were half empty. And the khederim [primary religious schools] – except for the "Foundations of the Torah" [schools] – had almost entirely disappeared. The majority of the young already were receiving a Polish education. They learned Yidishkeit [Jewish way of life] – as in the American way – from private lessons in the afternoon. Divisions even appeared in the fortress of the Shomrei Shabbos [Guardians of the Sabbath]. The excessive practicality and the chase after income left no place for Yidishkeit and for spiritual matters.

Before the outbreak of the Second World War, the social fabric in Kolomea again woke up to a great charitable purpose and for fraternal aid on a very large scale. At that time, hundreds of families were brought to Kolomea from Auschwitz. These were the Jews from Poland and Galicia who had lived in Germany for scores of years, but they did not have German citizenship. And as believable evidence has shown, the entire Kolomea Jewish population was very moved by the fate of the new refugees. They were generously provided with apartments, food and drink, just as the Jewish city had cared about the military that crossed through the city at the outbreak of the First World War.

And even more: as I was told by a believable man, our landsleit [people from the same town] showed great self-sacrifice in saving Jewish souls, even during the time of the Nazi government. At the beginning of the war many Hungarian Jews who had Polish passports were driven to Kolomea. The Nazi government issued a decree and threatened death to everyone in Kolomea who permitted one of the deportees to spend the night. But no one thought about this decree; the Kolomea Jews risked their lives and gave their persecuted brothers a home in which to hide, eat and live.

E.

Ending my memories and impressions of my hometown, Kolomea, I still want to remember a few people who were very close to me and from whom I have written documents. It seems to me that it is worth publishing them on this occasion:

[Page 173]

1.   First, a few fragments from two long letters from my esteemed comrade, Meirtsie Etinger, of blessed memory, who has already been mentioned. The following excerpts are the Yiddish translations from the Hebrew text. The first letter was written Khol Khomoed [intervening days] Passover 5687 [1927], before he came to Eretz-Yisroel.

"...my heart tells me that although we have chosen different roads in life and that we have parted ways – in truth, it is external. However, internally, in our hearts, we have common aspirations and goals – to discover and to purify the Jewish sparks in us and to bring them back to their source of origin. And on the way we will be able to unite the best of humanity and repair what we have damaged in the course of generations.

"I will describe for you in subsequent letters my work over the years, since we have not seen each other. It was a time of much energetic work: I studied a great deal and could learn about life not only from books but also as it is: cruel and difficult. When I ended my university studies in Prague, I received a travel stipend to the eastern countries from the university. But the sum did not suffice for the entire trip – and I did not have any other money – I had to postpone the trip for a year and I was compelled to take on a teaching post in the Hebrew gymnazie [secondary school] in Munkacs [previously in Hungary, now Mukachevo, Ukraine]. This is the city famous in all of the lands of exile and I am sure that you have also heard of it. I have been sitting in the sticks for a few months now. True, my work in the school is very fruitful and nice. But I cannot study personally to the degree to which I am accustomed.

"In the beginning of July I plan to travel to Eretz-Yisroel and I hope to see you there. But in the meantime, I still hope to hear from you details of your life and your deeds."

The lines of the second letter are dated the 9th of Chesvan, 5688 [4 November, 1927]. The letter was written after Dr. Etinger had been in Eretz-Yisroel for a short time:

"I am greatly grieved that I have left Eretz-Yisroel. I cannot describe for you how great my longing is for Jerusalem, for the center of education and elevation of the spirit that one attains there. I now find myself in a city without education, where the Hasidim rule

[Page 174]

without content. And, although I take part in the important work of laying the basis for a new Hebraic education, and although I have extraordinary success in my work – I do not have any satisfaction in this work because while here I have the influence, the highest authority in all matters, the "fear," I have a need to be a "student." The ideal of our people is the "learned man," "to study" and not to be the teacher. Here I do not have any possibility of continuing my studies; for this reason my decision is to come to Jerusalem after the end of the school year – that means the end of June – and what will be will be."

2.   An answer from my friend Leibish Heller, may the memory of a righteous man be blessed, to my letter in which I tried to convince him and other friends in Kolomea to come to Eretz-Yisroel and work with me in the Mizrakhi [religious Zionists] teachers' seminary; here in this letter he answered me (also in Hebrew):

"My dear friend!

"I have received your first letter from the land. It is difficult to describe the impression and the enthusiasm that I felt while reading; words do not suffice. Praise to God that you had the merit and you have seen the dream of your youth accomplished.

"About your proposal that a number of our talented friends come there – great yasher koyekh [congratulations]. This is the best evidence that you have not forgotten us. However, I regret very much, my [heartfelt one], to write to you that this 'suffering' over which you have always lamented, increases from day to day. The difficult economic conditions force each of us to help his family in the difficult struggle. For example, our very talented comrade, Sobel – he spends his days and years in his shop on the "canal" in order to help his mother, the widow. Or our friend Menakhmen Sheinfeld, the enthusiastic Hovev Zion [Lover of Zion], who also studied in the Pedagogium [teachers' academy] of the Rabbi, Professor [Zwi Perez] Chajes, of blessed memory in Vienna, sits here in a dark cellar and sells pelts to the gentiles. And if the gentiles stopped coming to him, he has decided to move to a distant village so he can bring them his goods 'to their nose' and so on. This, my friend, is life here. And as I described the proposal to our friend Eliezer Dovid, he groaned bitterly and looked at me with pitiful eyes and stammered: 'Yes, the door is open, but we are bound...'"

[Page 175]

3.   And now a poem from my talented sister, Miriam'tsia, may she rest in peace; she was the youngest daughter and helped a great deal in earning money. This poem, which originally was written in Yiddish, expresses, to a certain extent, the situation of our young people in Kolomea in the years before the outbreak of the Second World War:

I will my life
Lament – as consolation,
That I have given it
Such wretched spirit.

I believed that by age
Twenty and a few –
I would have [traveled] far
In the far distance...

Meanwhile, I have remained standing,
Here and I cannot go anywhere.
Although, you scream, although you shout,
They do not let you go free.

They need you
To [share] the suffering of pain,
To [join in] carrying the yoke,
You are still needed.

Histadrut haMizrakhi [Mizrakhi organization] in Kolomey, 1929

[Page 176]

Zionism in Kolomea

During the Period Between Both World Wars[1*]

by Dr. Zvi Heller, Tel Aviv

Translated by Gloria Berkenstat Freund

When I speak about Kolomea, I mean the environs that were called the political electoral district of Kolomea that was geographically known under the name Pokutia. Everything that took place in Kolomea had an effect on the shtetlekh [towns] and villages with large Jewish settlements in the mountainous vicinity.

Kolomea had its own Jewish representative in the state parliament, then the Austrian Reich's Council in Vienna, for many years before the First World War. The election district in Austria consisted of three cities in one: Kolomea (Kolomyya), Snityn (Sniatyn) and Beczucz (Buczacz [Buchach]).

The Kolomea Jewish deputies before the First World War were members of the "Polish Club" (Kolo Polskja).

After the First World War, the Kolomea election district in the newly revived Poland was represented in

[Page 177]

the Sejm by a deputy from the United Zionist list number 17, on which the general Zionist, Dr. Henrik Rozmaryn, Dr. Zvi Heller, the representative of Histadrut, the representative of Mizrakhi [religious Zionists], Dr. Shimeon Federbush were candidates. The other Jewish lists, from the Bund, Agudas Yisroel [anti-Zionist religious party], and Paolei Zion [Marxist Zionists] were incapable of carrying through their candidates.

The democratic elections to the Jewish National Council that were dominated by the assimilated [Jews] to the Jewish National Council that in the time of transition immediately after the war took the place of the earlier small kehile [organized Jewish community] houses of prayer provided a strong push to national-political organizing by the Kolomea Jews.

Contributing to the [Jewish] national turmoil was Hashomer Hatzair [the Youth Guard – Social Zionists], the Zionist youth movement that arose during the First World War in Vienna and then was transplanted to Galicia by the returning refugees, young men and girls. A group of Hashomer Hatzair was also founded in Kolomea that had its hakhshara [agricultural training for potential emigrants to Eretz-Yisroel] location in the area of the village Slobudka Lesna.

Immediately after the war, Kopl Gugik and his wife [reopened] the Hebrew school, Safa Brura [clear language – a movement to encourage the use of the Hebrew language] and organized classes for the young and courses for the adults.

In the large meeting hall of the Zionist party, Beit Yisroel [House of Israel], which had existed since 1903, would gather veterans of the local Zionist movement of the past such as the old Dr. Shlomo Rozenhek, the commendable Efroim Klarman, Dr. Marek Laks, Shlomo Scher and Yona Ashkenazi; also there were the younger leaders and the halutz [pioneer] youth, among whom, in a place of honor, were representatives of Hitachdut: Chaim Ringelblum, Kopl Gugik, Moshe Schneberger, Mikhal Hazelkorn, Lev Grebler, Yitzhak Teitelbaum, Meir Laks, Yakov Bender, Nakhman Palik, Shlomo Rares, Dov Sternberg, Etl Ramler, Yakov Schikler, Dr. Meir Etinger, Nety Eiferman and others.

The mentioned Hitachdut comrades headed by Mikhal Hazelkorn led the Keren Kayemeth [National Fund] commission in the city and in the area.

Hitachdut created a professional artisan's school that was led by Mrs. Gusya Horovitz.

The Herzl Library, at the head of which stood the famous Zionist activist Yakov Byter and his wife, Gitl Perminger Byter,

[Page 178]

was very beloved in the city. It possessed thousands of books in Yiddish, Hebrew, Polish and German.

A drama section [of the Zionists] was started with Dr. Marek Knap, Pinkhas Scheierman, Zindl Neiman, Hersh Neiman, Leibele Wolfberg and Neti Eiferman at the head. The drama group carried the name Halevi.

The lectures were begun again as before the war in the Jewish Toynbee Hall. Of the local people, Dr. Shlomo Rozenhak, Chaim Ringelblum, Kopl Gugik and Dr. Kramer often would appear with lectures. Dr. Meir Geyer, Senator Dr. Mikhal Ringel, Professor Binshtok, Dr. Zilberstein, Dr. Naftali Schwartz, Dr. Kopl Schwartz, Fishl Werber, Dr. Fishl Rotenstreich, Zalman Hering and Dr. Zvi Heller would come from Lemberg to lecture. Hundreds of Jews from various circles listened to these lectures.

There was a chess club with a considerable number of members in the Baron Hirsch Hall. Pinkhas Scheierman and Dovid Schreiber led the club.

Lively work went on and with it good success for the Keren Hayesod [the Foundation Fund] in Kolomea and in the surrounding area. The success mainly was thanks to the emissaries from Eretz-Yisroel, Natan Bistricki and Sura Berger. The Hitachdut worker, Lev Grebler traveled to the surrounding cities and villages with the delegation from Eretz-Yisroel.

There were often clashes with Agudas Yisroel in the small Vizhnitz, Ziditshov, Boyan, and Otynia synagogues. Agudas had its fortresses of anti-Zionist struggle in every Hasidic synagogue.

The first halutzim [pioneers] left Kolomea for Eretz-Yisroel in 1920. Among them – Yehuda Grunverg-Hurin, the current leader of Jachin [Prepare] and of Merkaz Hahaklai [Agricultural Center] at Hahistadrut in Eretz-Yisroel, Yosef Kuperman, Dov Sternberg, Sholom Laks and others.

There was a large hakhshara [training site to prepare emigrants for life in Eretz-Yisroel] settlement with the name Klasov that consisted of comrades from the Kresy [Borderlands – formerly territory in the eastern part of Poland], from Volyn, from Polesia, Podlasie and from the Vilna area.

Among the first comrades that Hitachdut sent to hakhshara to the landowner, Engineer Ayzyk Berlet in Gody-Turka, were Chaim Laks, Yakov Grin, Etl Ramler, Levi Grebler, Yakov Hamer and others. Most of this group emigrated to Eretz-Yisroel during the month of July 1925.

[Page 179]

The Hitachdut Central [office] in Lemberg strongly supported the Kolomea hahalutz movement through special cultural envoys. Among the Lemberg delegates were Engineer Reizer (today a high official in the Jewish Agency in Jerusalem), Dov Stok (today Dov Soren, professor of Yiddish at Jerusalem University), Menakhem Gelerter, Fishl Werber, Dr. Nusan Melcer, and the former Sejm [lower house of Polish parliament] deputies, Dr. Kopl Schwartz and Dr. Zvi Heller. The General Secretary, Minister Zigmund Herring, and the regular delegate from the Halutz Central [office], Lionek Braunstein (today in Kibbutz [communal settlement] Hulda), also helped with the cultural work.

The general Zionists, Mizrakhi and Revisionists [non-religious Zionist group founded by Ze'ev Jabotinsky], had their youth and halutz groups in the city.

Yehuda Kreps, Henekh Schecter, Yona Ashkenazi, the Rabbi, Reb Chaim Zvi Taumim, Hersh Rozenbaum, Efroim Klarman and others stood at the head of the Mizrakhi Party. At the initiative of the Hebrew writer, Reuven Fahn, delegates from Kolomea Mizrakhi (Hocher and Zinreich) traveled to Eretz-Yisroel to buy land.

Dr. Hesl, the lawyer, Yakov Heger and others, led the Revisionist group. They created a Betar [Revisionist Zionist youth group] group, as well as a group of Kayil Lemui [National Force] in the city.

The main workers from the leftist Poalei-Zion were: Shlomo Schmoys, Mendl Marksheid, Dutsia Landman, Krauthamer and others.

The Agudas Yisroel was a small group in Kolomea, as it was in all of eastern Galicia. However, it had several capable leaders and the most capable among them were Reb Yosef Lau and the lawyer, Dr. Ben-Tzion Fesler. However, Agudas was completely weakened and lost its influence after Dr. Yosef Lau was chosen as the local rabbi, at the initiative of the Mizrakhi social worker, Reb Yona Ashkenazi (Gedelia Biter's son-in-law and Yekl Biter's brother-in-law). But it still had a group of respected businessmen in its leadership, such as Dovid Zeidman, Lipe and Shlomo Heller, Lipe Ungar, Leibtsie Libman, Shmuel Ber Hener, Leibush Krys and Mendl Hirsh.

Kolomea had its own two Zionist newspapers, Nas Glos [Our Voice] in Polish from the general Zionists and Undzer Shtime [Our Voice] [in Yiddish] from Hitachdut.

The visit of Yosef Sprinzak, the present speaker of the Knesset [Israeli parliament], was an important event in the history of Kolomea Zionists.

Yosef Sprinzak came to Kolomea in 1935 to carry out the

[Page 180]

unification of Hitachdut and Poalei-Zion. Some from Hitachdut with Chaim Ringelblum, Moshe Schneberger, Lewi Grebler and Dr. Marek Knop were stubborn and would not embrace the unification with Poalei-Zion that had been carried out on a worldwide scale.

After greater efforts and more intensive theoretical doctrinal work on the part of the special messengers from Ikhud [Union], Dr. Naftali Schwartz and Yitzhak Fagenbaum and finally, Yosef Sprincak, the Ringelblum group as well as Kopl Gunik's group united with Poalei-Zion. The previously mentioned leaders of Hitachdut, Chaim Ringelblum, Kopl Gunik and Moshe Schneberger and the Poalei-Zion workers, Dr. Wagman, Shlomo Badler, Dr. Schnebalg and Shlomo Eizner, were at the head of the united party.

In 1934, Lewi Grebler created a hakhshara settlement of the Hitachdut comrades under the name Vitkinia.[1] The group became a part of Hitachdut halutz in eastern Galicia. The economy of Vitkinia consisted of four gardens near the Prut [River] and a house on Dzieduszycki Street. During the summer the group worked in the field. However, during the winter, the group was hired to do laundry in private houses. The group members were woodcutters during the winter.

It was very typical that the halutzim had to carry on a struggle for the right to work. The woodcutters organized by P.P.S. [Polish Socialist Party] often attacked the halutzim and did not allow them to work. The municipality helped to secure for the halutzim their right to work thanks to the councilmen Chaim Ringelblum and Moshe Schneberger.

Hitachdut and the women's organization, WIZO [Women's International Zionist Organization], created a people's kitchen in the city. Members of Hitachdut founded a credit bank for artisans and retailers, again with the help of Sejm-deputy, Dr. Avraham Zilberstein, who was the leader of the Jewish cooperative movement in Poland and with the help of the "Joint" [Joint Distribution Committee] representative, Yitzhak Niterman. The old communal worker Dugye Vizelberg stood at the head of the bank.

Yad haRutzim, the artisans' union that was under the influence of the P.P.S., split after the death of the well-known P.P.S. leader, Dr. Samuel Lazarcz Schor. A Zionist group emerged from the union and the comrade from the

[Page 181]

Hitachdut, Yitzak Teitelbaum, succeeded in organizing 15 young locksmiths for emigration to Eretz-Yisroel.

Most of the artisans reorganized under the leadership of the jewelry traders and the government-friendly city politician, Yehuda Borukh Feuerstein, in a union, under the name Rzemieslnik (the Artisan).

The Hitachdut under the chairmanship of councilman Moshe Schneberger created a separate union for artisans and retail traders. A Union of Private Employees that joined Lemberg Central was founded under the chairmanship of Chaim Ringelblum. The Hitachdut also created Jewish produce cooperatives in large villages surrounding Kolomea under the name Hema (butter) with the help of Dr. Avraham Zilberstein. These cooperatives were in contact with the cooperatives Tnuva [fruit] and Mashbir [to sell food] in Eretz-Yisroel.

Members of the Local Committee of Hitachdut Tseiri-Zion [Young Men of Zion] in Kolomea
Sitting from right to left: Munya Schumer, Wolf Weisbrat, Dr. Marek Knopf, Chaim Ringelblum, Levi
Grebler, Moshe Schneberger, Dovid Hilzenrat;
Standing under them: Zini Thau, Moshe Schikler, Dr. Zev Haber, Yitzhak Kern, Shama Tindel (Teicher), Itsye No
index entries found.No index entries found.**, Naftali Thau;**
In the last row: Yosef Reich, Yosef Ramler, Munya Bank, ...?, Bank

Footnote:

1. Dr. Zvi Heller was one of the leaders of the Zionist-Socialist party, Hitachdut in Poland and a deputy in the Sejm [Polish parliament] from Kolomea during the years between both World Wars. As a deputy, Dr. Heller often came to Kolomea and was in constant contact with Zionist society as a whole in the city and, principally with Hitachdut, which had the finest representatives among the Yiddish and Hebrew speaking intelligentsia, such as Chaim Ringelblum, Kopl Gugik, Moshe Schneberger and others.
    Dr. Heller's remembrances of Kolomea bring out several interesting facts and an abundance of names of well-known older and younger activists in the city.

Translator's footnote:

1. Vitkinia is named after Joseph Vitkin, Zionist author of the pamphlet, A Call to Jewish Youth who Love their People and Zion, in which he encouraged immigration to Eretz-Yisroel based on the ideal of agricultural work.

[Page 182]

Socialist Demonstration in Kolomea
on the Eve of Voting, 1907

by Levi Grebler

Translated by Gloria Berkenstat Freund

Three days before the voting, on a Shabbos [Sabbath], the Z.P.S. [Zydowska Partia Socjalno Demokratyczna – Jewish Social Democratic Party] under the leadership of Dr. Schorr, together with the P.P.S. called a mass meeting in Lyeblyk Room on the Sobiejski Street to question why the city council was not carrying out the [recent] Austrian law requiring that three weeks before the election, the city council was to distribute a stamped voting card to each citizen so that he could take part in the election.

This was to be the first, general, secret, direct and proportional election that was battled out with great effort in the Reichsrat [Austrian Parliament in Vienna]. However, the municipal authorities in Kolomea deliberately and consciously neglected their duties and three days before the election, the citizens still had not received their voting cards. The crowd was very agitated by this action on the part of the city managing committee and everyone came as one to the protest meeting. Kolomea had not seen such a gathering until then! Artisans, merchants and workers came from all strata to demand that the municipal authorities treat them as the law demanded – as free Austrian citizens.

Dr. Schorr gave an inspired speech. He proposed his program to the large assembled crowd, which he intended to carry out in the Reichsrat [Austrian Parliament] as the representative of the working masses. At the close of his speech, he enjoined those assembled to march in closed ranks to the city hall. The crowd responded to his speech with strong applause. The several thousand assembled immediately formed rows and, singing the Czerwony Sztandar [Red Banner], they marched with the red flag, carried by Anshel Weitz.

[Page 183]

Yosl Glazer, Fishl Thau, Haber, Dr. and Mrs. Schorr with a Ruthenian female teacher and Dr. Oster walked in the first row. Fuks, Ciper, Ehreman, Mikeitin, Bialas, Korski, Simcha Weitz and his wife, Leib Biger, Mordekhai Leibowitz, Borten, the younger Thau, the shoemaker's son, Shaul Freier, Gabrial Ziegenlaub, Naftaler Kesten, Haker the shoemaker, Hilzenrat the weaver. The enthusiastic masses called out various slogans: "Niekh zywo, Dr. Schorr, hoorah! Precz z kliki magistrackiej! Hanba! Wstyd! Tchórzak! The Ruthenians sang: and "Hei tam na hori Sich ide" ["There upon the mountain Sich marches," a Cossack song] and so on.[1*]

New people constantly joined this marching mass, Jews in their Shabbos [Sabbath] clothing, in long, coarse coats and shtreimlekh [fur hats worn by members of some Hasidic sects]. These were the Jewish weavers, mostly pious Hasidic Jews. All were ready to fight.

When the demonstrators reached the city hall with the cry, "We demand our voting cards!" the Jewish vice mayor, Funkenstein, gave an order to the firemen to close the gate and he telephoned the military. Meanwhile, still more people joined in. The crowd became larger and larger. The clique in the city hall also quickly called a meeting of its people to decide what to do in such a tense mood. Meanwhile, several demonstrators noticed that the officials from the city hall on the second floor were standing near the window and laughing. There was shouting:

"Look up, they are laughing at us!" The masses started for the city hall and began to storm the gate. Some threw stones and broke the windowpanes of the windows of the city hall. Dr. Radecki arrived during this. When he had to pass the Hotel Grand, the masses threw rotten, stinking eggs and began to beat him. However, Herer came to his aid and pushed him into the gate of the hotel. After everything, the masses stormed the gate of the city hall until they broke in and several hundred people entered inside. The military came immediately, a company from the 24th infantry regiment with the Lieutenant Colonel Count Czukowski at the head. They

[Page 184]

called out the 24th regiment, not the landwehr [militia], because there were many Jews and city bourgeoisie in the landwehr and they knew that the landwehr would not dare to shoot at the masses.

The company commandant demanded that the demonstrators disperse, if not he would be forced to order shooting. Dr. Schorr and his wife left immediately, but the demonstrators did not move from the spot. Even the doctor's bodyguard remained in place with a firm decision to present the demands of the masses. At the commandant's second demand to disperse, the masses slowly withdrew from the city hall and stopped near the gymnasium [secondary school]. The lieutenant colonel demanded for the last time that the masses disperse and threatened that he would give the order to shoot. As the masses still did not leave, he did give an order to the military: "Attention, load the weapons! Secure the bayonets!" And the trumpeter began to blow with such power that a fear fell on everyone. The crowd began to draw back in the direction of the Ring Platz. They ran in all directions in the greatest confusion. Hundreds of brave people remained standing in the Platz. Here, some kind of miracle took place: at the moment when the company commander made a gesture to the soldiers to open "fire," we heard a strong whistle and we saw our dear Field Commandant of the city of Kolomea, Colonel Sir von Pfeifer, come running with all his power. (It could be that the Colonel von Pfeifer was a Jew and, perhaps, not. We cannot know. But it is certain that he was a very liberal person.)

Meanwhile some cried: "Shoot!" And tore open their shirts and stood unbuttoned at the chest ready to perish for their rights. There was a great tumult. People pushed and were pressed so closely together that it was impossible to move from the Platz. Even I, an onlooker, could not free myself from the vice. The people did not consider what kind of danger to life hovered over them, standing against the armed soldiers who were ready to shoot at any second.

The Colonel von Pfeifer was seen running out of the restaurant that was in Moshe Breyer's house. He was a good looking,

[Page 185]

tall man, so he could be seen among the entire mass of people. When the top lieutenant Czukowski, who was ready to give the order to shoot, saw the Colonel von Pfeifer running with his sword in his right hand, he was puzzled. The colonel came and called out to the company: "Attention! Weapons to the feet! Back three steps! Halt!" And he called to the company commander: "Who gave the order to shoot at unarmed people?" The company commander could not answer. He was pale as a wall. The colonel gave the soldiers an order to turn around and withdraw. He told the company commander to take over the command to call the soldiers back to their barracks in full order. And this all lasted only several seconds. The soldiers withdrew and marched away.
When the people noticed this, some began to gather again. However, the colonel remained standing on the stairs of the gymnasium with his sword in his outstretched hands. The crowd

began to come out of its hiding places and again began to shout slogans: "Niekh zywo, Dr. Schorr!" "Precz z kliki." "Hanba! Wstyd! Tchórzakomi!"[2*]

The colonel gave a sign to the crowd to calm down. He wanted to say something. As soon as it became quiet, he began: "My men! I ask you, tell me, what pains you and why have you gathered here?" Everyone shouted out an answer to his question at once: "Voting ballots!" And a great tumult began again. The colonel shouted at this: "My men, I do not understand any words. Let two or three of you approach, lay out your complaint; I will see what I can do for you. However, be calm!" Three respected middleclass citizens appeared. They were: Yosl Glazer, Naftali Kesten and Hersh Eisenthal, an iron merchant who had his business at Bitman, near the canal. He came from Bukovina, an intelligent man who spoke German well. He was the spokesperson.

Eizental called out as follows: "Respected Sir Colonel! Our majesty, the Kaiser, for the first time in history, had permitted us, as Austrian citizens, according to the decision of the

[Page 186]

Reichsrat – universal, secret and direct voting rights. The elections will take place on Tuesday. According to the order of the Reichsrat, the city hall has to distribute a stamped voting card to each citizen three weeks before the voting and now it already is three days before the voting and we have not received our voting cards! Therefore, we gathered to demand that the clique in the city hall carry out its duty. When the leaders in the city hall saw us coming, they locked themselves in and would not even listen to us. And because of that [there] is great agitation!" To the colonel's question of who was responsible for not carrying out the order, came a shout from the masses: "The clique, the propinatarski-clique![1] The straw mats! Down! Disgrace!" And so on.

The colonel shouted: "My men! Calm yourselves. I do not understand a word you are saying. I will have to leave if you do not calm yourselves." It immediately became quiet. And Eisenthal called: "Sir Colonel, you want to know who is responsible? The vice mayor, Josef Funkenstein!" The colonel answered this: "Let several of you go with me to the mayor and you will present your complaints in my presence. I assure you that I will strongly demand of the mayor that he carry out his duties."

They immediately elected a delegation of five people: Dr. Oster, Yosef Glazer, Herer, Hersh Eisenthal and Haber (an official at the Export Bank). The colonel walked in front and the delegation after him. The firemen, seeing the colonel, moved aside and opened the gate of the city hall. The delegation and the colonel immediately went up to the mayor on the first floor.

While the delegation lingered in the city hall, the crowd outside again began to sing fight songs and called out slogans. When the delegation and the colonel came back out, they went up to the balcony of the Hotel Grand. They asked that it be quiet because they had something to report. It became quiet. And Dr. Oster and Herer reported that the Colonel Sir Pfeifer had demanded strongly of Vice Mayor Funkenstein that he carry out his duty unconditionally and provide every citizen with a voter card. If not, a military managing committee would take over the city hall and itself carry out everything. The rights of citizens cannot be violated! The colonel also warned the mayor

[Page 187]

that he would hold him responsible for calm and order in the city.

The crowd accepted the report with a shout of hurrah and great ovations for the colonel. The colonel saluted and left.

The Jews of Kolomea have the Colonel Sir Pfeifer, to thank for the prevention of a blood bath before the Reichsrat voting in the summer of 1907. He appeared as an angel of the people and a miracle for the Jews of Kolomea happened through him. Who does not remember what happened in Drohobych on the same Shabbos when in a similar case, under mayor Feuerstein, 21 Jews fell dead and many were wounded![2] However, thanks to the Colonel, Sir Pfeifer, area commandant of the city of Kolomea and commandant of the 36th landwehr [militia] infantry regiment, the Polish top lieutenant, Count Czukowsk, could not carry out his murderous intentions and destroy hundreds of families.

Later, when the colonel parted with the assembled, Dr. Oster, in the name of the mayor, reported that every citizen should go up to meeting room of the city hall where he would receive his voting card. He, Dr. Oster, asked the crowd to stay calm, not to disturb the work of the city council.

Those authorized to vote left for the city hall in closed ranks and everyone received their voter card, stamped for the voting. When a thousand Jewish citizens had received their voter cards, the secretary said that from now on only the Christian voters would receive their voter cards at the city hall. The Jewish voters would have to go to the Jewish community council for their voter cards. The Jewish voters left for the [offices of the] kehile [organized Jewish community] en masse. It was closed because of Shabbos. They saw this was a new trick by the community leaders and they again went to the city hall en masse.

It appears that in the further course of events, the following occurred:

When the clique saw that it had lost, they turned for help to the district chief, Dr. Poblikowski He again made contact with Count Potocki, the governor. When Count Potocki heard the report from the district chief about the situation in the city and what had occurred

[Page 188]

with the Colonel Sir Pfeifer, he communicated with the corps commandant of the 11th Corps in Lemberg, General Sir Kolossváry von Kolosvár (of Hungary) and he pulled strings in such a manner that the kehile would accomplish its goal. The following occurred:

When the Jewish demonstrators again returned to the city hall, they were told that the voter cards were being given out at the kehile and they should go there. When they arrived for the second time, they met the well-known kehile shamas [sexton] [and] informer, Shlomo Dovid, standing in a shtreiml [fur hat worn by some Hasidim], before the Jewish community building gate. He shouted in Deitsch-merish [Germanized Yiddish] to the demonstrators: "Komen zi morgen. Heite ist Shabbos!" [Come tomorrow. Observe the Sabbath now.] When they heard this, they understood and the humble Jews again raised their heads; they had been turned away again. They again left for city hall singing songs and calling out their slogans. Some shouted: "Long live Dr. Schorr!" Others shouted: "Long live Dr. Thon!"

Meanwhile, evening fell. At around eight o'clock, when they approached the gate of the city hall, the gate was closed and no one was permitted to approach. The police did not get involved and remained neutral because this was the municipal police. However, the firemen and the gendarmes did take part, protecting the city hall from the outside and the inside because they were working in the villages and employed by the Kolomea district. The well-known lawyer, Dr.

Havrilo Trilovsky, leader of the Ukrainian Social Democrats and also the leader of the Rutenian Radical Party, Ivan Lobruk, campaigned there. The gendarmes had enough work in the villages.

Two squadrons of dragoons with drawn sabers suddenly came running when the demonstrators before the city hall demanded their rights and they stormed the demonstrators from the right and the left and demanded that they disperse.

There was a great tumult and a wild stampede. Shtreimlekh and caps were mixed up on the ground along with pieces of kaftans and sticks. However, thank God, no victims fell. This also was thanks to Colonel Feifer because although he had to carry out the order of the corps commander, he probably ordered the dragoons to be careful that no human victims fell. In addition, the 14th Dragoon regiment consisted for the most part of Czechs and a small number of Germans. To our good luck, not

[Page 189]

Hungarians, as had happened in Czernowitz [Chernivtsi] at the election of Lucien Bruner.

After the crowd dispersed, the Ring Platz looked as if there had been a battle. However, we had pulled through well.

The clique won a great victory. They sent entire wagons, loaded with beer, whiskey and sausages to the Christian streets. Meanwhile, the German anti-Semites banged on Jewish skulls on the Menechevka.

Thus ended the first public election demonstration of Jewish workers, artisans and citizens, after the first large election meeting that was called by the Socialist candidate, Dr. Schorr. He was beloved by all workers and toilers. However, because of the machinations of the clique in Kolomea, he was never elected to the Reichstag.

————

Footnotes:

1.   Long live Dr. Schorr! Down with the municipal clique! A disgrace! A shame! Away, cowards! (They called the candidate of the clique "Tchórzak." [Tchórz is the Polish word for coward.])
2.   [Long live Dr. Schorr.] Down with the clique! A shame and a disgrace with the cowards!

Translator's & Coordinator's footnotes:

1.   "propinatarski" is derived from the Polish word "propinator" – a person licensed to produce and sell liquor [Tran.]
2.   Drohobych sources report that the shooting took place on election day in 1911 also, of the 21 killed, 11 were Jews [Coor.]

————

[Page 190]

Vienna Rothschilds and Kolomeyer Taleysim Workers[1]

by David Yesha'yahu Silberbusch

Translated by Gloria Berkenstat Freund

A young Jewish man got married in 1876 in Kolomea, the well–known city of approximately 13,000 souls with a majority of Jews, unpretentious Jews from the old generation. He was supported by his own parents and by his father–in–law and mother–in–law for several years. He became a man with the burden of children and a long, yellow beard already grew on him. He searched for his own income for himself and the members of his household. He had an ingenious idea in 1883. He imported looms from Germany. He brought trained weavers from there for the period of several months, until he could teach the [working] Jews the business of the weaving trade and until the Germans would no longer be needed.

Taleysim [prayer shawls] were woven. The Taleysim weaving factory grew from year to year. It already was called a Taleysim factory. And soon the owners were called "the manufacturers."

The manufacturer with the yellow beard was a respected naïve

[Page 191]

Jew. He was a Boyaner Hasid with a little bit of learning and a great fear of God, and his workers were mostly Hasidic Jews. A number of them were elderly, former teachers, learned men.

The bosses behaved well with their workers outside of the work time in the traditional Jewish customs and they with him.

All through those years life went on according to traditional Jewish practice in the Taleysim factory. On a wintry eve before Purim, they paused their work for the daily late afternoon prayers known as Minkhah and Maariv. The manufacturer often led the prayers from the podium in front of the worshipers and his workers were proud of their boss's God–fearing manner. One of the workers sometimes spoke up to present a dvar Torah [a comment on the religious text] or to tell a Hasidic story. The manufacturer was not disturbed by a little criticism from the worker. In fact, as he stood alone on the podium, he listened with great pious interest. And what is more, on a special holiday, when it was the old rabbi's yahrzeit [the annual memorial on the date of that rabbi's death], the manufacturer provided whiskey and cake after the afternoon prayers and drank along with all the workers in a brotherly way and told a marvelous story about the old rabbi, of blessed memory.

The workers disguised themselves at the Purim feast. They bent their peyes [side curls] behind their ears. They rolled up the coattails of their kaftans, tied them behind with their gartlen [belt worn by pious men] to the knee. And thus they disguised themselves as Germans. The entire group went to the home of the manufacturer. They distorted their mouths to speak hoch–Deutsch–merish [high German–infused Yiddish] with swollen lips. The manufacturer laughed. The manufacturer's wife laughed and the manufacturer's small children actually rolled with laughter. The Purim spirit brought happiness to the house. They ate; they drank. They sang The Rose of Yakob and they merrily began a little dance with the boss.

Things went very well at night on Shemini Atzeret [the eighth day of Sukkos – the Feast of Tabernacles]. The Taleysim–weavers gathered with the manufacturer. They devoured hot stuffed cabbage, blowing it with their lips and burning their tongues. They drank alcoholic beverages, "on which the world stands and on which the world does not stand." And thus they carried on drunk. The workers, the owners, manufacturers, went singing and frolicking through the streets with flaming torches in their hands to their small synagogue for hakofus [circular precession with the Torah scrolls on Simkhas Torah].

*

* *

The talis–worker stood for years and years, day in and day out, naively, innocently at the loom. With his hands, he wove

[Page 192]

Taleysim, Taleysim–kotnim [small pray shawls usually worn under a man's clothing] and large taleyisim. And his brain weaved its own thoughts, small thoughts and great thoughts: the wages are stingy. But praised is the Lord God for it. He has a noble occupation. He is not a shoemaker and not a tailor, not a carpenter and not a blacksmith...

However, times change. New birds flew in from afar, far away and with them new songs.

It was not too long before social democracy in Austria would "raise its head," show what it was capable of, gather around itself its wandering comrades, until then in various party camps, and prepare for them the program of organization that had long ago been achieved in other nations.

This party worked with all its strength.

Socialism also entered the Kolomea Taleysim factories.

A young man, half–intellectual, fiery, pretentious, was the successor of an elderly deceased comrade. The young man immediately became a big shot among his comrades. They even grinned sarcastically at the start. They called him the "Taleysim philosopher." However, they listened to his words. He explained that in Vienna there is a group of worker–contractors and when one joins it [the group], they get all benefits as members.

They accomplished: 1) a raise in wages; 2) no more than eight hours a day of work; 3) to be paid their entire wages even at the time when, God forbid, the worker "collapsed" and he could not come to work; 4) the bosses became intransigent in accepting the demands of their workers, so all of the workers stopped working at their trade at the same time – and received their wages from the society in Vienna for as long as it takes for the bosses to give in.

In the Taleysim weaving factory could be found a tall, slender Jew with a grim expression and with a thick, black beard, a Jew who stood sullenly almost the entire day at his loom, his heavy black eyes downcast and his lips always clenched. This Jew heard these words; he became inflamed, flashed

[Page 193]

his two large, dark eyes. His lips opened. He explained the matter to his comrades in his own Kosower–Hasidic style. He called them together for a meeting on the same evening at the small Sharagroder synagogue. A thick, dark cloud settled on his face. He opened the Aron Kodesh [Torah ark] with his lips clenched. He was the first to swear on a Torah scroll to stick together. "All for one and one for all," and then his comrades did [the same].

And on a hot summer day in 1892, suddenly, all Taleysim workers wiped the sweat from their brows with their right sleeves. They donned their caftans and caps. And ——with the canes in their hands, all together, they left the weaving factory.

*
* *

"The talis–weavers donned their caftans and caps in Kolomea – Vienna was gripped with excitement: A strike had broken out in the Kolomea talis factory! The socialist ideas had infiltrated the Jewish neighborhood from the distant east!"

The socialists laid out this matter and explained it in detail. They made every effort. They photographed the workers with their beards and peyes [side curls], with their talis-katan hanging out over their pants, as if they, the "wretched ones," were standing wearily at the looms. They distorted the face of the Taleysim manufacturer, with the yellow beard, into a caricature of a leech. They put up these images in the Vienna streets and sent them to their comrades in all their groups in other countries.

In Vienna, two young parties, the Hovevei Zion [Lovers of Zion] party and Austria's newly prosperous Socialist Party quarreled and were at each other's throats. Each party wanted to become the only power in the Jewish neighborhood. They stood opposite each other like angry roosters. The socialist rooster found the best opportunity to give a peck with his hardened beak to the Hovevei Zion rooster in the very middle of his forehead. On the contorted face of the Kolomea talis manufacturer he painted a large Mogen Dovid [Star of David, literally Shield of David] – this was to signify: Here, this is a Zionist!

And their organization carried out another nasty trick:

[Page 194]

*
* *

A hit! "Blood runs from the nose of the Hovevei Zion rooster..."

In Vienna Dr. Natan Birnbaum was the editor of a German news weekly entitled Selbst-Emanzipation, and I was the editor in Kolomea of the Hebrew biweekly entitled Ha'am. Birnbaum published an open letter to me in his newspaper (number 17 of 1892)... He stroked me "under my double chin." He praised me highly. And finally he let out a frightening "howl" –

"How come?! Why did I permit the Taleysim workers to fall into socialist hands and did not grab them earlier for Zionism?!!!"

Understand that as a matter of course, when the editor in Vienna questioned me in his newspaper, I, the editor in Kolomea, had to give him an answer in my newspaper. To tell the truth, I was in not too small a dilemma. If I had a thousand heads I could not explain to a Viennese what a Kolomea manufacturer denotes and what "Hasidic socialists" signifies. In short I answered:

– Our socialists did not cease reciting three times a day the Shmoneh Esreh [central prayer], "May our eyes behold Your return to Zion in mercy" and at the prayer after the meal "rebuild Jerusalem." There even were present among them those who rose at midnight for khatsus [midnight study and prayer in memory of the destruction of the Temple]. Socialism did not injure in the least their sense of being Jewish. However, they wanted not only a dry piece of bread for themselves, for their wives and children, but a little bit of butter, too, for their work... Meanwhile can they not earn a pair of shoes for their child despite their love of Zion and Jerusalem... If we want to do something tangible for them, there is another piece of advice: we collect for them a sum of money to create a talis factory where they can work in partnership and divide "equal portions for all" with the gains from their work.

When writing the last several lines I did not think about Ferdinand Lassalle and not about Karl Marx. I only remembered a Hebrew poem by Samuel David Luzzatto entitled, Portions for Portion Shall They Eat. In addition I must tell the truth that the writings in the last few lines were just like this. A clever Jew always needs

[Page 195]

to be prepared with clever advice. I do not think that I could believe for a second that the Viennese Hovevei Zion would consider my advice. Furthermore, this had no connection to their program [of Hovevei Zion]; they themselves, begging your pardon, were poor people and their influence was a lot less than nothing.

However, there was a surprise! A Hebrew written bomb was thrown as far as Vienna and [it] exploded; this means only that it was fired in Kolomea.

There was no doubt in Kolomea that the Viennese Jews were great "experts" in such things... There were still Rothschilds in Vienna. We only needed to find a smart solution and – they immediately would obey.

The first was the manufacturer with the long, yellow beard who came to me with a complaint; why did I want to decrease his income?

– In short, the Viennese "gentiles" do not know. But you, a local Jew, know that I have not made a great fortune from my weaving factory. I can tell you a secret: I made a match for my oldest daughter a year ago. I did not promise a large dowry. The agreed date for the wedding on the Shabbos [Sabbath] after Shavous [spring holiday commemorating the giving of the Torah] was written into the engagement contract. However, I had to seek pretexts for delaying the wedding for later. I tell you however, that the real reason is simple: because it is difficult for me to pay the dowry. And I know that my in–law is a "merciless" Jew. He will not relent [for even] a penny.

Hearing these words, I controlled myself with all of my strength and did not even smile. On the contrary, I was very happy with what he meant, that now the Viennese Jews would create a talis–factory for the Kolomea workers. I only made a stern face and I said:

– I believe you that it is too difficult for you to make a wedding for your daughter. However, I think that the mitzvah [commandment] of communal help for young women without the resources to marry is not the obligation of your workers. They have the first mitzvah of responsibility for their wives and children... Yet, I will point out that you and your household eat a good lunch and good supper from the [profits of] the Taleysim weaving shop. And your workers also want the same for themselves and their households... You should not forget for a second that your Taleysim weaving shop cannot run without your workers. Not one talis can be made for you without them. However, without you, if they were given the necessary sum of money they could and would...

[Page 196]

At my words the manufacturer became soft as dough: "he gave me a proxy to reach an agreement with his workers."

But – frankly, with them, with the workers, it was not so easy for me. They, the workers received my "written advice" with very little interest. They believed the same as their manufacturer.

With great effort I persuaded them that meanwhile they should go to work, until... yes... until the Viennese Rothschilds would make their own Taleysim factory for them.

Footnote:

1. The famous Hebrew–Yiddish storyteller, publicist and memoir–writer, Dovid Yeshaya Silberbush (born 1854 in the eastern Galicia shtetl of Zaleszczyki, died in 1936 in Tel Aviv), was a Kolomea son–in–law. At the end of the 1880s and in the first years of the 1890s he lived in Kolomea and published Ha–Am [The People], a Hebrew bi–weekly.
    The chapter about the Kolomea Taleysim workers that we take from Silberbusch's memoir-book, Mentshn un Gesheynishn [People and Events] (from the Literary Friend publishers, Vienna 1922) had a connection with Silberbusch, the editor of Ha–Am, and with the first strike of the Taleysim workers.
    The Editors

Coordinator's footnote:

1. For more information about this historic strike in Kolomea in 1892, see <u>Diaspora Nationalism and Jewish Identity in Hapsburg Galicia</u> by Joshua Shanes, Cambridge University Press, 2012, pp. 104–108. This was the most important of the Austrian socialist strikes in the 1890's and the most successful of that time with 1000 gulden raised for the strike fund. Hundreds of tallis weavers had been working 15–16 hours a day for the meager pay of 1–3 gulden per week. The instigator of the strike, Max Zetterbaum, originally from Kolomea, and an assimilationist socialist, was a law student in Lemberg (Lvov/L'viv), who returned to Kolomea and got a job in the factory to organize the workers. As to how the strike ended, Joshua Shanes has found no other sources that confirm Silberbusch's account of being the negotiator who ended the strike. One socialist correspondent reported that ten workers with large families crossed the picket line to break the strike. A Yiddish memoir by Abraham Locks, who was in Kolomea then, recalled that the striking workers prevented Russian weavers from taking their jobs but the owners eventually outsourced to factories in Bohemia and replaced other workers with non–Jews – CHS

[Page 197]

The Hechalutz[1] in Kolomea

by I. Teitelbaum (Haifa)

Translated by Gloria Berkenstat Freund

The start of Hechalutz in Kolomea is connected with memories about general events in our city during the first years after the First World War. A short time after the disintegration of the Austro–Hungarian Empire, Kolomea seemed to experience the excitement of a Ukrainian regime, of the Romanian occupation army until the establishment of free Poland. The economic situation was very difficult; factories, tanneries, weaving factories, mills barely managed to operate; artisans kept looking for a few tools, a little material for their workshops; there was almost no possibility of earning something; the new rulers began to show their true face; they began to throw Jews from trains going at full speed, cutting off Jewish beards in the street; Jews were removed from all government posts. The Polish apprentice institutions seemed to be closed to Jews.

The young Jews fell into despair. What next? There was no chance at any kind of life. Some young people left for the borders; they left for Germany, Austria, across the ocean, to South America, Argentina and other lands. Many of those who remained threw themselves into the retail trade, took up the so–called intelligent professions: dental technician, weaving, printing and others. A number succeeded in entering the Polish gymnazie [secondary school]. The Ukrainian gymnazie was open to Jews because the Ukrainians felt discouraged because of the failure of their independence. However, the majority of Jewish young people walked around idle and sat at home supported by their parents.

[Page 198]

Halutzim group in Kolomea 1924–1925

The group in Kolomea 1933

Histadrut Gordonia[2] in Kolomea 1933

[Page 199]

It was in this environment that the news of the Balfour Declaration reached Kolomea. Things seemed brighter for Jews, in general, the young particularly. The young saw the Balfour Declaration as the redemption of the Jewish nationalist question and the opportunity for an existence in the future. The enthusiasm was great at all levels of the Jewish population.

The Jewish young people in Kolomea began to dream of ways of emigrating to Eretz–Yisroel, particularly the former students in the Hebrew school, led by Kopl Nunig and his wife.

The start of the halutz emigration from Kolomea was made by a female pioneer, Milke Zaydman, the daughter of Yehuda Ber Zaydman. She left in 1921. I remember that at her departure a comrade called after her: "Go and we will follow en masse." Milke's emigration made a great impression in Kolomea. Many were envious of her courage and boldness. Today, Milke Zaydman is one of those who lives in Kibbutz Ein Harod.

There was a small group of comrades in Kolomea at that time who were called "the professional halutzim." They completed the Hachshara in Słobódka Leśna and Sigiovke, near Lemberg. Returning to Kolomea they began to search for an opportunity to emigrate. At that time such possibilities were bound up in a measure of difficulties. At the beginning of 1922, Dov Shternberg, Yehuda Rat and several others traveled "oyf shvarts" [illegally]. The first stop on their itinerary was Presburg [Bratislava]; from there they left for Vienna where they worked baking matzohs in order to put together the needed sum for the further trip. They reached their goal after almost 12 months. Yehuda Grunwerg, the later Yehuda Chorin, the director of the citrus company, Yakhin, joined the group in Vienna.

Yosef Kuperman was a halutz, in a double sense, the one from Kolomea [who went to the land – Eretz Yisroel] and the one who "pioneered" a road across Romania. His itinerary was from Kolomea to Chernovitz [Chernivtsi]; from there to Constanta. He arrived in the land [Eretz Yisroel] in 1924.

In 1922 a group of halutzim from Brod appeared on the streets of Kolomea. These were Dov Sadan's students. They came to Kolomea for agricultural training. They were housed with Nusan Bishel in his egg warehouse on Klebanya Street. The cooperative life of the group, their lack of care for comfort created

[Page 200]

a sensation in Kolomea. There was constant talk in Jewish homes about the group from Brod. The young people listened to the talk and, infected by the example, they decided to leave their homes and also go for agricultural training. At that time the Histradrut Hehalutz [Pioneer Organization] was found in Kolomea. The halutzim from Brod, 163 in number, were taken to Godi Turka, to Yankl Bretler's farm where with fervor the group took to worship and education at the same time.

Hehalutz became the strongest Zionist organization in Kolomea in the interim. Young people from all classes flooded into Hehalutz: those employed in trade, locksmiths, tinsmiths, weavers, village children to whom work was not strange. All of them wanted to go through agricultural training to be ready for all the heavy work that was in store for them in [Eretz Yisroel]: drying the swamps, working in the orchards, at the construction of houses, at furnaces and others. Feverish cultural work was carried out at the premises of Beis Yisroel. Yitzhak Ramler, Meri Etigner, Chaim Ringelblum and others carried out widespread political work. The young Halutzim became acquainted with all of the Zionist and Jewish problems. The members of Hechalutz became among the most active coworkers in all Zionist institutions: Keren Kayemet [Jewish National Fund], Keren HaYesod [the Foundation Fund], Ezra; they were extremely active in Zionist election campaigns, at elections to the Jewish kehilus [organized Jewish community] and to the Polish Sejm [lower house of Polish parliament]; the Hechalutz took over the maintenance of calm and order at all Zionist meetings and presentations.

A group of Kolomea Chalutz joined the Akhdes [unity] collective in Stanislav and studied in the Barzel [iron] workshop. On a rainy day during the summer of 1924 they crossed the Cheremosh to Kitev and went from there to Chernovitz and then further on. Among others, those in the group were: Yitzhak Feder, Shimeon Likvornik, Sholem and Meir Laks, Tspora Shiber, Dovid Krauthamer, Nusen Fridler and others. Yitzhak Feder was an exceptionally interesting type. His enrollment at the time in Hechalutz brought a great deal of feeling and recognition from all who knew him. He was a merchant. He denounced foreign currency on the stock exchange in Kolomea and Lemberg in the years after the [First World] War and caused a great stir. On a beautiful morning, in Chalutz work clothes, he joined [Akhdes] and became one of the most active, leading strengths in Akhdes in

[Page 201]

Stanislav. He learned to be a locksmith with the group that "split" the Cheremosh, and left.[3]

The group worked as porters in a grain warehouse in Chernovitz. They lived in constant danger of falling into the hands of the Romanian Siguranţă [Kingdom of Romania secret police] and if one of them was arrested it would lead to a "bribe" so as to be arrested again in the morning. The group remained in Chernovitz under such conditions for a few months until they collected the money for their expenses and acquired the documents necessary to be able to continue on their trip, with a payment of money it should be understood. The also arrived in the country [Palestine] in 1924.

The Jewish and non–Jewish farms, which surrounded Kolomea on all sides like a belt, very quickly became a center for the agricultural organization of halutz, not only for Kolomea, but also for a number of other cities and shtetlekh [towns] in Galicia. The agrarian school in Słobódka Leśna founded by IKA [Jewish Colonization Committee] in 1901 was a very important place for Chalutz training. The economy was partly ruined during the First World War. The remaining and newly annexed buildings were adapted for Hachshara. Hechalutzim flooded here, not only from Kolomea, but also from all of Galicia and Poland. Kolomea was the main center for the school. There was limited contact between Kolomea and the school. Słobódka Leśna was an excursion spot for the young people in Kolomea; they would go on excursions there on foot. The honorary administrator of the school and the authority for all Hechalutzimin general was Dr. Shlomo Rozenhek. Słobódka Leśna, along with its well–known agrarian school, also experienced the tragic events of 1919, when the Polish military of [General Lucjan] Zeligowski's army killed the martyrs Yosef Bal, Rotenberg and Preser, of blessed memory.

Kolomea became an important center for Hechalutz, not only in regard to Hachshara, but also as a leg of the journey for Chalutz emigration from all of Galicia and Poland. The emigrants stopped here on the way to Kitev across the Cheremosh, or to Sniatyn across dry land. The emigrants received their final instructions in Kolomea. It sometimes occurred that sneaking across the border was unsuccessful and the emigrants would be brought back to Kolomea in a procession of convicts. In such a case, they were first of all provided with food, then

[Page 202]

Bnos Agudas Yisroel, the Hachshara collective for girls in Kolomea in 1935

A group of Hanoer Hatzioni [Zionist Youth] at a summer colony in the area of Kolomea in 1934

NA BANKIECIE W BEJTARIE Z OKAZJI
WYJAZDU 2 BEJTARCZYKÓW DO EREZ.. Kołomyja,
[KITNERÓWNA - ROZENBAUM]. 2.III. 1933.
Fot. M.D.

A departure banquet before the departure for [Eretz Yisroel]
by the Betarists[4] Kutner and Rozenbaum in 1933)

[Page 203]

with legal help. The regular Hechalutz lawyers were: Dr. Marek Laks, Dr. Meir Gelbart. And Dr. Marek Knopf.

During an election campaign in Kolomea I often had the occasion to meet with a group of young artisans who were close to the Bund [Jewish socialist party]. I established contact with them and after several meetings I succeeded in convincing them that their place should be in Hechalutz. And their purpose – emigration to Eretz Yisroel. At the end of 1923, Zaynwl Eizner, Mendl Bochner, Wolf Grinberg, Maks Gelert, Gershon Rot, Yosef Habicht, Wolf Laks, Sura Bretler and others from the group joined Hechalutz. These comrades later created the famous agrarian collective Kherut (freedom). They could be found every evening at Beis Yisroel where they truly swallowed the talk of our best mentors; Comrade Levitas taught them Hebrew.

The [members of the] Kherut agrarian collective went through hachshara in Kolomea with a group of halutzim from Stryy. Due to a lack of certificates, several members of Kherut tried to cross the border near Stryy–Lavodshnye. However, they were stopped in Mezherichi–Ostroh and they again were placed on the Polish side. A number of them had to serve in the Polish military. In 1930 the group finally arrived in Eretz Yisroel. Three of them did not succeed in emigration: Habicht died after an illness; Wolf Laks and Gershon Rot perished during the Hitler years. May their souls be bound in life.

The Trumpeldor Agrarian Collective

The Trumpeldor[5] agrarian collective was founded at that time by the following comrades: Shimeon Krinits, Shimkha Shmid, Kalman Gredinger, Yona Hashpil, Yitzhak Wilner, Naftali Wilner, Zehava Rozenkrants, Yona Teicher and others. The comrades from the agrarian collective did their agricultural training at the Zabolotiv farm. They arrived in Eretz Yisroel in 1926 and worked in Zikhron Ya'akov at various jobs. The agrarian collective failed because of the economic crisis that broke out then in the settlement in Eretz Yisroel. Some members of the group made a fatal error – in 1927 they returned to Poland.

Meanwhile there was no end to the creation of more and more agrarian collectives in Kolomea: Hitachdut [Zionist–Socialists], Bulia, Vitkinia,[6] Klosov, Gordonia[7] and others. In 1925

[Page 204]

Lev Yitzhak Shancher, Yakov Grin, Yeshaya Feder, Etl Ramler, Yosf Domb and Chaim Laks of Hitachdut came to [Eretz Yisroel].

I left Kolomea on the 6th of May 1925 and emigrated to Eretz Yisroel. I visited Kolomea several times in 1931–1937. The Hechalutz and Hechalutz Hatzair [Zionist youth movement] were still strong and had strong young people in their ranks. However, the limited possibilities created a condition of despair and helplessness among all the comrades. At that time the English already had guards on the shores of the settlement [Eretz Yisroel] aided by radar. Ships with immigrants would wander aimlessly at sea for weeks until they succeeded in reaching the shores of Eretz Yisroel.

The boat "Welos" with which we tried to reach the shores of Eretz Yisroel along with other Hechalutzim from Kolomea – Lev Grebler, Mendl Bachner, Shmay Tindel – had to return to its point of departure after wandering aimlessly for many months. The emigrants were forced to return to Poland. Some of them later did receive certificates and arrived legally in the country. Today a thousand souls are counted in the Kolomea family in the Land of Israel. We find our Kolomea landsmen [people from the same town] at agrarian settlements, kibbutzim [communal settlements] and moshevim [farmers cooperatives]; we find Kolomeaer in workshops, factories and also in responsible state posts across the entire country. While all were placed in important Jewish communities, the Kolomea family in the Land of Israel is, to our great sorrow, a small one that could have been immeasurably larger…

Translator's notes:

1. Hechalutz – The Pioneer – was a movement with preparatory training for young Jews hoping to settle in Eretz–Yisroel. Hachshara were Zionist agricultural training farms that prepared potential emigrants for work in Eretz–Yisroel.
2. Zionist youth movement – Histadrut ha–No'ar ha–Amamit ha–?alutzit Gordonia – the People's Pioneering Association of Youth – Gordonia.
3. "Spliting" the Cheremosh River and leaving is an illusion to the parting of the Red Sea and the exodus of the Jews from Egypt.
4. Betar is a Revisionist Zionist youth organization founded by Ze'ev Jabotinksy.

5.   Joseph Trumpeldor was an active Zionist and hero of the defense of the Tel Hai settlement in Eretz Yisroel in 1920.
6.   Vitkinia is named after Joseph Vitkin, Zionist author of the pamphlet, A Call to Jewish Youth who Love their People and Zion, in which he encouraged immigration to Eretz–Yisroel based on the ideal of agricultural work.
7.   Gordonia is a Zionist youth movement named after Aron Dovid Gordon who encouraged the use of manual labor and called for a revival of the Hebrew language.

[Page 205]

The Martyred Chalutzim
from Slobodka Leshna (1919)

I. Teitelbaum

Translated by Claire Hisler Shefftz

During the Polish-Bolshevik war in the Ukraine, a Polish division under General Zeligowski tore through Bessarabia and Bukovina and stopped in Kolomea during its winter march to Poland.

Kolomea was then temporarily occupied by the Rumanians and the border was near the shtetl Otynia between Stanislav and Kolomea.

During their stay in Kolomea, General Zeligowski's soldiers ("the wild division", they called them) often attacked Jews. But Jewish workers organized a civil patrol and gave the hooligans quite a few beatings.

During the march to Otynia, Zeligowski's soldiers carried out a pogrom against Hachshara HaKibutza from HaShomer HaTsair which was an agricultural school owned by the Jewish Colonization Association in the village of Slobodka Leshna.

On the sixteenth of June, 1919, the hooligans killed three student Halutzim: 1) Joseph Bal- the son of butcher Moshe Bal from Franzishkaryuzifar Street, 2) Tsvi Rotenberg, the son of the restauranteur Rotenberg from Yagielanskai Street near the Post office, and 3) Shmuel Presser from Stanislav. Members of the Bartfeld family were also murdered.

The dead were brought to Kever Israel in the new Kolomear cemetery on Klebanye Street. Almost the whole city took part in the funeral. Adjoining graves were prepared for the martyred near the main entrance to the cemetery.

[Page 206]

Even officers of the Austian army who had been former Halutzim, delivered eulogies: Lieutenant Engineer Shlomo Rores, Lieutenant

Teacher Poizer-Dresher, and an Oberlieutenant from Prague, a son-in-law of Kolomear resident Max Vaykselboim.

Hachshara Group [Hashomer HaTsair] in Slobodka–Leshna in the year 1919

When the Polish army turned toward Kolomea in September 1919, the three Jewish officers who had spoken at the funeral were taken before a military court and accused

[Page 207]

of insulting the Polish people and the Polish army. The sentence was a relatively light one. Rores and Dresher were demoted to a lower rank and the Prague lieutenant was sent out of the country.

The "hero" of the "wild division", General Zeligowski, was the same one who later, in 1920, plundered Vilna for Poland and carried out a pogrom against the Jews there.

Translator's note:

1. For another account of this incident, see Shtetl Memoirs by Joachim Schoenfeld, New Jersey, Ktav Publishing House, Inc., 1985, p. 212. General Lucjan Zeligowski (pronounced Zheligovsky) is mentioned on page 221 as having occupied Wilno (Vilna). The author, born in 1895 in Sniatyn which was some miles west of Kolomey, lived in that Galician town until World War I. He provides historical background about Jews in Galicia as well as accounts of typical Jewish life in Sniatyn and his service in the Austrian army. He also describes how Jews fared under independent Poland in the years between the two world wars.

[Page 208]

At Kol Nidre in the Boyaner Kloyz[a][1]

by Dr. Stanisław Vincenz (Paris)

Translated by Gloria Berkenstat Freund

In antiquity it was believed that blood spilled by murder, absorbed in the earth, awoke the sleep of the holy goddesses of revenge, the shadowy, quietly slinking Erinyes.[2] Let these Erinyes reach not only the guilty but also the indifferent. They demand not only revenge, but also memory! They demand a struggle against hate. And against indifference, too.

There was a belief among Jews that at Yiskor [memorial service] on Yom Kippur the corpses at the cemetery stand up. Let them also be present today and participate in the Day of Judgment at the trial of the world.

*
* *

One wants to remember Kolomea from various eras, in various situations. I remember that once, after a long sojourn abroad, I traveled to Kolomea and went to the coffee house that was named Tsentral [Central]. My attention was immediately drawn to the fact that the coffee house was empty. I looked through the window: the only guest was asleep, sitting with his cheek [on his arm] and his horse had apparently also fallen asleep. At first, I was surprised that the city was so empty. In about a second, I understood: it was Shabbos [Sabbath]. I remember exactly that I thought: "This is how Kolomea would look without Jews."

[Page 209]

An old Ukrainian folk song says: Kolomyia ne pomyia, Kolomyia misto [Kolomea is not slops, Kolomea is a city]. And still, what a city. An eternal fair, a tumultuous one, a surging one. Every village would arrive in its own clothing, with different harnesses, even the types of people were different. Every corner was a characteristic for an ethnographer. We usually think superficially that Kolomea Jews were mainly involved in trade or only in trade. Alas, no one has tried to create statistics about artisanship. And yet there is no doubt that the majority of Kolomea artisans were Jews. Shoemakers, tailors, furriers, tinsmiths and others. At the small number of factories, Jews provided the greatest amount of the city's needs and of the wider area, because the importance of Kolomea reached the Dniester, [reached] the highest peak of the Carpathians under the Chornohora [mountain range]. I also now remember various artisan personalities. I remember everyone with whom I was involved. But about this, later.

From my young years until ripe old age, I was interested in spiritual professions. During my school years I was a constant and avid client of the institution that was called the "great library." One axis of my aspirations was the Kraszewski Library and the second actually the "great library." It was at the market not far from the city hall and it was founded by the Kolomea bookseller, Yankl Ohrenstein, later a famous publisher of Ukrainian books. We would borrow Polish books from the Kraszewski Library and books in foreign languages from the "great library." However, its attraction was that at that time, at the beginning of the 20th century, it had serious books, particularly philosophical. The philosophical advisor to Yankl Ohrenstein was a certain Kohn, as it happens, an Orthodox Jew, because he walked around in a long, loose robe and wore a beard. However, he was extraordinarily well read in the philosophical literature of that time. From the "great library" I borrowed the thick volumes by Kuno Fischer [historian of philosophy], the magnificent History of Philosophy [six volumes] and monographs. There I first learned about all of the books of [Henri] Poincaré about the problems of science. I borrowed them and studied. From there the works of Bernson, James and many other reached me.

[Page 210]

Several alleys further from the market was located the modest and unremarkable kloyz [house of study] of the Boyaner Hasidim. It carried the name of the shtetl Boyan [Boiany] in neighboring Bukovina, where a famous rebbe once lived. His Hasidim were mainly relatives of the small artisans and merchants. However, they were difficult to recognize, because there they were changed, almost uplifted. In my youth I knew nothing about this kloyz. I was completely uninterested in it and, certainly, neither were my friends or colleagues. I first "discovered" it in my ripe older years when one of my colleagues, by chance from the sphere of small merchants, invited me there and I came to the prayers for Yom Kippur. There I found the phenomenon of such fervid, exaggerated prayer and so different for each of the worshippers that all of my "modern" ideas about prayer disappeared. A little later, at my suggestion, the same acquaintance invited a friend of mine, a guest from Switzerland. Becoming acquainted with the text of the prayers (which they had hospitably given to us in the German translation), hearing the singing of the old khazan [cantor], whose voice broke tragically, seeing the faces of the old men and also of the young people, exhausted from fasting and from constant prayer, I sat through the evening until the late hours, together with my Swiss friend, and the following day until evening. However, we, Christian guests, left to eat and the worshippers fasted the entire time and even the old men, even those who fainted from exhaustion, did not take a drop of water in their mouths.

I had never felt in the presence of a Godly Day of Judgment – the fundamental idea was difficult for my Catholic concepts or Platonic conceptions – but I had never been so close to being persuaded as then.

How much spiritual power was hidden behind these unremarkable kapotes [caftans]. In one alley that was near the "great library," they observed the advance of the newest ideas and in another, an old fire was unextinguished for even a minute and apparently flared up no less than in prior generations.

[Page 211]

Saying goodbye to Kolomea, how I would like my greeting to reach the other shore, to reach those who have not lived for a long time or fell as victims during the war.

I remember the professor of Greek, Skharye Dembicer, who taught us to love Homer. I remember my neighbor, the pious old man, Berl Lenter, who calmed the frightened and murmuring Christian witnesses when the members of the Gestapo led him away: "Children, this is all from God, do not complain."

I remember my school friends and friends from among the Jews, those who died in their youth before the First World War, such as Marsel Ritigstein, Misha Hules, Mishel Sucher, about whom the priest, catechist, would always say to us: "Look at him, he has Jesus' face."

I remember the Bobeshi [diminutive of grandmother] Hules who would traverse Kolomea with small steps and erected a home for Jewish orphans with the donations she collected. She, at the age of 80, was deported with her great grandchildren. I remember the poor couple from outside Kosów [Kosiv] who, almost unrecognizable, invited us during the occupation to spend the night in their underground cabin. Tens and hundreds of faces from that side of the shore elbow their way to me. I greet them.

———

Original Footnote:

a.   At the memorial service for the dead that is observed every year by the Organization of People from Kolomea in Haifa, a landsman [man from the same city], Dr. Stanislaw Vincenz, the Polish folklorist and researcher of the legends of the Baal Shem Tov [founder of Hasidism] in the Carpathian Mountains, sent a eulogy from France. We provide here a summary of this generous Polish memory of a city of Jews that disappeared.

Translator's notes:

1.   A kloyz is a house of study
2.   The Erinyes, also known as the Furies, are three sisters in Greek mythology who personify divine vengeance

———

[Page 212]

The Apostate Newcomers Are Honored and the Resident Apostate is Trounced[a][1]

by Shlomo Bickel

Translated by Gloria Berkenstat Freund

Kolomea was a pious city. There were present, it should be understood, also a considerable number of members of the Enlightenment. However, they mostly behaved with dignity. They were enlightened, but they did not separate themselves from the remaining Jews, not with their clothing, not with their way of life and not even with the education of their children.

Even the pious associated with and boasted of the arriving Maskalim [followers of the Enlightenment], Reuben Asher, Broydes and Hersh Leib Sigheter. Reuben Asher was a sharp wit and recited witticisms, and the pious ones would often forget about his heresy because of his comments. Hersh Leib Sigheter was a splendid badkhan [wedding jester] whose humorous rhymes and curious stories were enjoyed. While his literature was close to the heart, the heretical touch in his songs and stories was disregarded and his entertaining with his jokes and with his learned insight was thoroughly enjoyed.

Hersh Leib Sigheter was, it appears, himself a little bit amazed by the mild climate he met in the Galician city. As he underlines particularly in his autobiography that when "he came to Kolomea, he was embraced by the Maskilim as well as by the scholars with great respect. In his Hungarian birthplace Sighet [Sighetu Marmatiel, Romania] he had had to endure persecutions and finally had to escape from the rage of the rabbi who placed a ban on his newspaper, Hashemesh (The Sun), and here in Kolomea, not only did they pretend not to know of the Sighet rabbi's ban, but Hersh Leib was invited to Shlomo Halfen's home on a Shabbos [Sabbath] night and he recited Torah [Five Books of Moses] to a group of scholars who scalded

[Page 213]

their tongues by doing two things at once: eating hot borscht with potatoes and laughing at Hersh Leib's jokes and badkhn–like antics.[2]

One of my uncles, who spent several such Shabbos evening meals with Shlomo Halfen and who remembered a considerable number of Hersh Leib's songs and jokes until his death, would often tell me about the famous Sighet badkhn and people's poet, who spent three fortunate years in Kolomea paradise.

Hersh Leib Gottlieb[3] already was then a Jews of about 70 and his clever, sad face was encircled with a grey beard that was cut short, which looked like a wreath of wilted greens.

– If you saw him in the street – my father said – you would never in your life think that this Jew had such a golden mouth. He had a clever, Jewish face, but his eyes showed his fear and therefore he gave the impression that this Jew must be a person who does not speak. And he was the true silent one... a fiery tongue and as soon as he opened his lips, there was the desire to laugh. To begin with, he started – it was at the home of Misnagid Shlomo Halfen – with cutting remarks about observant Jews and Hasidim. His host [Shlomo] smoothed his beard with pleasure and the sons–in–law and the sons laughed with great pleasure; and when he, Hersh Leib, felt that the audience was his, he began slowly to include in his witticisms and in his songs so much heretical poison that it became awkward to sit through it. They were ashamed to look at Shlomo Halfen, in case it was painful to him. And once – my uncle recorded in his memoir – Shlomo hit Hersh Leib lightly on the shoulders and half in jest and half earnestly said:

– You must atone, Hersh Leib!

Hersh Leib did not ask why, but turned to Reb Shlomo's son–in–law, Simkha, who was a gentle Jew, very knowledgeable about Tanakh [Bible] and a grammarian, and asked him in a totally serious tone:

– Reb Simkha, what gender is atonement, male or female?

And, as Reb Simkha, as was his manner, calmly and with an embarrassed smile answered: "Female," Hersh Leib raised his back and covered his face as if to show despair and roared:

[Page 214]

– The devil knows! And I have so little of the yeytser–hora [evil inclination] toward her [atonement]!

Everyone laughed heartily – My father assured me – And forgot that the joke was nor only heretical, but that it reeked of quite a lot of foul language. But my father himself had surely laughed at Hersh Leib Sigheter's wisdom repeated more than 30 years later in Chernowitz [Chernivtsi].

While Reuben Asher Broydes and Hersh Leib Sigheter had so much success in the city, [other] well–known members of the Enlightenment during those years did not have such good fortune, particularly among the pious. At the same time that Reuben Asher's pointed witticisms were going around and respect was given to the Sighet heretic, Hersh Leib, Khaskl Itsik Rosenstock[4], a local follower of the Enlightenment, had to endure suffering incited by the Hasidim. Khaskl Itsik was not a source of jokes and did not dazzle with humor. He was a poor melamed [religious school teacher] in a long caftan with a shtreiml [fur hat worn by some Hasidic sects] and never missed the afternoon and evening prayers in the small synagogue. In general, he spoke little and what he thought, he never spoke except with a few chosen ones. Nevertheless, this quiet Jew drew the rage of the pious as if through human magnetism. As is said, he prayed every day in a group, but pious young people furtively observed him and "knew with certainty" that he did not even move his lips. On a Yom Kippur [Day of Atonement], when Khaskl Itsik again sat as did all Jews covered with his talis [prayer shawl] at his reading desk, the same pious young men observed furtively that the teacher was reading a newspaper. It probably only appeared that way to some since Khaskl Itsik would not dare to bring anything but a Makhzor [prayer book used on Rosh Hashanah and Yom Kippur] to the synagogue and there never was any direct proof of heresy against him. However, the community had the holy spirit. Khaskl Itsik Rosenstock was the deepest, the most educated and the most obstinate heretic in the city.

He lived for all his years on Spinoza Street because he had great respect and love for the Amsterdam gaon [often a title of respect for someone learned in Torah] and was a complete expert on his works. Khumashim [Five Books of Moses], Gemaras [commentaries] and other permitted books lay on the table and on several shelves near the wall in the front room, where Khaskl Itsik studied with his students. In an alcove that the sun never reached and which was pitch dark, he

[Page 215]

kept his philosophical books. He usually would drop in there after the afternoon prayer and sit by the flame of a candle end and study the entire night. And Khaskl Itsik was not only interested in philosophy, he truly, breathlessly read and could not tear himself away from books about mathematics and physics.

The spirit of Salomon Maimon[5] lived in the poor religious teacher from Kolomea's Spinoza Street. Perhaps he was just as proficient as [Maimon] in Talmud and in knowledge, but he lacked the other's tempestuous boldness, the other's intellectual rigor and certainty, as well as Maimon's writer's splendor. Like Maimon, Khaskl Itsik learned German through the difficult language of Kant and Hegel and like him, while learning the language, recorded the ideas in the book with penetrating philosophical questions. However, he did not have the courage to carry his questions over the threshold of his alcove because he was afraid of losing his teaching job and he was even more afraid of the fury of the Sadagorer and the Boyaner Hasidim who, God knows why, as is said, considered him a terrible enemy. Khaskl Itsik shared his ideas with a select few people in the city. And these people, among whom was my father, connected with the religious teacher–philosopher with a deep love and with such a deep silence.

And remarkably the less we heard from Khaskl Itsik, the more he would come to pray even more and on time, so his students could better study a page of the Gemara and they were surer of his piety, and the Sadagorer enemies seethed more and more at the silent and mysterious teacher. A bit of the psychology of the police lived in the young Hasidim who were ready to destroy a criminal when his crime could not be proven.

Until one summer day, Shabbos at the third meal, when the young people in the small synagogue were overtired, threw sharp–witted aphorisms and towels at each other and did not know what to do with their energy, which gushed from their bodies, just then Khaskl Itsik Rosenstock strolled in with his stately, fine stride. It happened as such cases of mass psychosis always happen. One of the young people shouted that "one whose lack of piety brought shame to the Jewish people" had come and no one later knew when

[Page 216]

and how 10 hands grabbed the poor teacher, turned him with his face down and attacked him with lashes from yarmelkes [skull caps], blows with gartln [rope–like belts worn by pious men] and even several fleshy blows. It became a riot ... Fathers uttered bitter words of reproach to their excited sons and a quarrel almost broke out with the elders, who condescendingly tried to reproach the fathers of such sons. However, two good things came out for both sides in that twilight. The Hasidim finally had certain evidence of Khaskl Itsik's heresy. How? The most secret students of the philosopher finely came out of hiding and publicly began to praise their rabbi [Khaskl Itsik], that he is just as great as the Rambam and... that he had his ways of Yiddishkeit [a Jewish way of life]. Khaskl Itsik was finished both in the synagogue and in the kheder [religious primary school]. [His] clandestine students gave the philosopher a monthly salary and he spent the several years that he remained alive in his house on Spinoza Street and occupied himself with the books of the Amsterdamer [Spinoza] and in other books through which he could better understand the five parts of his [Spinoza's] Ethics.

Khaskl Itsik now lived calmly and without concerns about income, but he could not overcome his fear of the Hasidim who had punished him previously. He rarely appeared in public and he read quietly with his visitors, as if he were whispering a secret. My father, who was one of Khaskl Itsik's close friends, once told me about an event that throws a particularly sharp light on the fear that the Hasidim inspired in the poor teacher and of the strange way of revenge with which he quieted his heart against his enemies.

My father, who after his marriage lived in a small shtetl [town] near Dniester in Galicia Podolia, always visited his rabbi when he came to Kolomea. One night – he knocked on the door of his [Khaskl Itskik's] house on Spinoza Street. The door was locked and he felt as if Khaskl Itsik was afraid to open it. He asked who was there several times and did not believe my father when he answered. The way the poor Jew fluttered around the room in fear and could not decide to open [the door] because it could be a Hasid who was pretending to be one of his good friends. In fear, he did not recognize the voice of one of his close

[Page 217]

friends and when my father finally entered the room, he saw lying on the table a copy of the excommunication against the Hasidim that the parnasim [trustees] and rabbis of the Brod kehile [organized Jewish community] issued during the large yearly market of 1772. The excommunication could not in essence have any more value for the follower of Spinoza, than, for example, In Praise of the Baal Shem Tov [stories about the founder of Hasidism]; both were for him the products of demons. Yet the human weaknesses cooling the heart led Khaskl Itsik to reread several times a year the sharp precepts against Hasidim of over a hundred years earlier, and he felt lightness in his heart [knowing] that the great–grandfathers of his torturers had received the true judgment. And perhaps this was not any human weakness, as can be seen, but really true philosophical greatness that the teacher from Spinoza Street had the rare strength to console himself with such a confused comfort as the excommunication of 100 years earlier. If those young Hasidim had possessed Khaskl Itsik's historical vision, perhaps the excommunication of Spinoza of two hundred years earlier would have been enough on that dawn in the synagogue.

However, that Khaskl Itsik was in fear when he read the excommunication and that he closed and locked the door and gate behind him, this surely was not like Spinoza... And something else also was not according to [Spinoza's] Ethics. After the teacher calmed down, he again considered if there was anyone in the room besides him and his student and, trembling violently, he began to curse with pointed, barbed curses, particularly against the Hasidim from Sadagora and Boyan.

* *

*

How did Khaskl Itsik Rosenstock look during my time, that is, in the years just before the First World War? Completely different, totally different. He was called Mekhl Kon and was dressed according to the latest male style. An elegant, round beard, a well cut afternoon jacket or Schwalben coat, as it was called then, and a thin cap. He did not speak Yiddish or Polish. He spoke German and read the newest novels that appeared at the book market. He was not fond of

[Page 218]

Bernard Kellerman's Der Tunnel [The Tunnel] (Kellerman was too in love with technique) and saw that the Jewish–German writer, Jacob Wassermann was marching downhill in his literature in his last work, Die Juden von Zirndorf [translated as The Dark Pilgrimage]. He was a great admirer of Richard Dehmel, but he explained to us that the profound poet–personality of our time was the young, pure one, [Rainer] Maria Rilke.

We went home from the boring literature courses that we heard in the gymnazie [secondary school] and we encountered Mekhl Kon on the street. If he was in the city, he strolled two or three times a week around noon to Mickiewicz Street and met some of his young friends there. Young Jewish students from the fifth, sixth classes seeing "Herr Kon" raised their hats with joy and approached him. He began to talk about German literature and everyone listened to him with open mouths. They first began to realize that Professor Wishniewski's course of an hour or two earlier [had taught] them nothing. Then, the master group scattered and a few, three or four young people, remained. They all accompanied "Herr Kon" home and they made an appointment to meet in the Folks–Garten [public garden]. In the afternoon, around five, they met in a side alley and Mekhl Kon opened new horizons for the students. He gave us a lecture about philosophy; he led us to [Friedrich] Nietzsche's and [Arthur] Schopenhauer's works. He criticized their ideas for us and inspired us with their language and once suddenly launched into a long speech about Hasidus. And I saw before me a miracle worker, not the kind I had read about in [Heinrich] Graetz's Jewish history and, of course, a completely different one than those that had reached me through the tradition of my enlightened family. He spoke about "wonder rabbis" [rabbis capable of performing miracles] with such tolerance and such a thoughtful love that at the first opportunity when the Vizhnitzer Rebbe came to Kolomea for Shabbos [Sabbath], several of us students went to the Vizhnitzer synagogue, mixing with the joyous enthusiastic Jews and took part at the table like true Hasidim with fervor and rapture. And something more: He told each of us something nice and interesting about our deceased grandfathers and great–grandfathers, whom he knew and woke in us a strange feeling and insight and pride in our family and for those "who had gone on the eternal road."

[Page 219]

And Mekhl Kon was a quiet one, hidden and a timid person as once was the remarkable teacher of Spinoza Street. And he was the most effective teacher not of a generation (it was not in accord with his temperament), but among several individuals of a generation. And I think the individuals learned everything from him and that without him their private lives would have looked different, much slighter and much noisier.

Original Footnote:

a.   From the book, A City of Jews, New York, 1943

Translator and Coordinator's notes:

1.   This story appears in the table of contents of Bickels's book as "The Newcomer Apostate's Honor and Resident Shpinozams – Trouncing – page 108. – CHS [Coor.]
2.   A badkhn is an entertainer who performed at weddings and holiday celebrations [Trans.]
3.   Hersh Leib Gottlieb was also known as Hersh Leib Sigheter, indicating that he was from Sighet. [Trans.]
4.   The Khaskel Itzig Rosenstock of this story may be the one listed in the Kolomea vital records (AGAD JRI) as Chaskiel Izak Rosenstock who died in 1900 at the age of 70. – CHS [Coor.]
5.   Salomon Maimon (1753–1800) was a Jewish rationalist philosopher born in Lithuania who did most of his writing in Germany. He was influenced by Maimonides whose last name he adopted as well as by a brief stay with the Hasidic Maggid of Mezrich. – CHS [Coor.]

[Page 220]

The Jewish Workers Movement in Kolomea

by Dovid Landman (Tel Aviv)

Translated by Gloria Berkenstat Freund

A Jewish workers movement began to arise in Kolomea around the last quarter of the 19th century. Jews already were employed as wage workers in almost all of the Kolomea branches of industry during the period before the First World War; Jewish workers could be seen in all of the larger and smaller factories and, of course, in the workshops where the owners worked together with three or four workers. The factories in which Jews worked mostly belonged to Jews where non-Jews also often worked; a small number of Jewish workers also were employed in non-Jewish factories. The Kolomea Jewish workers had not created any strong, organized professional organizations during that era; the small number of those among them who were class conscious took upon themselves the difficult mission of attracting the wide-ranging Jewish workers group to fight to better their economic and social conditions.

At that time, before the First World War, there were two leading influences on the Jewish working class in Kolomea: the Zionist-Socialist movement, led by Poalei-Zion and the anti-Zionist, Z.P.S. [Jewish Social Democratic Party] and also in part by the Jewish section of the P.P.S. (Polish Socialist Party). The leaders of the P.P.S., Dr. Schorr, Herer and others, were popular with the Jewish and non-Jewish workers in Kolomea, particularly among the large number of Kolomea Jewish artisans.

Until 1914, the focal point of political life in Kolomea was the periodic elections to the Austrian parliament where the central government had designated one seat for Kolomea. There usually were three candidates: from the Jewish-National movement (a Zionist), from

[Page 221]

the P.P.S. and one of the "cliques," a Jew who was obsequious to the non-Jews or a Polish landowner, According to a simple accounting of the number of followers, the chosen candidate was supposed to be, if not the Zionist, the candidate of the P.P.S. However, the election committees always had in their arsenals various machinations and the winner always turned out to be the candidate of the reactionaries. Kolomea really did not have the good fortune to have a socialist or liberal as its representative in the old Austrian parliament.

The economic and political proportions changed in Kolomea after the disintegration of the Austrian Empire when the League of Nations gave all of eastern Galicia to the new Poland. The workforce in Kolomea was politically aware at that time and influenced by the victorious Bolshevik Revolution. After the split in the Poalei-Zion party into right and left, a left Poalei-Zion party also arose in Kolomea; an illegal Communist Party also existed. The majority of the Z.P.S. organized in the Bund, joining the general Jewish Workers Bund in Poland. The right and left Poalei-Zion, the Bund and the Jewish division of the Communist Party now fought for influence among the Jewish working class in Kolomea. Cultural institutions began to rise - libraries and evening courses; the largest according to their scope were the Y.L. Peretz Library and the communal evening courses that were created by left Poalei-Zion. The Bund created the Medem[1] Library, the communists – the Karl Marx and the Sholem Asch Society. The communist institutions would be closed by the Polish regime after a short time.

At the head of the parties stood the activists, known from before the First World War and, also, the younger, newly arrived. With the left wing Poalei-Zion party, the leaders were Yuda Langemas, Miler, Y. Shleier, M. Marksheid, Avraham Parnes, Shmuel Winkler, Berl Krauthamer, Shlomo Shmois, Leib Elenberg, Leib Meizler-Weitz and the writer of these lines. The leaders of the right Poalei-Zion were: Shlomo Badler, Dr.Wagman, Shpiegel; of the communists, known were: Shike Shechter, Yidl Greif, Heizer, Nusan Meizler, Sheyndl Shechter; at the head of the Bund stood: Gizelo Herman, Naftali Kesten, Leah Rozenshtreich, Feywl Loiber, Dr. Adolf Frish. There were many other party workers; however, I do not remember their names.

[Page 222]

The existing parties, as well as a number of impartial worker activists, made great efforts to create professional unions in Kolomea and drew into them an even larger number of members. Others in the unions of needle-workers, bakers, weavers, woodworkers, those employed in trade and others were active. However, Jewish workers, after all, for the most part were scattered in the various smaller workshops. Therefore, the fight for better working and wage conditions would end with only small successes. They did not always succeed in drawing all of the workers in the designated trades into the fight. In such trades such as bakers and hairdressers, a "general" strike by the workers did not stop the enterprises from functioning. The owners would mobilize their family members and somehow continue working. However, as a result of the strike something would be achieved: a little higher wage, better conditions and the recognition of the existence of the professional organization.

As a rule, the state labor inspectors were not very fastidious in the application of the existing labor laws. The only function of the police was to make sure that the businesses and workshops that opened up into the streets closed at the prescribed hour of seven o'clock in the evening.

Kolomea belonged to that part of the new Poland where the Poles were in the minority. The Polish regime, therefore, was on the lookout for unrest and did not permit any open gatherings and demonstrations, principally the 1st of May demonstrations, unless they took place in a locked meeting hall. Such a locked First of May demonstration took place in Kolomea for the last time in 1923. The hall was packed with Kolomea workers, Jews and everyone else, city dwellers as well as village dwellers. At that time the old Austrian law about the right to speak in public only in three languages, German, Polish and Ukrainian, still was valid. The demonstration ended with a march to the city hall through the main street in Kolomea, where the leaders of the demonstration had decorated the balcony with the red flag and gave speeches. This was the last time that the red workers' flag waved over the Kolomea city hall.

Coordinator's note:

1. The Bund's Medem Library was named for Vladimir Medem (1879-1923) a Bund leader and activist for Jewish workers. Since his Jewish born father had converted to Lutheranism, Yiddish was not allowed in his home and Medem did not learn Yiddish until he was 22 years old. He emigrated to New York in 1921 and is buried in Mount Carmel cemetery in Queens, NY near the grave of Sholem Aleichem's and other Jewish writers. The Medem Union was a group of Jewish writers and activists which helped found the Medem Library in Paris which still exists today since its members hid the books in basements all over Paris during World War II. [Coor.]

[Page 223]

My Little Street and My Youth Organization

by Leib Weitz

Translated by Gloria Berkenstat Freund

I travel to Kolomea in my imagination and here I stand on Osa Street where I spent my youth. It was a small street, a muddy one, unpaved and the only sidewalk on the street is full of mud and holes. Small houses on both sides, some of which were ready to fall. The street itself was not yet very old.

My mother still remembered how the old Prut [River] alleys were not yet streets, but fields. Past the fields [there were] paths on which we went to the Prut to swim.

However, it seems that the houses were older than the street. Most of the houses had crooked doors and windows, peeled walls. There also were several new houses. I myself remember how they were built. The new houses [belonged to] the "aristocrats" among the people.

"Common Jews" lived on our street: shoemakers, tailors, wagon drivers, water carriers, shop owners, butchers and horse traders (koniares). There were several shops in the small street where herring, bread, butter, salt, kerosene, glasses for lamps, soap, coal and lumber was sold. Everyone earned their livelihood from [this] work, but earning was difficult, although no one died of hunger.

On the right side of our house lived Dudya Henigsberg or, as the Jews in the street called him, Dudya Telep [tremble] because when he walked he shook or, as we said, trembled. Dudya was a tall Jew, a solid one of middle age with a partially grey, small beard and always laughing eyes. He had five sons and two daughters. The sons were all as tall and as solid as their father and also butchers like he was.

[Page 224]

Dudya was not learned and also not too skilled in world questions. But everyone looked to him and everyone loved him. If someone in the street became ill and did not have money for a doctor, he went to Dudya. If the water-carrier's horse died and he did not have enough money to buy another one, he went to Dudya. Dudya did not refuse anyone.

Dudya Henigsberg was a busy man. He would wake up early when it was very dark outside to go to the slaughterhouse. Later, during the day, he stood at the covered market and sold meat. He came home very tired. Therefore, when Shabbos or a holiday came, he beamed with joy. He became a different man. His house was full of Jews. They spoke about politics, about helping Jews who needed help and meanwhile gemakht a l'Chaim [literally made a l'Chaim – a toast; had a drink]. Dudya, himself, did not drink much. But he loved for the Jews to drink and there was no lack of what to drink in Dudya's house.

I leave my small street and drop into the city where there was commerce, where the workshops stood, the small factories as well as the communal institutions and the places of entertainment.

So, this is "Di Neye Welt" [the New World], the street that led from here to the market. There were houses on both sides, not ugly ones, the doors beautifully painted, the walls whitewashed, clean and tidy. Jews lived in all of the houses, only Jews. There were no gentile houses. The Komarner Rebbe lived on the left side. There was also a synagogue in his house. It was always full of Jews on weekdays and self-evidently on the holidays. The Komarner Rebbe was a Jew in his late fifties, with a white beard, not tall, with dull, blank eyes. He was surrounded with much love and simple, ordinary Jews. He prayed alone at the pulpit. With his entreating voice he quarreled with the passersby in the street. It was said that his oldest son wrote surreptitiously for one of the Yiddish newspapers.

And so I was on the bridge across the "Potiek" that once arose [there] and became a great [body of] water. It poured out over the banks, flooded entire streets and caused much damage. A great deal of wild grass grew on both sides and it

[Page 225]

gathered a great deal of dirt. Only in the middle of the flow was there a little green water. However, a small bridge over the "Potiek" led to a large spring. There were always many Jews and non-Jews here. But below, near the "Potiek," was a drinking trough. The horses of the local wagon drivers and the village horses drank here. There were many people and horses present here during the market days. There was no room then to throw a pin. A few steps further stood four pumps and at each pump stood a water carrier who pumped water.

I knew one of the water carriers very well. He was a small man with a yellow face and yellow beard. He was lame in one foot. He was called Borukh the krumer [lame one]. He was a quiet and a pious Jew, could pray well and observed Yidishkeit [Jewish way of life]. He had many children, boys and girls. When the children were small I could never tell which of them was older. They grew to be important people and took part in communal life in Kolomea.

When Borukh the water carrier's father was still a boy, he fell in love with a Christian girl and married her. After the wedding, she learned the Jewish laws, kept kosher, celebrated the Jewish holidays and provided a room for a synagogue and he, Borukh's father, had a religious book written. When I knew her, she already was very old. One could not recognize that she did not come from a Jewish family. She spoke a good Yiddish just like all of the Jewish women of Kolomea.

It was different at the market than in the back alleys. The streets were paved and clean. Wide sidewalks with trees were on both sides, gardens, memorials and squares. The streets were clearly lit with electric lamps and there were Jewish shops on all sides. The streets were full of people, with wagons, horse-drawn carriages and autos. Here the life of an entire generation lay ahead of them.

Opposite the city hall the A-B line[1] begins. Grinberg's paper shop is here. Here we get all of the Yiddish newspapers, daily newspapers, weekly publications and journals. Foreign newspapers, including American, can be gotten here.

The A-B line was always full of people. Workers gathered here very early with packs of food under their arms. Here, journeymen tailors and workers from other trades strolled around. They carried on discussions about world problems, carried on fights between the left and the right. When the city clock struck seven, they dispersed, each to

[Page 226]

his direction, each to his work. In the middle of the day the A-B line was full of merchants from the city and from the provinces, with customers and at night it was impossible to pass through here. Workers were coming from work, trade employees were coming from the businesses and there were strollers – boys and girls. It was joyful in the evening at Line A-B. Dressed up people walked through the street to the café-hall. Theater was presented there. Brides and grooms, young couples walked on Line A-B. Workers dressed in holiday clothes stood peacefully in discussions. The discussions often led to shouting. The police who kept order here were not so friendly; they drove, pushed and sometimes let loose with their rubber sticks.

*
* *

Pilsudski Square was located in the center of Line A-B. My heart begins to beat faster. Here stood the house of my young dreams and of my communal work. This was a large two-story building whose windows looked out onto three streets. Almost every apartment was occupied by private residents, by doctors. Only one apartment, whose windows opened onto the small alley that led to the Hey Platz [Hey Square], was occupied by the Jewish Workers Library named for Y. L. Peretz.

The entire meeting hall consisted of three large rooms. The library, the evening courses for workers, the collection group for the Jewish Scientific Institute (YIVO), the Poalei-Zion Party [Marxist-Zionist] and the youth organization, Yugnt [youth] here are concentrated in these rooms. The library was in the first room.

Various posters about events were always pasted on the walls. Here hung a large red poster that announced a reading by Y. Zrubbel on the theme, "From Y.L. Peretz to H. Leivik." In another corner – a large poster about a reading by Z. Sonalowicz. A third poster was about a report by Yoal Mastbaum. Another poster was about a theater performance with the famous artist, Aleksander Granach, and still another poster called the young to a reading about youth problems by Yakov Kener. And dozens and dozens of other posters, printed and self-made that told about small and large political

[Page 227]

and cultural undertakings, about dozens and dozens of discussions and evening courses that were organized through the years by the Y.L. Peretz Society and through the Poalei-Zion party.

The library room was full of people who came to read books. On the other side of the table stood comrades and they gave out books to the readers. Among them was Rayzl Merbaum, a worker in Shimshon Heler's talis [prayer shawl] factory. Comrade Chana Birnbaum sat in another corner. She sat bent over and wrote something. Not far from her sat Comrade Reicher. He worked with the statistics of which books were loaned the most [often].

In a corner on another side sat a person deeply absorbed in his thoughts. This was Moshe Elenberg. He founded the library. He built the most beautiful Jewish library in Kolomea from a small number of books, gathered from among his own comrades. He was a weaver by trade, worked at Shimshon Heler's factory. Moshe began to work when he was very young. He worked hard in the factory during the day and he devoted his entire free time to library work. He studied at night like someone who is thirsty and he swallowed books, in Yiddish and in other languages. It was difficult to mention a serious book that Moshe Elenberg had not read. He had a lung illness from too much exertion and was forced to remain in bed for many years. But despite his illness, he led the cultural work of the Poalei-Zion youth.

A fervid argument occurred not far from the door. They were discussing the most recent events in Eretz Yisroel. Everyone shouted at the same time, but Maks Rot always shouted over everyone else. Maks Rath was small, short with a pale face, straight hair combed down. He had a high forehead with deep wrinkles, with greenish eyes. He was a sick man. It was rare when he did not have a cold. He was good by nature, genteel in character, an idealist and a terrific optimist. He lived with his parents on Sloneczna. The room in which Maks lived with his parents looked as if it had been rebuilt from a wooden cell.

Maks' father was a free person, a socialist. He was a member of Poalei-Zion (right) for many years. He was a brush maker by trade. He worked in Kiva Hener's factory for many years. Because of a strike that broke out in the brush

[Page 228]

factory, Maks' father lost his job. He was forced to work at home in a small spot in his small room that was divided by both beds. A hand-machine to cut the bristles from the brushes stood there. Thus Maks lived. There he read books, read poetry that he loved so much.

It was dark in the other room of the meeting hall; only a strip of light from the third room made its way in. The meeting of the committee that led the organization, Yugnt [youth] took place here. The committee consisted of the comrades Chaim Bal, Leibel Elenberg, Moshe Herman, Mekhl Lichtn, Y. Latner, M. Cweig, Leib Meizler, S. Kamet and Josef Biber. These were the leaders of the organization. Hundreds and hundreds of young people in its ranks were educated. Many of them first learned to read and write here at the evening courses. A large number of the young people actually were wrested from the underworld and turned into [socially] conscious, useful people.

The organization worked according to a plan, according to a purpose. All of its members were divided into groups with 15-20 members in a group. The selection of the groups was according to age and according to the knowledge the member possessed. Group meetings would take place at least once a week in addition to gatherings and lectures. The main themes were political, economic, history of the Jewish workers movement, history of socialism, Eretz-Yisroel problems, Palestinographia [the study of Palestine] and Borochovism [socialist Zionism]. The lectures were appropriate to the level of the members. In addition to this, there was a presentation circle where the comrades would learn to speak at a meeting and gatherings.

A committee sat in another room of the premises and discussed a plan to carry out a questionnaire among the young people in the city to find out about the life of the young, the work of the young people and the number of grades in school they had finished. This was a giant undertaking but they had to do it because the Polish government was not interested in doing this, so they had to do it, said Chaim Bal who reported now about this plan. Chaim Bal, a solidly built young man, with red checks and a high forehead, looked a great deal older than his age. He was a true idealistic type. His mother did not permit him to learn a trade because it was

[Page 229]

not appropriate for her son to be an artisan. He became a komi (business employee) in a shop. He worked in the shop until he became a member of the Yugnt [youth]. There he learned that there is no shame in work. Chaim Bal immediately left the shop and went to Avraham Zimmer to learn carpentry. He did not know Yiddish from his home; he learned mama-loshen [mother tongue, Yiddish] and became an expert on Yiddish literature. He became one of the most beloved leaders of the youth organization. His fervid dream was to settle in Eretz-Yisroel.

Mekhl Lichtn sat at Chaim Bal's right hand. Lichtn was descended from a poor, respectable home. His father died when Mekhl was still very young. His mother sewed shirts and cared for him and his sister and young brother. Mekhl studied industriously in a kheder [religious primary school]. His mother hoped that he would become a teacher. However, his mother's dream was not accomplished. Instead of becoming a teacher, he became a business employee at a leather shop. Mekhl Lichtn was one of the best and most substantial speakers and lecturers among the young.

Next to Mekhl Lichtn sat Leibele Elenberg, a young man of middle height with a worn out face and with a warm human heart. He stood there and spoke before the young people. He loved the young people as much as his life. Perhaps that is why he never had his own youth. He always was an adult. He worried about his younger brothers and sisters. He worried about his old father. He was raised without a mother. He did not even remember her. She died when he was still very small. They lived on Rogatke Street in a house that should have already collapsed with age.

Leibele Elenberg was a bright, transporting speaker and the best of all of the activists. The young loved him as much as their own lives.

The brother and sister, Dovid and Loti Reichman. were noticed immediately among the arriving readers.

Dovid and Loti Reichbach remained alone in Kolomea after their parents and sister left for America. They were not allowed into [America] because their eyes were not healthy. They were members of the Y. L. Peretz Library. After a short time, the brother and sister became active

[Page 230]

members of Yugnt. There was no area of work in which they were not the first ones.

When Dudya and Loti left for Warsaw, Dudya became one of the best instructors in the Poalei-Zion children's organization, Yungbor [Young Borokhovists], and Loti became an active comrade in the Warsaw Yugnt.

All of my dear comrades, whom I have mentioned, perished.

Moshe Elenberg, who was the founders of the library, committed suicide. Chaim Bal was shot in the courtyard of the factory where he worked even before the start of the aktsies [deportations]. Leibl Elenberg perished with all of the other Jews; Mekhl Lichtn was also among them. My dear comrade Maks Rot tried to commit suicide after his wife, Comrade Chana Gartenlaub, had been taken away. However, he was not successful. He perished along with the other Jews. Loti and Dovid Reichbach, who returned from Warsaw before Hitler took Kolomea, also perished.

Two classes from the evening school organized by the Evening Courses for Workers Society

Translator's note:

1. Line A-B refers to the designation of the buildings on the perimeter of the market.

———

[Page 231]

Memories of a Young Kolomeyer Tailor[1]

by Leizer Walder (New York)

Translated by Gloria Berkenstat Freund

We lived on Walow Streeet opposite the Baron Hirsch School where I was a student.

My father, Moshe–Leib, was a baker. He worked hard through the night and barely earned a livelihood. The flour dust and the difficult work undermined his health little by little. However, he never complained although he knew how weak and sick he was.

Once, I was then not yet 12 years old, my father had a conversation with me.

– You know, my child, while I would want you to study, what can I do?

I do not see any possibility for you to continue going to school; there is no purpose in it for you.

– You will remain neither here nor there. I will give you [as an apprentice] to a tailor; you will become a good craftsman and not know from need.

My father chose a tailor, a good craftsman; he was named Yakov Hersh Kalechstein. He was a genteel man, a learned man. He was called "the Hasidic tailor" because his children were Hasidim and he would sew silk kapotes [long, black coats which are worn by Hasidic men] for them. My father apprenticed me to the Hasidic tailor for two years and also paid 20 krones. He had to borrow the money as a loan.

The day on which I went to the tailor to work for the first time was a holiday to my father. He said he had "provided for his child."

[Page 232]

However, he was not destined to see his child taken care of; he died during the same year and left my mother a desolate widow with three orphans.[2]

One of our neighbors was Shlomo Dovid. In the city, he was called "Shlomo Dovid der shtot–balebos" [important man in the city]. After my father's death, Shlomo Dovid's wife called in my mother and consoled her in pious Yiddish: "God is a Father of orphans and widows. He feeds all creatures and He also will feed you." She persuaded her husband to provide us with a bit of housing and, after Passover, we actually did move into a small house in Shlomo Dovid's courtyard. This was a true ruin; the walls had holes, the doors were without doorknobs and did not close properly. Shlomo Dovid was an important person at city hall and he pushed through a proposal that the kehile [organized Jewish community] pay him rent for my mother.

This Shlomo Dovid was one of the Kolomea elite. He was dressed like an elegant young man. His boots were always shiny. Whenever one met him, he was carrying a portfolio under his arm and a pen was behind his ear. Besides being a meddler at city hall, he was an intimate of the district chief and influential at the kehile. He approached everyone from above, never answered anyone's "Good morning, and said "Du" to young and old alike.[3] In general, he carried all of Kolomea in his head. He had a list in which he recorded everyone's behavior. In the "main synagogue," where he was, it should be understood, an important person, he, tall and proud, would go to the Torah reading desk on Shabbos [Sabbath] and call out the weddings that were scheduled for the coming week.

And we were lodgers of this Shlomo Dovid.

After my father's death, my mother became the bread–winner for the family. She would help flick goose feathers during the winter and in addition to [receiving] a few kreutzers, she would also earn several feet, wings and a few gizzards from the geese. During the summer she helped middle–class women with the cooking, washing, polishing and thus we lived in need and in poverty.

During the two years in which I learned tailoring, I did not completely leave school. I worked with a needle from early in the morning to around six at night. I went to school from six to eight; from there I went back to work until around 11 at night. My mother, exhausted and broken from a day of heavy labor, would wait to take me home. My mother's only hope at that

[Page 233]

time was that I become an artisan and be able to earn my own bread and, with Shlomo Dovid's influence, I would not have to go to serve in the military.

* *
*

In order to become a tailor, a young boy had to be apprenticed to a tailor for three years. The first year, the young boy worked without pay. The second year, only for food and the third year the young boy received two kronen a week along with food.

The first year the boss's wife made use of the young boy. He needed to carry water from the well, chop wood for the oven, help carry the laundry to be washed, coddle the children, run an errand, and do other such work that had nothing to do with tailoring.

The second year, they would little by little begin to break in the fellow in tailoring. First, they would bind the middle finger of his right hand for a few weeks. This was a means for him to hold the needle well in his hand. The young boy took pride in his bound finger – he already was like a tailor. In addition to this he also would run to the bathhouse for hot coals for the press-iron. He was taught little by little to sew on the sewing machine during the second year, so that by the end of the second year he could make a pair of pants and he could legitimately earn the food he would get. But the food was woefully poor. One consolation was that the boss himself did not have better food.

During the third year, the boy was a full journeyman and he was trusted to make a jacket, so that in addition to food, he received a suit and a pair of shoes.

The workday would begin at 6–7 o'clock in the morning and last until 10 at night – approximately 16 hours a day. Holiday evenings were irrelevant. They would work until 12 o'clock at night and the week before Passover, the entire night. At the Seder [Passover meal at which the Hagadah containing the story of the holiday is read], all of the apprentices would sit around the holiday table, but immediately after the Kiddush [blessing of the wine], they all fell into a sweet sleep. They waited long for the holidays, the poor things, so that they could sleep well.

[Page 234]

You will find a large number of former apprentice tailors from Kolomea in the New York Garment Center. Some of them are now rich manufacturers. Others remained workers. I hope that reading this writing will remind them of that time and they will again relive their dear younger years.

*

* *

Singing songs at work was always a part of the tailoring trade. I still remember many of the songs that we would sing at the time in the workshop in Kolomea. And here is one of them:

> Sleep my child, sleep well,
> I will sing you a song.
> If you rest, my child, you will grow older,
> You will know the difference.
>
> If you, my child, will grow older,
> You will become equal to people.
> Then you will learn,
> What poor is and what rich is...
>
> The most expensive palaces, the richest houses –
> All of this is built by the poor.
> But – do you know who lives in them?
> Not him, but the rich man...
>
> The poor man – he lies in a cellar.
> The moisture runs from the walls
> He gets rheumatism
> In his feet and in his hands...

Songs were written for every important event that happened in the city. One such song was composed when a strike broke out in which a victim even fell – a young girl named Chanala was killed then.

[Page 235]

Here it is:

> Chanala went to work
> And did not know of anything.
> They called out the militia
> And Chanala was shot for no reason...
>
> Chanala fell dead –
> Her eyes, her lips closed...
> They wrapped her in the red flag –
> She fell in the sacred battle!...

A tragic event once happened near Kolomea, at the gasworks. A young man, a Jew, was killed there because of an explosion and they sang about his tragic death in all of the Kolomea workshops. Here is this song:

> Perhaps you saw or perhaps you heard,
> What happened here?
> A young man, a bridegroom,
> Was standing at work,
> And the gasometer [storage tank holding natural gas] discharged.

When the gasometer discharged at him,
He ended up like clay.
He asked that they send for his beloved bride,
Because he wanted to see her again before he died.

*
* *

My two years as an apprentice passed. I could sew a pair of pants and a waistcoat by myself.

Our friend, Hershl the tailor of women's clothes, presented me to the best tailor in the city. His name was Zeyda Pesler from Budapest. The agreement was: He would pay me three krone a week for the first half year and five kronen a week for the second half of the year.

My mother could barely make due end meet with my salary. There was only bread during the week and challah [Sabbath bread] and a piece of meat for Shabbos.

[Page 236]

Her luck did not last for long. The First World War broke out in 1914 with all of its terrors.

The government mobilized everyone who could carry a weapon. The young were taken into the army. There was an effect on income. The tailors and the shoemakers were the first to be affected. They wandered around without work, without income, full of poverty and fear.

The worst was when the Russians entered the city. They showed what they were capable of doing. They robbed, tortured, murdered. No one's life was secure. Everyone lost hope. Everyone walked around with a gloomy face. Whoever could, escaped. Whoever could not escape looked for a place to hide wherever they could find a hiding place.

In 1915, two weeks before Purim, the Germans drove out the Russian troops. The Austrians returned and we were a little more calm, but not for long.

During the same year on the 15th of May, the Russian hordes recaptured Kolomea. The tumult that was brought to the city cannot be described. All of the residents of the city were scattered and our friend Shlomo Dovid took his talis and tefilin [prayer shawl and phylacteries] and in a whirlwind ran with everyone else to find a more secure place.

I escaped to Bohemia then. My mother, my brother Avraham and my sister Rywka also ran to Bohemia after me. But they did not find me there. The Austrians mobilized me and sent me to the Italian front.

———

Footnotes:

1.   Leizer Walder sent us this manuscript a short time before his death in 1956.

Translator's note:

1. In Yiddish a child is considered an orphan when one of its parents dies.
2. "Du" is the familiar form of "you" and usually is not used when speaking to an older person. The formal form "Eikh" would be used as a sign of respect.

[Page 237]

My Streets

by A. Sh. Yuris (Tel Aviv)

Translated by Claire Hisler Shefftz

1. Ulica Ciasna

My cradle stood on Ulica [Street] Ciasna, which means narrow street, and I do not remember if the house was numbered 4 or 6, but I am inclined to number 4. The street was not actually a street, but an alley; in Hebrew one would have called it simta and in Russian, pereulok. The alley connected two beautiful streets in the very center of the city that went to the very central square of the city, to the rynek, which means the market, with the city hall in the middle and the train line for the small train, kolejka, which cut across the market and the entire middle of the city. Yes, I almost would have forgotten the name of the city: Kolomea. Eastern Europe, more correctly, "Pokuttya."[1] Incidentally, the city earned a well-known reputation in Polish and Yiddish literature. It was immortalized by Sholem Aleichem in his famous humorous story, S'a Lign ["It's a Lie"] and Stanislaw Przybyszewski, characterized one of his heroes in his novel, Synowie Ziemi [Sons of the Earth] (The Children of the Earth), thus: "He looks like some sort of Englishman from Kolomea." For him, it appears, my city was a synonym for a backwards corner at the end of the world.

I was born accidentally. When there are poor parents who live in barely one room with an alcove that also serves as a kitchen and who already have nine children, they do not excessively long to sow another, tenth child. However, as I was born on a happy day, in the middle of Purim, it seems that my appearance in the world was met with love. Go figure, a tenth child, but they would not throw it out. And for the sake of the true historic record, I here provide the date: the 8th of March

[Page 238]

1890. Formally, the two-story house belonged to us, but as the burden of a mortgage and debts of all kinds lay on this house, an [impounder] collected the entire rent money from all of the neighbors for a bank account [in payment of] the debts, which had a tendency to keep increasing. A poor house. My father was a small broker of large houses. Prosperity was rare. The income – minimal.

I spent my first childhood years in this house. I would always run out into the larger world and, for me, this was two streets into which my street ran. On one side was Jagiellonska Street, which was a noisy street of businesses and I was enticed by its noise and tumult. On the other side was Kosciuszko Street, which was impressive with its elegance and on which was found the salon of the Kasa Oszczędności [savings bank], where all of the important communal-literary undertakings, Jewish and non-Jewish would take place.

A childish soul longs for experiences that will pull it through the monotony of great poverty. Exactly across lived a baker with a beautiful daughter, Ruchla. On Friday nights, she would often pull me into their house to their comfortable dinner, about which we could not even dream [in our house]. Her small blond head and her sweet smile are forever engraved in my heart and memory. And when some sort of house began to be built on the street and childish fantasies longed for blazing flames, the children and I from the same street and the same poverty started a small fire of wood chips, which engulfed the entire scaffolding with its fiery tongue-like flames. The city firemen arrived just in time to put out the fire. However, the small "igniters," including me, were not found. I was very frightened, lying hidden under the bed for hours. And we, the mischievous boys, could not bear that the middle class in the city would prepare the fish for Shabbos [the Sabbath] and hide them in the cellars because of the natural coolness – we decided to punish them for their fish-wealth and avenge our fish-poverty in a characteristic, conspiratorial manner. On a Friday evening, when it was a bit dark, we sneaked into the cellar of a member of the middle class, stole the good

[Page 239]

cooked fish and ate them ourselves. However, to add to the mockery, we filled the pots with stones and covered them with the fish remains. In the morning it was a Yom Kippur for the "rich," but Simkhas Torah – a celebration for we poor children.[2] Those, who did this also were not discovered.

And a rare, nice family, nice and genteel, lived in the house on the right side of our house: a man and a woman and their wonderfully beautiful daughters – the Henish family. In later years, Gabriele D'Annunzio's splendid novella, Three Graces, fell into my hands; the slender figures of the three sisters surfaced in the field of vision of my memory.

And when, for the first time in the history of my city, gas lighting was brought in on the streets and gigantically tall poles were erected, it became my favorite pleasure to climb up to the very highest height of the gas pole on my street – to the great fear of my mother. In this way I wanted to be closer to the heavens. My mother was afraid that, God forbid, falling down from such a pole could truly lead to my departure, falling into heaven – for eternity.

The heavens drew me for my entire life, to this day. And will until I draw my last breath.

2. Ulica Rejtana

The debt and mortgage on our house exceeded the real worth of the house. This house was auctioned and we left it without a groshn of money, penniless. For lack of a choice, we moved to a still smaller residence. What is a still smaller residence? In any case, the residence consisted of barely one room, but much smaller and of barely one alcove that was identical to a kitchen and, in addition, an oven, but also much smaller than on Ciasna Street – much more crowded. And in addition, one brother, a bookbinder, placed his worktable for cardboard in the only room. The street, Ulica Rejtana also had its patriotic name.[3] However, the street itself was smaller and more narrow – in addition stifling – because opposite the house in which we lived was the

[Page 240]

workshop of a shoykhet [ritual slaughterer]. The cry of the slaughtered chickens caused shudders. The flying feathers crept into the nose and eyes and ears. The smells nauseated and choked us.

I am only left with sad memories of not being on the street for very long. When my older brother, Yosef, and I needed to go from the folks-shul [public school] to the gymnazie [secondary school] and the payment was three krone, our mother had to pawn in the pawnshop the only pair of candlesticks that we had. And on Friday she blessed two candles that were stuck in two potatoes.

3. Ulica Zamkova

We moved to a very romantic street: Ulica Zamkova. And we lived in a very romantic courtyard in which a row of houses was located, divided into the highest and lowest parts of the courtyard. This was a more gentile street, close to the gymnazie and there was always a danger in passing through at night because of the angry dogs in the Polish houses.

I was inebriated by the romance of the courtyard. My romantic feelings were ignited here for the first time for a small girl and her name was Lorka. I was then 12 years old and she was about 10. But this strange feeling, and call it what you will, prematurely made me into a "poet" because it was in poems that I poured out my heart and was stirred up for the first time and it should be understood that there were rhymes and they [the poems] were in Polish.

And on the street I lived through the premature death of my brother, Kalman. Although, a very capable and good brother, Hersh, died on Ciasna Street. But that death was at the beginning of my first years of childhood; it did not shock me like the death of my brother, Kalman, at a time when I was a student at the gymnazie. Since then I have been a principled opponent of death and an absolute proponent of life. Death is the saddest and most excessive thing in our, in any case, so short lives, which are given to us only once by His Dear Name [God]. This life is a gift from heaven. Why does heaven take it back so quickly?

[Page 241]

4. My First Slap

Again because of poverty, we changed our residence – and moved a little further from the Jewish center – onto a completely gentile street, right down after the "spring." No many memories of this street remain in my memory because it hurt my soul deeply. One evening I returned home and some sort of gentile boy, even an intelligent enough Pole and a brother of my colleague in the same gymnazie class, approached me by chance from the opposite direction, and without any reason, slapped me, saying: "Masz Zydku!" – there you have it, Jew-boy. This is a classic illustration of the Jewish tragedy of exile: a minority among gentiles and, therefore, persecuted. The slap on my face still burns for me to this day as an earlier "momento." I do not remember what the street was named. Perhaps Ulica Szewczenko or perhaps Ulica Orzeszkowa or perhaps another name. However, whatever name it was, the street and the Jewish person in me was defiled by it. And this is one of the internal, physical factors of my Zionist conception: I will no longer be "the one who gets slapped," not being able to answer them. My Zionist concept says: not a slap for a slap, but a double and triple slap for a slap. I regret now that I have forgotten the name of the street as the name of the street also was defiled. I have since avoided that street in my home-city. It only remains an angry nightmare.

5. Back to Ulica Zamkova

We lived on the gentile street for almost a year and then moved back to Ulica Zamkova. I spent all of my gymnazie years up to my certificate of graduation here. I formed my essence here. I was a "celujący," that means an "excellent" student. I was especially captivated by history and literature. I began prematurely to write a diary during all of my gymnazie years. I wrote many poems in Polish. They, both the diary and the poems, disappeared during the stormy years of the First World War. A shame.

[Page 242]

I was prematurely absorbed into the secret Zionist cultural circle, Bar Kokhba, which was connected with the Galicianer student movement, Tzeiri-Tzion [Youth of Zion]. In my 15th year of life, I wrote a large report in the form of a brochure in Polish on the theme, "Poalei-Zionism [Workers of Zion], what it is, where did it arise and what does it aspire to." Incidentally, my first paper made a deep impression in our student circle. The chairman of our circle, also a student, but in a higher class, Feywl Shternberg, with great enthusiasm, then equated the beauty of my presentation of ethical standpoints to the cry of the lost 10,000 Helenes when they suddenly saw the sea, a cry of spiritual ecstasy: "Thalasai! Thalasai!" (Sea! Sea!).

Comrade Juda Langenmas was a student in the same class. He was a great follower of Yiddish literature and a Yidishist [proponent of the Yiddish language, literature and culture] "on principle." In time, he began to translate all of [Jiliusz] Slowacki's poems, among them Ojciec Zadżumionych [The Father of the Plague Stricken] and [Adam] Mickiewicz's Pan Tadeusz [Mr. or Sir Tadeusz]. He lived not far from us, I think on Bernarska Street. Near the courtyard where I lived was a large pole with a gas lamp. We stood there until deep into the night, spoke and discussed everything and everyone, politics and literature – we discussed everything!

I was in love with my street, Zamkova, because of the romance of the street and the romance of the courtyard, which certainly once was a kind of zamek [castle]. University studies carried me to Vienna. And Ulica Zamkova was my last street in my home city.

6. The Longing for Streets

University and then the First World War, in which my family was "mandated" to go to Vienna, finally ended this chapter of my home city as a home for me and [my] young friends and the experiences of my youth. However, a burning longing for the street and the house where my cradle stood, Ulica Ciasna 4, particularly remains to this day. And when I would come by chance, but rarely, to my home city for various party missions and missions

[Page 243]

for Eretz-Yisroel in general, I would first find the street and apartment of my birth on Ciasna Street and immerse myself in a sea of childhood memories. I turned my steps first at the B-line[4] to the courtyard at Zamkova Street, where my entire being slowly ripened as a Jew and a man, as a socialist and Zionist. These young ideals were expressed and carried out on this street of the beginning of my life, Ulica Ciasna, and on this last street in my home city, Ulica Zamkova, to which I have remained devoted for my entire life.

Translator's and Editor's Footnotes:

1. Pokuttya is historically the area between the Prut and Cheremosh Rivers, of which Kolomea was considered the historical center.
2. Yom Kippur, the Day of Atonement, is a fast day; Simkhas Torah, the holiday celebrating the completion of the annual Torah reading, is a joyful holiday. Therefore, because the "rich" did not have their Shabbos fish it was like a fast day.
3. The street was named for Tadeusz Rejtana who was a Sejm (parliament) member in opposition to the first partition of Poland in 1773 and dramatically blocked the doorway with his own body. A painting of this by the artist Jan Matejko in 1866 was very well known.
4. B-line refers to the designation of the buildings on one side of the perimeter of the market.

[Page 244]

Two Russian Jews in the City
Yona Shamas and Motl Fonya, the News Seeker[a]

by Shloyme Bik

Translated by Gloria Berkenstat Freund

Like almost every city in Galicia, Kolomea also possessed its small colony of Russian Jews. Among the immigrants from Fonya [Russia] long present here, there are those who have lived here for dozens of years and yet floating around each of them is still an atmosphere of secrecy, of fear and sometimes also a wariness.

For example, take the shamas [synagogue caretaker] of the small Itsikl synagogue, Yona the Russian, whose strange existence was permeated by secrecy. He came here [to Kolomea] when he still was a young man. He did not run from the military because why would he have to run when he had a severely crippled foot? It is certain that he left a wife at home; firstly, he came in a talis [prayer shawl] and put on a shtreiml [fur hat worn by some married Hasidim] here. Secondly, he remained in Kolomea for 50 years without a wife. He must have been descended from a rich, middleclass family because during the half century of his being a shamas, not one crumb of income stuck to him and [he was not dependent on anyone]. He spoke with the members of the middle class as an equal and from above with several of them, not as an equal. That Yona was not an ignorant person could be seen easily during one's first conversation with him. But how far he had gone in his education was difficult to know because he avoided discussion of words of Torah with anyone.

Why did he run from his home, somewhere in a shtetl [town] in Podolia gibernia [province]? Who were his family? Why did he never correspond with it and how had they sinned against him that he never even

[Page 245]

spoke of it? A sort of Yoshe Kalb[1] lived among a city of Jews for 50 years. But, unlike I[srael] J[oseph] Singer's literary figure, the mysterious shamas from Kolomea was spiritually nimble, a person with clear senses and with a smooth tongue who knew everything and did not forget anything about himself and his family, but simply did not speak [about them]. In addition, it is strange that no one was curious enough to learn [about them].

A person who is overloaded with so many secrets and silence usually has a tendency toward melancholy. Yona Shamas had not unburdened himself for tens of years and yet (truly, wonder of wonders!) had not lost his easy-going mood in dealing with people. He was always ready for a joke with the adults and always with a prank for the kheder [religious primary school] boys in Reb Itsikl's small school. Yona Shamas created so much joy for we young boys with his call to the hakofus [circular procession with the Torah scrolls on Simkhas Torah]. When he finished with the first difficult names for the first and second procession, Yona then had a thin cutting remark for those newly called, which truly did not did not cause any hurt [to those who received the remarks], but a smile of joy and pleasure appeared on their faces. The ranks of young boys came for the fifth and sixth hakofus; each boy received a compliment or a small tweak of his nose, which awoke their ambition to study.

Zarekh Rauchwerger, who was taught privately [at the] gymnazie [secondary school] and knew several pages of Gemara [Talmud] by heart, was called up by Yona as follows: the esteemed Torah scholar, the young man Zerakh [son of Menashe], whose name will shine in the Torah and among the non-Jews. Yona invited my friend, Shimshon, who was known for having exceptional knowledge of the Tanakh [the Torah, Prophets and Writings], with this call: the young man Shimson [son of Moshe], the strong man of the Tanakh.[2] However, they really laughed and had pleasure when Yona did not forget to call himself for the seventh hakofah: the esteemed Torah scholar, I honor myself with the honor of the Torah. Today I think "I, myself" was both an ideal mockery for the person who finds himself in the comical situation of honoring himself and as a jest about the difficult Jews who had a presumption of receiving an honor, for which each of them had already been named, yet they could not receive the honor without a command from Yona Shamas.

What did the Jews think of Yona? I often heard it said

[Page 246]

about him that he was a villain, an embittered Jew. It could be that this thought came from the fact that there was a lack of trust in Yona's seriousness and of faith in his smile. And perhaps he actually was a villain, a person who kept all of his grief to himself, buried his own cries in his own depth and never cried out his protests. Perhaps, human goodness, the very little real humanity, begins with a tear that someone else can also see and with the cries that someone else can also hear? Then the genteel, human language, the language of compassion is born!

The second Russian Jew whom I knew, my uncle, Motl Fonya, had, of course, spoken a great deal and told a tremendous number [of stories], but we did not learn much about his home and we also did not know much about his family. He came from Kiev. Shlomo the money-changer brought him to Kolomea as a son-in-law. Motl Fonya was not a crafty person, as the Galicianers considered the Russians, but instead a wild visionary. He brought a large number of rubles with him from his home. His rich father-in-law added a considerable amount of Austrian money and Motl began to dream about [increasing the value of] the money doubly and a hundredfold, about becoming a rich man. Later, the Kolomea Jews joked that Motl probably had not wanted to become rich, but to show the Galicianers of what a Russian was capable. Motl felt like a stranger in his new environment and it bothered him that the Galicianers took pride in their [Emperor] Franz Josef. Nothing less than love for the Russian tsar remained with Motl for his entire life. Motl had no greater joy (even in his old age when he had given his Galicianer sons and daughters in marriage) than from being able to sit with a hot glass of tea and talk about the greatness and richness of the Russian tsar. These were fantastical stories that Motl had heard when he was a child in Tulchyn, and then, over the course of years, with his literary talent expanded, leading even more and more to terrible, complete fictitiousness.

The first, and I think, the "only one" who 50 years ago befriended the young, Russian son-in-law with his stories about the tsar and with his dreams about wealth was Benyamin the royfe [old-time barber-healer]. Benyamin was a small Jew with a large water-head [large head, possibly suffering from hydrocephalius], with a

[Page 247]

a pointed beard and with such a large hump that he could barely be seen from under it. I remember his cruelty. I was sitting on a stool. He was so small that he barely reached my hair with his small [hair cutting] machine. He asked me:

"How do you want me to shave [your hair]?" I answered: "Half short." I actually did not have any conception as to what this meant. Benyamin pulled [my hair] "half short" so ruthlessly with his machine that the tears always suffocated me. Several years later, I happily escaped from Benyamin the royfe and I could get a haircut from Moshe Bal, who was a communal worker in the city and spoke to all of the gymnazie [secondary school] students as with an adult about Zionism and socialism.

However, 50 years earlier, Benyamin the royfe, it seems, was not yet a malicious person and such a puller [of hair] and he enchanted my young uncle, Motl, with beautiful Hasidic melodies and, chiefly, with listening to his [Motl's] stories about the tsar. Motl lent Benyamin all his money at a high interest and, in addition, he also receive a firm promise that he [Motl] and his entire family would be able to have their hair shorn for free. Benyamin never paid any interest. The principal, understand, was lost because the royfe was a poor Jew and could never pay back such a large sum. It would have been useless to even try. But he kept his word about cutting [Motl's family's] hair for his entire life. It had been agreed for my Uncle Motl and his children, but Motl would send even more distant relatives including me to have our hair shorn by Benyamin without payment.

Motl remained a poor man for his entire life. And for his entire life he also remained with a deep fervor for dreaming and for fantastical news items and stories. Without a doubt, he had the substance in him of a traveler to distant wonderlands and of a great newspaper reporter. Never in his life was he anywhere else but in Tulchyn and in Kolomea; he must have encountered these wonderlands in the city in which he lived. As he had no newspaper, he told the news, fresh and current, to his wife and his children and if there was no news available, he found it, composed it.

The city of several tens of thousands of residents without news items was too quiet for his effervescent mood as a reporter. He was tall, thin, with a grey beard plucked out in the middle, with an intense, pensive face. Motl carried himself like a whirlwind

[Page 248]

in the morning hours from Hamer's Bank to Gralink's grain warehouse, from Meshulem Welwel's grocery to the butcher shops in pursuit of news. He had not had any income for many years. He even had given up worrying about income. Now he was only passionately interested in finding out if an event had happened that would interrupt the stillness in the city so there would be something to talk about, something to discuss.

Finally, I think, around noon, he got hold of something. He ran home at full speed. The discovered news burned in him like a deep secret that both wanted to remain a secret and wanted to be told. He ran breathless into his house and from the threshold he was eager to tell his only reader – his wife – the sensational news he had discovered.

– What Motl? What happened?

– I know everything! I learned everything!

And when he was sure the "reader" had reached the highest level of eagerness and reacted like someone hungry for the "Extra," he would blurt out the news:
– They want to move the butcher shops. They are too close to the synagogue. Last night Yosl Funkenstein had a consultation with the mayor.
And now came the greatest socialist reportage of Motl's reporting career. In the middle of the city, facing the A-B Line [the A-B Line refers to the designation of the buildings on one perimeter of the market] (the street where the young people strolled on summer nights) and facing Hamer's Bank and Cukerman's jewelry business (the sidewalk which was the temporary exchange where Jews walked around with their canes and looked with longing for a brokerage), stood the stone memorial of the Polish poet, [Franciszek] Karpinsky. Noise was made, people hurried, they spoke and they bustled around the stone he-goat and the he-goat himself remained solid and stared. For Motl Fonya who was entirely [involved in the socialist] movement, Karpinsky in the middle of the market was something of a symbol of mockery against life. The entire Jewish city hated the stone he-goat, Karpinsky. Karpinsky became a curse word.
– A mother shouted to her son - Why do you remain standing all of a sudden like Karpinsky?

– The wagon drivers and porters at the market cursed: Stoney Karpinsky!

[Page 249]

I think, more than anyone, Motl Fonya hated Karpinsky. He thought about how to move Karpinsky from the spot, how to make a ruin of his lustrous importance. Motl, in general, did not believe that someone could stop and remain for years. One night when the city was asleep and the train that passed through the main street and caused the windows of the nearby houses to shake as usual, Motl thought that Karpinsky had stirred. This was his most sensational reporting. Pragmatic, unbelieving Jews laughed at his news, but Motl did not stop his fantastic reports. The opposite, he built them up wider and further every day and every day using commonsense, he fortified them more strongly and with more certainty. The listeners who laughed at him did not understand. They believed rigidly and he, Motl, believed in the strength of fantasy, from his fantastic stories that could even move Karpinsky from the spot. Motl is now already in the World of Truth [he has died] and, perhaps, Kolomea Jews have forgotten him. But the saying remains, that when the train shakes Karpinsky in the market, we remember the great dreamer, Motl Fonya.

And now in order to round off and end the portrait of Motl, I will in short explain that while the city was too quiet and too uneventful for him, he used the cemetery as a source of help with the news. Every Shabbos afternoon, when Jews had finished their kugel [usually a baked potato or noodle pudding or casserole] and had lain down to sleep, Motl Fonya dressed up in his Shabbos clothing and went to chase after news. The streets in the city were empty, the shops closed and Karpinsky, the "king of nothing," ruled over the stillness.

He went past Hersh Puzer's grave and from there he could see the headstone of his [Hersh's] wife, Tsipa. Hersh had lived at odds with Tsipa for all their years [together]. She had not wanted to marry an unreasonable conservative from Krakow. They were about to divorce. Now she had to consider that Hersh had been correct because the Krakow son-in-law was the pride and joy of the family. And Tsipa told it to Motl,

[Page 250]

and Motl, while he did not write on Shabbos, recorded it only in his head. It was sensational news that would shock the city.

And this was not the only sensational news that Motl brought from the cemetery. Death did not exist for him. If life was too quiet, in his fantasy death made noise, because it [death] could not bear that nothing happened, that everything would remain frozen, that nothing would move from its place.

In the 1920s, after the First World War, I saw my Uncle Motl Fonya for the last time. He already was in his deep seventies and the blinding whiteness of his beard waved with the legend of a white winter land. He also told me a good piece of news then, but one could see and feel that his fantastic world about which he had so much to tell had been somewhat destroyed.

And for a long time he could not no longer provide the noisy, clamorous news from the cemetery that had the virtue of not causing pain.

My uncle died quickly. He was joined to the rigidity of which Karpinsky was the symbol, a rigidity, that he, Motl, had hated all his life.

———

Original Footnote:

a.   From the book, A Shtot mit Yidn [A City with Jews], New York, 1943.

Translator's Footnotes:

1.   The title character in I.J. Singer's novel, Yoshe Kalb, leaves his wife and wanders as an atonement for his sins.
2.   Yona is describing Shimshon – Samson – as a strong man, a play on words because Samson was the strong man in the Torah.

———

[Page 251]

Yosl Klezmer Saved the City from a Fire[a]

by Naftali Gross

Translated by Gloria Berkenstat Freund

Once at night in Kolomea
A fire broke out, may we be spared –
The city almost went away with the smoke,
And who knows what would have, God forbid, happened,
If Yosl klezmer [musician] had not been there, –
Oh times of wonder!

Yosl stood in the middle of the marketplace,
[He] played so fervently, so strongly on his fiddle –
That the fire immediately left the roofs. –
Who knows what would have, God forbid, happened.
If Yosl klezmer had not been there, –
Oh times of wonder!

When Yosl klezmer saw the fire,
He suddenly received strength from his heart, –
Oh times of wonder!
Yosl took his fiddle from the wall, –
Who knows what would have, God forbid, happened.
If Yosl klezmer had not been there, –
Oh times of wonder!

The firemen hurry and ring the bell,
And the fire goes from corner to corner, –
Oh times of wonder!
The firemen extinguish and extinguish, one after the other,
But who knows what would have, God forbid, happened.
If Yosl klezmer had not been there, –
Oh times of wonder!

[Page 252]

Yosl stood in the middle of the marketplace,
[He] played his fiddle so ardently, so strongly, –
Oh times of wonder!
The fire immediately came down from the roofs. –
Who knows what would have, God forbid, happened.
If Yosl klezmer had not been there, –
Oh times of wonder!

The fire was seduced by the music –

[It] wandered over to Yosl at the marketplace, –
Oh times of wonder!
And [it] began to dance around in a circle. –
Who knows what would have, God forbid, happened.
If Yosl klezmer had not been there, –
Oh times of wonder!

Yosl klezmer plays in the middle of the city,
And the fire dances around Yosl in a circle, –
Oh times of wonder!
Who knows what would have, God forbid, happened.
If Yosl klezmer had not been there, –
Oh times of wonder!

And just as the fire entered the earth,
Yosl left for the wine tavern, –
Oh times of wonder!
And first Yosl played and played
Who knows what would have happened with the tavern,
If Yosl klezmer had not been there, –
Oh times of wonder!

Yosl played and drank without end,
And friends – with him; they forgot about sleep, –
Oh times of wonder!
And if they have not stopped – they are frolicking still.
Thus, thus this once happened, –
When there was a fire in Kolomea. –
Oh times of wonder!

———

Original Footnote:

a.   From the book, Yidn [Jews], New York, 1929.

———

[Page 255]

My Companions from Kolomea[a]

Translated by Gloria Berkenstat Freund

They study Torah, they read books and newspapers,
And trains come day and night from all over the world;
And what was hidden and disguised
Reveal invisible heralds every day.

A people of pure visionaries and poets!
Always seeing in dreams what is missing.
The humble dwelling place becomes a palace –
The towers and gilded minarets glow.

Wonders flower from everyone's scribbles
And enter as if invited into everyone's soul.
They even know what is happening on the planets,
And the most hidden and deepest sources become clear.
The world lies open before everyone's threshold,
But it is difficult to cross this tiny distance.

———

Original Footnote:

a.   From the book, Yidn [Jews], New York, 1929.

———

[Page 256]

Between Stopchet and Kolomea[a]

by Itzik Manger

Translated by Gloria Berkenstat Freund

Between Stopchet and Kolomea
(Oh, quiet joy of my childhood years)
My grandfather sits on the coachman's seat and is silent –
Giddy up blockhead, giddy up! And we move.

The young willows along the road,
Quiver piously and are silent –
I see an old willow bend
The moon between the branches.

"Mazel Tov [Congratulations] Grandfather!"
My grandfather is silent,
The horses go faster, faster –
I dream of blackberries and sweet cream
In a white moon–dish.

My grandfather is silent. The wind chatters
From fields, mountains and caves.
My grandfather is old, the wind is young
And has a great deal to tell.

I dream and listen. The moon is large
The roads as bright as snow –
Where are the horses? My grandfather runs
Between Stopchet and Kolomea.

———

Original Footnote:

a.   The poet, Itzik Manger, was born in Czernowitz, but his father, Hilel, was a Stopcheter [from Stopchet] (Jabłonówer) and his mother, Chava, was the daughter of Itzik Voliner, the upholsterer of Krawiecka Street, after whom the poet was named.
We publish the poem here with the poet's permission. We believe that this poem along with the poem of our Kolomea poet, Naftali Gross, may his memory be blessed, serve as the most beautiful introduction to the "Portraits" section [of this book].

Portraits

[Page 257]

Chaim Gross
(1904)

by B. Tsh.[1]

Translated by Gloria Berkenstat Freund

It can be said about the widely acknowledged and well–known sculptor, Chaim Gross, that he was without a doubt, an even greater "miracle from Kolomea" than his brother, the poet, Naftali Gross, long may he live. Actually, Chaim Gross was a resident of Kolomea only for a few years during his earliest childhood years, but the influence of the Kolomea Hasidic environment in Chaim Gross' extensive artistic creation becomes even clearer and more distinct.

[He] was born in the Carpathian village of Wolowa [Mezhgorye, Ukraine] in 1904. Chaim Gross was three or four years old when his family of many children – Chaim was his parents' 10th child – settled in Kolomea. His father, Reb Moshe, already was impoverished at that time and there was little attention given to Chaim's education. Meanwhile,

[Page 258]

the First World War had began. In the panicked and the chaotic escape from the pogrom of the Cossack invasion, Chaim alone remained a 10–year old boy alone in "a world in flames." After innumerable torments, the lonely young boy reached Budapest where he entered into an apprenticeship with a jeweler and even received the ability to begin to draw and to paint.

When the reactionary [policies] began to rage in Hungary, Chaim made his way to Vienna. There he suffered hunger and hardship until his brother, Naftali, who had emigrated to America shortly before the outbreak of the war, enabled him to come to New York in 1921.

A new world opened here for the 17–year old young man. He really had to labor very hard in order to earn his livelihood; but at the same time, he became a diligent art student at the Educational Alliance [and], later, also at other superior art schools and with relentless stubbornness and rare perseverance, Chaim reached the very important position in the art world, which he has to this day.

Chaim Gross soon received American and international prizes for his wonderful sculptures in wood, stone and bronze. He arranged frequent exhibitions, which always caused a sensation in the interested circles. His studio in Greenwich Village, in New York was always a meeting place for local and not local art critics and art dealers. The fact that he was officially invited to create a sculpture of the first Israeli president, Chaim Weizmann, shortly after the rise of the State of Israel, shows how popular Chaim Gross was across the ocean, particularly in the Jewish world.

Professor Josef Vincent Lombardo, the famous American art critic, published a large biographical–critical work (in English), Chaim Gross: Sculptor.[2] In this work we find, in passing, these remarks:

[Lombardi p. 105] "Chaim Gross's philosophy is very simple indeed. He believes that his sculpture should stir the observer's imagination and awaken in him the consciousness of form and beauty hitherto unknown to him."

[Lombardo p. 132] "To Chaim Gross, the human body is a source of abstract invention; nevertheless he always preserves

[Page 259]

some aspects of its representational character..."

[Lombardo p. 221] "Chaim Gross is an artist of unusual creative imagination and productivity..."

[Lombardi p. 222] "...new subjects will in turn suggest new forms and only through this process of creative evolution will he continue to produce original work of indisputable artistic merit."

The influence that the Kolomea Hasidic environment left forever on his artistic spirit [is evident in] Chaim Gross' observation in his conversation with a New York art critic:

"I was raised in the joy of the Creator and in spiritual pleasure. I do not understand the artists who are ruled by productivity and the grotesque. Why should the artist behave like a corpse as long as he is alive and creates?"

Translator's footnote:

1. These initials belong to Baruch Tshuvinsky whom the editor, Shlomo Bickel thanks in his preface to the yizkor book.
2. The following quotes have not been translated from the Yiddish text, but are taken directly from Professor Lombardo's English–language book, Chaim Gross: Sculptor, Dalton House, Inc. 1942, 247 pp.; the book includes photos of and comments on Gross's sculpture up to that date. A "Biographical History" chapter starting on p.73 describes Gross's early life and influences as told to the author by Chaim and his older brother Naftali.

Coordinator's note:

1. Chaim Gross drew and contributed the title page drawing to the yizkor book. He died in 1991 and was buried in Mount Lebanon Cemetery in Brooklyn–Queens NY.
    The Renee and Chaim Gross Foundation maintains a repository and display of his work in NYC and can be reached at www.rcgrossfoundation.org.

The Poet Naftali Gross
(1897–1956)

by Shlomo Bikel [Solomon Bickel]

Translated by Gloria Berkenstat Freund

Naftali Gross was born in Kolomea on the 10th of Tevet 5657 (January 1897).

He spent his early years in Slobodka–Lesna where for several years his father, Reb Moshe, was the treasurer of the sawmill not far from the Jewish colony and agricultural school named for Baron Hirsch.

At first Gross studied with private melamdim [religious teachers] and with his father, later in khederim [religious primary schools] and in the Polish school in Kolomea. He prepared the gymnazie [secondary school] course privately. Gross began to write poems at 12–13 years of age. The Hasidic and folk stories that he had heard at home and had read in storybooks influenced Gross' poetry.

Gross left for Canada in 1913 and from there came to New York. At first he worked as a typesetter in a printing shop. In 1917 he became a teacher in the schools of the National Workers Union; later – over the course of 15 years – in the Arbeter Ring [Workman's Circle] schools and middle school. For a short time he also was teacher in the Sholem Aleichem Schools.

[Page 260]

Gross debuted in the Keneder Adler [Canadian Eagle] in 1913 with his poems. In 1915 he began to publish poems, stories and essays in the newspapers and journals: Fraye Arbeter Shtime [Free Workers Voice], Onheyb [Beginning], Oyfkum [Rise], Velt Ayn, Velt Oys [World In, World   Out], Zukunft [Future], Kunds [Customers], Veker [Waker] Yidish   Kemfer [Jewish Fighter] Di   Zeit [The   Times]. Forverts [Forward], Der   Fraynd [The   Friend], Tog [Day], Morgn Zshurnal [The Morning Journal],

Kinderland [Children's   Land], Kinder–Velt [Children's   World], Kinder–Zshurnal [Children's Journal], Indzel [Island], Studio,   Epokhe [Epoch]   – all   in   New   York; Der   Tsvayg [The Branch], Filozofia [Philosophy], Renesans [Renaissance]   –   in   London; Kritik [Criticism]   in Vienna. In 1943 Gross became a worker at the Forverts. He published his work, Mayselekh un Mesholim [Little Stories and Parables] over the course of 1946–1952. In 1918 he translated the first of three parts of [Heinrich] Heine's Buch fun Leider [Book of Poems] (Yiddish Publishing House); of Edgar Lee Masters, of Edward Arlington Robinson, Kahlil Gibran, and other American poets. With Avrom Reizen he translated poems by Reb Solomon Ibn Gabirol for Dr. A. Ginzburg's Poets   and   Thinkers   in   the   Middle   Ages.   Gross   edited   the   journal, Kinder–Ring [Children's Ring], published by the Teachers Union of the Arbeter Ring in 1929–1930. In 1936 he edited the weekly children's section of Tog; in the 1930s [he edited] the children's and women's   section   of Fraynd,   New   York.   In   book   form: Psalmen [Psalms], Lider   un Meditatsies [Poems   and   Meditations],   New   York; Lider [Poems], New   York, 1920; Der Veyzer Reyter [The White Rider],

[Page 261]

poems and ballads, New York 1925; Yidn [Jews], poems and ballads, New York, 1929; Eugene Debs (a story about a man), New York, 1933: Vladimir Medem (the legends of the Jewish workers movement), a biography, New York, 1938; Mayses [Stories], with drawings by Chaim Gross, New York, 1935 ([later in] Hebrew [translated] by Shimshon Melcer, Tel Aviv, 5710 [1950]; Yidn, second book of poems and ballads, New York, 1938; Di Finf Megiles [The Five Scrolls], Yiddish with an introduction and explanations for Eykhe [Book of Lamentations], New York, 1936; Tehilim [Psalms], Yiddish with an introduction and Hebrew text, New York, 1948; Shir haShirim [Song of Songs], Yiddish, Yosem Tsvi Publishing House, Rio de Janero, 1949.

Although Gross' books of poem were warmly received by the critics, some of his writing comrades had complaints as to why "in the time of revolutions and barricades," he was occupied with religious themes (Di Psalmen) and too much with the shtetl [town] (the two Yidn books). Years later, the same writers changed their opinion toward life and toward Yiddish life and turned to Naftali Gross' themes.

"He was shy and reserved," his poet–comrade, Efroim Auerbach, writes about Naftali Gross, "but in his shyness was a spiritual strength, which did not bend nor bow, but with the most internal light illuminated himself."

This strength that shone from Gross' dark eyes with his tenderness and with his soulful relationship to people, along with his naivety and simplicity, made him beloved to everyone who knew him.

The Second World War and the Jewish catastrophe in Europe severely affected Gross and destroyed his health.

Notes left on Gross' writing table, had written on them – "If only I had known all of the Kolomea Jews, the wonderful figures, people and types who each in his way affected Jewish life there in the city, I would have tried to save as many as possible of the magnificent people, but I did not know them."

In the summer of 1948, Naftali Gross suffered his first severe heart attack and in June 1954, the second one. From then on he had to give up the greater part of his work little by little.

[Page 262]

In 1955 Gross' book, Mayselekh un Mesholim, was published, from which he still received much satisfaction. The book was very warmly received by the critics and readers.

However, he did not live to see the completion of the work on the Kolomea Yizkor Book. Sunday, the 8th of April, 1956 (27th of Nisan 5716), around two o'clock in the morning, Naftali Gross breathed out his illustrious soul.

Speech Given at his Funeral
Tuesday, the 10th of April 1956

Once at night in Kolomea
A fire broke out, may we be spared –
The city almost went away with the smoke,
And who knows what would have, God forbid, happened,
If Josl klezmer [musician] had not been there, –
A time of wonder!

Josl stood in the middle of the market,
[He] played so fervently, so strongly on his fiddle –
That the fire immediately left the roofs. –
Who knows what would have, God forbid, happened.
If Josl klezmer had not been there, –
A time of wonder!

Josl klezmer, the alter ego of the poet Naftali Gross, was there and in the times of wonder, served the city and its wonderful Jews with his poems.

And as I stand now at the coffin of my beloved comrade, friend and fellow townsman, Naftali Gross, I see the shadows of our common holy community embrace the deceased and envelop him with love and thanks.

They come, the shadows, one by one – the rabbi and the magid [preacher], the respectable middle class man and the impoverished man, the bride and the old servant, the old tailor and the fiddle player – now they all come, as we say good–bye to their celebrator, their immortalizer in beauty; they come to welcome him with honor, come to console his family; they also come to give us, his comrades and friends, a word of consolation and to the

[Page 263]

entire Jewish literature, which has lost one of the most respected representatives of the modern Yiddish poem, lost him at the age of barely 59, lost him just at the blossoming of his creativity.

In the 30 years of his poetic and Biblical translation activity, Naftali Gross was one of the Pleiades of Yiddish, Galicianer poets, who remained a complete and utter romantic; I mean a poet whose romanticism was classic and did not exhibit the foolishness of all of the divisions and fractures of tragic mockery and the grotesque that was so characteristic of Jewish singers in Galicia.

He was our Naftali Gross, the calm Galicianer of our literature, who never had an unfriendly argument with the images and visions from the old home that accompanied him; he was right with his God in his creations, always welcoming with piety the poetic gift with which he was gifted. He was the poet who created wonder by forming the same happy calm with which his most beautiful hero and alter ego, Josl klezmer, deceived the fire in the middle of the market on the strings of his fiddle and saved the city from a fire.

The poet, Naftali Gross, was a rare artistic portraitist and artistically painting a portrait for him meant tearing out the image from the surrounding noise, smoothing over his own unhappy distress and transforming it into a monument of calm and beauty.

Naftali Gross left us a magnificent garden of created calm and beauty. This poetic beauty, whose creator was our dearest deceased, will blossom for as long as Yiddish lives. And Yiddish, the Yiddish poem, will live eternally. The Yiddish poem will never be erased from the soul of the Jewish people, never be erased from the spirit of our people.

[Page 264]

The Musical Child Prodigies

The Brothers Sigmund
(1900-1952)

and Emanuel Feuermann
(1902-1942)

by Dr. Isaac Shchor

Translated by Gloria Berkenstat Freund

Among my relatives, who mainly were butchers, was one named Mendl Henigsberg. Mendl Henigsberg's daughter married the musician Meir Feuermann.

Meir Feuermann was a gifted player of several musical instruments, but his two sons, Sigmund, born in Kolomea in 1900, and Emanuel, born two years later in 1902, achieved fame.

At three years old, Sigmund already was playing the violin; at four years he tried to read musical notes and at five he appeared in public as a violinist at the Kolomea Zionist Women's Union, "Rachel."

To be able to perfect his wonder-child in music, the father moved his family to Vienna. In Vienna Sigmund studied with the music professors Roze, Feist and Shepczik and at age eight he gave his first violin concert in the Austrian capital.

In 1911, at age 11, Sigmund had colossal success with a violin concert with the London Philharmonic Society, which was under the patronage of the English king.

From London, Sigmund Feuermann's triumph over Europe and America began. He came to America

[Page 265]

in 1925 and had a great success there with his concerts. He also became a teacher at the New York Music Academy.

Sigmund spent five years in America. In 1930 he returned to his parents in Vienna.

However, he only benefitted from his virtuoso glory in Vienna for a few more years. The difficult pre-Nazi and then the horrible Nazi years immediately arrived. It should be understood that there could be no talk about appearing publicly as a musician under the Nazis.

One day before the deportation of the Vienna Jews, thanks to the intervention of his younger brother Emanuel, who then lived in Zurich, Sigmund and his parents crossed the Austrian-Swiss border.

Sigmund only spent four months in Switzerland and he emigrated from there to Eretz-Yisroel. And in Eretz-Yisroel it was apparent that the glory of the once famed wonder-child had been harmed considerably.

Sigmund took a position as music professor at the American University in Beirut, but the growing hatred by the Arabs forced him to return to Tel Aviv.

Sigmund Feuermann's last years in Tel Aviv were sad and then tragic. There were few concerts, few lectures, little income and little peace with his wife.

One day at the beginning of 1952 he became paralyzed; he lost his ability to speak. Sigmund died several months later.

2.

Emanuel (Munya), the younger brother of Sigmund, reached even more glory, but he was cut down at a younger age.

Emanuel was a cello virtuoso. He studied music with his father and with Professor Anton Walter. Emanuel gave his first public concert at the age of 11 as a soloist with the Vienna

Symphonic Orchestra. Emanuel later studied with the well-known musician Julius Klengel in Leipzig.

[Page 266]

At age 16 Munya Feuermann himself was a professor at the conservatory in Cologne. And it did not take long for him to lead the cello division of the Berlin Music Academy and strengthen his name in Europe as one of the most important cello virtuosos.

In 1934 Munya Feuermann gave a series of concerts in Eretz-Yisroel and evoked great enthusiasm. Then he lived in Vienna for several years and from there he traveled around for concerts in France, England and America.

In 1938, when Hitler entered Austria, Munya Feuermann settled in America permanently. He appeared in many cities and played with many orchestras with great success. In 1941 the 39-year old cello virtuoso became the leader of the chamber music department at the Curtis Institute in Philadelphia. A year later Munya Feuermann became ill, went through an operation and died at the early age of 40.

The Nationalist Educator of Two Generations

Laibel Taubes
(1863–1933)

by Meir Henish, Tel Aviv

Translated by Gloria Berkenstat Freund

Laibel (Arya Leib) Taubes was born on the 19th of Adar 5624 (1863). His father, Reb Yitzhak Ayzyk Taubes, was the rabbi in Otynia and his grandfather was the famous gaon [scholar] and Iasi Rabbi, Reb Ahron Moshe Taubes, the author of [a book of] questions and answers, Karnei Re'em [The Horns of the Wild Ox]. His mother was descended from well–known righteous men, back to the Rozhiner [Rebbe] and the Baal–Shem [Tov] [founder of Hasidism].

Even as a very young man, Laibel Taubes already had begun to feel that besides [concern for] the after life, we Jews lacked the feeling and comprehension

[Page 267]

of the "pintele Yid" [essential feeling of Jewishness]. And thus he came to Zionism before the Zionist movement. At the beginning of 1890, as one of the first 10 pioneers, he began to work on publicity for the Jewish national idea. He sent an appeal ".And the Jews according to their writing, and according to their language," [Esther 8:9] in which he declared the necessity of a Jewish newspaper. And soon he also created the first Yiddish newspapers in Galicia – Di Yidishe Folkszeitung [The Jewish Peoples Newspaper] and the Folks Freynd [People's Friend], both in Kolomea, and the HaAm – Dos Folk [The People or The Nation]. The first Zionist generation drew its basic ideas of Jewish nationalism and Zionism from these newspapers. Taubes also participated in the first National Jewish Conference in Lemberg in 1891. He also immediately stood in the service of Theodor Herzl and of his political Zionism and translated Herzl's Judenstat [State of the Jews] into Yiddish.[1] Herzl greatly valued Taubes' work and engaged him as a speaker and propagandist for Zionism.

Thanks to his rabbinical background and traditional way of life, as well as his great knowledge of Yiddish, Taubes was very successful with the middle–class Jewish circles that were then the majority of Galician–Bukoviner Jewry. His sermons and speeches particularly inspired the young generation Zionistically in the Jewish cities and towns and many of those who were drawn by the spirit of the speeches, are today in the ranks of Jewish leaders and activists in the Jewish centers of various countries. Taubes spoke at more than a thousand Jewish people's gatherings in almost every city and town in Galicia and Bukovina before an audience of more than a quarter million Jews.

Taubes lived for several years in Chernowitz [Chernivtsi], where he published the Judishe Vokhnblat [Yiddish Weekly Newspaper]. At the beginning of the First World War he and his family moved to Vienna and he also was active there as a Zionist activist and speaker, particularly in eastern Jewish circles. In Vienna, thanks to his initiative and work,

[Page 268]

the union Zion was created with the public Jewish library, around which gathered the Zionists of the eastern countries who lived in Vienna. Taubes was a delegate to many Zionist Congresses and also took an active part in the Zionist national political work in Austria. He also was a candidate to the Reichstag on the Zionist side during the parliamentary elections.

In addition to many Zionist appeals and brochures, Taubes published the minutes of the Katowice conference in Hebrew in a new edition with a preface as well as a book on Talmudic elements in Yiddish proverbs (in Yiddish) and Dos Judishe Jahrbuch fur Austreich [The Jewish Yearbook for Austria] (together with Chaim Bloch, in German). During recent years Taubes was an official with Keren Kayemet [Jewish National Fund].

Laibel Taubes' two sons, Dr. Dovid and Dr. Yisroel, live in Tel Aviv. The youngest [his third] son, the Yiddish poet, Yakov Shmuel, is a resident of America.

Coordinator's note:

1.   This information about Taubes' Yiddish translation of Der Judenstaat may be in error. Joshua Shanes writes: "Taubes himself recognized that even traditional Jews tended to view Yiddish as inherently less sophisticated than German or Polish. That is why he deliberately chose to transliterate Herzl's Der Judenstaat rather than translate it outright in order to preserve a sense of seriousness and realism that he hoped Herzl's status would invoke... [Taubes, according to Gershon Bader] fearing that had he produced a true Yiddish translation, Galician Jews would have viewed it as 'laughable, to treat in jargon, such a deep diplomatic question as the founding of a Jewish state.'"

2. p. 133 in Shanes, Joshua, Diaspora Nationalism and Jewish Identity in Habsburg Galicia, Cambridge University Press, 2012. See the book's index for more information about Taubes and his work.

The Last Kolomea Rabbi

Rabbi Joseph Lau

by G.P.

Translated by Gloria Berkenstat Freund

The rabbi, Reb Joseph Lau was born and raised in Lemberg [Lvov, Poland from 1918 to 1939; L'viv, Ukraine from 1991...]. He was the son of Reb Hirsh Leib Lau, of the respected residents of Lemberg and was descended both on his father's and mother's sides from great rabbinical ancestry. Reb Joseph Lau's brother Moshe was a son–in–law of the Vizhnitzer [Vyzhnytsia] Rebbe and rabbi of the Bukowiner city of Shutz (Sutshava [Suceava]), and in the years before the disaster in the Hungarian city of Eperjes. Reb Joseph Lau's brother–in–law, Reb Mordekhai Fogelman, is today the Rabbi in Kiryat Motzkin near Haifa.

As a boy, the future Kolomea Rabbi showed great genius and was entrusted with the office of rabbi by such great Talmud scholars of that time as the Lemberger Rabbi, Reb Yitzhak Shmelkis, the Berezhany Rabbi, Reb Sholem Mordekhai haKohen Shwardron and the Chernowitz [Chernivtsi] Rabbi Reb Benyamin haKohen Weis.

[Page 269]

In 1911 Rabbi Joseph Lau married the daughter of the rich banker and mill owner, Reb Yakov Beidaf, in Kolomea. The young son–in–law was busy in his father–in–law's large business during the first years and the Jewish community only knew him as a great scholar and a [teacher] of Talmudic lessons for young men in the small Vizhnitzer synagogue.

After the First World War, Reb Joseph Lau was drawn into communal work. The Agudas Yisroel [Orthodox anti–Zionists] was founded then and Reb Joseph Lau appeared at its head as a spokesperson and leader, and leader of the fight against Zionism in Kolomea. He himself was an exceptional speaker and a first–class organizer. The pious young men and a considerable number of the Hasidic middleclass gathered around Reb Joseph Lau. He created a yeshiva [religious secondary school] and founded a Bais–Yakov [Orthodox school organization] and Bnos Yakov [daughters of Jakob] School and made Kolomea a bit of an Aguda fortress. Rabbi Lau's main co–worker was the lawyer, Dr. Ben–Tzion Fesler, who helped him organize the pious talisim [prayer shawls] weavers and created a union of Poalei Emuni Yisroel [Religious Workers of Israel].

The bank of his father–in–law, Reb Yakov Beidaf, no longer existed then and Reb Joseph Lau and his brothers–in–law carried on business by exporting poultry, which went from bad to worse because of [Polish Finance Minister Wladyslaw] Grabski's tax penalties against Jews.

Around 1930 the city began to talk of hiring a rabbi. The rabbinical seat in Kolomea had remained vacant for over 20 years since the Rabbi, Reb Gedaliah Schmelkes left the city in 1907 and returned angrily to Przemysl.

The Agudah leaders, among them the Lipa brothers and Avraham Shmuel Heller, Dr. Ben–Tzion Fesler and Leibush Krys, negotiated about bringing the Smapolner Rabbi.

This was learned by the Zionist circles and Reb Yona Ashkenazi, one of the leaders of Mizrakhi [religious Zionists], thought out a plan of how to prevent Agudah from getting its rabbi and neutralizing the Agudas work of Reb Joseph Lau.

The Mizrakhi leader Yona Ashkenazi offered Reb Joseph Lau the rabbinate on the condition that he not be politically active. The representatives of the Zionist parties agreed to Yona Ashkenazi's proposal and Reb Joseph Lau also agreed.

On another day, the Zionist parties began to make efforts in support of their candidate. The Agudah was surprised. It did not expect Mizrakhi to put forward the

[Page 270]

candidacy of its sharpest opponent. The Agudas Yisroel split and some of the leaders held stubbornly to the candidacy of the Sampolner Rabbi. However, the majority went over to Reb Joseph Lau.

The kehile [organized Jewish community] council unanimously chose Reb Joseph Lau as rabbi. After an interval of 23 years, Kolomea again had a rabbinical authority, who was worthy to sit on the seat of such scholars as Reb Hillel Lichtenshtein and Reb Gedalia Schmekles.

The city was very satisfied with the new rabbi. Rabbi Lau was a big hit with his Polish speeches at state celebrations and even more with his sermons at der Hoykher Shul [the Great Synagogue] every Shabbos haGadol [Sabbath before Passover] and Shabbos Shuvah [Sabbath between Rosh Hashanah and Yom Kippur]. Rabbi Lau also was an exceptional organizer in the area of Jewish education and of teaching among adults.

All Jews saw their spiritual leader in Rabbi Lau and he "found favor with the multitude of his brethren: he sought the good of his people..." [Book of Esther 10:3].

Eliezer Unger talks about Rabbi Lau during the Nazi time in his book, Zikhor [Memories] (Tel Aviv, 5705 [1945], pages 74 and on):

"One of the most frightful edicts during the first months of the Nazi occupation was the edict that Jews must tear out the headstone at the cemetery and pave the streets with them. Hundreds of old and new cemeteries in Poland were destroyed as a result of this edict. I remember that day during the 10 Days of Repentance 5702 [days between Rosh Hashanah and Yom Kippur 1942], when the Gestapo entered the office of the chairman of the Judenrat [Jewish council] and demanded several hundred workers to rip out the headstones. The head of the Judenrat informed the local rabbi, Rabbi Joseph Lau, about the order. The members of the Judenrat assembled on the same day in order to consult on what to do. The majority of those assembled wanted to oppose the order. Most argued: no matter what happens to us, we will not desecrate the graves of our parents. But Rabbi Lau declared that the sin does not belong to the three, of whom it was said ya'avor v'al ye'hareg [guiding Jewish principle of "transgress and do not be killed"]."

Those assembled listened to the rabbi's words with grief and pain. A fast was called for the next day and –

"We all stood around the graves and the rabbi among us. Before we began to tear out the headstones, the rabbi went to one of the older graves and said approximately thus: "Sacred graves, sacred bones! Forgive us for desecrating your honor. It is an edict on us to desecrate the sacredness of your

[Page 271]

graves and we must carry out the edict so that our children and grandchildren will remain alive. We ask mercy from the Divine Throne on the people of Israel on whom tragedy has been poured..."

And raising his trembling hands, the rabbi called out: "God is my witness, we are anusim [Jews forced to abandon Judaism]." The rabbi could not finish his words. He began weeping and everyone wept with him. And then the rabbi, with tears in his eyes and with trembling hands, went to tear out the first headstone. The heads of the kehile [organized Jewish community] helped him."

At the end of the year 5702 [1942], Rabbi Lau together with other Jews were sent to the Belzec death camp.

It was said that on the way to the train station, the rabbi found himself walking near the leader of the left Poalei–Zion [Marxist Zionists], Yitzhak Shlomo Shmoys, whom everyone in the city called "Rabbi Shmoys."

Rabbi Lau is supposed to have said to Rabbi Shmoys, "You see, all these years, I went one way and you went another way and today we are all going on the same path. We are all Jews and we are all doing the will of the Holy One, blessed be He."

Rabbi Josef Lau, may the memory of a righteous man be blessed, was the last Kolomea rabbi. He sat on the rabbinical seat for 12 years, from around Shavous 5690 (1930) until his death al Kiddush haShem [in the sanctification of God's name – as a martyr] at the end of 5702 [1942].

Only one of Rabbi Josef Lau's sons, Shmuel Yitzhak Lau, survived. He now lives in Tel Aviv.

Coordinator's note:

1. Based on what is stated about his family, we can assume that Rabbi Joseph Lau was briefly the uncle of Israel Meir Lau who was 8 years old when freed from Buchenwald, and went to Israel in 1945 where he lived with his Aunt Bella –Joseph Lau's sister–and her husband, Uncle Mordecai Vogelman in Kiryat Motzkin. Rabbi Israel Meir Lau was Chief Ashkenazic Rabbi of Israel from 1993 to 2003 and published an autobiography in Hebrew in 2000: "Do Not Raise a Hand Against the Boy."

The Rebbe-Bokher
(188? -1917)

Translated by Gloria Berkenstat Freund

The Rebbe-Bokher [Hasidic rabbi who was a young man] was one of the most colorful pious-Jewish personas in Kolomea. He was the Rebbe, Reb Mordekhai Nadverner's grandson and himself a rebbe in Kolomea. He was called the Rebbe-Bokher because he began praven tish [led a communal meal at which a rebbe's followers are present] before he was married.

The Rebbe-Bokher was a people's rebbe. His Hasidim were completely from the poor. The Rebbe himself was an impressive figure, a handsome man, a sharp nay-sayer with wonderful commonsense, evoked admiration on one side and, from the other side, considerable contempt on the part of the Hasidic spiritual world and on the part of scholars and rich men.

[Page 272]

Legends about the Rebbe-Bokher spread while he was still alive. One legend saw in him a great philanthropist, who would give the small pidyones [gifts given to a Hasidic rebbe after meeting with him] he received from his poor Hasidim to the needy, and others saw in him a kind of cynic who made fun of the world and his Hasidim and of himself.

Much was written about Rebbe-Bokher, who stimulated the fantasy of the city dweller, and each writer provided his legend. (See: Shlomo Bikel in his Shtot mit Yidn [City with Jews], New York, 1943; Meir Henish in Reshimes [Lists], volume 2, Tel Aviv, 5717 [1957], Avraham Yitzhak Braver in his essay, Kolomea, haTzofe [The Observer], Tel Aviv, 5714 [1954] and Moshe Rat in Reshimes, Tel Aviv, 5717.)

Each writer gives his own version and each one has a remarkable amount of good and pertinent stories to tell about and in the name of the Rebbe-Bokher.

We will provide only a few facts about the Rebbe-Bokher, as they are told by Levi Grebler who was present at the wedding of the Rebbe-Bokher and knew his family, and several characteristic lines from the pen of the writer, Meir Henish, because we think that they come the closest to objectivity.

Levi Grebler writes from Tel Aviv: "Summer 1903, a large rabbinical wedding took place at Leib Zenenreich's in the large inn at Jagielonska Street opposite Mota Pesakh's house – a wedding that had never before been seen by the city. Everyone ran to watch the wedding. Reb Mordekhiale Nadverner made the wedding of his grandson.

"Several days later, a large plank bed with furniture pulled up in Reitana Street, near the house of the widow Miriam Shneier, and a young man, a handsome one, a tall person with a brown beard and with a high fur hat on his head and a kaftan with a velvet collar and velvet cuffs on the sleeves, stood near the porters and told them how they should carry the furniture into the house and not damage it.

"Here I will list the Rebbe-Bokher's first Hasidim, in addition to me and my playmates: Ayzyk Frid, a son of the grain merchant, Reb Shmuel Frid; Chaim Becher, Moshe Yehuda Becher's son, and Moshe Fan (today in America). The rebbe's adult Hasidim were: Dutsia Bandel and his son Gershon, who has been in America since 1909; Khaskl Fliker, the butcher Hersh Shofter, who was called

[Page 273]

"Hersz Noz [nose]" or "Hersh Pan [Mister] Kolomea"; the shtreiml [fur hat worn by members of some Hasidic sects] maker, Avraham Hersh Cygelaub, Tevl the fisherman, Ayzyk the deaf one, who sold butter; Borukh the baker, who was called Labik-Baker; Hersh the porter, Itshe the coachman's father (in America since 1911); the butcher, Henekh Szifter and Pinya the soda-water carrier.

"As the Rebbe already had Hasidim, he rented two small rooms from Dutsia Bandel for a men's synagogue with a women's. The Rebbe was a good singer and Torah reader. He himself would pray at the reading desk and it was a pleasure to listen to him. On Saturday evenings he liked to play his violin.

"No rich Jews nor Talmudic scholars crossed the Rebbe's threshold, although a considerable number of them lived near him. The Rebbe-Bokher only acquired one well-to-do Hasid. This was a Jew with the name Zegenreich, an insurance agent from the Adriatika Society. He would visit the Rebbe for Havdalah [concluding Sabbath ritual] and the Rebbe played Gut Vokh [good week] for him on his violin. Zegenreich would leave a nice gift for him and Cuban cigars for the entire week. The Rebbe also smoked a large, beautiful amber pipe. Many women would come to the Rebbe for remedies and ask for a healing for an illness. Often, one would hear crying from women who came to ask the Rebbe for the salvation of sick children.

"Later, in the years before the First World War, the Rebbe-Bokher lived better. He bought a house on the Klebanye, near Yona Zager's talisim [prayer shawl] factory.

"The Rebbe had four children – three daughters and one son, Meirl. The Rebbe was often seen strolling near his house, speaking with Jews as well as Christians. The Germans spoke German with him. The Rebbe did not interfere in politics, not even at elections. When I came home from the First World War, I did not meet the Rebbe. He had died during the time of the war. Many of his Hasidim dispersed, mostly to America. Others died. The rebbitizin [rabbi's wife] married her oldest daughter to the son of a rabbi. The second daughter married the son of Zayde Landman, may he rest in peace, a large cloth merchant in the city.

[Page 274]

The Rebbe-Bokher's son, Meir, who was supposed to be his father's successor, turned from Yidishkeit [a Jewish way of life] after the premature death of the Rebbe; he became a communist. He evacuated from Kolomea with the Soviet Army and was murdered on the road by Nazi bombs."

* * *

The writer, Meir Henish, relates in his memoirs, that –

"The Rebbe-Bokher did not exalt himself over his Hasidim, who were all common people. He maintained his folksiness and behaved simply and modestly. He prayed more and commented on the Torah less. He had a sense of humor and instead of miracles and tales of wonder, his Hasidim spoke of his witticisms and sharp jokes."

According to Dr. Avraham Yakov Brawer, the very exuberant humor that the Rebbe used with his Hasidim he did not use with his own wife, the rebbitzin [rabbi's wife]. He constantly quarreled with her and he cursed her: "May you live through hard times in this world and in the other." And his words came true, because after his death, she endured hardships. Before his death, he also issued a decree for her that every erev Shabbos [Friday night] she should go to his oyel [tomb] at the cemetery and bless the [Shabbat] candles. And this unfortunate woman carried out his will, she went to the grave in the heaviest downpours and frosty blizzards, when no person was seen on the street.

The Zionist Veteran
Dr. Shlomo Rozenhek
(1862-1934)

by T.M.

Translated by Gloria Berkenstat Freund

The Folks-Doktor [people's doctor] Shlomo Rozenhek was a veteran of the Zionist movement in Galicia and the symbol of Zionism in Kolomea. He was the senior delegate from Kolomea to the First Zionist Congress in Basel (the younger of the two delegates was Peysie Zinger's son, Shlomo Zinger, then still a student at the Juridical faculty in Lemberg.

[Page 275]

During the first years of the Zionist Congress, when there was a quiet and also half-public quarrel between [Theodor] Herzl and the Hovevei Zion [Lovers of Zion] movement under the leadership of the Tarnow lawyer, Dr. Avraham Zalc, Dr. Shlomo Rozenhek was on the side of Dr. Herzl and Kolomea was a political-Zionist fortress. Dr. Rozenhak was a member of the broader shareholder's committee and Herzl's close co-worker in Galicia.

Dr. Shlomo Rozenhek had Dr. Herzl's Judenstaat [Jewish State], which accidentally fell into his hands, to thank for his Zionist convictions.

Dr. Rozenhek writes about this in his essay, "Why did we go to the First Zionist Congress?" (1922):

"I already was politically active as a student in university. During my time as a student in Vienna, I was a German national, and as I began my medical practice in Kolomea, I became a Polish national. At the end of the year 1896, doubts about assimilation stole into me, mainly because I had read Judenstaat.

"In 1897, I was sent as a delegate to the first Zionist Congress in Basel by the union, Yishuv Eretz Yisroel [Land of Israel Settlement], to which I belonged only for philanthropic reasons. I traveled to Basel more because of Switzerland than because of the Congress. On the way I met my childhood friend, Dr. M.T. Shnirer (in our joint time of study in Vienna, Shnirer, who traveled to Basel together with Professor Maks Mandelshtam, had not succeeded in drawing me in as a member of the student union, Kadimah [Onward]). The conversation with Dr. Shnirer awakened strange feelings in me that grew stronger and more positive after I became acquainted with Dr. Theodor Herzl in Basel.

"After the First Zionist Congress I changed completely spiritually. Coming home to Kolomea, I became one of the most passionate Zionists. At a large people's gathering I

[Page 276]

evoked such enthusiasm among the young gymnazie students that they enrolled as a body as members of the Zionist union, Beis Yisroel [House of Israel]. As a result, Kolomea became the center of Zionist life in Galicia. This Zionist centrality lasted until the end of 1901.”

Dr. Rozenhek did not exaggerate anything in his report about his own great contribution to the rise of Zionist work in Kolomea.

For all the years, Zionism in Kolomea remained identified with the name, Dr. Shlomo Rozenhek. During the first 20 years after Basel, Dr. Rozenhek was the active stimulating power of Zionist work. Later, when he grew older and younger strength arose, Dr. Rozenhek, until his death in 1934, was the respected symbol of Zionism in the city.

From a report that Mikhal Hazelkorn published in the Lemberger Togblat [Daily Newspaper] (28th September, 1922) about the celebration of Dr. Rozenhek's 60th birthday, we extract several points about the celebrant's devoted and self-sacrificing work for Zionism in Kolomea and in Galicia.

At the celebration, representatives from all Zionist parties appeared and all unanimously spoke about Dr. Rozenhek as Herzl's first friend in Galicia, about Dr. Rozenhek the co-founder of the Colonial Bank (Dr. Rozenhek's signature was on the shares of the bank), about Dr. Rozenhek's propaganda trips through Galicia and Bukovina on behalf of Zionism and to the harm of his own large medical practice, about Dr. Rozenhek, the president of the kehile during the most difficult time of the Ukrainian regime and president of the national council during the no less difficult time of the Romanian occupation, about Dr. Rozenhek, the Joint [Distribution Committee] activist and doctor at the Jewish hospital, about Dr. Rozenhek's earnings for Keren Kayemet [Jewish National Fund] and Keren Hayesod [The Foundation Fund – United Israel Appeal] and for the maintenance of the Hebrew School.

In a word, there was no corner of Zionist and Jewish national work in the city that was not connected with Dr. Rozenhek's work or with the prestige of Dr. Rozenhek's name.

[Page 277]

Dr. Shlomo Rozenhek died in 1934 in Lemberg after an operation in a hospital there. His remains were brought to Kolomea, where he was buried. Dr. Rozenhek's funeral was one of the largest funerals in the history of Jewish Kolomea.

The Creator of the Religion Yirat Elohim[1]

Moshe Yakov Schwerdscharf
(1858-1922)

by M. A. Shulwas, Chicago

Translated by Gloria Berkenstat Freund

Moshe Yakov Schwerdscharf was born in Bilgorai near Lublin on the 2nd of Tevet 5618 [19 December 1857] (beginning of 1858). He was descended from a rich and illustrious family. His father from his great grandfather, Reb Mordekhai Hajlpern from Kaidan, was a brother-in-law of the Vilna Gaon [genius] and, on his mother's side, he was a descendent of the Hokhem Tzvi, the famous rabbi from Amsterdam.

Our family legends still circulate today about Moshe Yakov's brilliance and about his clear commonsense. It appears that he also had capabilities as a painter. It is said that when he was a boy, he would cook eggs in coffee and would with a needle engrave on the brown area [of the eggshells] in miniature and with great accuracy faces of those close to him. One of the lords from whom Moshe Yakov's father, Reb Dovid Tevil, would lease a whiskey distillery wanted to send the boy to an art academy. However, his pious parents would not hear of it.

When Moshe Yakov was 20 years old, he married Sura Hirsz of Kolomea, a daughter of Shaltiel Ayzyk haLevi Hirsz, of a prestigious Kolomea family. Moshe Yakov settled in Kolomea, where his family remained forever. He wandered all over the world, but he would constantly return to his family.

[Page 278]

At first, Moshe Yakov was a merchant, a rich man. But, as his head did not lay in commerce, he lost his possessions and almost always lived in need. In 1895-1897 he was in Budapest where he apparently did physical labor and lived in great poverty. At the inn in which he lived, he did not even have his own room. Despite this, he wrote his small book, Daas LeNevonim [Knowledge for the Wise], a commentary on Ethics of the Fathers.

Moshe Yakov returned to Kolomea in 1898. It is certain that he also was in Kolomea in 1900, 1906 and 1909, because he published several of his small books there. His three children were also born to him in Kolomea: a son Shaltiel, a daughter Chava Raitsa, who later lived with her family in Bilgoraj, and the youngest daughter, Ryvka Chana, who lived with her mother in Kolomea. I do not know where Moshe Yakov spent his later years. It appears that in 1919, he was in Krakow because he published his, Birkat Hamazon Hakatzar [Short Grace after Meals], according to religious prayer Halakhot Tefilah [Laws of Prayer] of the Rambam. Around 1921 he came to Warsaw, old and sick but still full of great plans. His dream was to prompt the non-Jewish world to adopt a new religion whose basis would be the Sheva Mitzvot B'Nei Noakh [seven Noahide Laws]. For this purpose, he published a pamphlet of 72 sides with the name Emuna Hakduma [Ancient Religion] with a title page in Hebrew, Polish, German, English, French and Russian. The Hebrew version is: "This Hebrew book contains the holy and pure religion of the people called The Fear of God, the believers of which will be called The Fearers of God. I beseech those who find interest in the religious question in this book to translate it into all languages, and I hope that it will provide you with pleasure and satisfaction."

We also see that he gave the believers of the new religion a name, Yerai Elohim [God-fearing people]. In the introduction he asserts that this is not a new religion, but he wants to lead all of humanity to a pure belief and to peace. In the last chapter, he writes exactly who his parents were, when and where they were married and when and where he himself was born. He does this, he writes, in order that after his death it is not said that he was born supernaturally.

H.D. Fridberg records in Beis Eked Sforim [Bibliographical Lexicon] seven of Moshe Yakov Schwerdscharf (he was not familiar with Emuna Hakduma and the Kitzur Birkat Hamazon [Shortened Version of Grace After Meals), mainly small, pamphlets of 16 sides.

[Page 279]

One of these he published anonymously three times (the first time in Kolomea, 1890) under the name Torath Ha'amim [The Wisdom of the Nations]. I never saw this book, but according to its name, I surmise that this was an earlier, anonymous version of the Emuna Hakduma. Among the other treatises, it is worthwhile to remember Drosh vaTefila Keter Melukha [Essential Prayers for the Royal Crown], published in 5669 [1909] in Kolomea, in honor of Franz Joseph's 60th state jubilee.

In the preface to Emuna Hakduma, Moshe Yakov Schwerdscharf asks that his pamphlet be translated into various languages. He was sure that the great universities of the world would disseminate his idea. In the middle of his dream, he suddenly fell in the street in Warsaw and died. I do not remember the exact date, but it must have been in the summer of 1922. His daughters and grandchildren still lived in Kolomea, Bilgoraj and Warsaw at the outbreak of the Second World War.

[Page 279]

The Teacher, Reb Wolf Rozenkranc

by Dr. Moshe Elihu Nhir (Klarman) Tel Aviv

Yiddish translated by Gloria Berkenstat Freund

Hebrew translated by Sara Mages

Wolf Rozenkranc was born in 1846 in the shtetl [town] Horodenka near Kolomea. His father, Moshe, maintained an inn in the shtetl. When the inn burned, Reb Moshe Rozenkranc and his family moved to Kolomea. As a youth, Wowa [diminutive of Wolf] was a child prodigy. At the age of 25 he took part in the Rabbi's Conference in Chernovitz in 1871.

In 1883, when the future deputy from Kolomea, Dr. Josef Shmuel Bloch, was victorious in the trial against the anti-Semitic Professor August Roling, respected members of the Kolomea middleclass with the very wealthy man, Reb Yakov Bretler, at the head, sent a congratulatory letter to him. The highly pompous letter was written by Reb Wolf Rozenkranc and he signed it:

"Dr. Shoshanim [Dr. Roses - Dr. Rozenkranc], teacher of young children of Yeshurun [Jewish], here in Kolomea."

Reb Wowek [diminutive of Wolf] was the author of many Hebrew poems and he translated poems from German to Hebrew. Among the translated songs was the Austrian anthem. The most important one of the books Reb Wolf Rozenkranc published is Sefer Moreh Shevile ha-Lashon [a Hebrew grammar book for language teachers].

[Page 280]

The introduction to the book is in rhyme and reads thus:

> My notebook! Sail between the Hebrew camp
> Bring a greeting to all seekers of wisdom,
> Don't be proud of your mistakes, my daughter,
> Because a net of error is slanted on every book.

> The eyes of your lovers will explore you
> Will see in you all the pleasantness and beauty
> Those who envy you will look at you
> All good and helpful - defect and blemish in their eyes.

> Don't recoil from critics who will meet you
> Tell them an excuse that is already known:
> How hard it is for a man to do something with wisdom
> And how easy it is to find a flaw in everything.

When my father, Efroim Klarman, of blessed memory, together with several pious and enlightened members of the middle class in the city founded the first Kheder Metukan [modern religious school] under the name Torat Chaim [Theory of Life], Reb Wolf Rozenkranc became one of the main teachers there.

At the time of the First World War, Reb Wowik [spelled Wowek above] was a refugee, first in Vienna and then in Carlsbad.

He traveled from Carlsbad to his children in the city of Mannheim in Germany. There, Reb Wowik died on the ninth day of Kislev 5676 (1916) [actually 1915, on the 16ᵗʰ of November] at the age of 70.

He prepared the inscription on his headstone himself. We provide here a part of the wording:

Here
In the depths of the earth
In the Hall of Silence
A dwelling
For a man respected by his community
He also wrote useful books for the Jewish people
In the glory of the language that God has chosen
And always used his logic wisely
The writer of the book "Moreh Shevile ha-Lashon"
And the book "Time to talk"
And the book "The grammar rules in a way of singing,"

Translator's footnote:

1.   Fear of God

[Page 281]

Member of Suchnot[1]

Dr. Fishl Rotenstreich
(1882-1938)

by Y. D. (Tel Aviv)

Translated by Gloria Berkenstat Freund

Dr. Fishl Rotenstreich was a child of the Kolomea hey-platz [hay square]. He was born and he was raised there. His father, Yehoshua, a pious Jew, who prayed and studied at the Roytshulekhn [small, red synagogue] died young and left his wife, Sora née Rotenstreich, and his only son, Fishl, in poverty.

Fishl studied at the Baron Hirsch School and then at the Kolomea Polish gymnazie [secondary school] at Mickewicza Street.

Fishl helped his mother with their livelihood when he was at the gymnazie by giving "private lessons." At one such "private lesson" he became acquainted with Manya Eiferman, the daughter of the rich grain merchant Yisroel Eiferman. Manya later became his wife.

When in gymnazie [secondary school], Fishl Rotenstreich was occupied with Zionist work. He founded the organization Betar with friends. The organizations at the Jewish gymnazie in Kolomea and in other Galicianer cities then united and under the name Tseiri Zion [Youth of Zion], became the secret national movement of the educated young people in Galicia. The central committee was in Lemberg and there, in the capital, at the beginning of summer vacations the yearly vietsn (congresses) were held.

Fishl Rotenstreich made his first appearance in the public arena as a student from Vienna University. He came to Kolomea then (1907) and took an active part in the election propaganda of the Zionist candidate to the Reichsrat [Imperial Council], Dr. Yehosha Ton.

[Page 282]

After graduating from the Philosophy Faculty in Vienna, Fishl Rotenstreich became a gymnazie [secondary school] teacher at first in Hungarian Brod, then in the shtetl [town] of Bursztyn and finally in the middle Galician city of Sambor.

Rotenstreich was an extraordinary gymnazie teacher; he spoke Yiddish publicly and took an active part in the Zionist work in the city.

The Poles remembered Rotenstreich's Jewish nationalism and when Austria crumbled and Sambor became Polish, the new rulers arrested Fishl Rotenshtreich and held him for several months in a concentration camp.

He was freed through the intercession of Chaim Weizmann and Nakhum Sokolov at the English Interior Ministry.

Fishl Rotenstreich was elected on the Zionist list to the Polish Senat and then to the Sejm. His specialty was economic questions of the Polish Jewry. He also wrote a well-read article in the Warsaw Heint [Today] about these matters.

As the leader of the General Zionist Group B in Galicia, Fishl Rotenstreich was chosen as a member of the Jewish Agency at the 19th Zionist Congress in Lucerne and he settled in Jerusalem with his family.

Rotenstreich took over the leadership of the Department for Industry and Commerce at the Jewish Agency and remained at the head of this important division until his premature death in 1938 at the age of 56.

Fishl Rotenstreich left two sons: Natan and Yehosha. Natan is a philosophy professor at Jerusalem University and Yehosha – a lawyer in Tel Aviv.

————

Translator's footnote:

1.   Jewish Agency

————

[Page 283]

The Jewish Teacher in Vilna

Dr. Yisroel Biber
(1897-1942)

by Shin Beis

Translated by Gloria Berkenstat Freund

Yisroel Biber was a friend of mine from the Kolomea gymnazie [secondary school]. I remember the new wooden house that his parents built on Morka Street. Biber was not communally active in gymnazie. He did not belong to the secret student organization, Tseiri Zion [Youth of Zion].

After many years, I met him for the first time during the winter of 1935 in Vilna. He occupied a respected place there in the Jewish school and cultural world.

There are three articles about Yisroel Biber in the memorial book about the teachers from the Tsysho [Tsentrale Yidishe Shul-Organizatsye – Central Yiddish School Organization] schools in Poland who perished.

We provide here short citations from all three articles to characterize Yisroel Biber and his work.

"Yisroel Biber actually came to us from afar, from Kolomea in southern Galicia to Vilna in northern Lithuania; this is quite a distance. However, he very quickly became a "Vilner" with heart and soul. His systematic methodical education was far from our yeshiva [religious secondary school] traditions, autodidactic, enlightened. All of us at the Seminar were folkslerer [teachers of the people], who themselves had climbed up to higher levels of knowledge. Biber came with a great deal of knowledge and an even greater love of nature. For others, for us, natural science was a part of our pedagogical communal ambitions. For him, this was a direct love, planted in him from childhood on, more knowledge

[Page 284]

and fewer impulses and urgencies. Two worlds, and I often marveled at how quickly he grew to feel at home among us.

"We led the Jewish Teachers' Seminar along with Biber for an entire nine years.

"Yisroel Biber took an active part in the cultural work in Vilna, in general. He led the evening courses for workers of Vilbig (Vilner Bildungs-Gezelshaft [Vilna Education Society].

"Yisroel Biber wrote a great deal and enriched our poor Yiddish natural-scientific literature. The bibliography of his works in this area is very large."

Regina Weinreich relates:

"Yisroel Biber came to Vilna in approximately 1924 at the invitation of the Teachers' Seminar as a teacher of natural science and geography and he later became the director of the Seminar. When the Polish regime closed the Seminar, Biber took over the same subjects at the Real Gymnazie [secondary school emphasizing the sciences] of the Central Education Committee and worked there until the Germans arrived in Vilna. During the vacations, Biber would travel to the Medem Sanitorium (Miedzeszyn, near Warsaw) to direct the natural science work there.

"From the start Biber found it was not easy to impart in Yiddish the knowledge that he received in Polish. He gave a great deal of effort to overcome the difficulties and did this, as everything, very thoroughly: working out terminologies for his subjects, taking part in terminology commissions, putting together teaching and reading books on zoology and anatomy and systematically writing popular scientific articles in Folksgezunt [People's Health].

"Yisroel Biber was a real expert in his trade, a stubborn and systematic worker. He helped to raise Jewish study in and around the school with his activity and equalize the level of instruction to the highest European standards.

"Biber was idealistically inclined, but he never was a militant Yiddishist; in general, he did not have a combative nature, but he obviously brought his complete honesty and consistency to his private life. His house was full and completely Jewish. The Germans took Biber from Vilna to Estonia before the liquidation of the Vilna ghetto."

[Page 285]

Sh. Giligski describes it:

"Dr. Yisroel Biber was connected with the Medem Sanitorium for over eight years. He would spend almost all his summer and winter vacation there, as well as other times when he was free of his work in the Vilna schools.

"Thanks to Biber working with it, the sanitorium became rich in content and the life and pleasure derived from it for the children was fuller and deeper.

"Dr. Biber was among the few teachers who, with their work and talent and with their strong love of children, elevated the education of children to such a high level that the institution became famous first to the tens of thousands of Jewish children in Poland and then in the pedagogical world."

I note books from B iber's published worls: 1) Zoologie [Zoology], first part of Onshedredike [Invertebrate], Vilna, 1934; 2) Anatomie, Fiziologie and Higiene fun Mentsh [Anatomy, Physiology and Hygiene of People], Vilna, 1945

————

The Leader of the Bund

Dr. Adolf Frisch
(1891-1943)

by Ed.

Translated by Gloria Berkenstat Freund

Dr Adolf (Bunjo) Frisch was the oldest son of an esteemed fabric shopkeeper, Motl Frisch. The house in which the future leader of the Bund in Kolomea grew up and was educated was a pious, enlightened house. The sons studied in khederim [religious primary schools] and also graduated from the Polish gymnazie [secondary school] and then one studied medicine and another engineering. One of the three sons, Elihu (Eltsie), born 1896, did not succeed in attending a university. He fell in June 1916 at the Austrian-Italian front, in the mountains of southern Tyrol.

Adolf Frisch studied medicine in Vienna and served in the Austrian Army, receiving his doctoral diploma in 1916. The same year, he also got married in Vienna to Ida Shor of Kolomea. Their only child, a daughter Miriam, was saved

[Page 286]

from death in the ghetto and lives today in Stockholm as the wife of her landsman [person from the same town], Ervin Saudek.

In 1930 Adolf Frisch settled in Kolomea. He immediately became one of the most esteemed and beloved doctors in the city. He was beloved and esteemed by all of the rich and middle-class patients, beloved and truly idolized by "the common people." Adolf Frisch was a people's doctor in the nicest sense of the word. He was more than a doctor to his poor patients. He was their friend and their consoler. He healed them without payment and if it was needed, he left the necessary coins to buy various remedies.

A very busy doctor (Dr. Frisch, over the course of years, also was the director of the Jewish hospital), Frisch found time for communal and literary work.

Between both World Wars, he was the leader and the gem of the Bund in Kolomea. He was the Bund's spokesman and the most important communal envoy to joint ethnic institutions and he diligently did literary work. He took part in Bundist publications with short stories and articles and he tried to make a reality of a great literary plan: translating all of Shakespeare into Yiddish. He had already completed several of Shakespeare's dramas. As Dr. Frisch's brother Zigmund, who lived in America in the city of Lancaster in Pennsylvania, asserted in a letter, Dr. Frisch held these Shakespeare translations as his most important literary achievement.

According to the information from friends who lived in Kolomea on the eve of the catastrophe and during the catastrophe, Dr. Frisch was also busy with the translation of Goethe's Faust and he had read the translation of several scenes from the first part of Faust to a group of friends.

In 1938, Adolf Frisch's poetry collection, Libe nisht Mer [No Longer Love], 120 pages, was published in Kolomea by der Bloyer Shtrokh [the Blue Stroke].

Dr. Frisch remained in Kolomea the entire time until the liquidation of the ghetto. He perished at the hands of the Nazi murderers on the 26th of March, 1943.

————

[Page 287]

The Minister of Education of Tel Aviv

Dr. Elihu Maruz-Rozenbaum
(1897-1952)

by Shlomo Bikel

Translated by Gloria Berkenstat Freund

Elihu Rozenbaum was born on the 30th of May 1897. During his gymnazie [secondary school] years he was one of the leaders of the student education group, Tseiri-Zion [Youth of Zion].

In 1921 he received his Doctorate of Philosophy from Vienna University. He graduated from Dr. [Adolf] Schwarz's Vienna Rabbinical Seminary the same year.

He was one of the main founders of the Hashomer Hatzair [the Youth Guard – secular Socialist Zionists] organization in Vienna and chief editor of the Polish publication, Hashomer [The Guard].

From 1922 to 1923, Rozenbaum was the director of the Jewish-Polish gymnazie in Bialystok.

 He was then the director of the gymnazie in Plock and of the Yavne [religious Zionist] middle school in Lodz and inspector of all Tarbut [secular Hebrew language] schools in Poland.

In 1929, he emigrated to Eretz-Yisroel and at first became a teacher at the famous gymnazie in Haifa and from 1940 until his death, the leader of the municipal education department in Tel Aviv.

On the 1st of July 1952, Elihu Maruz-Rozenbaum died after a severe heart attack.

[Page 288]

I do not know why an official title is connected with the managing society of the municipal education department of Tel Aviv, but in the autumn of 1950, when after a long, long time I met with my childhood friend, Elihu Rozenbaum; he looked like the expert government ministers with whom I also met then – preoccupied, bent under the burden of responsibility and a mountain of plans, with realistic and Menakhem Mendl-like plans.[1]

And another similarity to the government ministers: friends were also concerned about him, the Minister of Jewish Education of Tel Aviv, that he was working beyond his strength and quietly let him know that he needed to take care of himself because his heart was not "fine."

Eltsie (that was what we called him during the years shared in kheder [religious primary school] and shared at the gymnazie [secondary school] in Kolomea) came to me at the hotel several times with the clear intention, he said, to have a conversation about "old times," about gymnazie teachers, religious teachers, school Jews, about friends, those without number who perished and the few survivors and about everything that we remembered together as a pair about the days and nights at the "convent" (representative council) of the gymnazie group, Tzeiri Zion, and the library in his parents' house, at the Hebrew club and at the annual viets (congress) summer-time in Lemberg.

We sat on the terrace of the Hotel Irkun and had made, so to say, the introduction to conversation. We calculated how long we had actually not seen each other since the several years of close friendship in the Kolomea secondary school.

In one flight of our memories, we put together 36 full years, from the beginning of the First World War and up to the conversation on the Irkun terrace at the end of 1950.

Both of us, I think, simultaneously remembered that the 36 years had had an interval – an interval of one hours-long winter night that Eltsie had spent in my house in Bucharest when he came on a special mission from the Keren Kayemet [Jewish National Fund] Directorate from Eretz Yisroel to somewhere in Romania for several days at the beginning of the 1930s.

– And remember, then – Rozenbaum said to me as if with a reproach – we said almost nothing about Kolomea.

[Page 289]

I spoke then about Eretz Yisroel and then I sang Eretz Yisroel songs for hours on end (although I was asked if I had been invited or had I myself rushed to the synagogue lectern? – Eltsie smiled sadly with his eyes and with his dimples on both cheeks) and then it became late and I went to my hotel in Bucharest and then 19 years later I again came to you for a conversation in the hotel in Tel Aviv.

We were already, as I said, at the beginning of a conversation about "those days," but just then when his eyes and dimples smiled auto-ironically, I saw a hidden paleness on his face. I remembered what friends had told me, this his heart was not "fine" and I felt a need to caress him with warm and friendly care.

Eltsie, they tell me – I started a second introduction to "conversation" – that you work too much, that you exceed your strength both in the office and in traveling. So we – I tried to speak jokingly – remembered the 36 years that we have not seen each other. What do you mean, 36 years are only an abstract time and not 36 steps down in physical health nor 36 measures less energy and strength?

With my few words of concern about Eltsie's health, I was not willing to move the conversation away from the theme that we both desired so much and for the several times thereafter, that we saw each other, by no means could I return to it [the subject of his health].

Rozenbaum listened to my humorous words of concern and honestly confirmed that he often did not feel well, that he made frequent visits to the doctors about his heart and that the doctors, and mainly his own brother, the doctor, asked him to take good care of himself and to work less and less. However, how was this possible? How could he take care of himself when there was so much work, so much endless work that had to be and must be done?

And my friend Elihu Rozenbaum began to talk about this, how the educational needs during these recent several years had grown in Tel Aviv, about the scarcity of school buildings, scarcity of good teachers, scarcity in school benches and so many other scarcities for which he had the duty and responsibility, as far as possible, to evaluate

[Page 290]

in order to argue for budget increases with the municipal managing committee and until he finally succeeded in persuading them and as he came to terms with the finance minister about foreign currency and he left for Switzerland to buy comfortable chairs, it had cost him some of his health.

The number of children grew, the number of teachers grew and also the number of school buildings and, along with them, Rozenbaum's work hours, Rozenbaum's communal difficulties and the symptoms of his heart ailment also grew.

But in one detail – he had taken over one of the conversations from me – I did not have problems. The opposition is the municipality, your Histadrut [General Organization of Workers in Israel] – his eyes brightened with satisfaction, no, with joy, and the dimples on his checks shone as always – is not a problem for me. With my party comrade, the mayor, Rokach, there was actually a war, but not with me and with my school department.

Why is "my Histadrut" so good and gentle to him, the devoted party comrade and coworker of Yisroel Rokach? Rozenbaum's answer to my question was a clever smile and a quiet utterance, more to the table than to me: It seems, that I have luck. (I remember Eltsie's father, Reb Hersh Rozenbaum's clever and smiling to the table when he would speak about the successes of his successful daughter, Frida, and her successful brother.)

Friends we had in common and people from Histadrut later explained to me that Rozenbaum's luck with the opposition was not only miraculous. The Education Minister of Tel Aviv made it very difficult to engage in opposition because he was the most capable, most energetic, most loyal and most responsible leader in the [educational] area that the city had ever had. And a close friend of mine from Histadrut added something of his own: Rozenbaum – he said – added to the luck of the city and to the difficulties of the opposition in that he was not concerned with politics, only with education.

When I saw Rozenbaum for the last time at the home of our common young friend, Dr. Shemaria Elenberg, Director of the Geule Gymnazie [secondary school], he did not seem to be particularly

[Page 291]

filled with good health. He sat quietly and sadly in a corner and barely said a word.

But once in the course of the evening we happened to sit close to one another. Then he bent over to me and spoke to me as if from somewhere in the middle of an already long drawn-out conversation: the old, pious Jews who you described in your Shtot mit Yidn [City of Jews] all remained devoted to the people and to Yidishkeit [Jewishness, connoting an emotional connection to Judaism and/or to the Jewish people and their history, beliefs and customs], but the young Jews from Tseiri-Zion [Young Zionists], from the library and from the congresses in the majority withdrew from the front. From our generation, from those who were spokesmen, who remained? Only a few.

I wanted to tell him that of the few who had remained devoted, he was the most devoted and that we, the survivors, were succeeding him and [continuing] his good work for the people and the country.

However, I was not successful in doing so. The woman of the house called us to tea and the friends at the table drew me into their conversation.

Translator's footnote:

1.   Menakhem Mendl is a Sholem Aleichem character who is an impractical man with lofty aspirations.

[Page 291]

Khaver[1] Shmoys
(1887-1942)

by Yakov Mendl Marksheid (Tel Aviv)

Translated by Gloria Berkenstat Freund

That is what we called Yitzhak Shlomo Shmoys in all of the groups of Jewish Kolomea and with it we expressed recognition and even love for one of the most devoted leaders and pioneers of the Poalei-Zion [Workers of Zion – Marxist Zionists] movement in the city.

Yitzhak Shlomo Shmoys was born in Kolomea to poor parents who were only able to allow him to study for no more than a few years in a kheder [religious primary school]. However, with the strength of his innate will to learn, Shmoys was able to graduate from the nine-class folks-shul [public school] in Kolomea and then the commercial school in Krakow.

Krakow had a crucial influence on his further life cycle. Krakow, at that time, was a revolutionary center. At that time and in all cities in Galicia, the Polish Socialist Party P.P.S. in considerable numbers and its well-known leader, Ignacy Daszyński,

[Page 292]

supported the Jewish workers, toilers and also to an extent the Jewish assimilated intelligentsia. The literary-political journal, Krytyka [Criticism], edited by the Jewish Wilhelm Feldman, also was published in Krakow in the Polish language. The leader of the Jewish workers parties and escapees from pogroms and Tsarist Russia would also at times settle there.

Shmoys returned to Kolomea; he came already "baked" [matured]. He was a young man with serious character traits, an idealist and, seized by those ideas that were nurtured during that romantic epoch at the beginning of this [the 20th] century, he threw himself with "body and life" into the struggle for "his" ideas.

A little later he was under the influence of an anarchistic atmosphere and ideologies. However, he quickly found the way to Poalei-Zion. He then served the Poalei Zionists, the Poalei-Zion movement for all his years.

A strong influence on him were the visits from Sholem Alechim, Dr. [Chaim] Zhitlowski, the Yiddish language conference in Chernovitz and then the tour of Galicia by the "four great ones" – Y.L. Peretz, Sholem Ash, Avraham Reizen and H.D. Nomberg – that was arranged by "his" Comrade Khasriel during those years.

Already as a serious worker at the Kolomea Poalei-Zion organization, he also was one of the founders of the apolitical Jewish Culture-Union in Kolomea that was created after the Chernovitz conference and that led to the Kolomea Jewish Socialist Party (Galicianer Bund) becoming the national opposition in the Jewish Socialist Party movement and, after the First World War, the three leaders of the Bund, Hersh Habacht (tailor, former chairman of the Jewish Socialist Party Congress), Moshe Bal (chairman) and Shaya Ernman (baker), members of Poalei-Zion. Khaver Shmoys also had a large part in this.

Then Shmoys became a recognized worker and leader not only of Poalei-Zion. He gave lectures on literary and political themes. He was one of the most active workers in the professional movement of the trade employees and private officials; in the people's movement for being registered during the census of 1910 in a column with Yiddish as one's mother-tongue, he was

[Page 293]

one of the fieriest speaker-propagandists. He earned his popular name, Khaver Shmoys legitimately and honestly.

He thus worked tirelessly in all areas until the outbreak of the First World War. Because of his weak body – he was tall, thin as a stick, in addition to being very short-sighted – he was mobilized at a later time and designated for a labor battalion, in addition to the annotation that he was "political, unkosher."

However, at this time, despite the serious danger for him, he did not keep his anti-militaristic position a secret and he did not stop his political education work. In 1918, half a year before the end of the war, he was freed and he returned to Kolomea.

Shmoys returned at the right time. During this leg of his journey, a political and military state of emergency still reigned there. Shmoys was an employee of the district administration. He was not afraid and it did not stop him from doing further political propaganda work. He and I – together – organized flying propaganda meetings in secret in the synagogues and houses of prayer during and after prayers. We proposed an initiative to create a Jewish national council in Kolomea as the representative and protector of the Jewish population.

On the 1st of November 1918, at the downfall of the Austrian monarchy, the Ukrainian military formations seized power in Kolomea and proclaimed its annexation to the Ukrainisher Folks-Republik [Ukrainian People's Republic].

A new era began at a time of serious dangers and also with certain hopes. On the same day, a national council was constituted in Kolomea, thanks to our previous preparation with the representation and chairmen from three parties: Zionists (Dr. Laks), Poalei-Zion (Marksheid) and Bund-Jewish Socialist Party (Zeinfeld), with equal rights and duties. Shmoys was unanimously elected as manager of the cultural division at the first constituting meeting of the Jewish National Council. There he showed his capabilities and devotion. The Ukrainian regime organs prevented him from continuing as an official at the district administration and, thus, he had the opportunity to be watchful, to influence

[Page 294]

and to obtain from the new regime a certain agreement for the needs and necessities of the Jewish masses.

The Jewish kehile that until then was in the hands of the "obsequious Jews" and allowed a constant disruption of Jewish national aspirations, was taken over by the Jewish National Council with the help of the Jewish military division. A Jewish national representation was built with all of the prerogatives and attributes, and Shmoys, as the cultural manager, immediately took on constructive work in this area. He organized a Jewish public school with Yiddish as the language of instruction, recruited teaching personnel among the Jewish intelligentsia who were returning home from the war front, helped create a teaching program for the school; he won over Aleksander Granach (who found himself then in Kolomea as one who had been demobilized) and they created a good Yiddish dramatic group at Poalei-Zion. And when the party decided to publish its own press organ named Di Royte Fon [The Red Flag], Shmoys was one of its most important editorial members.

The Ukrainian People's Republic episode was of short duration. After this came another Romanian occupation of several months and then the joining of all of eastern Galicia in the newly arising Polish state.

Shmoys not only lost his place of work, he also was persecuted by the new people in power because of his political past and position and they also could not forgive that he was an official in the Ukrainian county leadership. He was arrested several times and each time released under the pressure of public opinion.

It was a long time until Jewish life began to "normalize" a little. Shmoys made his great contribution to Jewish communal work during this transition time.

The struggle at Poalei-Zion began – "left-right." Shmoys remained devoted; he fought devotedly against a socialism that supported force and that turned to violent means. He would always argue that socialism and justice cannot be built with bayonets.

After the split, Shmoys became a member of the right Poalei-Zion Central Committee; he moved to Lemberg, became an editorial member of the Yidishn Arbeter [Jewish Worker], wrote articles on literary and political

[Page 295]

themes, and for several years he was found on propaganda tours through cities and shtetlekh [towns] of eastern Galicia, until he again longed for his home city of Kolomea. Returning, he was no longer an old man, but a young man with a girlfriend. He arranged a home, opened a beautiful lending library in the nicest part of the city with a separate division and to sell Yiddish books, newspapers and journals.

He remained principled for all his years, even a fanatic Yidishist [advocate of Yiddish culture]. This is, perhaps, one of the most important reasons that brought him closer to and drove him to the left Poalei Zion [Marxist Zionists]. Here, he also showed much activism, writing articles about cultural problems in the Warsaw Arbeter Zeitung [Workers Newspaper], the central organ of the left Poalei Zion, gave lectures at the "society evening courses for workers" at the Y.L. Peretz Library in Kolomea, gave public lectures, appeared at various opportunities at political gatherings.

When the Polish regime sealed and confiscated the Y.L. Peretz Library, the Society for Evening Courses, and arrested a number its activists, held trials for them, it did not forget Shmoys; they made frequents searches [at his home], warned him, but he, Shmoys the fighter, the idealist, went bravely and consistently on his well-trod way; his library was the meeting point for all workers and the populist element in the city, without exception. He was surrounded with honor and recognition by everyone.

Thus it was until the outbreak of the Second World War. The Ribbentrop-Molotov Pact divided the former Polish state and, on the 17th of September, 1939 Kolomea was occupied by the Red Army and the Soviet regime.

A few days later, Shmoys was destined to taste the flavor of the "Soviet Paradise." He was arrested after appearing with a serious speech at a gathering of people of culture who were going to organize the new school system for the three peoples who lived in Kolomea – Ukrainians, Poles and Jews – and also the new cultural life in the city. At the gathering, he demanded full rights for the Jewish public schools with Yiddish as the language of instruction, warned of Ukrainian nationalism, warned of idealizing the Cossack culture, which was a general phenomenon in Ukrainian literature,

[Page 296]

and he voluntarily made available his library and, when necessary, himself.

He was arrested at night; he sat in jail for half a year; finally, they did not have anything with which to accuse him. He left jail a broken man.

On me, his fighting and like-minded comrade for many years, fell the fate in his time of emergency to stand by him. I then led a textile cooperative that I had organized, taking in former merchants and making textile workers out of them, and I easily convinced them to accept Shmoys as a member. He became the secretary and treasurer of the cooperative. We worked together there until the last second, when the Soviet troops and the Soviet Union left Kolomea in chaos.

I did not see him again. He – Shmoys, the Jewish revolutionary, the fighter and idealist – was politically unkosher in Imperial Austria, in the new Polish state, in the "socialist fatherland" [Russia]. This was what his tragic fate wanted. In 1942, in one of the annihilation actions, he perished with his Kolomea Jews who he had served so devotedly and faithfully for thirty-something years. From 1906 on, the history of Kolomea Jewish life was tightly connected and bound to the person and name of Khaver Shmoys. He is a part of the history of Kolomea Jewish folks-lebn [folk-life].

———

Translator's footnote:

1.   Comrade

———

The Silken Jew

Chaim Ringelblum
(1894-1942?)

Translated by Gloria Berkenstat Freund

Chaim Ringelblum was the son of a gemore-melamed [teacher of the Talmud] on Kaminker Street and the son-in-law of Feywl Stampler, who moved to Mielec, western Galicia after the First World War.

The ideologue and one of the founders and leaders of Hapoel Hatzair-Tzeiri-Zion [the Young Worker-Youth of Zion] (later Hitachdut [Zionist Socialists]) in the city, Chaim Ringelblum emerged at the very front of Jewish society. He was one of the most beautiful personalities in

[Page 297]

Kolomea at the time between the two World Wars. He was beloved by all strata of the Jewish population and also by the Christians for his honesty and affability. Everyone recognized his devoted work on behalf of the community.

There was no social institution in the city for which Ringelblum was not among its managers. Be it the rescue committee, the gemiles-khesed [interest free loan fund], the orphan's home or the cultural institutions under the name Toynbee Hall – Ringelbaum had a hand in the work everywhere.

In addition to this, he was the chairman of the Hitachdut Central Committee in Lemberg, a member of the city managing committee and of the kehile council, chairman of the Union of Private Employees, delegate to the Zionist Congresses and a member of the managing committee of the cooperative bank, Preminger, Bergman, Biter and Frenkel.

During the last years before the catastrophe, he was the bookkeeper at this bank and he drew his livelihood from this.

That there was general recognition among the Zionist parties for the youngest of their leaders can be seen in that he, Chaim Ringelblum, was designated to be the chairman of the famous city banquet given by the Zionists for Yitzhak Grinbaum during his visit to Kolomea in 1932.

Ringelblum was esteemed and loved for his learning (he was a man with a great deal of Jewish and secular knowledge, knowledgeable about Spinoza and Kant) and his good, humane traits.

We called him the silken Jew. He was "silken" because he was a Jew with a warm heart and with a generous hand. He had to be well-guarded to make sure he did not distribute his wages as soon as he received them. He was ready to give away his last groshn if someone needy turned to him.

I saw Chaim Ringelblum for the last time during my visit to Kolomea in 1924. I remember the evening that I spent with him at his home in hot, Yiddish debates and in still hotter Yiddish singing.

I remember his quiet and mild persona that glowed with readiness for self-sacrifice.

Eliezer Unger, in his book, Zikhron [Memorial] (Masada Publishing, Tel Aviv, 5708 [1948]), provided several lines about the persona of Chaim Ringelblum.

[Page 298]

Eliezer Unger lived in Kitov in 1941. At the outbreak of the Soviet-German War, he, his wife and child moved to the larger city, to Kolomea. There he met Chaim Ringelblum. And he told the following about him on pages 51-53:

– In August 1941, the commandant of the Kolomea area, the Nazi Folkman, told the Ukrainian city leaders to provide him with a list of Jews who were eligible to be members of a Judenrat [Jewish council] (the communities of Kitov, Jablonow, Horodenka, Zablotow, Sniatyn, and Zabie belonged to Kolomea County). The Ukrainians immediately submitted the names of the Jews who stood at the head of the community and were distinguished workers during the time of the Polish regime. The next morning, very early, Folkman called these Jews to his office. Then, after they had waited in the waiting room for a few hours, the chief of this area came out of the office and told them to choose a Judenrat [Jewish council] and presented them with a slate of members for the council. He proposed Chaim Ringelblum as the chairman of the council. He spoke about the responsibility that lay on the representatives of the Jewish community on behalf of the German regime. He threatened them with the penalty of death and left. All those invited were imprisoned in a room. The doors were opened for them at night and they were permitted to go home.

Chaim Ringelblum – a relative of the historian Emanuel Ringelblum in Warsaw – was chairman of the Hitachdut group in the city, a member of the city council of the Polish regime, a fervid Zionist and a devoted communal activist, a refined and spiritual man.

That evening I went to Ringelblum's house. Several of his friends and neighbors were assembled there. All were apprehensive and distracted; it was almost night and he [Ringelblum] still was not there. His wife paced from one corner to another, each time lifting the curtain at the window to see if perhaps he, her husband, was coming. Their daughter lay in bed. The day before, while working, she had received terrible blows from the German bandits and got a fever. Her heart trembled for the fate of her father.

[Page 299]

Hunger infiltrated this house just like the other Jewish houses. The small reserves of food products had run out weeks before and the family was starving. All of the carpets in the house were taken to the peasants, exchanged for cornmeal and vegetables. Every day they cooked a meal that was called kulesha (a kind of cooked dish made of cornmeal). The good-hearted residents divided their small reserve with everyone who came to ask them. And the reserve ran out in a short time. The comrades and friends of Ringelblum knew what was happening in his house. They brought what they could in a way that he would not know. He would argue with his friends: "There are hundreds of families in the city who are dying of hunger and why should food be brought to me and not to the other families?"

Ringelbaum returned home late at night, pale and breathless. Full of concern, he spoke about the offer of the rulers. He had struggled with himself: should he take on the management of the Jewish council from the Germans or not? Many of his friends advised him to accept the proposal. They argued that as a crystal clear, honest man who had great moral influence in the city, at this fateful hour he needed to take over the kehile [organized Jewish community], which along with the smaller communities in the area, numbered 40,000 Jews. He desperately struggled with himself. He decided that he could not look in the faces of Nazi animals and that he would not in any way agree to their proposal, even if he were risking his life and the lives of his family.

After a sleepless night of reflection and of inner-most struggle, Chaim Ringelblum left and notified Folkman that he refused his offer of the office. With this decision, Ringelblum showed great moral strength. Many Jews did not have such inner courage... A short time later, during the extermination actions in the Morka part of the city, the Gestapo members caught Ringelblum and his entire family and traces of them disappeared...

Ringelblum was a good soul. During the days of hunger and need in his own house, he had an open ear for all the

[Page 300]

people who came to him to pour out their bitter hearts. He sympathized with everyone's sorrow and he made use of his personal influence with the rich men in the city to help the needy. Until his last second of life – just like many others – he was filled with illusions and with false hopes that despite the pain in his body and soul, the Jews in the captured nations would live to see the defeat of Hitler. He believed in the victory, the victory of good over evil, believed in the redemption and freedom of people. In the darkest moments he found words of consolation for the broken and despondent who would come to him.

There were two types of leaders in the ghetto: pessimists who predicted bad and inspired despair in the hearts of their listeners and optimists who strengthened and encouraged the mood of the fallen people and stilled their pain. "Chaiml" – as they called Ringelblum – was the head of the optimists in the city. People who were looking for a word of consolation in the most difficult minutes assembled around him.

Traces of Ringelblum disappeared at the time when the city already numbered hundreds of victims, thousands doomed, when there no longer was a house without a corpse... At the time after the two deportation actions in the city. The hearts of the people were horror-stricken in great sorrow and burning pain and their feelings became numb. Everyone was in his own pain and mourned for their closest ones. However, after the disappearance of Chaim Ringelblum, everyone cried and grieved. The man who consoled, cheered up everyone was gone. He had infected the hearts of those who listened to him with his own belief. This was the belief that the democratic countries, and particularly the workers' movement in the free nations would not permit Hitler to annihilate a people who had given the world the idea of fairness and justice...

———

[Page 301]

The Hebraist

Yakov Biter
(1894-1941)

Translated by Gloria Berkenstat Freund

Yakov or (as he was in general called) Yekl Biter was from his student days a Zionist and a devotee of the Hebrew language. In the Tzeri Zion [Zionist youth organization] student organization he was one of those who primarily emphasized learning how [to speak], to read and to write Hebrew.

He was the manager of the Hebrew library of the Safa Khaya [Hebrew the living language] Union and the most fervent propagandist for Hebrew among the young.

The youngest son of the rich wood merchant and industrialist, Gdalya Biter, Yekl was able to order every new Hebrew book and every new Hebrew journal and he lent to everyone who could and wanted to read [Hebrew].

Yakov Biter

In 1913 Yekl graduated from the Kolomea Polish gymnazie [secondary school] and then studied jurisprudence at the Vienna University.

After the First World War, he married Gitele Preminger, the daughter of the bead merchant, Reb Nota Preminger. Gitele also was a Zionist and a Hebraist and the Biter couple gave their children a Hebrew education not only with teachers in school, but also themselves, through the Hebraic atmosphere that reigned in their house.

During the years between the two World Wars, Yekl Biter quickly became known in the city as an industrialist and communal worker.

[Page 302]

As an industrialist, he and his older brother, Hersh, led the largest wood business in the entire area. Several hundred people worked in the Biter business.

In the communal area, he immediately after his arrival in Kolomea in 1919 founded the academic union, Avoyde [worship]. He was the president of the union. He organized all cultural undertakings and he was the lecturer at all literary evenings and the director of all theater presentations.

Yekl Biter belonged to the general Zionist group. He was a member of the Zionist city committee the entire time and several times was also the chairman of the Zionist organization in the city. Biter did a great deal during the Polish election campaigns.

He was often a delegate to the Zionist congresses in Poland and several times to the Zionist World Congresses.

Jekl Biter's private Hebrew library, which possessed its own particularly considerable number of antiques, was well known in the city.

At the time of the first Soviet regime (1939-1941), eminent Zionist leaders would come together in secret at Yekl Biter's house.

When the Nazis entered Kolomea, Yekl Biter was one of the first victims. On Hashana Rabbah [the seventh day of Sukkous – the Feast of Tabernacles], 1941, he and his family were taken to the Sheporovicer forest and there they were all shot.

The Pious Maskil[1]

Efroim Klarman
(1874-1928)

by Nun Beis

Translated by Gloria Berkenstat Freund

Reb Efroim bar [son of] Moshe Klarman, was born in Krakow in 5684 (1874). As a young boy he already had a good name in his home city as a child prodigy in Talmud and commentaries. As a young man, Efroim Klarman secretly acquired great general expertise and knowledge from older friends.

[Page 303]

The friends that helped Efroim Klarman to a broad general education were Dr. Dovid Rotblum, later one of [Nakhman] Bialik's closest friends and Hersh Malter, later professor of Talmudic literature at Dropsy College (died in Philadelphia in 1925).

In 1895 Efroim Klarman married the daughter of Reb Hersh Ramler, one of the very richest men in Kolomea, and thus became a resident of Kolomea.

Reb Hersh Ramler's young son-in-law quickly became a known and beloved personage in his new home city. He distinguished himself from all of the other pious Jews with his secular education and behavior and from all of the followers of the Enlightenment in the city with his deep piety. In the middle of the eastern Galicianer city of Kolomea, Efroim Klarman was the type of Orthodox Jew from the western German city of Frankfurt.

No one spoke a more beautiful Polish than Efroim Klarman and no one doffed his hat for a woman more elegantly, but at the same time, no one observed the daf yomi of the Gemora [daily study of the Talmud] more and no one recited the Shemoneh Esreh [central prayer of Jewish worship] with more religious ecstasy than Efroim Klarman.

After Reb Motia Herman's death, the leaders of the patrician Reb Ayzykl prayer house chose for their leader (synagogue manager) the Krakow young man, Reb Efroim Klarman.

Efroim Klarman also was one of the early Zionists in Kolomea and, also, one of the founders of the first Kheder Metukan [modern religious primary school] in the city.

Efroim Klarman was a refugee in Vienna during the First World War. When he returned to Kolomea from there, he was the chairman of the Jewish National Council and of the kehile managing committee during the Romanian occupation. Until his sudden death at the age of 54 in the summer of 1928, Reb Efroim Klarman was one of the Jewish spokesmen in the city.

[Page 304]

Both friends and opponents related to Efroim Klarman with great respect.

Characteristic of the general love and respectful relationship to the person of Reb Efroim Klarman was an incident that took place at his funeral. A quarrel broke out at his funeral between the Agudah [Orthodox anti-Zionists] and the Zionists. The members of Agudah argued that they did not want to permit an apikorsim [heretic] to trouble himself with the funeral of such a devout person as Reb Efroim Klarman. The Zionists argued that Efroim Klarman was an active Zionist all his life and a spokesman for the Zionist movement in the city.

Thousands of Jews as well as non-Jews accompanied Reb Efroim Klarman to his grave at the new cemetery.

Efroim Klarman's oldest son, Dr. Moshe Elihu Nhir, lives in Tel Aviv, where he is a well-known pedagogue and secondary-school teacher.

———

Translator's footnote:

1.   Follower of the Enlightenment

———

The Chortkover Hasid

Hanokh Shekhter
(1878-1955)

by Shin

Translated by Gloria Berkenstat Freund

Reb Hanokh Shekhter was born in Chortkov. In 1904, in Kolomea, he married the daughter of Reb Leibl Eiferman and his wife, Mesholem Velvel's Reyzl, who was known for her piety and charity and also as the owner of the largest millenary shop.

Reb Hanokh Shekhter quickly became well known in the city as a great scholar and as a fervid Chortkover Hasid and a leading activist in the Mizrakhi [religious Zionist] Party.

[Page 305]

Zionism was a major challenge for Reb Hanokh Shekhter. When he became the official propagandist for Mizrakhi in 1930 and traveled through the cities of eastern Galicia as an envoy for Keren Eretz Yisroel [Land of Israel Organization] from Mizrakhi, he had to carry on a difficult struggle with Agudas Yisroel [Union of Israel – Orthodox party].

His opposition to Agudas Yisroel created a wall between him and the Chortkover Rebbe, Reb Yisroel. Reb Hanokh Shekhter remained with Mizrakhi and he stopped traveling to Chortkov. But he remained a Chortkover Hasid for all of his days, not less fervid than his father, Reb Avraham Shoykhet [ritual slaughterer] of Chortkov.

The book of memoirs that Reb Hanokh Shekhter published in Tel Aviv in 5703 [1943] (with an introduction by the famous Hebrew writer, Dov Sadan) breathes not only with Hasidic warmth but also with his unyielding partisan spirit, so that he is known not just as a Hasid [follower] of a rebbe but as a Hasid of the Chortkover Rebbe.

This was both incomprehensible and intelligible with such Jews as Reb Hanokh Shekhter. Incomprehensible because the Mizrakhi activist, Hanokh Shekhter, was a man of wide national horizons. And understandably, because he was a Jew deeply rooted in the old family tradition and the inherited ball of fire did not cease to burn.

Reb Hanokh Shekhter and his family emigrated to Eretz Yisroel in 1933. He died there at the age of 77 in the summer of 1955.

Reb Hanokh Shekhter's children live in Israel. His son-in-law is the well-known Hebrew poet and translator from Yiddish to Hebrew, Shimeon Melcer.

[Page 306]

The Socialist

Mikhal Herer
(1885-1942?)

by L.G.

Translated by Gloria Berkenstat Freund

No one in Kolomea from before the First World War was a socialist with [as much] knowledge as Moshe Herer's oldest son, Mikhal, who wore a beautiful, black beard, a wide black hat and a black, artistic cravat, strolled with a Ukrainian woman dressed in national dress, publicly smoked on Shabbos [the Sabbath] and, as Jews would say by way of exaggeration, sat in jail every Monday and Thursday.

Mikhal Herer's father, Reb Moshe, was a rich grain merchant, wore a shtreiml [fur hat worn by Hasidic men] and prayed at Yekl Beidaf's synagogue.

Mikhal attended the Kolomea gymnazie [secondary school] and then studied jurisprudence at Lemberg University. He did not graduate from the university because he and his comrade, Oster, were expelled for carrying out socialist propaganda. Herer was the secretary to the famous leader of the P.P.S. [Polska Partia Socjalistyczna – Polish Socialist Party], the Kolomea lawyer, Dr. Shmuel Eliezer (Samuel Lazarcz) Schor. He and Dr. Schor took part in international socialist congresses and also were at the congress of the Austrian Social-Democrats in Vienna on the eve of the outbreak of the First World War.

Herer was one of the most capable worker organizers in the city. He organized the artisans of Yad Harutzim [Arm of the Diligent], as well as the Polish railroad workers, bricklayers and weavers and Jewish talisim [prayer shawls] weavers.

Herer was a regular speaker at the First of May celebration, where he spoke Polish and Ukrainian. He spoke Yiddish at Yad Harutzim.

Herer led a demonstration from the Leiblech Hall to the city hall during the parliamentary elections with the demand that the voting slate be issued. He and Simkha Weic and Oster were then arrested and sentenced to jail.

[Page 307]

A convinced member of the P.P.S., Herer appeared against Jewish separatism. The Zsh. P. S. section (the Jewish section of the party) was created against Herer's will. He also was a later opponent of Zionism, but despite this – a warm Jew.

After the First World War, he moved to Lemberg, where he was an employee at the Polish firm, Nafte. The Nazis murdered him there in Lemberg.

———

The P.P.S. Bookbinder

Moshe Sak
(18?-19?)

by Lamed Giml

Translated by Gloria Berkenstat Freund

I do not know when Moshe Sak was born. And I do not even remember when he died. But I know that during the 14 years of our century before the First World War he was a renowned person in the city.

Moshe Sak was a Jew, a poor man, burdened with children and a number of them were sick. Moshe Sak lived with Betz, the shoemaker, on Szpitalna Street in a room with a small kitchen. The bookbindery was located at the [house] of the widow Heller on the Ring Platz. And there in the bookbindery, was the main room for the Polish Socialist Party (P.P.S.) in the city.

Moshe Sak, a Jew in a long jacket during the week and in a long, coarse men's coat and shtreiml [fur hat worn usually by Hasidim] on Shabbos [Sabbath], was a fervid Polish Socialist. He prayed with Yad HaRutzim [Arm of the Diligent], went to hear a sermon by the city preacher, Reb Yitzhak Weber, on Shabbos and went to the tish [table – communal meal with a Hasidic rabbi] of the Rebbe-Bokher [Hasidic rabbi who was a young man]. However, in addition to this, Moshe Sak was a follower of the P.P.S. [Polish Socialist Party]. He did not speak or read Polish, but he nevertheless trusted the Krakower Naprzód [Krakow Forward] and the Lemberger Głos [Lemberg Voice] and was an opponent of bringing a Yiddish newspaper to the Artisans' Union. The bookbinder, Moshe Sak, was an assimilated Pole. The Jewish division, the Jewish Socialist Party, was created in the Polish Socialist Party, against Moshe Sak's will. He was for complete integration.

[Page 308]

At Moshe Sak's bookbindery the policy of the P.P.S. in the city was decided, as well as for the artisans' union, Yad HaRutzim. At election time, the main room for socialist activity was in Moshe Sak's bookbindery.

Every decision, before it was made by the city committee, was discussed first in Moshe Sak's bookbindery by Dr. Schor's Leib-Gvardii [imperial guard]: Mordekhai Leib Weitz, Shimkha Weitz, Fishele Thau, Mikhal Herer, Naftali Kestn, Shmuel Hilzenrat and Chaim Bretler and his wife.

Chaim Bretler was an insurance agent for Viktoria and Feniks and was the only one among the people meeting in Moshe Sak's workshop who lived well, lived in an apartment of six rooms and dressed elegantly.

Moshe Sak held the authority at the meetings. The strike of the talisim [prayer shawl] weavers was carried out from his workshop. Moshe Sak for all his life remained a consistent member of the P.P.S. Even during the time of free Poland, after the death of the famous leader of the Kolomea P.P.S., Dr. Samuel Lazarcz Schor, when the anti-Semitism of the P.P.S. strengthened, Moshe Sak, and a number of comrades, remained a Polish socialist – an opponent not only of Zionism but also of Bundist nationalism.

Moshe Sak, the P.P.S. member, bookbinder, had many enemies in the city, but no friend and no opponent doubted that Moshe Sak was an honest and devoted socialist who was ready to give his life for socialism, as his Rebbe, Dr. Samuel Lazarcz Schor, had preached and explained for him.

The Leader of the Merchants

Yehuda Borukh Feierstein

by G.B.

Translated by Gloria Berkenstat Freund

Before the First World War, Yehuda Borukh Feierstein was one of the better known watchmakers in the city.

In 1918, Yehuda Borukh Feierstein returned to Kolomea from Vienna where he had been a refugee during the war

[Page 309]

with his family. During the war years, the jewelry merchants in Vienna left for good and Feierstein, the jewelry merchant, returned to Kolomea with money. He bought Shaul Breyer's house on the A-B line [designation of the building on the perimeter of the market] and there arranged one of the largest jewelry shops in the city.

Feierstein was a young man with many temperaments, with great communal initiative and with a feeling for all roads and paths of politics. He truly, quickly became an important activist in the city.

He began to organize the merchants and created a Merchants Union with a well- functioning apparatus that was concerned with a very important matter to Jewish merchants under the Polish regime – taxes.

The Merchants Union grew greatly under the leadership of Yehuda Borukh Feierstein and of the lawyer, Dr. Izidor Bar, and of the managing committee in which sat among other well-known shopkeepers in the city, Shlomo Elster, Yosl Lederfeind, Ayzyk Fund, Zelig Sperber, Heinrich Reisman, Zisie Ziskind, Chaim Bortn, Motie Bank and others. The union doubled its membership and was a political power that had to be considered by both the Jewish parties and the Polish state.

Yehuda Borukh Feierstein, during the years between the two world wars, was a true, the true mediator of the small Jewish merchants and artisans, whom the state tax machine was trying to destroy.

Feierstein's devoted humanity was recognized by all, even his Polish opponents, who fought him, because his politics as a mediator was a moment of respite for the Polish power holders.

Feierstein occupied important offices both at the city managing committee and at the Jewish kehile [organized Jewish community]. He was appointed and also elected as assessor at the city hall, a member of the kehile managing committee, treasurer at the municipal savings fund and delegate to the chamber of commerce in Stanislau [Ivano-Franivsk]. And he served every office with distinction.

"I cannot forget, Mr. Feierstein" – Chaim Ringelblum, the leader of the city Hitachdut [Zionist Socialists] group, once said to him in a public quarrel – "that the boundary of your political

[Page 310]

work is the boundary of Kolomea, the Werbish Bridge. Because beyond Kolomea, no Jews stand behind your shoulders."

This was actually true. However, it also was true that in Kolomea, for the poor of Kolomea, Yehuda Borukh Feierstein was a devoted intercessor and helper.

Yehuda Borukh Feierstein and his family were among the first victims of the Nazis. The German murderers annihilated Feierstein, his wife Nety and four of their children in 1941 in the Szeparowicer Forest.

Only one of Feierstein's daughters survived. Feierstein's brothers, Leib (today in Israel) and Ayzyk (today in New York) survived.

The Financier

Emanuel Luft
(1893-1941)

by Sh. B.

Translated by Gloria Berkenstat Freund

I remember him somewhere from the third class of gymnazie [secondary school]. Until then, Emanuel, the son of the rich mill owner, Shlomo Luft, of the firm Asderbal and Luft, studied with private teachers. One of his private teachers was none other than the future well-known Jewish philosopher, Professor Dovid Neimark.

Emanuel Luft was the oldest of our class in years, the tallest in height and the most mature according to knowledge and commonsense.

He did not belong to our Jewish educational groups, Tseiri Zion [Zionist Youth]. But a year or two after his arrival, he created a group in our class with the name Europe for, in general, the most essential philosophical education. Of the members of that group who would come together from time to time and mainly under Luft's leadership, in addition to Luft and me, I remember two Poles, the son of the Kolomea court president, Jasek Bernacki, later an

[Page 311]

officer in the Polish Army and the son of the Kolomea tax director, Stanislaw Liphardt, later a doctor and a man of letters, and of the Jews, the son of a rich egg exporter, Karol Bishel, and the later lecturer at Vienna University, Philp Mandeles-Merlan.

After those young, philosophic discussions at Europe, 27 years later, approximately a month before his death, Emanuel Luft and I met in America at a hotel in the eighties around Columbus Avenue, where he struggled with a relentless stomach illness under the care of a nurse.

Here we began to talk in a few half hours about what had happened to each of us in the more than a quarter of a century that had passed.

For Emanuel Luft it had passed thus: in 1923 he received his doctorate in political science, specializing in economics and in financial matters.

He worked at the large Warsaw bank, Bank Diskontowie Warszawskie [Warsaw Discount Bank] and he quickly became the chief director there and the expert on international financial matters.

In the early summer of 1939, the Polish government sent him to America and to Canada to seek a loan from the banks there. Luft carried out the mission with success and returned to Warsaw on the last ship that sailed to Poland from New York on the 8th of August.

After the German invasion he was successful in escaping to Romania and from there he crossed Italy and arrived in New York in spring 1940.

Here business friends who were eager to make use of Luft's extraordinary abilities as a financial visionary and as a financial technician waited for him.

However, his severe illness clouded the road for the 48-year-old man. Luft fought the illness like an opposing party in a great confrontation: with cool dignity, with commonsensical, resigned indulgence and without the least expression of self-pity.

[Page 312]

The great finance man, on his sick bed in New York, was sustained by the knowledge of stoic philosophy he acquired during his childhood, which was drilled into his head and ours in the "European" social circle in Kolomea.

Five days after the outbreak of the Soviet-German War, which he greeted as the beginning of a possibility of Hitler's defeat with the weak voice of his last day, he died on the night of the 27th of June 1941.

The Writer

Dr. Anselm Kleinmann
(1882-1942?)

by Z. R. Lek

Translated by Gloria Berkenstat Freund

In the years before the First World War and in the first few years between the two World Wars, Antshel (Anselm), the son of Mordekhai Hersh the toker [turner], was the most popular Kolomea writer.

Mordekhai Hersh Toker (Kleinmann) was also a people's poet in his youth and wrote Purim-shpiln [Purim plays] and presented them with friends.

Antshel (Anselm) Kleinmann graduated from the Kolomea Polish gymnazie [secondary school] and studied jurisprudence in Chernovitz and in Lemberg. Under the influence of Leibl Toybsz, Kleinmann became interested in Yiddish literature and was a co-worker at Toybsz's Yidishn Vokhenblat [Yiddish Weekly Newspaper] and at Lemberger Togblat [Lemberg Daily Newspaper]. In 1906, Kleinmann was a member of the editorial committee of Gershom Bader's Nayes Lemberger Togblat [New Lemberg Daily Newspaper] and there, at that newspaper and also at the Polish-Yiddish periodicals and at Voskhod[Dawn] and Moriah, he wrote articles, short stories and theater reviews.

Anselm Kleinmann was one of the secretaries of the Chernovitz Language Conference in 1908 and then co-editor of Dr. Nusan Birnbaum's periodical, Beshas der Milkhome [During the War], he was a co-worker and, then, editor of the Vienna Yiddish newspaper, Di Viner Morgenzeitung [The Viennese Morning Newspaper].

[Page 313]

At the beginning of 1920, Dr. Kleinmann came to America and remained until the end of 1921. During the two years, he wrote in the New York Yiddish newspapers, Yidishes Tageblat [Jewish Daily News], Tag-Varhayt [Daily Truth] and the Tsayt [Time].

Between the years 1922-1924, Anselm Kleinmann published three yearbooks in Lemberg named Yidisher Literarisher Kalendar [Yiddish Literary Calendar] and with them he tried to carry on the tradition of Gershom Bader and Moshe Frostig's Almanakhn [Almanacs], which over the course of years became the centers for Yiddish literary creativity in Galicia.

Kleinmann translated two songs from Goethe's famous poem, Hermann und Dorothea. The translation was published in the Lemberg weekly, Der Yidisher Arbeter [The Jewish Worker].

At the end of the 1920s, Dr. Anslem Kleinmann withdrew from literary work, moved to the city of Jaroslaw and there practiced the legal profession until the end of the community in 5612 [Translator's note: 1952 – this is an error, the date should be 5702 – 1942]. Dr. Anslem Kleinmann perished there together with the holy community of Jews.

Surgeon and Philosopher

Dr. Eliezer Bickel
(1902-1951)

by Shin

Translated by Gloria Berkenstat Freund

Eliezer Bickel was born on the 8th of May 1902 (Rosh Khodesh [new month] Ayer 5662) in a village in southern Bukovina to his father, Reb Itsie Bickel, a Torah scholar, a follower of the Enlightenment, a [member of] Poalei Zion [Workers of Zion – Marxist Zionists], a Hovevi Zion [Lover of Zion], and then a fervid political Zionist.

His father sent him at the age of six to study in his home city of Kolomea. In Kolomea, Eliezer remained in the house of his grandfather, Reb Mordekhai Bickel until the second Russian occupation in 1916.

Eliezer attended the folks-shul [public school] in Kolomea and the Polish gymnazie [secondary school] to the fourth class. He finished the secular subjects in Chernovitz in 1920 and then studied medicine at Bucharest University.

[Page 314]

In 1926, the young Bucharest doctor left for further studies in Berlin. There he became an assistant to Professor Wagner, the director of the gynecological division of the "charity" clinic. He wrote a series of works in the area of gynecological research. The Berlin Medical Faculty gave Eliezer Bickel its doctorial diploma without an exam.

In April 1933, Eliezer returned from the Germany that had become Nazified to Romania, and in Bucharest quickly became one of the leading gynecologists and surgeons in the area of women's illnesses. He was the director of the gynecological division in the Jewish hospital, Mentshn-Libe (Jubirea de Omeni[Loving People]).

In addition to medicine, Eliezer Bickel was interested in philosophy. His knowledge of Spinoza led him to a friendship with the philosopher, Constantin Brunner, the author of Di Geistigen und das Folk [German title is Die Lehre von den Geitigen und von Volke – The Teaching of the Spiritual and of the People] and other books for expanding and deepening of Spinozism.

Constantin Brunner took Eliezer under his wing and he was one of his most beloved and most important students. In his will, Brunner designated Eliezer (Lothar) Bickel as trustee of his literary estate.

After the death of Constantin Brunner in 1937 in The Hague, Eliezer Bickel published and wrote introductory words to three books by his teacher: 1) Undzer Kharater [Our Character] (publisher Di Liga, Zurich, 1938), 2) Kunst, Filosofie, Mistik [Art, Philosophy, Mysticism] (publisher Humanitas, Zurich, 1940), 3) Der Entlarvte Mensch [The Exposed Man] (publisher Nishzhof, the Hague, 1951).

Eliezer published two of his own books during his life: 1) Zur Renesans der Filosofie [To the Renaissiance of Philosophy] (publisher Guchtov Kifenhauer, Berlin, 1931) and Probleme und Ziele des Denkent [Problems and Goals of Thinking] (publisher Humanitas, Zurich, 1939).

After his premature death, another two books were published, to which his good friend, Moshe Sterian of Toronto, wrote

[Page 315]

introductory words: 1) Wirklichkeit und Warheit des Denkens [Reality and Truth of Thought] (Diana Publishers, Zurich, 1953), and 2) Kultur [Culture] (Diana Publishers, Zurich, 1956). Two more books from Eliezer Bickel's literary estate were prepared and published by his previously mentioned friend, Moshe Sterian.

In 1949, Eliezer succeeded in leaving Sovietized Romania with his wife and child. He settled in Montreal, Canada, and prepared to revive his medical practice.

A serious heart attack made an end of Eliezer Bickel, who had not ended his 49th year, on the first day of Kol Hamoyed Pesakh 5711 [the first intermediate day of Passover] (23rd of April 1951).

In his introduction to Eliezer Bickel's book, Wirklichkeit und Warheit, Moshe Sterian writes:

"Thinking and doing were identical for Bickel and it meant the development of all his strength of intellect and feeling. This came to expression illuminatingly. Everyone who knew him was under the strong force of his personality. His incomparable insight went hand and hand with the ethos and emotion that flowed in his warm heart. In his last years, he spoke very little, but the silence was a result of his quiet, creative depth and of the most internal harmony. Goodness and wisdom were loving sisters who love each other and were worthy of being loved."

The Talmud Professor

Dr. Yisroel Osterzetser
(1904-1942?)

by Sh. A.

Translated by Gloria Berkenstat Freund

The son of Reb Ruwin Osterzetser and the grandson of Reb Leibush Osterzetser, the young Yisroel had behind him the tradition of an illustrious and scholarly Kolomea family.

Yisroel Osterzetser studied with the former head of the Lublin Yeshiva [religious secondary school], Reb Meir Szpira, and, in addition, he studied subjects at the universities of Krakow and Warsaw. In 1927 he received his doctorate

[Page 316]

in history and classical philology. In 1928 he made contact with the Institute for Jewish Studies in Warsaw and there became the assistant of the Talmud Professor, Dr. Avraham Weiss. In 1935, Yisroel Osterzetser became the lecturer on Talmudic and Hebraic Literature of the Middle Ages. He was the youngest lecturer at the Institute.

Dr. Osterzetser published a series of research works in the area of students' rights. At the university itself, Dr. Osterzetser took upon himself the heavy burden of practical examination work and maintained personal contact with the students who, for the most part, were the same age as he.

In 1936, Dr. Osterzetser was elected the vice president of the Union of Hebrew Writers in Poland.

Yisroel Osterzetser was a young, educated man with great talent and a great deal more was awaited from him in the area of Talmudic and Hebraic literary research.

The Editor of Di Rote Fahne[1]

Heinrich Ziskind
(1895-1934?)

by Shin Beis

Translated by Gloria Berkenstat Freund

Chaim Ziskind's youngest son Hershl, or Henrik, as he was called at the Kolomea Polish gymnazie [secondary school], or Heinrich, as he was called during his residency in Germany, was my gymnazie friend. He was the son of a rich father and was himself a stately and well-dressed young man.

He together with the majority of gymnazie students belonged to the secret organization of the Jewish educational circles, Tseiri-Zion [Youth of Zion].

With him, with Henrik Ziskind at home on Sobieski Street, in the spacious, beautiful kitchen, we held the meetings of our educational circle, Palestine, every Shabbos [Sabbath] afternoon. At the head of the small group in 1913 were gymnazie students from the sixth class. Henrik Ziskind was the secretary (he wrote useful and exact

[Page 317]

minutes), Shmai Manger, then a young Yiddish poet (died in America in 1954) – the vice chairman and the writer of these lines – the chairman. Benyamin Praiz, who wrote dramas (he fell in the First World War) was also among the leaders of the group.

Shmai Manger, Praiz and I struggled to be writers. Ziskind dreamed more about publishing in Germany.

His older sister and brother lived in Germany and Henrik was always their guest at vacation time. Henrik really liked this and spoke a good German and he was the Germanist in gymnazie.

After graduating from the gymnazie, I lost trace of Ziskind. However, during the 1920s, the news reached me that he had settled in Berlin after the First World War, that he had joined the Communist Party and obtained a prominent position there. At the end of the 1920s, Henrik Ziskind achieved the high position of chief editor of the communist central organ in Germany, Di Rote Fahne.

Here in New York in 1941, I was told about those few years of Henrik Ziskind at the height of his party success by our former gymnazie friend, Emanuel Luft (see his portrait in the same section, "Portraits"), who would meet him in Berlin from time to time. Luft said how Henrik Ziskind had grown intellectually, what a brilliant orator and writer he was and how high he therefore rose in the hierarchy of the Communist Party in Germany.

Henrik Ziskind's party success, as said, lasted no more than a few years. After Hitler came to power, Ziskind along with most leading communists left for Russia and there –

The only news they we possess about Ziskind in Russia comes from the book of the former communist, Jan Waltin, Aroys fun der Finsternish (Out of the Night), Alliance Book Corporation, Chicago, 1941). And there, in Waltin, it is written that Henrik Ziskind was liquidated together with many other German communist refugees in Stalinland about a year after his arrival in Russia.

———

Translator's footnote:

1.   The Red Flag

———

[Page 318]

Lawyer and Orator

Dr. Feywl Shternberg
(1887–1948)

by Sh. B.

Translated by Gloria Berkenstat Freund

He was a pioneer in Poale–Zion [Workers of Zion – Marxist Zionists] in Galicia before the First World War and he was the main spokesman for Poale–Zion in Romania immediately after the First World War.

When I became personally acquainted with Feywl Shternberg in the summer of 1919 in Czernowitz [Chernivtsi], I actually had been acquainted with him for a total of 10 years. He had belonged to the group of Zionist-Socialist students who very strongly influenced we Kolomea gymnazie [secondary school] students.

The young Kolomea student, Feywl Shternberg, was one of the most important propaganda workers for Yiddish [to be used in taking] the government census of 1910. He appeared on the same dais with Shlomo Kaplanski and with Nusan Birnbaum and had exceptional oratorial success. The young Kolomea student was a co–worker at the Poale–Zion party newspaper, Der Yidisher Arbeiter [The Jewish Worker], in Lemberg and even the editor for a time of this weekly publication.

At the end of the First World War, Shternberg moved to Czernowitz, where he was the editor of the Poale–Zion weekly publication, Di Freiheit [The Freedom].

Shternberg lived in Czernowitz for only a scant two years (from Autumn 1918 to Summer 1920). However, during the two years, he achieved prestige and importance for himself and for the Poale–Zion Party that is usually not easy to attain in ten times the time.

Along with the Bundist Yakov Pistiner and the General Zionist Meir Ebner, he was surely the most popular personality in the city. And on the dais, Shternberg had no equal.

[Page 319]

The late young Yakov Pistiner was the most politically experienced among the Bukoviner Jewish party leaders; Meir Ebner distinguished himself from among everyone with his writing talent; the youngest among them, Feywl Shternberg, possessed oratorical fervor and brilliance and took his listeners by storm.

I actually remember Shternberg's stormy success for Poale–Zion at the Jewish National Council in Czernowitz, summer 1919, when he spoke in the name of Poale–Zion, and both the Bundists and the General Zionists kept increasing his speaking time, did not want him to leave the dais because they stood under the spell of his argumentation, of the way in which he built and expressed his arguments.

In the summer of 1920, Shternberg left Czernowitz and moved to Vienna, where he quickly occupied an esteemed position in the legal profession.

At the Folks–Universitet [People's University] of the Social–Democratic Party in Vienna, Shternberg had the ability to make use of his great lawyerly zeal for the socialist world vision with great success and pleasure.

Here in New York, an escapee from Hitler's Vienna – one pulled from his Galicianer–Bukovina and from his Vienna environment – he could not find a way of active cooperation with Poale–Zion nor with the Viennese refugees.

Feywl Shternberg [known as Philip Sternberg in New York] died of a heart attack on the 18th of June 1948 in New York.

The older of his two sons, Daniel, is a music professor at State College of Waco, Texas, and the younger one, Eli, is a professor at the Technical High School in Chicago.[1]

Translator's footnote:

1. Daniel Sternberg was a professor at the College of Music, Baylor University; Eli Sternberg was at the Chicago Institute of Technology.

[Page 320]

The Actor

Alexander Granach
(1891–1945)

by Sh. B.

Translated by Gloria Berkenstat Freund

I was still a gymnazie [secondary school] student, a student in the higher classes of the Kolomea gymnazie, when the news spread that Yeshaya Gronik [Alexander Granach's original name], a beker–yingl [baker boy] from the nearby shtetl [town], Horodenka, had left for Berlin and all of Germany had gone topsy–turvy because of his talent.

Understand that at that time this was an exaggeration. However, the exaggeration quickly became true. In pre–Hitlerist Germany, Granach occupied a leading place in the German theater world. It was not possible to list Germany's ten greatest dramatic actors and to leave out the name of Alexander Granach.

Granach was not the only Jew among the great, but almost certainly the only one with a vigilant intuition and with a consciousness of his historical Yidishkeit [Jewishness, connoting an emotional connection to Judaism and/or to the Jewish people and their history, beliefs and customs]. Granach never tried to wipe away Yeshaya Gronik, the poor baker boy from Horodenka, from Zolishtchik [Zalishchyky], from Kolomea and from Stanislav.

The familiar tone was always articulated from Granach's stage persona and it was noticeable in his familiar gestures of a Jewish man of the people who combined the philosophical gentleness of Sholem Aleichem's Tevya the Milkman, the strength of [Joseph] Opatoshu's Kivke Gonif [Kivke the thief] and [Zalman] Shneur's Noakh Pandre and the stormy protest of a modern Jewish proletarian defender. Somewhere this element of Granach, the Jew from Horodenka and from Kolomea, was sublimated in all of his roles: in Faust, in Shylock and in Professor Mamlock. Granach's Jewish color and sounds were always noticeable and could be discerned in them.

Alexander Granach was a Jewish man on the German stage who acted in German. But in his core, he always interpreted the persona of that sad–smart and stormy–

[Page 321]

loquacious Shaya from his village of birth, Wierzbowce [Verbivtsi], after which his father named him[1] and which he himself immortalized in his book of memoirs, S'geyt a Mentsh [published in English as There Goes an Actor].

I became acquainted with Granach in 1915 in the Austrian military in the "Joint Division" (division of officer candidates). He served the officers there in the casino, did recitations of Faust for them and earned applause and enthusiasm from them.

After the [First World] war I met him in Kolomea. He was active at the Jewish Social Democratic Party and was a beloved speaker at their meetings. And he reached the very apex of oratorical success. He stood at the Torah reading desk at the large synagogue and thundered a protest against the pogroms against the Jews in Lemberg. It was an unforgettable speech. Granach expressed Shylock's irony and revenge, the self–sacrifice of Kivke Gonif and the clever wisdom of fate of Tevye the Milkman. In short: This speech in the Kolomea synagogue was the prelude to Granach's later 20–year–long theater [career], where the previously mentioned elements of persona occasionally emerged in succession and occasionally together.

At the time of Hitler, he wandered to the Soviet Union; from there (after months in prison) to Switzerland, and from Switzerland to America, first to California and then to New York.

He tried to act in the Yiddish theater, but the glory days of Yiddish theater in America had long passed. There was no place for Granach in the theater.

He began to write his memoirs. The book of memories was published in German and Swedish. He could not find a Yiddish publisher during his lifetime.

This grieved him greatly – but was this bitterness drawn into his heart?

Granach died suddenly after an appendectomy on the 14th of April 1945. I saw him dead in his coffin. A smile was frozen on his face, which gave evidence that Granach left the world without complaint and in the very fervor of hope, of faith and with love of the people.

Translator's footnote:

1. It is possible that the author is referring to the root of the village's name, Verbe, the Yiddish word for willow, and that Granach's given name, Yeshaya or Isaiah, echoes Isaiah 44:4: "...and they will flourish among the grass like willows by streams of water."

Khurbn [Holocaust]

[Pages 325-356]

Khurbn [Holocaust]

by Chana Weinheber-Hacker

Translated by Claire Hisler Shefftz

Edited by Benjamin Shefftz

The Annihilation of the Jews of Kolomey June, 1941 - February 1943

The Beginning of the Holocaust in Kolomey

(This account includes testimony from Sally and Sigmund Tager and Andi Lederfeind, Kolomeyers who survived the Holocaust and now live in Israel)

After the Soviet army left Kolomey, the Ukrainians took control the city. They immediately began to persecute the Jews and carried out a small pogrom.

The Ukrainians savagely hunted for Jews in the streets; they bound them with rope and chains; they bloodied them; and with laughter and mockery, they drove them to the statues of Lenin, Stalin and other Soviet leaders in the city park, on the Ringplatz, and on Vollnastzy [Wolnosci] Avenue.

They tied the Jews to the statues and they forced them to use all their strength to remove the stone and cement monuments along with their foundations and drag them all over the city.

That day, the Ukrainians also robbed and plundered the Jewish houses. Luckily, no Jews were killed. Many, however, were badly hurt and had to spend weeks in bed with broken ribs. Others went around with beaten heads, swollen and wounded.

Soon afterward, the Hungarian army took over the city. The Jews relaxed and breathed more freely. The Hungarians merely forced Jews over 12 years of age to wear a white armband with a blue Jewish star.

In July, 1941, automobiles with Gestapo appeared in the city. The German murderers caught 110 Jews in the streets, in the shuls, and took them away to the nearby village of Koroloavke. There they forced the Jews to dig a grave for themselves. When the Jews finished the graves, the murderers ordered them to undress and crawl naked into the graves.

Just as the murderers raised their rifles to shoot the Jews, the Hungarian commandant of the city appeared and with a stern voice demanded that the Jews be turned over to him since he was in charge of everything in the city. In this way the commandant managed to save the Jews from a certain death. And after they were held in prison for several days, they were all freed.

This attack by the Gestapo murderers resulted in the death of two Jews.

Germans Take Over the City and Begin to Torment the Jews

On the eve of Rosh Hashanah, 1941, the Germans took over the city and immediately began to persecute the Jews. On the first day of Rosh Hashanah, entire streets were emptied of Jews. The Germans drove the Jews out of their houses into the street just as they were. They didn't let the unfortunates take a single thing with them. The mood of the Jews was heavy and strained, and the suffering great.

They began to round up Jews for "work." They caught Jews in the streets, and with blows, mockery and insults, they drove them to the railroad station to unload freight trains and to switch rails.

Before starting work, they beat them with fists and sticks, and later they forced the Jews to unload heavy barrels and other things from the wagons with wild urgency. They hounded and wore out the unfortunates so much that they were left without strength and could work no more. Then the murderers began to scream that the Jews were lazy and did not want to work, and they took the exhausted ones and threw them into ditches filled with water and lime.

In the evening, when they finally let the tormented ones go, not one of them could stand up without help, and friends and acquaintances brought them home fainting, more dead than alive.

At the same time the Germans began to take Jewish women to clean their quarters. So the women fared a little better than the men. They were given no pay and no food, but they weren't beaten and they came home in the evening with unbroken bones.

This "work" was done under the supervision and orders of a special group, which was called "Zonderdienst." The civil administration and the Gestapo came later.

Jews Are Forced to Give Up their Gold, Silver, Jewelry and Foreign Money

At the beginning of August, the Jews were somewhat relieved when the 26 year old Volkmann took over the city administration. He said he would do the Jews no harm if they were loyal and obedient to all the German orders.

His first order was that they were to give him all their gold, silver, foreign money, jewels, and other valuables.

The Jews obeyed and gave up everything. They believed that by giving everything away, they were buying their lives. For the next two or three days in a row, the Jews often stood in line from four in the morning until late afternoon so that their gold and other things could be taken from them and came home hungry and dead tired in the evening and collapsed. And the next day if they had anything left, they still went off to line up with their remaining worldly goods as ordered.

You must understand, that not everything which one owned was given away. And what was left had to be entrusted to Polish or Ukrainian "friends" to hide. For whoever had not given away everything was in danger of his life. If a Jew was found with a piece of jewelry or gold, he was punished with death. This was in the first half of the month of August, 1941.

The German "Wehrmacht" Appears in the City

In the second half of the month of August, one morning at about five o'clock, I looked out my window of my house on Legyonove Street, and saw it filled with German troops with helmets on their heads as though they were preparing for a battle.

I immediately woke up my family. At the same time I heard the creaking of the gates and the soldiers knocking and banging with the butts of their rifles and shouting, "Jews, Open!"

Soon after that we heard cries for help from the beaten Jews.

On another day, the German soldiers drove several thousand Jews to one spot and beat and tormented them. They threatened that they would soon kill them. But they didn't do it, since at the time there was no established government in the city to give them the right to do it. And the German murderers claimed they had killed and murdered only when they were ordered to do so. This time they rounded up the Jews to torment them and to shed their blood.

Several hours later, they allowed the Jews to go home. They said that they had carried out this persecution of the Jews because the Jews had spit on a German officer. You must understand that this was a false accusation.

An Order to Organize a "Judenrat"

The head of the city, Volkmann, ordered that a Judenrat was to be established in the city. Motye Horowitz was appointed head of the Judenrat. From then on, all German orders for the Jews were given through this Judenrat. (The murderers did this in order to carry out many of the robberies and bloody deeds with the help of the Jewish organization.)

To begin with, the Judenrat had to provide good homes for the German officials and Gestapo. Because of this, Jewish families were forced to move out of their houses. "Officials" of the Judenrat went from house to house, much to our shame and sorrow, to carry out searches, and if they found valuable things they took them away without pity. One must point out here, that these "officials" turned over only a portion of the stolen objects to the Gestapo. They later sold many of the valuables to the Poles and the Ukrainians, or they hid them for themselves.

The Judenrat also had the responsibility of providing Jewish workers for the Germans. These workers were beaten and tormented at work so much that they were all but crippled. Because of this, the Judenrat then had to replace Jewish workers.

On Shabbat, during the day of the eve of Hoshana Rabbah, 1941, the Gestapo began to search houses for Jewish teachers. The Ukrainians had prepared a list of names and addresses for them, and then led them to the houses and helped them find the teachers. They caught a few teachers then; the others hid in time. A deathly fear descended upon the Jewish intelligentsia but no one knew yet that death loomed over everyone.

Hoshana Rabbah 1941

On Sunday morning the Gestapo were seen on the streets of the city along with groups of Polish and Ukrainian "helpers," mostly 14-16 year old ruffians. A wild attack began on all who wore white armbands with blue Jewish stars. The caught women and men. The murderers went into the synagogues and with blows and curses they drove out the Jews, still wearing their prayer shawls, and chased them all to one place. Soon afterward, they set the synagogues and houses of study on fire.

No one could understand what the murderers wanted, since it was Sunday, and usually on Sunday they weren't taken out to work.

The murderers also broke into Jewish homes and dragged out the people just as they were. Some were dragged out of their beds and driven out naked and barefoot. Woe to those who decided to hide. They were killed without mercy.

In a few houses on Vollova Street and on Mitzkevitch Street, they did not disturb women who had infant children. The also didn't bother several families on Mokra Street when they saw that they were healthy and clean.

That evening, they drove together the men in the streets near the Prut [River]. These Jews, 4500-5000, were taken to the jail overnight.

The next day they asked those who were arrested if any of them wanted to volunteer for work. Many healthy young people who wanted to save themselves from prison volunteered for work. They did not know that this was just a trap that the murderers had planned in advance to do away with them. They took these young people to the Szeparowice forest, six kilometers from the city, and there they forced them to dig mass graves for themselves and for those who remained in the prison.

Digging the graves took a whole day. And as soon as they were done, they lined them up near the pit and shot them all.

In the city no one knew where they had taken the young people. The Jews thought that they had taken them away to Germany to work in the factories there.

The murderers did this day after day, nine days altogether. Every day they took hundreds of Jews away to the forest and killed them.

The Jews who remained in prison lived in the most frightful conditions. They stuffed them into rooms like herrings. There was no place to sit or stand. They were given nothing to eat or drink. They became so hungry and dirty that they wished themselves dead. On the ninth day they were released from such a life forever. They were taken to the forest in trucks and there they were all killed. The slaughter lasted a whole day.

In the city, they did not know what had happened to these people. They spoke of letters that were supposed to come from Germany, Krakow, Viyelichke. But no one had seen or read such letters. Some even spoke of the names of workplaces where the people from the transports were employed.

It wasn't until weeks later that they found out what the murderers had done with the Jews and that all the stories about the letters had been false.

Great anguish was felt in the city after the terrible massacre. Everyone felt the nearness of death and everyone looked for a way to save himself and his near ones. The houses of the gentile inhabitants seemed as though they were holy buildings and it was everyone's dream to find himself under the roof of sucha house. Whoever could still afford it paid any price to a Pole or Ukrainian who was willing to rent a room or even a corner. An exodus from the Jewish streets had begun

"Mokra" Action At number 9 Shkarpove [Szkarpowa] Street, there lived a Jew who was in the militia during the Russian occupation. The Gestapo searched for him. They did not find him in his house since he had hidden himself elsewhere. Because of this, the Judenrat was given an ultimatum: If the suspect did not give himself up in one hour, all the Jews in that street and in the neighboring streets would be killed. The family, who knew exactly where he was, let him know about the ultimatum. The Jew soon left his hiding place, appeared before the Gestapo, and was immediately shot on the spot. But the search for the former militiaman, was no more than an pretext for a greater undertaking. Ignoring that the Jew had been immediately killed, the murderers soon went into the Jewish houses and without pity they dragged out Jewish men, women, and children and herded together 500 souls and imprisoned them. The next morning they took them away to the Szeparowice forest and shot them there.

The Collection of Furs

Having seen what had happened, the people lived in constant expectation of new extraordinary tricks and deceptions. Days passed with no end to beatings, and confiscation of dwellings, furniture, clothing and so on.

In the month of December, shortly before Christmas, it was revealed that arrests were to take place. According to an official command, the most prominent and the richest Jewish householders in the city were taken to jail. A day later, it was learned that they were not in danger, they were only being held as prisoners for 14 days, until the Jews would hand over all their furs, their fur hats, fur trimmed clothing, and so on. If they were deceptive and didn't honestly hand over everything, the Jews who were being held as hostages would all be punished.

The Judenrat took care of all this "work." The "officials" knew very well those who owned a fur coat and if someone chose not to give up the furs or tried to hide something, he was arrested by the Judenrat and put in the Jewish jail. The jail was in an unheated room in the Judenrat building. The prisoner was kept there without food or water, until he gave up everything that the Judenrat demanded and they turned it all over to the Gestapo. For hiding furs, the sentence was death.

The Jews gave away almost everything. Seldom did anyone hide anything with a Christian. They did not want to live in fear. And the fear of death was great. The German rulers, giving the appearance of "honest people," kept their word and freed the hostages after they had all the furs. They freed the prisoners, although a few days later, they arrested them again to condemn them.

Intelligentsia Action

Early in the morning on January 24, 1942, small groups of Jewish intellectuals escorted by Gestapos could be seen on the streets. It became known at 10 a.m. that they had used a list to collect doctors, teachers, and lawyers. The names and addresses, all precisely given, gave them no chance to hide themselves. If they didn't find the ones they wanted, they took the best substitute member of the family in his house.

They didn't only take the intellectuals. They also took those who had been held as hostages during the fur confiscation. Other rich and prominent Jews from the city were also taken,

But the rich were not badly treated. This time the Gestapo behaved "properly." They allowed them to take their coats and a meal with them. The families of those who were arrested had the right to bring warm clothes and food to them.

This action took a whole week. Everyone trembled lest he should happen to qualify as an intellectual or a wealthy man, and lived all week in fear of death. They couldn't believe that this category of people would be killed. These people were certainly in learned positions. And it was believed that they would be very differently treated than the other Jews who had been killed.

A week later they took them all away. They did not take them to be killed in the forest by the usual route; therefore people began to believe that they had been sent to a concentration camp in Germany. It was later revealed that they took them to Szeparowice by a different route and there they killed them all. A small part of the intelligentsia that the Germans still needed remained in the city.

The Ghetto

In February, 1942, it was announced in the city that a ghetto was being prepared. News came from Stanislav that there was already a ghetto there, and that Jews in the ghetto actually fared better than they had previously. In truth, they were suffering but they weren't destroyed, and for the time being they were not in fear of being killed. So people wished that the ghetto would soon be established.

The arrangements between the Gestapo and the Judenrat took a few weeks. No one realized that it was all a farce and the ghetto was not meant to be a dwelling place in which to live, but only a collection center from which to be taken to die.

The Gestapo had chosen only certain streets and houses and the Judenrat wanted more. In the end it was settled. Three Jewish quarters were planned and closed off from the outside world with wooden gates. The last day for moving into the ghetto was March 24, 1942. Anyone who was found outside the three Jewish quarters after that date would be shot to death. Only workers whose workplace was outside the ghetto could leave the ghetto. Groups of workers who were employed in a factory had to go out together under the supervision of an "arishn kolege," which escorted them from the ghetto gate each day. For single workers, their work pass was enough to get them to their workplace.

The gates were guarded by Jewish or Ukrainian auxiliary police, who were organized at the same time that the ghetto was established.

Jewish Police [Ordnungs Dienst] (A.D.)

Several weeks before the move into the ghetto, the Judenrat began to recruit the A.D., and in order to be a member of the A.D., money or influence was needed. People believed that membership in the A.D. would give them a better chance of going out from the ghetto more easily and thus enable them to provide their families with all they needed in order to survive. And by then each Jew had already suffered great need and hunger. People had also heard from other cities where ghettos had been established earlier that the Jewish police had earned a lot of money. The members of the A.D., however, had abused their power. They were supposed to watch the ghetto gates. But they used to help the Ukrainian police search the Jews when the Jews came back from work in the evening. They searched to see if the Jews had hidden a little bit of food in their clothes for their families in the ghetto. And since each worker, out of great need, was forced to "smuggle," the A.D. extorted from him a portion of the food or all of the food, or a cash payment. The A.D., also took away or, better said, robbed the Jews who were taken away of their remaining possessions; they could step out of the ghetto without being stopped and trade or sell the items. They also helped the Gestapo in the time of the "actions".

Their task was originally to maintain order in the ghetto and to accompany the Jewish workers.

The Passover Action and the Days from April 3-6, 1942

On Friday morning, April 2, all the workers who left the ghetto to go to their workplaces were brought to the gathering place at Kopernika Street and brought before a commission. The older and weaker people were taken to prison right away; all the others were murderously beaten and sent to work. Chaos and panic on the streets went on all day.

In the morning the Jewish quarter was cut off from the world. The gates were locked and Ukrainian auxiliary police and some S.S. stood by the first Jewish quarter. Gestapo and Schutzpolizei from Tarnopol entered the ghetto. They tore down the gates and wildly dragged out whoever they found in the houses, both grownups and children from their cradles and drove all of them to the gathering place in the High Synagogue and there sorted them out again: in one area the old people and in another the young people and those able to work. The sick people were shot in their beds during this action. The Jewish A.D. was soon active in the action. And again they were told that they still did not intend to send the people directly to their death.

They crowded hundreds of people into one room in the Handlers Synagogue; those who did not suffocate in the first few hours were loaded into cattle wagons three days later, 100 to 140 in a wagon, without water or food (the dead were also taken along), and were taken away to an unknown destination. This was the first transport to Belzec.

The same thing happened on Shabbos, April 4, in the second Jewish quarter. In ice cold weather and snow, they took half naked people to a small place on Mokra Street. They forced them to do various "exercises" and afterwards they took them away.

Monday, the second day of the Christian Pesach, was the day for the third quarter. This time people tried to hide themselves. But it was hell for anyone whom they found hidden.

So as not to waste time on the hidden Jews, the Gestapo threw fire bombs into every house and in a few minutes almost the whole Jewish quarter was engulfed in flames. The S.S. kept watch all day to make sure that no one put the fire out. And the A.D. took part in all the actions.

On the second day, the dead bodies of those who fled the flames and were shot by the Gestapo could be seen lying on the streets. Hundreds of burnt bodies were found in cellars, in closets, and in other hiding places.

Hunger-Death

After these gruesome events, everything "quieted down" a bit. The emptied-out houses filled up again with Jews driven out of the provinces. Not many of them could find a safe haven in these houses. Many of them settled for the meantime in the synagogues, in the ruins of the houses which the Germans burned and in the attics. The had no linens or clothing. They were infested with vermin. Their money and valuable things had been taken away by the Germans. They had no way to earn any money. They were forced to beg. But the original residents also suffered from lack of food. Even if someone were given a few kilos of flour to hide in his clothes and smuggle through the ghetto gates, he did it at the risk of his life, and the bit of food had to be kept frugally. The same guards was not always at the gate. There were several weeks when it was absolutely impossible to bring anything into the ghetto.

So truly the strangers, meaning the Jews from the surrounding areas, who brought nothing with them, were the first victims of hunger. With them also perished longtime residents. First they became famished and gaunt. Then they became swollen. Their facial features became prominent. The swelling spread to their eyes, nose, and mouth, the cheeks grown large, and the feet covered with open sores. And so in such a way, they went about and begged, as long as they could still move their feet. Afterwards they remained lying in one place, and begged further unit they gave up their souls to hunger. There were 50 - 60 such deaths each day. For days they lay until the truck picked them up and buried them in the Jewish cemetery in one mass grave. Almost every day someone from the Gestapo came to find out how the "hunger death" action was coming along. They must have had enough deaths to be happy with the results.

How They Dealt with the Jews from April 7 to September 7, 1942

As was said, after the actions that were carried out on Pesach, no more mass murders took place. They made it clear to the Jews that whoever worked would have no hair of his head disturbed. But anyone who did not work would be killed. So the Jews were eager for any work. And for every position, they were ready to pay with their last bit of money, with clothes and with other worthy things. The workers gathered in certain places: some were brought to their existing jobs by their escorts; others were taken as day laborers by the Germans to clean the streets, hospitals, and public institutions, to load and unload freight at the railroad station, and to make munitions. In the fall when there weren't enough horses, they hitched the Jews to heavily loaded wagons, and with blows they forced them to drag the wagons for miles at a time. The workers often went home badly hurt and with broken bones. Everyone had to take food from home with him. Whoever didn't have any, worked without eating. In the factories where they had steady work, they were "paid." The pay was between eight and 250 zlotys a month. A bread that weighed two kilograms cost 60 zlotys in the ghetto.

Not everyone could get work. Not everyone had enough money to but a job somewhere. In such a case, the person without a job had to sit in the ghetto and wait for his death. Anyone that had anything left to sell or trade for bread, did so. For a new unused men's suit, one could get 12 kilos ungrounded grain. For a pillow case, two kilos of potatoes; for a decent woolen dress, four kilos grain, and so on.

Those who had sold everything became swollen and starved to death.

In order to get "premiums" for their "wares," others even risked taking off their armbands and sneaking out of the ghetto to go to gentile houses. It often happened that they were caught and shot. Most often the deals took place near the ghetto gate. If the guard did not notice or turned aside for awhile, the Jews came out on one side of the gate, the Christians on the other side, and the trading began. If they were caught by the Ukrainians stationed there as guards or by the Jewish A.D., they bought their way out with half of their "earnings," or sometimes with all of their "earnings," and thus were overjoyed to have escaped with their lives. A Gestapo would ask no questions and, right on the spot, do away with the person, or set his dog upon the "Jewish swindler" to tear him to pieces (Knackendoerfer). Not a single day passed without a bloody sacrifice. Thus, for example, on a nice summer day in 1942, the Gestapo brought 120 Jews, men and women, into the Jewish slaughter house and killed them there. Afterwards, they dragged other Jews there to take the slaughtered ones – some of whom were still breathing – outside and lay out the bodies for the Judenrat.

Thus the "rest period" lasted until the beginning of September. At that time news came from Lemberg and other cities that fearful actions which had never been heard of before were taking place there. And that work is no longer any protection, and that every Jew must prepare a good hiding place, since that would be the only way to save his life.

In Kolomey they began to talk of a new "registration." A fear of death engulfed the ghetto, and paying no attention to the frightful news from other cities, everyone scrambled to find work. In great haste, and using their last remaining resources, every Jew made an effort to get himself a work card. Jewish delegations went to the German work officials. The officials again assured them, that Kolomey, due to all the previous actions, had lost enough Jews, and that the remaining ones who wanted to work could count on their protection for themselves and their families. In the middle of July, 1942, all the men were ordered to a "registration." Anyone found at home or in the street that day at one minute past six in the morning would be immediately shot.

That day there were many corpses. But all those who assembled in the gathering place to register before a Gestapo committee were only praised and they sent the lucky ones home. The sick and the weak ones were shot. This was supposedly a sign that the Germans needed the Jewish workers and had no grudge against them. And the Judenrat persuaded the Jews to believe this.

The President of the Judenrat Takes His Own Life

But suddenly, the leader of the Judenrat, Motye Horowitz, attempted suicide. He took poison. The poison, however, was too weak and the doctors saved him. At the beginning of

November, he again attempted suicide by taking poison. This time he died in the hospital after much suffering.

On about the third of September several factories were told to bring all the Jewish workers' work cards to be stamped. Those with such a stamp and their families would then be protected from death. The factories collected the cards and brought them to the head of the Gestapo (Leideritz). There they stamped the cards of only one or two factories. The others were supposed to be taken care of a day or two later.

In the meantime it was ordered that on September 7 all Jewish workers and their families had to come to a second "registration." Every factory had an assigned place. The workers went first, their families came after them, according to the factory or the shop. Meanwhile they were considering: To go or not to go? In view of the outcome of the previous registration, yes, they should go, since those who had not gone paid a heavy price. Besides that, they had told the Jews frequently that those who did not work would be considered "scum" and would be eliminated along with their families. That meant that remaining in the ghetto was one hundred percent death. Going to register gave them a weak chance of remaining alive. The work officials and the Judenrat had assured the workers that no bad end awaited them.

On the morning of September 6, they went to their usual work with a heavy heart. They went with the feeling that they were leaving the ghetto gates for the last time, and that they were with their fellow workers for the last time in their lives. What will tomorrow bring? Which one of us will go to work again tomorrow? A quiet deep resignation reigned. And in the evening, they still packed a few scraps in their rucksacks to prepare the last, and certainly meager, evening meal. I also did this. When I came home, my sister's little one-and-a-half-year-old boy was already waiting for me. He could not speak yet and he could not stand on his little feet made crooked by hunger. But one thing he understood: When I come home in the evening, the fire is lit, something is cooked, and he also gets something to eat. He pulls me by my skirt to the stove, opens the little door, and with his little finger on his little mouth, he shows me that he wants to eat. Around the stove were also my remaining living family members: my husband and my two younger sisters. We drew out our last small dregs of weak coffee and left nothing for morning. Each one of us knows that this is the last evening that we will be together, and no one wants to remain alive knowing that the other died hungry. So, shall we for once eat until we are full, for once free ourselves from that gnawing feeling of hunger in the face of death? None of us dared to look at the other, for each glance might be saying farewell. And never before was there such a strong feeling of togetherness and never before was it so clear to everyone how dear we were to each other. With eyes full of tears, we sat by the light of candles (there was no electricity in the ghetto) at our last evening meal.

We were weary and heartbroken and tried to go to sleep. But fear and sorrow drove us from our beds. These were then the last hours we could be together and probably the last night of our lives. Heavy sighs rose among us from time to time. A despairing search for some kind of resolution. Should we go to the gathering place or stay at home?. We decided: My husband and my younger sister would go to the gathering place; the second sister, the mother of the little boy, would hide herself and the child in the bunker. Several days ago, she had tried to get some poison for the child so that he could have an easier death without suffering. Since she could find no poison, she decided to die along with her child. But soon after we arrived at the gathering place, she appeared there with the child. She couldn't stand the fear of death all by herself and she came to die together with all of us.

On September 7, 1942, at five o'clock in the morning, thousands of men, women, and children were assembled at various sites. All of them wore the best clothes they had in order to look good and appear to be healthy workers. They were mostly young people since the older ones did not want to leave the ghetto.

On the Kopernika gathering place, across from the city park where the registration was supposed to take place, there were eight thousand people at six o'clock in the morning. At eight o'clock, Leideritz, the head of the Gestapo appeared, with all the Gestapo, S.S. men, and the Ukrainian auxiliary police. The gate of the gathering place was locked, and we all knew we were doomed.

The registration began. A Gestapo came to each factory group and read out the names of certain workers from a list and those chosen were taken out of the lineup in order to go to the "good side." The chosen ones would remain alive. There were 1600 of them. All others remained on the "bad side," and their great suffering had begun. It was very hot and no water was allowed. Every few minutes an order was given: "Get up!" "Run!" Pregnant women, women with children in their arms, did not run fast enough. Bloody blows from whips and clubs fell upon their heads and nearly the whole area was soon red with blood. Many tried to escape. But it was not possible. The deadly coil reached everyone and soon there were dead bodies underfoot.

The "get up," "run," and "sit down" lasted several hours. After that they began collecting the clothes and belongings the people had. The searched all the people. The coats and clothes were thrown into a pile. The men were left only with a shirt, a pair of pants, and also shoes, which were by then worthless. The women were left with only the clothes they wore. All over the area could be seen scattered and torn money: Polish zlotys, dollars, and other foreign currency. They threw their jewelry and watches over the gate in order to keep them out of the hands of the Gestapo.

The cries of the children for water were impossible to bear. The adults also thirsted for a drink. But all that was surpassed by the suffering of the children and the despair of their mothers.

The 1600 who were selected to live were taken to a building on Volnastzy Avenue. The others, those destined for death, were tormented until five o'clock in the evening. Afterwards, they were brought to the railroad station, guarded by hundreds of armed guards, and were loaded into freight car to be sent to Belzec.

The streets were strewn with the dead. Every effort to run away was of no use. From 100 to 140 people in one freight car. No space to stand of lie down. Since the little slits of windows were nailed shut, it was soon stifling, and almost all the children and older people fell down fainting. A hard struggle with death began. Almost everyone concentrated their thoughts on longing for a drop of water. Some had spells of madness. The older people become suffocated; the children, who come to after having fainted, called out the words "water" or "tea." Their little bodies begin to shake, and soon again lied weak and motionless. Mothers put their hands around the little throats of their children in order to choke them. This is the only help they can give to their little ones. In one wall there is a split board. A little bit of air comes through the opening. People almost kill each other to get to the opening. The dead remain lying with the living. One can't tell which one has fainted or which one is dead. At night it's dark and no one has a match. In some freight cars people have matches but the air is thick that as soon as a match is lit, it goes out.

This is how it was until Lemberg. There the stronger men were taken to the work camp at Janowska Street. All the others were sent stark naked, men and women together, directly to the gas chambers at Belzec.

The Liquidation of the Second and Third Jewish Quarters
Children Go Out on the Streets from Hunger

After the number of Jews was reduced in this way, the authorities decided that the first Jewish quarter would be enough for those who were left. And this is how it happened. Some carried only as much as they could with their hands to their new "dwellings." Whole families were already rare: parents had lost their children and children had lost their parents. Nevertheless it was impossible to drive everyone into one corner. There were still too many Jews to crowd into the few small streets. And those who still owned something paid large sums to get housing. The destitute ones were thrown out into the streets. Despite the harsh cold, people had to live in destroyed synagogues, in cellars and in attics. Typical of those times were the homeless children. Without parents, without a home, they lived on the streets. With a little dish and a little spoon in their hands, they went from house to house and constantly one heard their little cries: "Lady, lady, only one little spoon of food," "Housewife, only a little bit of bread," "Lady, only some hot cooked soup." Only seldom was there found a warmhearted person for almost every woman was just as hungry as the begging child.

They wandered about forlornly until they perished, swollen from hunger.

Sunday Action

After September 7, it was understood that only the legal ones – that is, the 1600 people who obtained stamps at the last registration – would be allowed to live. There were still Jewish functionaries who received such stamps through the recommendation of the Gestapo head of Jewish affairs, Frost, for large sums of money (1500 zlotys). There were people who truly believed that such a stamp could protect them from death. The majority, however, soon stopped believing the Germans.

On Sunday, October 3 or 10, 1942, at five o'clock in the morning, the whole ghetto was surrounded by Gestapo, S.S. men, Ukrainians, and others. An armed murderer stood at almost every Jewish house. It was too late to try to escape from the ghetto. People could barely get to their prepared hiding places. Most people were still sleeping when the Gestapo, the S.S., the auxiliaries and others burst into their houses.

And again one could hear in the hiding places – since one could hardly see – the beatings with the clubs and the pitiful screams of the tortured men, women, and children.

The lucky ones who had the stamps remained in their houses; they supposedly had nothing to fear. They were, however, almost the first victims. The mocking laughter of the Gestapo was their reward for their dutiful and simple trust.

Afterwards the ordeal was the same as it was on September 7. The usual torment at the gathering place, and again the registration, where 240 factory workers (umschlagshtele), with new stamps and with new passes, were allowed to return home. From 4500 to 5000 Jews were loaded off to Belzec.

The Factories Become "Juden-Rein" [Free of Jews]

Several days later, an order came down that all Jewish workers were to be dismissed from the factories. It was the responsibility of the factory manager to make sure that not a single Jew remained in his establishment.

All those who were sent away from their jobs were assigned to jobs in the Hallerbach group and had to report for work each day.

All knew that this meant that they were sentenced to death.

When the Jews went to the September registration, they left the few things they still owned in their houses, very few of them returned, and those who did return could not carry a single thing with them when they left the two liquidated Jewish quarters. The gates of those Jewish quarters were locked. Inside the Jewish quarter they kept the Jewish auxiliary police [A.D.] and later also the Volks-Deutsch militia in order to guard the possessions left behind. Neither Jews nor Christians were allowed to enter without special permission. The overseer Hallerbach was appointed administrator of this treasure.

The big houses were cleaned out and converted into storehouses. From 180 to 200 Jews left the ghetto each day in order to work at cleaning up the liquidated quarter. Furniture, dishes, and clothes were brought to various storehouses.

The Jewish workers were under the supervision of the Volksdeutsch, and they spared them no blows, clubs, nor insults. Hallerbach himself delivered quite a few blows upon the "dirty Jews" when he came to oversee the work. And he came very often.

The Hallerbach Action

Wednesday, November 4, 1942, all Jewish workers were notified that on November 5, at 7 a.m. they must appear at the ghetto gate and go to work under Hallerbach's personal supervision. An order had come from Lemberg, in regard to the to the Hallerbach group, and a commission had decided that the work in the Jewish quarter must be completed by January 1, 1943.

What happy news for us! That meant that they will and they must let us live a whole two months. Some thought that it was a good thing if it were true. And the news reached us from Stanislav that the work group there had indeed been liquidated.

And again a depressing realization, for it could be foreseen that on that day there would be a bloody action against all those who remained in the ghetto. Of the two evils, the smaller one was chosen. The members of the Judenrat advised that it was best to go out, since the danger lay only in the ghetto. Not only the workers, but also those who hadn't worked previously, went

to the assembly place. Hallerbach came to the place alone that day. Along with him came an unknown Gestapo from Lemberg. Behind the Gestapo gate stood an automobile with machine guns. Everything looked different than usual. The guard was weak and there were still opportunities to escape, but no one tried to run away. Death was everywhere. It was hard to predict where one would meet death sooner: whether outside the ghetto, or inside the ghetto. So following Hallerbach's signal, the column of workers left the ghetto.

As soon as they took their first steps, the workers' group was surrounded by Gestapo, S.S., Ukrainian militia, and others. They were all brought to the famous gathering place on Kopernika Street. The workers knew what that meant. But this time all of them were resigned. No one even tried to run away. Everyone knew that he was lost. And even if one undertook to run away now, in a few days or in a few weeks he would be caught again. So the understanding was that everyone must die, sooner or later.

This time the people weren't held at the gathering place very long. At about ten in the morning they were brought to the prison. They took their clothes. They robbed them of all their valuables. The searches lasted until evening. They had to remain lying on the ground in a windy rainstorm and watch while the Gestapo hanged a "dangerous" Jew for everyone to see. The Jew had hit a Gestapo while trying to run away. The body remained hanging at the gate until the next day – a warning for all who might think of saving themselves.

The soldiers also indulged in such "exercises" as cutting out an unborn child, piece by piece, from the living body of a woman in her eighth month.

Meanwhile, murderous scenes were played out in the ghetto. They searched through houses and dragged out people. Around noon, they set fire to the ghetto, and everyone who dared to come out of a burning house was shot. All the patients in the Jewish hospital were killed right there.

The night in the courtyard of the prison was frightful. The bitter cold, the heavy rain and wind, did their worst. The children screamed and their mothers were unable to help them.

First thing in the morning, November 6, the execution was carried out.

Halfway to Szeparowice, they undressed everyone half-naked, and led them thus to the place of their execution. At night everyone waited for his turn. The execution took a whole day.

The Action Against Old People

In the ghetto there still remained several hundred people. (When the ghetto was established, there were over eighty thousand, including those from the surrounding areas.) Some held that there were still 700 people in the ghetto and others said there were 1200 people. No more searches were carried out. Whoever could do so lived in hiding. Mostly, these were old people and children.

Four days after the Hallerbach action, the Judenrat received the order to shoot 500 old people. This time the Gestapo did not come to the action. It was given over to the Jewish A.D. to carry out and the A.D. copied their masters very well. Without pity, every hiding place was torn down. And if they couldn't find the hidden ones, they forced the sons and the daughters to give up their parents. And if the daughters refused to reveal the hiding place, took the mothers and their children to the slaughter. Shameful bargaining began. Sons bought back their mothers or fathers for several hundred dollars. They took the money and in place of an old one, they sent a young life, a child. For the required number of corpses had to be correct. There were also situations where someone took the ransom money, freed the old person, and soon told another A.D. about the hidden one, and the second one took the victim since there was no money left to buy back the person one more time. Every day they needed new victims. The childrens' action came right after the action against the old people which had lasted several days. It was claimed that the homeless and orphaned children were not productive and were a burden upon the city. So they all have to be put to death.

The A.D. also took care of this work. They did not only search for homeless and orphaned children. That would be too much trouble for them. Wherever they saw a child, they put an end to him. In some cases, if the parents had money, they were able to buy back the child. They brought the children to the prison, just as they had done with the old people.

Children Action

Shortly after the execution that the Hallerbach group carried out, a Gestapo delegation from the ghetto appeared in the prison courtyard in order to bring back to the ghetto a few "life-worthy" Jews. They had probably received a lot of money from the families of the people whose names were called out. And so those few were chosen, even though their days or weeks were numbered, to have their lives prolonged. Among the names was that of a woman who had just been killed a few minutes ago. I sized up the situation, grabbed my child and got up from the ground calling: "That's me!" In a hail of blows and beatings with rifle butts (those who were sorted out for death were not allowed to get up from the ground). I fought my way through to the prison exit gate. I hid my child under a piece of furniture that was there and soon I was in the group of 15 who were let out. They brought us to another part of the prison (I also managed to smuggle my child in). A feeling of relief swept over me for having escaped death and for having kept my child alive. (My husband and my last living sister remained in the courtyard and I could hear the preparations for their executions and their last steps to death.) It was the same for the other 14. Their loved ones were also being tormented and they could foresee with anguish their soon-to-be executions. But those who were inside the prison cell were happy with their poor little bit of life, painting pretty pictures for themselves of how good it would be if they only let them sit there for a year. There in that place they were reborn, there they were protected under lock and key and from prison guards.

But this "idyll" did not last very long. Only one night. As soon as they had taken the group in the prison yard to Szeparowice to be executed, Hallerbach showed up in order to identify the saved ones. He knew me well because I had worked for him for a long time. It was then his choice whether this Jewish woman or another one should remain alive. The money was already in his pocket. He counted the people- and discovered my child. Woe, woe, we are again lost. But my prediction was wrong. They didn't take the few unknown Jews to be killed. (Only the unseen were given that "honor." After they finished their work, they were killed.) They were sure that the sacrifices would not escape from the ghetto prison. Hallerbach counts..."Fifteen and a half" (half was my child). "So, dirty Jews, this is the right place for your heads, get up." Overjoyed, we left the prison gate; but where could we go? Death was everywhere in the ghetto. We went into the former Horowitz factory. That was the warehouse where we had sorted the clothes of those who had been killed. We felt safer there. The building belonged to the Gestapo and formerly there was always certain to be work there. The clothes of those who were now in Szeparowice were always brought there.

The A.D., which guarded us, had the right to come into the ghetto any time. Soon they brought us the news that the great slaughter was soon to end; and now they were looking for a few Jews, "personalities" who were Gestapo helpers, and they would be shot, one by one. Two Jews who had spent the previous night with us in the prison were forced to turn back and were taken away and killed. The A.D. also told us that the Gestapo were not interested in finding every one who remained. Some Jews were still left, and death and despair looked out from their eyes. The streets looked lifeless and were covered with unburied dead.

In the meantime they brought the "transport" from Szeparowice (that is, all the clothes and shoes of those who were killed), and we were off to "work."

I found there my winter coat, which had been taken from me before the execution, and my husband's suit; my husband had been killed in that execution.

The same day, in the evening, we went back to the ghetto. I quickly heated a little bit of coffee, and I put the child into a warm bed.

Typhoid Fever in the Ghetto

The old anguish began again. In frost and night, every day at five in the morning, I pulled my child out of bed, and quietly left the ghetto to find a hiding place for my child for the day. In the Hallerbach warehouse I used to hide my child under a pile of garbage, in feathers, under pieces of broken furniture, and in other places. I worked at "sorting." In the evening we went back to the ghetto. This is how it was for five days.

On the fifth day after the Hallerbach action, the child couldn't get out of bed. It had a high temperature and remained lying in bed. I, however, had to go out of the ghetto. I had to find a way to save the child. I had to bring a little bit of food. Would I still find the child there when I came home? And what would happen if they would find me out and the child remained in the ghetto, small, helpless, and sick? But what use is heartbreak and despair? I kiss my child (perhaps for the last time?) and leave the ghetto. After a day of maternal anxiety, I went back to the ghetto with a shaky heart. Was my child still alive? Will I see her again? My child met me in the room, dressed, with frightened eyes. "Mama," she said, "today the Judenrat ordered that all mothers must give away any children who are still alive. Will you give me away?" I answer her: "No, my child, either we will both save ourselves or I will go to die with you. Rest assured, my child, we will go on our final journey together." Her eyes lit up with happiness and gratitude. But soon the light went out. "Mama, why should you die because of me? You are still young and a lot of mothers save themselves without their children." In the evening, her fever went up from 40 to 40.5 degrees [104 to 104.9 degrees Fahrenheit]. On the second day, the Jewish A.D. men rampaged through the ghetto; they knocked on the gates of every area and each step of theirs meant death for my child. What should I do? I found a Jewish doctor. He examined the child and it was obvious: typhoid fever. There was no time to be lost.

The ghetto is small. Not many people – a few hundred, perhaps a thousand, and they know more or less which house still has a child in it. The truth is I had almost no chance of keeping my child alive. It was only six days after the Hallerbach action and I wanted to ease the child's death. On the second night, I dressed the child, took her in my arms, carried her out of the ghetto and brought her to our former dwelling. The snow was deep. It was hard not to leave tracks in the uninhabited former Jewish quarter. When I arrived, I laid the child down on the stone floor in the kitchen since that was the only place that still had walls even though there was no door or windows. The whole house had been plundered and ruined.

We had no bread and no water. The snow kept on falling. Every footprint could have given us away. During the night I brought in a little snow and ice and cooled off my child's forehead and lips with it. Four days later, my child's agonies began. Her whole body was all swollen and I decided that for her last hours I would bring her to the ghetto so that she could die in bed. Just then a Jewish work brigade went by. I told them what was going on and on their way back they took me with them. The dying child was stood on her feet (as though she were also coming from work) and two workers pulled her along. Returning to the ghetto, I quickly brought in a doctor. He cut and pulled the clothes and shoes off her body and assured me that in four or five hours the child would die. And how does one wait out these few hours? The child is known to them and the murderers can take her away any minute. Today is the last day of the children action. I begged the doctor to give me a little bit of poison. The child didn't need very much now. But the Jewish doctors didn't have any poison. I gave him the small amount of money I still had so that he could buy some on the black market from a Christian doctor outside the ghetto. But it wasn't worth his trouble. Not a single doctor wanted to talk to him and he brought the money back to me.

Under my bed was a deep hole. A nest of many rats. Quickly, with the doctor's help, I enlarged the hole and stuffed the child in there. Anything was better than death at the hands of the Gestapo. I put my living child in the ground and I waited. Three, four, and five hours passed and the very wished for death did not come. And the hiding place was very primitive. It could be found any minute.

The day went by. Night came. And the child did not die. At night I crept out of the hole, made a glass of hot tea, and luckily, the child drank it. In the morning, the fever began to drop. The child wanted to eat. In several days (the entire time in the hole) the illness went away. The child remained alive and the children's action had ended.

In the same house, 29 people lived in 3 rooms. All except me became ill with typhus. The disease spread quickly throughout the ghetto. The sick ones could have wished for nothing better than to die in their own beds. But unfortunately, even though no one succeeded in calling a doctor or taking medicine that couldn't be obtained in the ghetto, almost nobody died. They knew: By the time of the execution everyone would be well and go to his grave on his own two feet.

No Gestapo crossed the gate into the ghetto. Nevertheless, the epidemic reached the other side of the gate. Even though only one old woman died of typhus in the ghetto, in the Christian quarter, with the best sanitary conditions and medical help, there were many deaths.

Kolomey Is Declared "Juden-Rein" [Free of Jews]

On December 15, 1942, the Judenrat was notified that the Jewish A.D. had been rounded up and the Gestapo had taken them to the prison in order to kill them along with the old people and the children in Szeparowice that day. Kolomey was declared a Juden-rein [free of Jews] city. And the Jews who still lived there had officially ceased to exist. As to their future fate, few of them had any illusions. The majority awaited their death which could come any minute. But they didn't know if their epilogue would come before Christmas or soon afterward.

The Gestapo also celebrated the Christmas holiday, the holiday of giving. With full pockets of what were once Jewish goods, they hurried to bring the holiday presents to their wives and children.

From December 20, 1942 until January 1, 1943, the Gestapo were on furlough and the Jews had a whole 10 days of rest. That meant that one could properly lie down in bed and cook a "meal" as it should be, leaving the pots on the fire without fear. No one had to run to the hiding places or fall into the hands of the invading murderers. Full days of rest and stretching out. Eating until "full" and sleeping enough. One even began to hope that one might remain alive.

[Page 336]

Map Of Three Ghettos

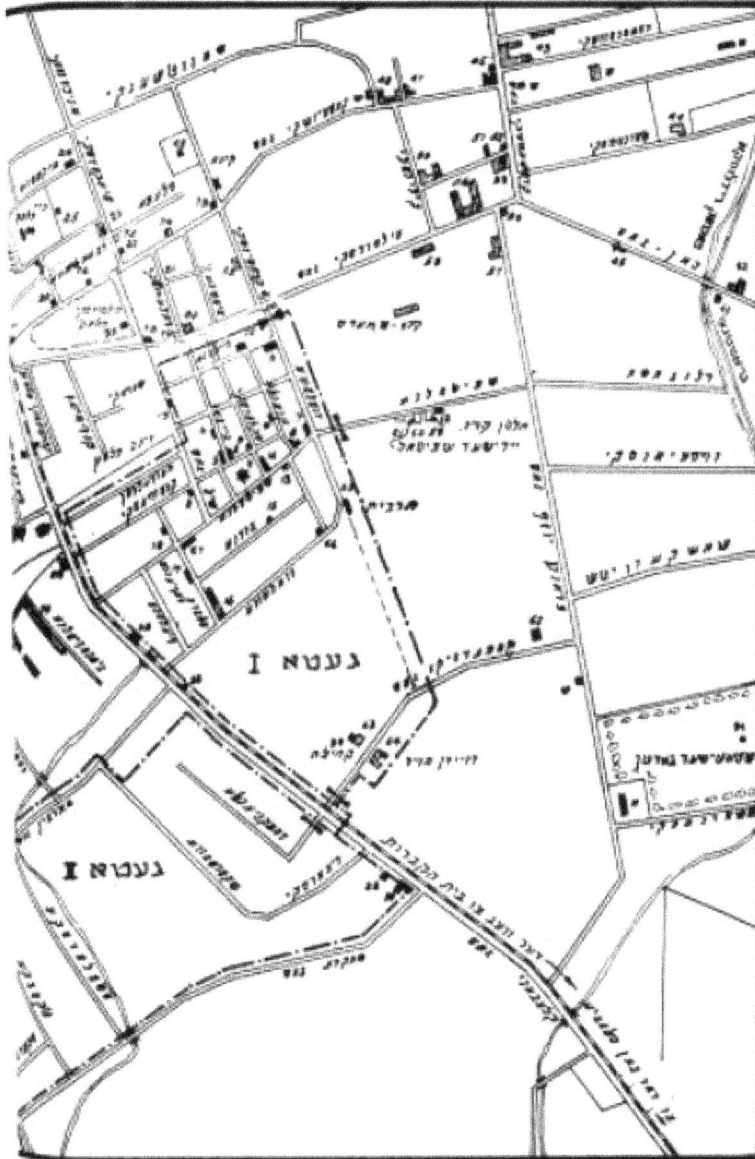

This rest lasted until January 1 and it was hard to believe that we were still alive. On January 20, 1943, discussions began between the Gestapo and the representative of the Jews, (Farbindungsman) Presser, about shrinking the ghetto and transferring Jews to other houses. The Gestapo chose for this purpose a part of Vallova [Walowa] street. Only a few hundred Jews were still alive and it was not possible to stuff them all into a few houses. The Jews interpreted this arrangement thus: The remaining workers and their families if such still exist, would actually go into the houses, and all others would probably find their place in a mass grave in Szeparowice.

This time we were wrong again. During the period from January 26 to January 31, all Jews had to go over to the "new" ghetto. Anyone who was found in the old ghetto after 6 p.m. on Janaury 31st would be immediately shot. So all the people went in together. From 30 to 36 persons in one room, hallway, or attic. But even in this way, all of them couldn't find a space. The cries and the wails were beyond description. They wished for an early end, and death was not long in coming.

Last Action

Soon after dawn on February 1, 1943, the first shots fell in the "new ghetto." The people who went out to work were caught right at the gate. The others were taken out of the houses. This time it was very easy for the murderers. First of all, no one expected such a quick liquidation, and second, there was no time to prepare a hiding place. Very few had prepared a place to hide.

The doctors and their families, who until now had lived outside the ghetto, were also taken in this action, and all were taken to the prison and sorted out there. Thirty people – eight doctors, two druggists, and 20 other skilled workers – were freed from the prison. They were given two houses where they had to live (without their families). All the others were taken to Szeparowice to be killed on February 2 at 11 a.m.

A pitiless search for Jews began again in the ghetto. The Ukrainian militia searched everywhere. Afterwards, the Gestapo searched with their tracking dogs. Those who were found in hiding were not shot, but were dragged over the snow-covered streets and were beaten until they could no longer move as punishment for not going willingly to their deaths on the appointed day,. Afterwards, they let them lie there like that until they expired. Under the threat of death, no one was allowed to give them food or water.

The Last Thirty

At the beginning of March, 1943, all the skilled workers, aside from the doctors, were taken out of their dwellings. They were brought to the Jewish cemetery and shot there. The doctors were all taken that same day and locked in a room that had been prepared for them, and told that they would be killed the next day. The seven doctors (one doctor, Dr. Gross, had run away somewhere previously) had poison with them and that night they all took their own lives. In the morning when the murderers came in order to take them to the cemetery, they found seven corpses.

[Page 336]

Khurbn [Holocaust] (cont.)

by Chana Weinheber-Hacker

Translated by Claire Hisler Shefftz

Edited by Benjamin Shefftz

Testimony from Sally Tager

Sally: While still young, a heavy fate was in store for me. In my sixteenth year I lost my father and in my eighteenth- my mother. Under this heavy burden, I struggled on with my life, without motherly love and fatherly protection. How lucky I was, when I was able to have my own home. And what a reward my children were, for all my burdens, loneliness, and solitude. I never dreamed that a person could be so lucky. All that I lacked in my youth, I gave to my children. That was many times over more than what I missed.

And my daughters were bright and accomplished. The elder, Rasia, was very musical. She was even more gifted in art. She studied in Lemberg in the art high school and she was considered a rising star there.

The younger one was also very artistically gifted. Still a student in the 7th class in gymnasium, she truly enchanted all onlookers with her dancing. The Soviet authorities tried to influence us to send her to Moscow so that she could get her artistic education there. But how could we part with the child? So we declined. But Hitler parted us. We lost both of our daughters.

On Shabbos, September 5, 1942, I went for my work as a hairdresser for the wife of a German officer. This was forced labor. I did not find her at home. I waited for her for a long time, and when she came, she was nervous and said that she had no desire to have her hair done. She also told me that in one or two days, all Jews would be brought together in one place, and they would all be shipped off to be gassed in waiting railroad cars. I left her house as though struck by thunder. Endless tears fell from my eyes and my mind kept working: How and where can I hide my children?

I looked around to see where on the streets I could find a shelter and a hiding place. When I came home, I found my daughter sick in bed with tonsillitis. Filled with thoughts of that tragic end, I greeted her with these words: "We are lost." According to the edict of the Gestapo, those who had a work card had nothing to fear. Since only three of us had work cards, and the younger daughter didn't, I decided that as a mother, I would share the fate of my lost child, remain in the ghetto and hide her there. My husband and my older daughter had to go to the "registration." On the night of the "registration," we went into the bunker. There were 12 people there. My husband nailed the bunker shut and we were cut off from the world. We stayed there until eight in the evening. We heard the "action" go on over our heads. Beatings, shots, woeful cries and the whistles of the railroad engines. The whistles still ring in my ears today; these were the signs of death – the last journey to the gas chambers.

Eight o'clock in the evening, a young man came, knocked on the bunker, and called out: "Mrs. Tager, all are alive and they have come home." I did not want to believe in such unexpected luck and I stifled the happy outcry of my younger daughter. To my great sorrow, my disbelief was correct.

When the bunker was opened, and when I saw my husband who had returned, I soon also saw my great misfortune. He had returned without our elder daughter.

Testimony of Sigmund Tager

At the time of the "registration" at the assembly place, I stood with my elder daughter, Rasia, in the "house servants section." The inspector of the house servants and his secretary came over to me, with trust and regrets, and assured me that all of us would soon be taken to our usual work. They took their leave of us and soon Leideritz, the head of the Gestapo, arrived. With his stick, he divided the group: a very small part for life and the rest for death. I was in the small group, and my daughter was in the large one.

I went to my inspector with a plea that he should intervene to save my child. He went to the Gestapo chief and was told: "Away!" His effort to help me was in vain. When I found out about this answer, I tried to go over to the "bad side" so that I could go on the final journey together with my child. Leideritz noticed my movement and with his foot he pushed me back to the "good side." The group destined to live was closely guarded and watched. At two o'clock we were taken over to the city park building. From there we were taken to an area between Lenyanova and Kopernika Street. There our work cards were stamped and we were sent home.

When we came out on the streets of the ghetto the next day, we saw many sorrowful faces and from everyone's lips we heard the question, "What happened with you?" "How many of you remained alive?" The answer was wordless: They held up only one finger of their hand.

Sally and Sigmund Tager Speak

There were very few houses set aside by the Gestapo for the last group of residents in the ghetto. It was impossible for everyone to find a spot for himself. Presser, who was in charge of the Jews who remained alive, asked the Gestapo authorities for more housing. To everyone's joy, Hertl, Eberhart, and Frost (all Gestapo officers) appeared in the evening. They observed the great need and added one big house to the previously chosen ones. That was again a sign that the sentence of death was postponed a little bit longer. But those who understood the situation very well knew that they must not fool themselves, and they hastened to leave the ghetto gate from the assembly place.

It turned out that the Gestapo officers had not come to make the Jewish living conditions easier, but to make note of the houses where the Jews lived, and, even on that same night, figure out how the easiest way of liquidating them.

We had a bunker in our house. We wondered, Should we hide in there after such a frightful day? Or was it better to wait and see what the night would bring? But our exhaustion took over and we fell asleep. But not for long. At three thirty in the morning we were awakened with loud knocks. It was a woman we knew who knew that we had a bunker. She ran to us after she found out that the ghetto had been encircled by Gestapo murderers. As soon as the woman was inside, we all went in to the prepared hiding place. Only two tailors who were still alive, because the Gestapo left them alone because they needed them, remained seated. Soon the Gestapo came and took them all, even the two tailors who were so sure of themselves. The murderers rampaged in the ghetto for three days and three nights, searched out every corner, knocked on every floor. At night we came out of the bunker. It was only a makeshift hiding place, intended only to save ourselves from the initial onslaught. We went to the better bunker that was prepared so that we could hold out there longer. As soon as we went in, a man with a three-year-old child came from somewhere. The frightened child began to cry. The father wanted to subdue him because the smallest noise could give us away. The child, however didn't understand this. The people there became upset, threw themselves upon the child, prepared to kill it; but the child kept on crying. The child's cry really did attract attention. The Gestapo were very close to the hiding place. The began to call: "Jews, Hebrews!" Suddenly a cat began to meow and that saved us. The murderers thought that the cat had been the one crying and carrying on, and they went away.

Meanwhile it began to be truly hell in the bunker. The small reserve supply of bread which was meant for a few people did not last very long. The newcomers, especially, threw themselves at the bread like wild ones, and ate it at night when the others were sleeping. Out of fright at the thought of being found, from regularly hearing the heavy treads of the Gestapo boots over their heads, everyone became nervous and suffered from diarrhea. The only pail for that purpose was always full. Once each night someone had to climb up a ladder, and the one who had to empty the pail was so overcome with fear and danger that when he lifted it to pour it out, he accidentally spilled some of it on himself. In the emptied pail we gathered some snow and pieces of ice which we used instead of water. With starved faces, covered with sweat from inner burning and thirst, the people used to throw themselves at the dirty pieces of ice and snow mixed with excrement.

After three days of such suffering and hardship, we began to realize that even death could not be worse. So we left the hell and were ready to die. On all fours, we crept from Vallova Street until the end of Legyanova [Legionow] Street, where the liquidation ghetto had been. We went into an empty house and stayed there for that whole night, and the next day until evening.

The struggle for life began with every step and with every moment. We went looking for a Christian driver we knew hoping to have several hours of rest there. But we didn't know where he lived. Our daughter, who was still alive then, saw two women. She was sure they were Christian women. So she began to ask them for the house of the driver. We were amazed to find out that they were two disguised Jewish women. They were also looking for a place to hide and they had been chased away. They warned us not to go there, because the driver would turn us in. Nevertheless, we went there. They really did let us in and hid us in an oven. In a few days they fell upon us, took our money from us, and drove us out of the house. So we went to another Christian to whom we had given our belongings. When she saw us she cried: "Jesus, Mary, what do you want from us? You are soon dead and we are still alive. Should we die because of you?"

And so we went from one to another. Our only home was the snow. After three weeks of such torment, we went to the railroad station to try somehow to get ourselves into another city. On the way we met Thaddeus Shklatchik, a former train engineer. He brought us to the railroad and promised to hide us in the coal car get us to Stanislav [Stanislawowa]. But he fooled us. He left us in the middle of an empty field and also forced from us our last bit of money and valuables. Only our daughter had a little bit of hidden money.

We ran to the Jewish cemetery where we found a broken down little house. We huddled close to our daughter with the hope of drawing some strength and will to live from her. Very early the next morning we went to the railroad station again. This time each of us stood in a different spot. If one of us were found out or recognized, the others could save themselves.

My heart stood still when I recognized the gate keeper as the son of a priest. He knew my children very well from school. There was no way to go back. We were waiting in line, first ourselves and then our daughter.

The gate keeper looked through our papers and let us through. But woe unto us! There was suddenly a disturbance. Everyone turned to see as my husband cried out to me: "We have lost our second child!"

The gate keeper had, it seemed, recognized our child; he did not let her through; he kept her aside until everyone had gone to the train and afterwards he turned our child over to death. Mad with grief, I screamed to my husband: "Come let us go with our child!" My husband, however, believed that we could help more by staying alive than by dying. Also, our daughter had enough money with her. Perhaps she could still pay to keep her life. We left the railroad station. After this, what meaning did our lives have and what was the sense of saving ourselves after we had lost both children? We had to find some people who could save our child from death. But how could we find such people, when death lies in wait on every street? And who wants to know us? And who will listen to us? When they catch someone who has spoken to a Jew, or even if they suspect him of having had anything to do with a Jew, he and his family have the same sentence as the Jew: They are all killed.

It so happened that once we crawled through a hole from a closet in an unoccupied house and from there over a wall into a house. We sat down on the floor to eat a morsel of bread, that we had found through a miracle and with great danger. The door opened and a Christian couple came in. They stood rooted in fright and speechless. Our fear and paralysis was beyond description. We jumped out quickly through the hole and began running in broad daylight. Convinced that we were being chased, we went as far as Szeparovke. There we looked around and saw that no one was coming after us. We saw a vacant spot with dried out corn stalks. So we stood them up, held them with our frozen hands (it was in the month of February), and stayed under them so that we would not be seen. Nearby that place, children were playing, and our hearts trembled hoping that they would not discover us.

Suddenly a hen came from somewhere to lay an egg and the hen's owner ran to look for her. He would soon be right next to us. With our last strength, we used our frozen hands to chase away the hen. And again we gained time. Was it minutes, hours? How could we know then?

The Gestapo headquarters were on Krashevska [Kraszewskiergo] Street, and opposite – the "Dom Ludovi" was the service building (the "Tod" organization [Death's Head], streets, and a brick building.) Many Jews had worked there (forced labor) for the ghetto liquidation process. Among them had been myself and my husband. Three young men were hidden on the roof of the building. The Ukrainians told the Gestapo about this and even though a Polish driver who lived and worked there warned the three; they did not run away. From the house across the way, the Gestapo came out and shot the three Jews there.

Three days later we were near this house. It was right at the time (8 p.m.) when they used to lock up the houses, and even the Christian residents were not allowed to be on the streets then. What could we do? In our great helplessness, we went to the previously mentioned driver, and begged him to find us a shelter for only that night. But how could he help us? The only thing he could do was to offer that same attic where those three Jews had been shot. He advised us that after going up there, we should drag the ladder along with us in order to wipe out every footprint. He also told us that at five in the morning, we should leave that place very, very quietly

The night was bitter cold, 40 degrees frost [-40 degrees Fahrenheit] and we also suffered from much hunger and fright that night. Before dawn broke, we set out quietly to leave our hiding place. But where to? The frozen ground crunched with every footstep and could have attracted the notice of the Gestapo. We came down and as just as we were by the railing, spotlight began to light up the area. It was the murderers searching the neighborhood. We clung to the railing and remained unnoticed. The light went out. The Gestapo patrol went into the house. And we again remained alive. We were already too exhausted. We wanted to die, just to be at rest. Every few minutes we decided to give ourselves up to the Gestapo. But death at their hands was so humiliating, so brutal, that against our will, we prolonged the torment of our being.

After many such shattering survivals and events, we came to the last 36 Jews whom the Gestapo officially allowed to remain alive. They took us up to an attic, kept us there until it was night, and smuggled us into a bunker through a fireplace.

In the bunker we found a bottle of turpentine. We were dirty and disheveled from the last few days. So we decided to clean and wash ourselves. Much to our misfortune, when we took the flask, a spark exploded. The noise from the spark gave us away to Dr. G. who officially lived under our hiding place. Very upset by our "carelessness," he began to search for our hiding place. He did not find us because two friends of ours quickly warned us, and got our persecutor out of the way. The Jews were afraid to keep us there and took us to a cellar that was in the same house.

We were not the only ones there. There were already several surviving Jews there. With them was a child. The child went to get some water. The Gestapo caught it. Alerted by the child's cries, the people began to run and were met by a hail of Gestapo bullets. We stayed in that hiding place, which was away from the upper hiding place which had almost been discovered.

In another part of the cellar, the last 36 Jews had built a bunker for themselves. Our friends Urvitch and Hacker brought us there. (The only one who survived was Urvitch. He now lives in Holon, near Tel Aviv.) Aside from us, there were three people there. (The 36 were still legal and didn't need to use the bunker.)

We told each other to keep still, quiet, because outside the bunker a channel had been built out, like a part of the bunker. There were, however, five of us, and because of our whispering, we gave ourselves away.

The previously mentioned Dr. G. quickly came to the door of the bunker and told us to open it. When we didn't answer, he began to speak: "Why are you afraid? I am just a Jew like you." We stubbornly kept quiet. So he angrily broke down the door and ordered us to leave by nightfall. If not, he would destroy the whole wall.

Where could we go? So we stayed there. At night Dr. G. sent one of his secret Polish helpers. He destroyed the concealed wall and we five illegals again were left unreprieved from death. One of us went away, perhaps somewhere else to seek her luck, and we hid ourselves with a six-year-old child behind the entrance door. Soon we heard the wailing scream of the woman who had been caught by the Gestapo; the murderers beat her with rifle butts and dragged her to the jail. We remained standing behind the door all day and had no way of getting a bit of food or water.

After several days of such hardships, a man who arranged for people to escape over the border came to the 36. He had been hired by others who had since died. Since the 36 were certain that crossing the border was a very dangerous undertaking, because the Jews were often robbed and afterwards killed, they sent him to us as a "possibility." We already had nothing to lose. So we hired him and chanced our luck to be rid of that hell.

We agreed to send a message after we crossed the Hungarian border. But our message never reached them. When the border crossing escort returned, he found only Urvitch alive.

Dr. G. was also alive. He had figured out how to find a good hiding place.

Testimony from Andi Lederfeind
(About the September 17 Action)

At the beginning of August all the men were ordered to register. They were all to be at Kopernik Place at 6 a.m. Right at 6 a.m. the next day the Gestapo came and began to look for the men who had not appeared. They immediately shot every man they found at home or on the street, young or old.

They came to my parents' house just when they were going into their bunker and at the time that my sister-in-law was locking the door. As soon as she left, she heard two shots. The murderers had found the hiding place and the two shots brought an end to their lives.

The order to register brought unrest and panic to the ghetto. People searched for legal ways to travel out to the villages. There were no ghettos in the villages and people felt they would be safer outside the walls. They hoped that in the villages there would be no searches. For large sums of money, the German work office issued "Cards for Economically Vital Work" (picking nettles for producing cloth and others).

Life in the village was a relief. Good nourishment and no Gestapo – until September 7th. On September 7th, Gestapo officials came and told the Ukrainian policemen (militia) to round up all the Jews. It did not occur to the village Jews who lived there (there were still some of these) that this was a danger to them. So they came of their own free will and presented themselves. They were soon brought to the railroad station and loaded into the waiting railroad cars and sent away.

In the same way, they also came to take me, my seven-year-old son, my sister and her eight-year-old little daughter and another three or four people to the registration. We bought ourselves off by giving the militia money and valuables. So the policeman looked the other way and we ran away. We hid in a cornfield.

There was a terrible storm that night – rain and wind. But we endured it. Before sunrise I went back to my village dwelling where I had some things. I took out some peasant clothes (a old outfit for peasants) and went to a peasant woman from whom I used to buy food. She agreed to hide us all in the dirty attic. In the morning, the woman's husband brought the news about the registration. There was no other alternative but to go back into the city.

Since we did not know what was happening on the roads, and especially what had happened meanwhile in the city, we sent out the peasant to bring us news. He brought the news that two ghettos had already been liquidated and that all the Jews who were left had to go into the remaining ghetto. We divided up and one by one went back to the city on foot. Not all of us arrived there. Several were caught and they "disappeared."

About the Sunday Action at the Beginning of October, 1942

A day before the action, all the German officers and their families ordered that all the Jewish craftsmen who worked at certain jobs were to send in all their work even if the work had not been completed. The women took their dresses from the tailors, the men – their unfinished suits and so on. There was panic because these were clear signs of a coming "action."

In the gray dawn the murderers came into the houses with the fearful cry: "Jews, Out!" They assured everyone that those who had a work card would soon be able to return. I and my little son also fell into their hands and were swept into the crowd. The several hundred people were herded along Kopernika Street to the railroad station. Along with the Gestapo and their dogs, we were guarded by Ukrainians and Poles.

One woman had a loaf of bread with her. Three young men attacked her and tried to take her bread. The woman resisted. The Gestapo shot. There was a disturbance in the crowd. I quickly took off my armband and I decided to run away with the child. I found myself in the Gentile section not far from the house of a Polish acquaintance who had relatives in common with me. But they didn't even let me into the house. The did allow me to hide in a closet that was outside the house. We sat there without food or water until evening and often someone outside tried to open the closet door. In the evening the owner of the house came and told me that the ghetto had been liquidated. (That was a lie.) I could no longer stay in the closet and had nowhere else to go.

As the wife of a doctor, I had some poison with me, and the sensible thing to do in such a situation would have been to use the poison. (he whole time, my seven year old boy cried: "Mama, yesteshmy strasteny!" – "Mama, we are lost.") I then took out some Luminal and told my son that he should swallow it because it would calm him and then he could sleep and rest. The Pole brought me a glass of tea. The child swallowed 18 Luminal tablets and in a few minutes he was covered with cold sweat, unconscious on my knee. (The closet was too small to lay him down.) When I saw that the child was comatose, I also took poison. The poison I took was composed of morphine, cocaine and atropine. I took quite a bit of it so as to quickly put an end to me. But I didn't know that this combination of poisons neutralizes itself. I became dizzy and in a few minutes I vomited heavily. Regardless of my effort to keep the poison in, I couldn't succeed. I vomited all of it up. And since I didn't have any more poison with me, I remained alive. All this time, the child lay unconscious – and so several hours passed.

I decided to carry the dying child to a place near the ghetto to find there the Jewish doctors who lived outside the ghetto. But as I came near I realized that the ghetto had not been liquidated and my doctor friends tried to revive the child. After four days my little boy regained consciousness, and the burdens and the struggles of the hours or minutes to come began anew

The Ghetto in Flames (About the Hallerbach Action)

After the Gestapo took over the Hallerbach group which was at the ghetto gate near Kopernika Street, the Gestapo and the Ukrainian militia went into the ghetto and threw fire bombs into the houses. An exception was made for the houses that bordered the gentile streets.

We sat in a small wooden room (on top of Pokucie) in a bunker with eight or nine people. Through the cracks in the boards, we saw the flames from the burning houses. An eerie "concert" rang in our ears: The murderers played on a harmonica and accompanied the music with song and dance. A wagon with liquor came after them and they drank heavily. The "concert" was broken up several times by shootings. They were shooting Jews who were trying to escape from the burning houses and bunkers. Zindl Naiman (then the head of the post office in the ghetto) left his job to look for his family. A shot found him. His wife saw him fall down from the bunker where she was and through my ears came her cry of woe: "Oy, vay, Zindl."

The flames soon became stronger. The whole ghetto burned like a bunch of matches. The smoke reached our distant room. For us there were now two possibilities: to stay in the room and suffocate or to go out on the street and get shot by a bullet. (The room was reached through a street that hadn't been burned.) We thought it would be easier to die from a bullet than to suffocate. In the dark we quietly went into the "Pokucie" buildings which were on the edge of the ghetto and we looked out at the unearthly sea of flames which engulfed the ghetto and its people. The fire lasted the whole night and in the morning the streets were covered with burned bodies and with pieces of burned houses. A white snow covered the tragic sight. The flames consumed about 5000 sacrifices.

The Escape
(Testimony from Chana Weinheber-Hacker)

On the day of the liquidation, as though heaven sent, there arrived a peasant acquaintance, Vasil Vaika from Kozmatch, to save me and my child. I could take several people with me, four or five, but no children. With a lot of effort I managed to arouse his pity and he agreed to take Mrs. Lederfeind and her eight-year-old boy.

We went together over the roofs as far as the Ringplatz. The irony of the situation was that we were brought to the attic of Andi Ramler's (Lederfeind) parents' house. Naturally, the house was Juden-rein [free of Jews], and in the former Ramler dwelling there now lived a Ukrainian militia member with his habitually drunk mother. She took us in for a lot of money and sheltered us only for the first night. In the morning we had to try to get out of the city. Bitter cold, anxiety and uneasiness tormented us the whole night. Our friends and our last few relatives were still in the ghetto. The children cried from the cold and fright. The little Lederfeind wailed and cried without a stop: "Mama, yesteshmy stratzeny." (Mama, we are lost). He wanted to go back to the ghetto with his mother even though he knew very well that death was inevitable there. He would rather die together with all the Jews than endure this precarious existence here in the attic.

At four o'clock in the morning, we heard shooting. It became clear that it was coming from the ghetto. The last extermination had begun.

Soon the old witch appeared and informed us that the blood of the slaughtered Jews was pouring all over the ghetto, and therefore she needed a lot more money than we had promised her. If we refused her, she would call her son, the policeman, and he would soon bring us back to the ghetto and turn us over to the Gestapo. We naturally, without a word, gave her more money. The worse it was in the ghetto, the more money she forced from us. With every hour, the price rose. But, to tell the truth, no price was too high to be able to escape from that hell. That day the peasant who was supposed to take us out came and told us that it was impossible to leave the city. The murderers were running around with their dogs; we had to wait several days until the tragedy in the ghetto would end.

Yes, wait. But how? The attic was a shared one. Several residents dried their laundry there. Even now, the laundry of a Polish family was hanging there. And what if they came and discovered us? Fortunately, there was a severe frost. The laundry was frozen and hadn't dried. And others didn't feel like washing clothes in such cold weather. We lay on the wooden boards in the dark for three days and three nights. The only sounds that reached us were the pitiful cries from the ghetto and endless shooting.

On the evening of the third day, our peasant came. He gave us different clothes to wear and led us to the Ringplatz where his wagon was waiting. The wagon was standing only a few yards away from our hiding place. But the short walk seemed impossibly long. The entire Ringplatz was filled with Gestapo policemen. All were armed; many with dogs. In deathly fear, we luckily reached the wagon. Our peasant remembered that he still had some unfinished business and that he had to leave us there for awhile. We remained alone on the Ringplatz. Our frightened eyes and the pale faces of the children could have easily given us away. Our suspicion that the peasant wanted to get rid of us, and that he had betrayed us, grew with every minute. And that every minute was an eternity for us is understandable.

But the peasant really did come back. He loaded us into the wagon; he hid the children under hay and straw, and we three women – Lederfeind, Feder, and I – had to look like peasant women whose husbands had been called to work in Kolomey that day. The wagon began to move and we were filled with fear of death and hope of being saved. Step by step, we passed through the murderous faces and left the city.

We were almost at the end of our journey when Ukrainian police and Gestapo stopped us to search the wagon. The peasant persuaded the police to let us through, and we finally came to our hiding place in Kosmatch. There we felt that we had been saved and were very lucky. Through the peasant we found a little attic over a cow's stall. Two Jews were already there. So there were seven of us. We had to lie still all the time – only lying down – because the smallest step, the quietest voice, might reveal us to the neighbors.

Night after night, the peasant brought us food. On nights when there was no moon, he took us into his house so that we could warm up a little and wash ourselves. Our children dreamed of such nights. A lighted lamp, a table, a bench... filled the children with longing. Above all, the lamp – light in the darkness. It was a hard winter, near the Carpathian Mountains. And the roof was not well covered. When we woke up in the morning, if we really had slept, we would be covered with snow and frost, with freezing hands and feet.

The peasant was a wonderful person. He rightfully wanted to keep us alive even though he knew very well that his head was at stake. He was a widower and his mother-in-law lived with him. They often quarreled. She used to run out on the street and scream the her son-in-law was hiding Jews and that she would report him to the Gestapo.

The peasant was also our contact with the city. He tried to seek out the Jews who were still alive and bring them to Kosmatch; he even prepared places for them to hide. He found the doctors and we began a correspondence with Dr. Frisch, Dr. Gross, and Dr. Lande. They sent us a few of their relatives. But they themselves couldn't decide to come because they had no news of those who had gone over the Hungarian border. And before they found out, they were liquidated. Dr. Frisch sent his 19-year-old niece to us.

Being forced to lie still without the least bit of movement became very unpleasant for her after several days. So in broad daylight she left the hiding place with the intention of going back to Kolomey. She aroused the suspicion of the peasants in the village. And they started searching for Jews. The suspicion fell on our peasant; he asked us to leave his house for awhile and go into the forest and he would also provide for us there. This, however, meant going up against death, and we hesitated to leave the attic. When he began to threaten us, we reminded him that he had gone too far with us to turn back. The danger was truly very great and each minute could have brought us a catastrophe.

So we decided to go over the mountains to the Hungarian border, regardless of the snow and the bitter cold. The didn't want me and Mrs. Lederfeind to go along: Our children were too small and unable to make such a difficult journey. Bringing them along could have been dangerous for the adults. And if we had lived up until now, we would remain alive.

Their arguments were persuasive. We were left with only one thing to do – bid them farewell as they went on their hard and dangerous journey, and remain alone. I had only one request for Dr. Gewirtz, that he leave me his poison, so that I wouldn't fall into the hands of the Gestapo while still alive. He did not do this, but said that he would send the poison back with the peasant if they succeeded in crossing the border.

Instead of the poison, I received a letter a few days later, that they did cross the border, but neither the Hungarian Jews or the Christians wanted to give them a roof over their heads. They were therefore in danger of being found by the Hungarian police and turned over to the Gestapo. (Hungary did not allow any Jewish refugees from Poland to enter.) A week later, the contact brought us the news that the border police found everyone, turned them over to the Gestapo, and they were all killed.

We all stayed with the peasant for four more weeks. At the end of April we also went on that trip. Two peasants carried to the children on their backs along a longer route. (This was the only possible way to avoid the border police on both sides.)

The way was hard and difficult and full of danger. During the day the snow was soft and deep. It was hard to pull our feet out once we had stepped in. At night the mountains were steep and slippery and we had to keep going without stopping.

Exhausted and desperate, I lay down and begged to be allowed to die. But they forced me to go further. After a week of extreme hardship and danger, we came to a Hungarian peasant on the other side of the border. Hritz was the name of the Humgarian and he was a wonderful person. He watched and helped us with each step until we came to Budapest where they took all of us "Aryans" into the Polish underground camp.

Hritz had built up an extensive bunker system in the Carpathians during the German occupation of Hungary in order to save the Hungarian Jews. He was in touch with us all the time. He finally was caught and the Gestapo killed him.

[Pages 376-413]

We Survived

Told by Yeshaiah [Schaja] Feder and his wife Shoshana [Rozia] Hecht-Feder

Translated by Claire Hisler Shefftz

September 1, 1939 was a black day for the whole world and especially for us, the Jews. On that day, the war that ended so tragically for us, broke out between Poland and Germany. The sudden attack on Poland and the bombing led to a wild panic. In less than two weeks all of Poland was occupied. A rather large part of the Polish military forces rushed through Kolomey-Sniatyn-Kuty, to escape to Rumania.

The frantic flight continued. On September 16, 1939- it was Shabbos- the entire Polish government was in Kolomey, in the "Burse" on Shenkevitcha [Sienkiewicza], and on that very same day, all the Polish ministers crossed the border into Rumania. The Jewish community was in a state of uncertainty. Jews did not know what to do. Only a small number of Jewish men succeeding in obtaining passports to Rumania. In any case, men were packed and waiting for some kind of a sign. The suspense was soon over. News came over the radio that our area was to be occupied by the Red Army and Jews breathed easier.

On September 17, 1939, the first heavy Soviet tanks appeared in Kolomey. Among those in the tanks, there were several Jews who reassured us; they told us that in the Soviet Union there was no difference between Jews and others people. Jews lived there as equals with others. After the first few tanks, big armies detachments began to march in. The main force went through Stanislav-Lemberg, and in accordance with to the German-Soviet pact, up to the San River. The Germans "forgot" about the border and went in further. But they did pull back because of the agreement.

After the red flag was raised over the city hall, a committee, a militia, and an administration was formed in Kolomey and Jews took part in all of them. Among the Jews in our city, very few were engaged in maufacturing; there was a larger middle income group of large and small shopkeepers, workers, and businessmen. In the towns, there were large landholders, small farmers and various other occupations. The nationalization of small businesses was hard on many Kolomeyer Jews. Jews suffered from being deprived of their businesses and their large and small stores. Many of the nationalized businessmen were ousted from their homes and were in danger of being sent to Siberia. But a substantial number of Jews became government officials. Many Jews joined cooperatives. There were some Jews who were better off than they had been before the war. Life became, so to say, normalized. The Jewish populaton in the city increased, since in addition to the German Jews, Jews came in from the other side of the San River which had been occupied by the Nazis, and some also came from other areas since it was easier for them to live in Kolomey than in their own cities where they were known to be previously prosperous people.

The Jews from western Galicia who found themselves in other areas were tricked into registering so that they could be sent home but one night they were all brought together and sent to Siberia. They suffered greatly from cold and hunger there and many couldn't withstand it, and died there. Those who remained alive, however, were saved from Hitler's murderous hands.

The Soviet administration built us a network of schools whose official language was Yiddish. Many Jewish teachers were hired for the Jewish schools. Jewish children were also allowed into the Lemberg [Lwow] high schools and even the children of "nationalized" parents received stipends from the government. And so life went on for Jews under Soviet power until June 22, 1941, when, disregarding all the agreements between the Soviet Union and Germany, the German-Soviet war suddenly broke out.

A day before that, Shabbos, a uneasy feeling of anxiety and fear gripped the Jewish population, and that fear soon proved to be well grounded. We felt that something was coming. It was as though there wasn't enough air to breathe. And in that same night, -we did not know of any war yet- the Hitler hordes bombed many Soviet positions, among them Kornitsch near Kolomey, where the Soviets had built an air base. Sunday, before dawn, I went out to the marketplace. The radios soon announced that the German army had crossed the Soviet border. Panic, fright, turmoil- all of these- gripped our Kolomeyer Jews. They didn't know what to do first. People ran to stand in line at food stores in order to put away some food for themselves. The main question was, what could be done and how could we escape? We hoped that eventually, the Red Army would counterattack and it would then be possible be able to escape with the Red Army.

We knew that Jews had been insulted and we knew of the decrees imposed by the Germans. We had heard of murders. We had heard that with the entrance of the German hordes, Jews were buried alive, but afterwards the situation had just about "normalized" itself. Jews lived in the ghetto, but they lived. We saw no alternative for ourselves. The possibilities for escape were very limited. The roads were bombed by the Germans. Many had died trying to run away. And some were forced to turn back. All in all, the German attack was so unexpected and strong, that a mass escape was not an option.

On the first day of the war, I received a "notification" from the military. I gathered everything together, said goodby to my dear mother, may she rest in peace, and all my sisters and brothers. At the designated place I found a large group of people my age who had been called up. We remained there all day until late at night. Afterwards we were called together and all sent home. We were told to remain ready. We would be called several days later. A group of Jewish young men came to join voluntarily to serve in the Red Army. Among them I remember Dr. Shloime Wolf. The second day a broader mobilization was carried out. Everyone was mobilized, given military uniforms, and sent away. My brother, Majer Feder, was also mobilized then, and because of that, he remained alive

The constant air attacks and the feverish retreat of the Soviets gave rise to a frenzied panic. People fled by train, in automobiles, with horses, and on foot. Many of our youth who had been mobilized fell into German hands. The non-Jews were allowed to return home. All the Jewish prisoners were shot by the Germans. Still another group was freed by the Red Army on their way back and the rest were conscripted into the work detail, "Trudarmiya". They were able to survive in Russia. Regardless of the difficult roads, full of fire and danger, many Jewish youths started out, mobilized or not, to reach Russia. My brother-in-law, Pini Hecht from Berezhov, who had been mobilized to build the air base in Kornitsch, was immediately sent home. My brother, Isaac Feder, who had been mobilized for the Red Army, was sent home, and our youngest brother Shayke, a student in the university in Lemberg, tried to escape on an evacuation train with some other young Kolomeyers. They let the young women travel to

Russia but the young men were thrown out of the train by the N.K.V.D. Some of them were shot on the road and the rest, together with my brothers, were killed in the ghetto. A group of Jewish doctors and young women joined the medical corps of the Red Army. Among those were Dr. Seller, Dr. Velvel Haber, Dr. Rosenkrantz, Dr. Krumholtz, Dr. Deligdisch, Dr. Neuberger, Dr. Katz, Dr. Rosenberg, Dr. Lederefeind, Dr. Fruchter, Dr. Heller, Dr. Sechestaver, Dr. Becher, and still others.

This state of mobilization, restlessness, and running went on until July 3, 1941. On that day the last Red Army soldiers left Kolomey. They had managed to destroy part of the Kolomey railroad station before dawn.

It was deathly still in the city that day. The streets were nearly empty of people. On the streets were seen young Ukrainians who still wore white bands on their left arms; they were following orders until the armed forces came in. The Jews were overwhelmed by the feeling that they were doomed. We were no longer free. We were at the mercy of all kinds of upheaval. We were abandoned. My neighbor, Sholom Blecher's wife, collapsed out of fear. I ran to consult Dr. Frisch. We could see a big fire somewhere in the hills and Dr. Frisch was so frightened that he couldn't tell me anything.

On July 4, 1941 the Hungarian army marched through Varachte Pass into Kolomey. Soon announcements were posted to confirm the orders.

On Friday, July 5, 1941, the Ukrainian nationalists, who regarded Hitler as their national savior, hung their national yellow and blue flag on all the buildings. People also had to display the flag with the swastika and the Hungarian and Ukrainian flags. For Jews, the swastika was forbidden. All the Jewish stores had to display a Magen David (Jewish star).

The Commandant, Volkmann, (from Vienna) gave out new orders against the Jews every day, and inciting the people against Jews with his announcements, declared that the Jews caused the war, and that the Jews were communists. Because of the these decrees, Christians were afraid to sell a Jew anything. They didn't let themselves talk to Jews very often. It was hard to buy a piece of bread. They began to break into Jewish houses and on many occasions they stole anything that appealed to them. Such events occurred often.

Soon afterward, the so-called "Judenrat" [Jewish Council] was formed. It had an office, a hospital, a Jewish police (Ordnungs-Dienst), a kitchen, a department of "Materials Procurement", and also a labor office. And, complying with constant orders from the Germans, the Materials Procurement department took the best property, furniture, carpets, drapes, cloth, leather, and other things from the Jews. They were then delivered to the Germans. For the Jews it was a difficult task. Every day the best things had to be brought to the Germans. Around the end of July, the city commandant Volkmann ordered that Jews had to give up all their valuables. People stood all day at the designated place so that not only would their gold, silver, and jewelry be taken from them but their foreign currency as well.

On July 21, 1941, it was ordered that all Jews over the age of 10 had to wear armbands ten centimeters in width with a blue magen david [Jewish star]. People who had a work number had to put that on the band also. If anyone forgot wear the armband, he was immediately shot. For this transgression many people were murdered. My cousin Chaytzi, Hersh Nateh Feder's daughter from Peczenizyn, forgot and came out on the doorstep of their house without the armband. It was enough that a Ukrainian boy saw this. Nothing could help her. She was immediately shot.

And so each day brought troubles anew. Our neighbors, the Ukrainians, were unable to quench their thirst for fury and blood. They couldn't get enough of it. They weren't satisfied with the German-Hungarian forces and regarded the Gestapo with great impatience. Like a wild horde, they descended upon the Jewish population of Otinye and carried out a violent pogrom. At the same time the local Ukrainians did away with all the Jews from Khlebitshin, which was located between Kolomey and Stanislav. Khlebitshin was just a village but it had a large Jewish population. The same thing happened to the Jews in the village of Harasimov Niezwiska. The hooligans there tied up Jewish children and threw them into the river. They also killed all the Jews from Keredov and Kosmacz, including my father-in-law Henech Hecht and his family. They were all awakened from their sleep at night and driven out of the villages. The murderers made themselves even happier by beating everyone brutally. Several of my father-in-law's Ukrainian neighbors told the mob that my brother-in-law Pichas Hecht, z"l, had buried gold. He was taken away along with his cousins Manye, Urcie, and Mendel Horowitz to the Szeparowice forest where they were forced to dig their own graves and then shot.

We tried everything we could think of, but we were unable to rescue them from those murderous hands.

I remember one Friday at the end of July 1941, the Ukrainian police with their so-called "heroes" invaded the Jewish streets and alleys, dragged young and old men out of their houses, and beat them murderously with clubs. The Jews were all taken to the marketplace where a big statue of Lenin stood (once there was a monument to Pilsudski there and another time a statue of Karpinskin). The statue was bound with rope and the Jews were forced to drag it around over the entire marketplace. Then the Jews were taken to the city park. A Lenin-Stalin monument stood there also. The hooligans tormented the Jews until it was night. They made them line up with their faces to the wall to be shot. The Jews all said their final prayers. Just then, the Ukrainian mayor, Alinkevitch, came and rescued the Jews. The Hungarian forces observed casually and didn't interfere.

All Jews from 16 to 60 were required to work. Young women also had to work. The work was arranged by the Jewish labor office. Jews worked at breaking stones on the roads, at the city hall, at sweeping streets, in all institutions. Every day 500 Jews were brought to the railroad. There the overseers were Germans who beat the Jews so much that every day, several severely beaten ones had to be taken to the hospital. Motek Horowitz, the president of the Judenrat, once tried to ask that they not be beaten so much. So they broke his hands and he went around with his hands in bandages for a long time. I had to work there just one day (since I obtained steady work in the bristle factory which had once been managed by my uncle) and I saw frightful things there. I remember: they brought us to a pit of lime that was full of water. They made us kneel there and the murderers enjoyed themselves at our expense. After that work we were forced to run, and when we were freed for the night, it was as though we were coming out of hell. Among the beaten ones on that day, was our friend Moshe Brettler.

Before dawn on August 5, 1941, a sudden turmoil and panic broke out. The Jews began to run away from the synagogue streets and Klebanye. They didn't know exactly what was happening. What had happened was that starting at 2 a.m, a group of German soldiers encircled those streets, dragged all the Jews out of their homes, and took them away. All of them had to go with their hands up to the work center opposite the city park. Several thousand Jews were brought together, tormented, and beaten. They made speeches to them and insulted them, because a Jew had supposedly spit on a German officer. They had to go on their knees over the sand and then they divided them up. Each group was supposed to be shot. Upon the intervention of the Hungarian commander, they were pardoned and freed. But several days later they were all called out again and soon they were seen no longer. They were all killed somewhere. Such things happened to us in our city very often then.

On August 16, 1941, they caught about two thousand Jews in their houses and study houses and took them to Kornitsch where they forced them to dig a grave for themselves. But thanks to the intervention of Miriam Horowitz -Motek Horowitz's sister- with the Hungarian commander, they were transferred to the jail, kept there for several days, and then freed. (Miriam Horowitz did alot for the Jews in the ghetto. But in the end, she and her brother Motek committed suicide.) The Jews who were freed had vowed to each other in jail that if they survived, they would all go to Eretz Israel. But none of them lived to keep their vows.

Many Jews from Hungary- thousands of people with their families, young and old, were brought to our city, because they were not Hungarian citizens. They arrived on trucks and trains. They were allowed to bring nothing with them and they were in great need. The Jewish soup kitchen at the Judenrat expanded. They were put up in private lodgings and also in synagogues and study houses. A large number just traveled through our city and were taken straight to the Dniester where they were killed. Several months later the Germans took all the Hungarian Jews to the Szeparowice forest and killed them. Only a small number of them were able to go back to Hungary with the help of Hungarian officers.

On the second day of Rosh Hashanah, Motek Horowitz (head of the Judenrat) came into the synagogue where I was praying, stood by the ark and spoke some reassuring words. He declared that according to a talk he had with the city commandant Volkmann, the Jews could pray without being disturbed and no ill would befall them. This calmed our spirits for the time being. The same thing happened on Yom Kippur. All the working Jews were at work. On the second day of Rosh Hashanah, a Gestapo office was established in our city.

Hoshana Rabah, TSh"B [5702]- 1941, is a tragic date. That morning when many were still praying in the synagogues, ominous news suddenly came from the synagogue streets where there was a concentrated Jewish population. The report was: They were caught; they were beaten. A young boy who tried to run away was shot. Jews took shelter wherever possible in cellars and in bunkers. I and my two dear younger brothers, Isaac and Shmeyke, ran to hide ourselves with Christians. They told us what was happening in the Jewish streets.

The action lasted until the night. This was the first deep cut. That day they brought together 2500 souls and took them to the prison. The Germans said nothing about their fate. But we soon knew that their final road was to Szeparowice, in the forest. They shot them all there and buried them. That day, the Germans, along with the wild horde, set fire to the Great Synagogue, which was famed for its beauty. On the morning of the second day, they ordered all the Jews to go to their work immediately.

On Simchas Torah, TSh"B [5702; 1941], two days after the action in Kolomey, the Gestapo surrounded the city of Kosow, and rounded up not only men, but also women and children. The people there didn't know what was going to happen to them. They took them all to a one place, and the same Ukrainians enthusiastically helped catch the Jews who had fled to the woods. They shot 2800 innocent Jewish souls that day. Half-shot, fainting little children were torn by their little feet and hurled into the mass grave. After that there were very few Jews left in Kosow. The Kosover rabbi lived in Kolomey at that time. I went to him then to ask about the fate of my wife's brother, Yaakov Hecht. The rabbi answered, "A fire from heaven came down on Kosov and everything, everything was burned."

A Jewish man who had been in the militia during the Soviet occupation and did not escape with the Red Army lived on Mokra Street. The Gestapo found out about him and ordered the Judenrat to give him up. The young man hid and did not go to them. The Gestapo brought together all the Jews on Mokra Street (Nov. 15, 1941), 500 men, women, and children. Very quickly the news spread throughout the entire city. The 500 Jewish souls were taken to the prison and then to the Szeparowice forest where they were shot. The poor unfortunates realized what their bitter, black fate was to be and where they were being taken. The former "Jewish-Soviet" militiaman was later found dead. He had committed suicide.

At the end of November, 1941, the Jewish inhabitants of Kolomey had a monetary assessment imposed upon them. A special committee was formed by the Judenrat and used all sorts of threats to get more and more money from the Jews. The Judenrat also held some Jews under arrest until they gave up greater sums of money. They had to bring foreign currency and valuables as had been required by a previous order; now they were considered law abiding as long as they brought things. Understandably, they brought more than was needed with the thought that perhaps they could save their a little bit of their lives.

At the beginning of December, 1941, there was a new order: "Fur-Action"- all Jews should immediately give up their furs. They were supposed to go to Frost, because the weather was very cold then and the German army at the front needed them badly. The Jews promptly gave up their fur things. Several Christians revealed that Jewish furs had been hidden with them and because of this, entire Jewish families were taken away and killed.

At the end of December, 1941, the Gestapo gathered two thousand Hungarian Jews and killed them in Szeparowice forest also, and that was how the Hungarian Jews in our city were liquidated.

In January, 1942, they suddenly began calling men and also women for a special plan. It was called, deceptively, "Geizlen" (hostages). The people were from the intelligentsia- doctors, lawyers, teachers and so on. There were 600 of them. They were kept in prison for several weeks, and then they were taken to the Szeparowice forest and killed there.

And so it went from one day to the next. Every day brought shattering tragedies. Nevertheless, we gritted out teeth and still hoped. Always, as if through a small crack, a weak ray of hope came into the ghetto, and Jews believed in it. Maybe then, a bit of a miracle would happen? They said that the plan for making a ghetto had been cancelled because the situation at the front had improved. Unfortunately, all these stories did not turn out to be true. It was announced that within three days all Jews had to move into the ghetto.

This was just before Pesach, TSh"B [5702- 1942]. According to the plan, three dzhielnice (quarters) were specified:

• 1st section: Walowa, Kopernika, Szklarska, all the little streets, a part of Legianowa until just before Koraloavka.

• 2nd section: the second part of Legionowa, all of Mokra Street, Mickiewicza.

• 3rd section: Dziedziuszycki, Slowackiego, Khalanievskich, until Wierzbawa. The gates of all the ghettos were guarded by Jewish and Ukrainian policemen.

The Christian inhabitants had to leave the area where the ghettos were established and move to the good, formerly Jewish houses, and since Jews had been forbidden to have horses, or animals, those were taken away and distributed among the Volksdeutsch. The Jews had to use baby carriages to bring only what they could fit into cramped quarters where several families lived in one room.

Jews were not allowed to leave the ghetto except to go to work. Very often, they caught a Jew who went out to try to find something to eat. They shot him immediately. From the second day of the move into the ghetto, the Gestapo were frequent guests. They rode around on their horses arrogantly.

On the second day of Pesach, it was ordered that all working men had to report to the work office in order to have their work cards inspected and stamped. From there they took a certain number of them away from us under guard. Later the same day, the first section of the ghetto was encircled. They rounded up young and old, men and women, into one area and then took them to the railroad, packed them into freight cars and sent them away.

The first day of Chol Hamoed Pesach [3rd day of Pesach], the second ghetto was surrounded by the Gestapo, and all day long the Gestapo and their helpers carried out an action (the Jewish police also helped the Germans). Then they set fire to a large area of the ghetto in order to drive out the Jews who were hidden away in the bunkers. There too, they gathered together a large number of Jews. After that we understood that the third section was next. It was a Christian holiday just then. So they made it a day later. Many people left early that day to go and hide themselves in the first ghetto where an action had already taken place. On the third day of Chol Hamoed Pesach [5th day of Pesach], the murderers burned most of the third section. The dragged out all the Jews: old, young, men, women, frightened children, and with wild screams, abuses and blows, they drove the beaten, starving people to the railroad. They put the poeple on the trains and sent them to Belzec death camp where they were killed. Six hundred souls were sent away. When we came home that evening, our house had not been burned but it had been robbed. Everything was broken, torn, or stolen, but that wasn't important.

After the Pesach action, severe hunger arose in the ghetto. Only a few remained alive in many families, and because of this, life became more difficult. Many people became swollen from hunger, fainted, and went into a death agony. Once well- to- do people were seen in the streets with swollen faces, dragging their two heavy swollen feet. Every day people died mainly from hunger. Every day the cart drawn by the white horse rode around, until it was filled with the corpses thrown into it; then they were covered with tselt and buried in the mass grave. People went through garbage piles to look for something to eat. "I beg you, give me something." There was no bread. So we took from our own mouths to give some cooked food. We thought that if this continued, everyone would certainly starve to death. Perhaps the hunger had also spread typhus. Working people took various things out of the ghetto and tried to trade with the Christians they met for something to eat. There were instances when people paid with their lives when Ukrainian police or Germans caught them doing this.

At the beginning of June 1942, the Gestapo again decended upon the Ghetto, collected three hundred Jews (they "justified" it by saying that only the swollen old ones would be taken), took them away to the Szeparowice forest, and shot them there.

Dear readers, I write because I was asked to do so. I write because I was one of the very few who survived. I write because I, together with our dear sisters and brothers, lived and suffered during that tragic time of mass destruction. I am one of the few who went with them on their final journey. But is it possible for a person to adequately describe that time? However reluctant I may be to write, it so insignificant and pale compared to what actually happened.

After the so-called "test registration", which took place on September 7, 1942, people were uneasy. The felt and guessed that something murderous was coming. News spread about about what was happening in other cities.

Then came the "registration." That was their deceptive name for it. In fact, it was the beginning of the end. It was the 7th of September, 1942 (the second day of Selichos, TSh"B

[5702]). That day, all Jews, young and old, men and women, were ordered to report in groups according to their jobs, to the work area at 6 a.m. There, on that large field, we were put into groups. The Gestapo had a list of all of us. All around the area there were German and Ukrainian police. They went to each group and took out certain people, and sent them to one side and the rest to the second side. The second side was the bad one.

I was with my work group. I worked in the brush factory with my uncles, who had owned the factory, and I was beaten and sent to the bad side together with my uncles, Joseph Isaac, Itche, and Shmuel Hager, and with the whole family. My wife's work was gathering medicinal herbs and various special plants that were needed for healing. She didn't know what to do. Should she go with me and my group, or with her group? Fortunately, she spotted her group which consisted mostly of women in the distance, and on the spur of the moment, she decided to go with her group, and was placed on the good side. Everyone in my group was taken away except for three factory workers.

It was a very hot day. The sun baked down as the Jewish people stood there. All day the Germans and the Ukrainians beat them mercilessly with clubs and fists. The Jewish police, who were one of the groups standing there, had thought that they and their families would be released. Their wives and children were soon placed on the bad side. And they themselves were quickly taken away to the ghetto to help out just in case there might be a Jew still hidden there.

There were some who tried to get over to the second side. They were brutally beaten for that sin. I must note, however, that there were cases where frantic men or women risked danger to get over to the bad side in order to die together with their families. The same thing happened with parents and children who chose to die rather than be separated.

I must add that everyone had started out that day freshly shaved and dressed in their best clothing, in order not to look bad because looking bad was always dangerous.

The bestial events that took place that day are impossible to describe. The Gestapo and their helpers were given beer and afterwards they aimed the bottles at Jewish children and cut their heads.

There were about ten thousand of us in that area. 1300 of us were sent to the good side and 8700 to the bad side. On the good side was my wife Shoshana (daughter of Henoch Hecht), my two dear brothers, Isaac and Shmeyke, and my sister-in-law, my brother Meier's wife with a golden little girl, Aliza. The 1300 were later taken away from the area to a school building and kept there for less than a week. They sat there beaten, shamed, ragged. Perhaps they envied those of us who were going to die together.

After they took them away, they turned to us again. First they announced that whoever had gold, silver, foreign currency, or vaulables would have to surrender it. When I saw my wife going over to the good side, I told her that we would not see each other again. I signalled good-bye to her. I can rightfully say that at the time I felt more pity for her than for myself. I pitied her because she was alone. Her whole family, her sister Fruma and her husband Mendel Bernheit and children were sent along with me to the bad side. We had hidden my mother Pearl, z"l, (from the Hager household) and my sister Henie, z"l, (from the Shimel household) somewhere in the ghetto and they had, through some miracle, survived there so far.

We all had to sit on the ground and then they arranged us in columns, ten in each column, and guarded on all sides by Shutzpolice and Gestapo, we were slowly taken down Kopernik

Street to the railroad. People who had poison with them committed suicide. With sorrow, I must remark, that this happened frequently in the ghetto.

When they led us along, I noticed that a little door to a yard was open. Without hardly a thought, I went into the yard to try to escape. A Ukrainian who lived there came out and ordered me to go out quickly or he would turn me in. That meant that I would be certain to be shot to death. I went out right away and slipped back into the line. My uncle Shmuel Hager told me that the guards hadn't seen me. Freight cars were ready and waiting for us at the station and before loading us they counted us along with blows and wild screams. We were driven into the freight cars where little children were lying, dead and half-dead. All were packed into the cars with the doors closed tightly. Someone came around and made sure the small barred windows were nailed shut. In the freight car, we could hear the wailing cries and screams of the innocent victims along with the curses and insults of the murderers. >From time to time, we could also hear a shot. They were shooting Jews who tried to escape.

I found a spot for myself in the freight car and soon dozed off while the train was moving. So be it, I thought, it's all over. I must die.

It was soon dark outside. It was the time of Selichos [before Rosh Hashanah]. The days of mercy...

Suddenly I heard a woman's voice on the other side of the freight car. I heard her plead with her husband, "Moshe, don't leave me all alone!" I struggled over to them and saw that the husband had taken the wire off the small window opening and wanted to jump out of the moving train. People went to the woman and pleaded with her, "What's bothering you? What harm will it do you Moshe saves himself?" She was stubborn, however, and did not want to die without Moshe! Regardless of the conflict between husband and wife, Moshe suddenly went out. The wife cried out, "Moshe!" but he was already gone and the train went on. Having seen what Moshe had done, I thought of doing the same thing. I didn't think very long. I asked people to lift me up a bit and soon I was sitting on the edge of the small window with my feet sticking out and then, turning around on my stomach, I slowly freed myself from the barbed wire with one hand so that I wouldn't remain caught on it, and in the dark I flung myself from the train in the direction the train was going. I quickly ran away from the train since the last car was full of Germans who had orders to shoot us in order to frighten us into not trying to escape. They really did shoot many who jumped out badly, fell down hurt, and gave up their souls on the railroad tracks.

Lying there in the dark, I watched the heavy freight train carrying away thousands of our Kolomeyer Jews to their death. I found a little stream to drink from. I found corn in a field and ate it. I breathed more freely and my feet carried me along in the deep darkness.

I followed a path through the field that went toward Kolomey, and as I went along in the dark, I suddenly heard, as if it were coming out the ground, a Ukrainian shout to me "Shtoi!" (Stop). And there he stood before me and asked, "A ve kuda?" [Where are you going?] I answered him, "Da Kolomey, pane." [To Kolomey, sir.] "A Vitki?" [Are you a Jew?] I understood that I had to answer, "Z'karashava". [Yes.] He looked at me and called out: "Aha! Te z' payzhdu utik!' [You're running away!] And he started to drag me to the police. I pleaded with him. I asked for his understanding, but it was in vain. I was all alone with him. I looked him over. He was healthier than I. I was hungry and worn out from the ghetto. Since he did not let go of me, I begged him to give me a minute to take care of a human need. It was very dark and even though he was two steps away from me, he could not see, and sitting there I decided that I had to fight with him since I could also die here. I decided that I still had a chance and I began to run. I ran through the fields and the peasant ran after me. I felt that death was two steps away from me. And so I ran and ran. Until I heard shouts of "Tebe zhere shlak trafet!" I understood that that he had resigned himself to pursue me further. Fear drove me further and I ran until I came to a field of barley. I went into the barley and lay down there. Lying on the ground that way in the still night, I could still hear from far, far away, the heavy train locomotive chugging along, carrying away the 8700 Kolomeyer Jews.

I had chosen this barley field because the grain had already been harvested in the surrounding ones. I lay and looked at the cloudy sky. I found myself in a situation where I didn't know what the next minute would bring.

Suddenly it began to rain. I was a little wet but it didn't bother me. I breathed the air deeply. I decided that even if I were to be caught tomorrow and have to die, it wouldn't bother me. I was caught up in the desire to live, to struggle, to fight, to grit my teeth, and make every effort as far as possible to take care of myself. I decided not to go any further until daylight so that I could see where I was going.

When it became light, I went on the road again but I couldn't figure out which way to go from the field and I wound up in a village where a peasant showed me which way to go. Along the way several Ukrainians fell upon me like hungry wolves, captured me and took me to a railroad inspector. I met several other Kolomeyer youths there, among them Bubi Kerner, Nachman Kerner's son, and from there we were taken to another train inspector. We pleaded with them to let us go. But we were answered with such blows that we said no more. On the way, following the train tracks, we saw many dead Jews who were shot trying to escape or who died jumping off the train. After several hours, they came with a small railroad car and took us to Kolomey. One of us had a broken foot. So they said: "This one we will bury somewhere". Unfortunately, he overheard their talk, but he could do no more than stare with his eyes.

In Kolomey we were turned over to the railroad police. They were opposite the railroad station. There they insulted us, beat us, and threw us into a room that was so dark that we couldn't even see each other. There were twelve of us. From there we were taken to the Gestapo on Krashevska Street and then straight to the ramleruvke in the prison yard, and there they began bringing transports of Jews from all the little towns: from Peczenizyn, Jablonow, Kosow, Kitev, Pistyn, Zablonov, and from other nearby areas. Each transport brought frightened Jews with women and children. The Jews obviously didn't know that they were being led to the slaughter since they brought provisions with them. They had again gathered ten thousand Jews. Among them were quite a few Kolomeyer Jews who had taken shelter from the so called "registration" in the outlying towns. They also rounded up some Jews from the ghetto and took them all to the prison.

At the prison we lay in the mud. At night we were not allowed to get up but had to remain sitting down. Every time they allowed the Judenrat to take out the dead ones, they didn't spare any beatings. The Ordnungs-Hiter (Jewish Police) brought something to eat but it was seldom taken because beatings came with it. They once brought a pail of water for drinking, but we didn't drink. They poured out the water.

On September 10, 1942, they told us to get up and called out: "Anyone who can't run has to step forward." All the sick people came forward. They came and took them away in large wagons. We did not know where. I spoke to those around me to try to persuade them that the only chance we had to escape was to run away. Later they took those of us who could still walk out of the prison yard and they also took the Jews we didn't know about out of the prison building. They took us out and counted us. They did not take us to the left to Szeparowice but to the right, to the railroad.

It took a long time until everyone was sent along the road. They sent several Jews from Obertyn with us; among them I saw my former friend Shlomo Provisar. We were then led along the Railroad Street. Doors and windows were not allowed to be open. Children were not allowed to be on the streets. We went along like a big quiet funeral procession, carrying little children, until we reached the railroad. There they put 160 souls in each freight car. That's what I heard the Gestapo officer call out.

I hoped to be in a freight car with barbed wire on the windows since the iron bars couldn't be broken so easily. And it turned out to be so. This time there weren't just 160 people in the freight car, but as many as possible were crammed in so tightly that I stood on only one foot. I had nowhere to put the second one. There was such a heat that hot droplets began to fall from the ceiling. The door behind us was tightly closed and people threw all their clothes off. Some people fainted and some were suffocated.

In the evening when the train began to move, I immediately removed the barbed wire and I was the first to jump out. I again threw myself to the side. First I drank some water and started out for home. I feared daylight. And again two Ukrainians ran after me and again wanted to turn me over to the police. I managed to influence one of them somewhat. I gave them what I had and they let me go. At dawn I went through the Turka woods and went through the village of Pyedin. I was afraid to go through Banigsberg. So I went by the way of Kosachov [Kosaczowka]. On the road I noticed a Ukrainian policeman coming toward me. So I hid until he went by, and soon came to a place not far from the railroad. I wanted to go to the cemetery because they were still bringing the dead there and I could go back to the ghetto with the hearse. Wanting to cross Kosachov Street before dawn (it was the eve of Rosh Hashanah, TSh"B [5702]), I heard someone tapping on a window to me. I turned around- a woman was calling to me. I was afraid to go. I hesitated, I wasn't sure. But she opened the window and said to me in Polish: "Nie boj sien, i chodz to. Tylko uwazaj ty niekaga nie uwdage!" [Don't be afraid, sir. I won't betray you to the Germans. Only be careful that no one should see you.] I went into her kitchen. I was so exhausted and beaten that I didn't even greet her. I began crying hysterically. I couldn't stop. The Polish woman said to me: " Widocznie ze panu przeznaczono zeby pan zyl." [Apparently, sir, you were destined to live.] And she gave me potatoes with sour pickles and a hot pot of milk. Afterwards the woman asked how she could help me. She got dressed and went to see my youngest brother Shmeyke, who worked in a big store for Otto Mayer in the Kneffers house but she came back with nothing. She told me that she didn't have the courage to go in and ask for a Jew. She took me into her garden where there was still corn and and handed out to me- careful that no one should notice- an iron pot with hot soup and crackers. I pleaded with her to let me stay there overnight and she agreed.

I spent the night in the garden. Toward morning -it was the first day of Rosh Hashanah- she fed me again in the garden. The Polish woman told me that a German lived in her house and he would be coming home after work. So she couldn't let me into the house. I looked upon her as an angel. In the evening she brought me a white arm band (shame-band) and led me to a group of Jews who worked nearby. I went home with them. "Home"- that meant the ghetto.

It was dark when I entered the ghetto. We were not allowed out in the street after 7 p.m. I went in to my cousin Isaac Kesten. At that time he lived with his sister-in-law; Sternberg, the dentist; and also Gisele Herman. They were very happy to see me. The gave me hot water to wash myself and I spent the night there. Early in the morning Isaac Kesten found my wife in the ghetto in the first quarter since the other two quarters no longer existed. And so I came home again to my wife on Zhelana Street on the second day of Rosh Hashanah. Food was easier to get. Several families lived in the building. At night we worked, digging a kind of cellar under the house so that we could hide there is case of an action.

The 1300 people who were left at the assembly place had been taken back to the ghetto. Their permits were stamped and whoever did not have such a stamp had no right to exist. My wife and my two brothers, Isaac and Shmeyke, moved over from the third quarter and the first quarter because those had been declared liquidated. With great effort and suffering- fearing even a Jewish policeman- my mother and my mother-in-law also came over.

My father-in-law Yekhiel Hecht from Kosov and many other close and distant relatives had been in the province-registration. Several of my uncle Hersh Nateh Feder's children and still others had been there.

I had no stamp on my work permit and I went about illegally. Later, other such illegal Jews also came in from the provinces; they were the hidden Jews who had been caught and sent to the Kolomeyer ghetto.

And again, every day we heard about Jews who fell into the hands of the Gestapo. Among them was Doctor Marmarash. They took him to the cemetery and shot him. We heard of such things almost every day. Those who were caught trying to escape over the Rumanian or Hungarian border were shot right on the spot.

Meanwhile the typhus epidemic spread in the ghetto. The last remnants of the Jews in Zablatov were brought to Kolomey as well as the Jews from other towns. Among them was my sister Ruchl. She was the wife of Leib Bloch of Zablotov. After the newcomers were kept at the prison for several hours, they were freed and taken to the ghetto. Jews struggled again to be hired for work, hoping to gain security that way. It was known, however, that entire groups had been taken away from their work. An epidemic of suicide began. That did not appeal to the scoundrels among the Jewish police who had to choose people for death. Since the ghetto had been greatly diminished after the actions, and the remaining Jews from the provinces who had been found somewhere had been brought in, as well as many Jews who couldn't stay with Christians any longer- there was great crowding. People lived packed together. Jews even were on the roofs of the houses.

And again we began to hear the dark news that they were again digging graves in Szeparowice forest. Such information was often passed along and it was always true. And again the air seemed heavy. We could not know what each moment might bring, and the fear, anxiety and knowledge of that from which there was no escape, made our hearts heavy. And nevertheless, we still, still, always hoped. We stood between life and death and at the same time we heard the voices of those who sold popular cigarettes. People ran to their work early every morning.

Then there came the black Sunday of September 11, 1942. That Sunday, before dawn- I slept in the attic then (on Zhelana Street)- my wife called to me with a warning: "Get down from the attic!" When I came down, the action was well underway in the neighboring streets. With wild cries, men, women and children were taken to their bitter frightful deaths. They didn't have to work hard that time, since the ghetto was in a small area and very compactly inhabited. As in the previous action, this time they also took the unlucky ones to the fenced in "Work Area". That day they took out nearly four thousand souls. My sister Leah from the Axelrod household in Halitch, with her golden little girl, Aliza, was also swept away by the black tide. The four thousand Jews were held until evening. Afterwards they were loaded into freight cars and sent to Belzec.

We spent days lying in our bunker, suffering from heat and fright, and afraid to stick out our heads. My brother-in-law, Leib Bloch, came to tell us that the action was over. Leaving the bunker we came across the body of a Jewish woman. The Germans had shot her. Whe we were in the bunker we had heard her pleading with the Germans for mercy and immediately afterward, we heard the shot from the revolver. Many dead still lay in the streets and in the yards. It took many days until the corpses could be taken to the cemetery and buried in the mass graves. Some Jewish children were found dead in the bunkers that the Nazis had set on fire. Afterwards, pieces of their burnt bodies were carried out.

On September 12th, they again captured - this time the work was carried out by the Jewish police with the help of the S.S.- two hundred people including plenty of older men and women; they were brought together in "Pacht" (the poultry slaughterhouse) and the Germans shot them there.

And even after all this, anyone who remained alive went on living.

The "Hallerbach-Group", named after one of the Gestapo, was a group of men and women who worked in the houses of the former ghettos collecting the clothes, furniture, and other things that had been left behind. It was considered the best work group. To get into that group was not easy since it was believed that whoever worked in that group would not be taken away. Every morning, the group assembled on Kopernika and from there they marched in columns to their work. On their way to work, the marchers often had to sing "Hatikva" and other Jewish songs. That was how the Germans made fun of the Jews.

This went on every day until Thursday, November 5, 1942. The group assembled as always on Kopernika near the ghetto gate. The Jewish Ordnungs- Dienster [A.D.] rushed out and herded even more people together. But instead of taking them to their work, they led them all to the prison. My brother-in-law Leib Bloch and his brother Avraham were also trapped then (people wanted to go out to work in order to stay in touch with the world outside the ghetto). After all their efforts to get into that group for protection from actions, now the whole group was caught. At 11 a.m. that same day, they fell upon upon the "Umschlagshtele" (the "Paka" house opposite the former Jewish hospital), and there they took all the craftsmen and skilled workers and with shouts and screams brought them to the jail as well. (The Umschlagshtele was the headquarters of the Judenrat. All the craftsmen were concentrated there and some worked for the Christians and some for the Germans.)

Done with the "Hallerbach Group" and the "Umschlagshtele", the Gestapo started to set fire to one house after another. Jews who tried to run away from their hiding places were shot and thrown into the flames. Many Jews, half-burnt and badly wounded, were also taken to the prison.

The ghetto stood in flames. One house after the other was set afire. We lay hidden in the bunker. After a long time I left the house and saw burning buildings all around. The former Talmud Torah behind us and all the houses around us were burning. A woman, the wife of a Gestapo, was riding on a horse, and was taking photographs of everything with obvious enjoyment

We were in great despair. We didn't know what to do now. Staying in the bunker would doom us to being burned to death. It would be easier to die from a bullet. I ran up to the attic, took the few gold coins and divided them equally among us so that in case someone could escape, he would have some with him. Soon the roof was burning over us, and the smoke was choking us all. I went first. I took my mother-in-law on my shoulders and ran out. After me ran my wife, my two brothers, Isaac and Shmeyke, our mother and our only sister Ruchl. Outside, the flames blinded our eyes. And to add to all this, rain poured down and a cold wind blew. Running with my mother-in-law, I slipped in the mud and fell. I got up quickly and we ran to the houses across the way, having no idea of what we were we were doing or where we were running. In a house on Legionova Street, in the attic, we came together and looked out into the dark.

We heard the city fire engines come to control the fire. We could see people's shadows. We did not know if they were Jews who were looking for a place to hide or Germans. We later found out that they were Jews. We sat there overnight. The action was over. This time all the Jews in the prison were taken to the Szeparowice forest where they were killed.

Our ghetto population was now barely 1500 Jews. We were left with nothing and without a roof over our heads. Chaim Teitelbaum's wife (he was no longer alive) and her father, Breier, took in my mother with the children. I, my wife, and my mother-in-law stayed with the Schiber family (they were already alone without their children). In the morning I decided to go out of the ghetto and my wife's former teacher, Sonoitza, gave me a loaf of bread. I brought bread, potatoes, fruit, and meat back to the ghetto and we ate. My two brothers were afraid to go out; I was the only one who risked going out without a work permit.

A new turmoil: the Judenrat received an order to collect a few hundred souls and Jewish police headed by Mendel Green, Shpiegel, Lany, Fisher and other "Ordnungsdienstler" grabbed anyone who looked bad. They caught a number of people every day. They sometimes released someone for alot of money in order to have something with which to live well. Avramtche Schiber was brought in all bloody after an encounter with them. The action took several days. My mother and my mother-in-law, z"l, were taken out of a cellar by the Jewish police. All the captured ones were taken to the jail. About 500 to 600 men and women were caught by the Jewish police. Our mothers had been hidden in a cellar when they were searching for old people and we did not even hear when they took them out.

The ghetto now consisted of a small number of people bordered only by Walowa Street. The few people who were left did not know when they would be taken to die. But perhaps they would leave these few alone. So we lived anxiously. We slept in our clothes. The president of the Judenrat, Motke Horowitz, and his sister Miriam committed suicide. We felt as though the end was coming

We got in touch with Ukrainian acquaintances to take us to Hungary. We had little to lose. But the deal with the Ukrainians was called off at the last minute. Later I was able to arrange a deal with a Shvertzer for our only sister Ruchl and my two brothers Isaac and Shmeike. In the meantime I met a peasant from the village where my sister, z"l, had lived. He was willing to take my wife to his house but only she. My wife did not want to go alone. We thought that after our sister and brothers were taken to Hungary, we would also go there.

On February 2, 1943, we slipped my sister out of the ghetto. It was in the evening. The brothers were supposed to go out the next day. But it was too late. Toward morning the next day, February 3, I was sleeping in one corner of the house along with my wife, my two brothers and our Mordchile Bloch. Suddenly, my wife heard a shot. We regarded that as a signal, and we were not mistaken. Soon we saw that we were were surrounded by Ukrainian policemen. We got together quickly. We understood that we could no longer hide. We had to get out of the ghetto and try to save ourselves somehow.

There was a bunker in the house where we lived. The other neighbors went into the bunker, but we tried to go out. We planned to go to the ghetto fence and jump over it. As we went out we noticed the great danger all around us, and also that there was rain falling on the frozen snow so that we could hardly put a single foot down. We ran back to the house and hid under the porch. I was the last one in and wanted to pull the board shut but I couldn't because it was wet and frozen. I closed it as much as I could. In the meantime Lomtzi Petraver came running and told me that he was closing another bunker with wood and would then come over to us. But he couldn't do any more. They caught him right away. I threw something on the loose board and we anxiously lay there.

We could hear the savage Gestapo with their helpers and their big dogs run from house to house and drive out the people. They were all assembled somewhere. We could hear the wild screams of the murderers mixed with the crying of our women and children. We could hear the Jews pleading with the murderers, but the murderers- with their bestial screams and clubs- only yelled: "Go! Go!." We heard screams from the next house where Isaac Kesten, Celia Herman, and Sternberg, the dentist, lived. We heard Sternberg, the dentist, pleading with them, but they cruelly chased them all out.

It was deathly still. They had taken them all away somewhere.

But suddenly a cry rang out again over the stillness. A Gestapo saw a woman somewhere and he shouted at her: "Come, come, you old witch!" She pleaded with him and it was all quiet again. Usually after an action, those who were left alive came out of the bunkers right away, but this time they didn't. The silence lasted the whole day. In the evening we heard footsteps. Someone went into our house and then went away. Who knows who that was? Perhaps robbers. We heard shooting at night. They were probably catching Jews who came out of their hiding places somewhere. Because of the frequent shooting, we decided not to go out. We stayed on in the cramped bunker without bread or water.

The next day, in the evening, horses and wagons came to take away the Jewish belongings. We heard someone come near our hiding place and say, " A mozhe y tu son zhidzhi?" [Perhaps there are Jews in here?] He stomped with his heavy boots above us. We held our breaths so that we wouldn't be discovered. We heard one Polak say to the other that he had never done such dirty work in all his life. They carried out the things over our heads and it was quiet again.

In this action in early February, 1943, the last few Kolomeyer Jews and the Jews from the provinces (about 1500 souls), were taken to the Szeparowice forest. And so this large venerable Jewish settlement became "judenrein" [free of Jews].

Several doctors like Dr. Bunye Frisch and a few others had been left alone. But a few days later, they were no more.

We stayed on under the porch. Around us was silence and frequent shooting. We stayed there another night. Before dawn, Grinstein's frightened young son ran to us and said that the Feders had hidden themselves in the burned houses and then he ran back.

We decided to leave that night. It was the third night. I told everyone that I would go first and they should follow me and do everything that I did. Halfway through the night I removed the board. I went out and everyone followed me. I saw that in the meantime a heavy snow had fallen and the houses here were far apart. We could be seen from somewhere. I told them to slip into the first house.

I watched and listened carefully, and we safely crept into the next house. And so we went along safely from house to house until we came to Legionova Street and to the emptied houses of the ghetto. We lay there quietly. We heard and saw the pre-dawn train on its way to Peczenizyn. The windows of the house looked out upon the street. We were already outside the ghetto and the windows were nailed shut because windows were not allowed to be open. We finally opened a window right outside the ghetto. My brothers Isaac and Shmeyke and

Mordechai Bloch went out to Kamionka Street where we once lived and hid themselves in the attic. My wife and I took off our Jewish armbands and quickly walked on Wintsetoavke to my wife's former teacher.

We arrived there safely. I stayed close to the wall while my wife tried to reach the teacher. She knocked at the kitchen where the old mother and the servant girl were sleeping. The girl was related to the teacher. She opened the door and we were taken into the new house which wasn't finished yet. Later the teacher found out that we had come. She was very frightened. She told us that her brother-in-law mustn't know about us. She told us that if she had lived alone with her sister, she could have kept us. But now it was not possible.

It was almost Friday evening. I borrowed a fur hat (since Jews had been forced to turn over all their furs) and went to an aquaintance of ours, a Ukrainian professor. The professor wasn't home. His wife crossed herself. She was afraid of me and said, "Dobre shtcho we zeyjsze" (It's good that you're alive). She told me to go near the high school with my wife on Shabbos at 6 o'clock. From the professor's house, I went to my two brothers on Kamionka Street. They were very happy to see me. I brought them food and decided to stay overnight in the attic with them. It was terribly cold. So we went down into the cellar. We settled ourselves into a corner and spent the night. Before dawn I parted with them and went to my wife. My wife was very worried about how I would survive such a dangerous journey and she arranged for the girl to go along with me since the dog might wake up all the neighbors when I came. I arrived safely and and repeated what the professor's wife had said: "Michiala skosov, treba byla was wzity." ("Michiala said that you must take us.")- were her words.

On Shabbos, we parted with the Sonoitza, the teacher. She dressed my wife in Ukrainian peasant clothing and her heartfelt parting words were: "Mani yednega boga." (" We have one God.") On Mickiewicza Street, near the high school, they were waiting for us as we had agreed. I went again to my brothers, told them where we were going and we went out through Slowackiego, Tarnovitzia, over the Werbishe bridge, to Werbish. We spent the night with my wife's acquaintances, who were of Ukrainian nationality. The wife had gone to school with my wife. On Sunday we persuaded the peasant Nikolai to take a big pot of hot food to my brothers in the attic. Then he took bread and apples to them and after two days he brought them to us.

Both of my brother Isaac's feet were frostbitten. We brought him up to us in the peasant's attic. The peasant's wife did not know about the brothers and Mordechai Bloch since the peasant was the one who brought us food. The wife just wanted us to leave as soon as possible since she was very fearful.

Finally a peasant came from the village of Berezov where my father-in-law, z"l, used to live, and agreed to take us to his house. He would take me and my wife first and then my brothers. He sat my wife, who was wearing a kerchief like a peasant woman, up on his wagon next to him, and I sat inside the wagon. We had decided that in case we were caught, we would say that that we had met him on the road and begged him to give us a ride.

As though to spite us, it was a moonlit night. Ukrainian police were travelling back and forth. We went safely as far as Jablonow and then the peasant saw several people he knew up ahead. We stopped until they went away and then went on, reaching Berezov near his house, and then we saw three policemen. They were going along peacefully, slowly approaching us, and our peasant also began to go slowly so that we wouldn't look suspicious. The policemen looked at us and didn't say anything. We breathed more easlily. The peasant took us into his cottage.

We were given some food. Afterwards we were taken to the stable and there we slept in the hay. Then the peasant took us into a bunker that he had made for us and we wrote to the brothers often. Isaac suffered so much from his frostbitten feet that we were afraid he might not succeed in crossing the border. The peasant promised to bring them. In those days there were frequent police raids in the villages. They would catch people- Ukrainians- to send to Germany to work. Because of that the peasant was afraid to go to get the brothers and decided to wait.

Finally, one time- when I was waiting for Michaila to come and give us a message- he decided against the plan. So we soon realized that something had happened. Finally he told us that the peasant with whom we had left our brothers had taken them to another house- an empty house, that only had hay in it. Another peasant noticed them there and turned them over to the police. So the Gestapo came with the Ukrainian police and took the boys away. They were killed somewhere in Werbish.

Our peasant was trying to find someone to take us to Hungary. One night he came to us, frightened, and told us that his wife had a dream. He took us out quickly and fled with us into the forest. My wife couldn't run uphill. Our peasant said that we had no choice. He said that since it would soon be dawn, he would hide us for the time being. He led us into a young deep little forest and the went home alone.

We both sat in the woods. We heard shouts. My wife said she recognized the voices of the forest guards. We sat huddled together. We were afraid to move from that spot. It was a nice day in March. The sun warmed us and soon we heard someone coming. We saw a dog and we were sure that someone was coming after him. He came very close to us- and we saw that it was a wolf. He came to us and we looked at him, and he quickly ran away. Good that it wasn't a two-footed beast...

We sat this way until the dark night came. The peasant came late at night and led us away. We didn't even dare to ask him where we were going. We felt ourselves to be alone, worthless, insignificant. Then we saw that he was taking us back to his house. He told us that his wife was against having someone else take us away at night because they would kill us.

We felt very lucky to be back in the little bunker in the stable even though it was terribly cramped and dirty.

Several days later the peasant again decided to take us into the forest and hide us there. And so it was. One Sunday night, he went away with his brother Haretzi and his brother-in-law. One of them stood and watched to make sure no-one could see them and the other two worked. They prepared a bunker for us.

That night the peasant took us into the forest. We went far, very far, deep into the forest, through valleys and over hills, in the dark, often falling, paying no attention, and going further. Finally we came out from the forest path to a deep, endless abyss. We went on this way downhill for several kilometers and then, in view of the Berezover forests, we came to a heavy rotting log. This was a tree which had been toppled by the wind and was about 80-100 cubic meters in size. We all stopped there and in the stillness I asked the peasant: "Ba sztyche dalka, Michailka?" [Hey, where's your shovel Michailka?] He laughed and said to me: "Uzhe nie daleka." [I don't have a shovel.] Then he told me to figure out what that was. I looked around in the dark forest and saw nothing. Then he bent over the side of the thick log and called out something into the ground. I small lamp was lit inside the log and he told us to crawl in there. We crawled in on our stomachs through a small opening and it became clear to us that he had been hiding a Jewish family there.

It was David Tillinger and his wife and ten year old little girl. The peasant had made the bunker very far from any settlement so that no one could travel there. And there was no reason to go there.

We were now five people in the deep hole in the bunker. It was very crowded. We had to lie on the narrow side and we couldn't sit there because if we sat, our heads bumped against the ceiling. But we were very happy to meet other Jews.

Every Shabbos, 1 to 2 o'clock at night, the peasant brought us food for the whole week. When we expected him, we could hear his heavy footsteps breaking the twigs under his feet. He used to come with his brother-in-law, both laden with heavy bundles- with bread, a little cheese, and sometimes two bottles of milk. This was our food.

The food was very limited. We lived on a little piece of salted bread. We had water near the bunker and we used to divide up the little pieces of bread. If it rained or snowed, we lay in water. We did try to arrange, as much as we could, for the water to drain out. Basically, if someone had placed another kind of material down there, iron instead of people, it would never have lasted. In the great heat of summer, we choked there.

The peasant brought us Polish, Ukrainian, and German newspapers, and we used to tell him that the war would eventually end. But the worst was that we didn't see that end. And thus the days, weeks, and months went by. The peasant often went to Kolomey and afterwards he told us that Jews had been betrayed and turned in there. This caused our peasant great distress.

The peasant used to remind us that we might be discovered. We used to assure him heatedly, that we would go to our deaths silently without ever betraying him. He used to say to us: "Never mind, I am ready to die with you. But my one and only child, my one and only innocent child- why should he die because of you?" (They used to threaten that if hidden Jews were found, the entire family would be liquidated.) We always reassured him.

Early every morning we used to go outdoors. We washed ourselves in the little ditch of water that we used as a reservoir. But we were still very dirty because we had only the clothes we wore.

We knew about what was happening on the battlefields from what we read in the newspapers that the peasant brought us. Then we got the news that Mussolini's Italy had surrendered. Our hearts grew lighter. Afterwards, we read in the newspapers that the Soviet army was advancing. We once more saw that we could afford to hope. Perhaps? Perhaps then? Perhaps we would be out of danger? And then we read in a newspaper that our peasant brought us that Kiev was in flames. They were fighting around Kiev, D. H. [Thank heaven]. We soon heard about places that were closer to us.

In the meantime the peasant found out that the area of the forest where we were hidden was to be cut down. He told us that he and his wife would come to us at night and take us to another part of the forest. He brought us to a temporary bunker and we lived there in fear and anxiety since it was closer to the village. We could hear the voices of the shepherds in the distance.

We stayed in the temporary bunker for two weeks. In the meantime the peasant built a better bunker, better hidden, better camouflaged. But once my wife saw a peasant not very far away and we were very frightened- who knew if he hadn't seen us?

Meanwhile, it was winter again. Deep snow came and our peasant couldn't bring us food. We lived on the little bit of bread we had hidden but we suffered greatly from hunger. Then once in the middle of the day when snow was still falling, the peasant packed two, three loaves of bread and with a saw and a hook in his hand, started out to see us. He did that so that if he met someone, it would seem as though he were going into the forest to chop wood. He came in the middle of the day, spent two hours with us and then went away.

He left and then suddenly, a frightened Michaila returned and said that judging by the footprints he had seen in the snow, someone had followed him, and even stood still to listen to us. Our peasant ran all over the forest to find that person. But he didn't find him and we were terrified. We were convinced that soon they would capture us and would mockingly, after much suffering, lead us to our deaths. We thought of running away somewhere into the forest, but the deep snow would obviously show where we had gone and we could be caught anytime.

Our peasant told us that we should wait quietly and that he would come and get us at night. And he did. The peasant took us to his home and hid us in his stable in the leaves.

The was around February, 1944. The front was coming closer. We were still in danger. Any second, we could have been seen through the walls of the stable. In the pile of leaves where we were hidden, it was different than it had been in the forest. We were given more food and cooked food. But we were very uneasy about other things. The peasant used to bring us our food in a container at the same time he gave the animals water. That was how he fed us. It was drafty there but we were glad because we weren't in the forest any longer and the front was coming nearer.

We heard that the Soviet army had crossed the former Polish border. We thought of freedom already, but our hearts were troubled. How many of us were left and who would be freed here-very few Jews!

I don't remember any famous dates- I do know it was a Friday- when we were told that Soviets were already close to Horodenka. On Shabbos, March 27, 1944, we were told that the high school in Kolomey was in flames and the Germans were pulling out. Our peasant called us out into the stable so that we could see how they were running away. The peasant was a Ukrainian nationalist. He even took part in an action to disarm the Germans.

The next day, March 28, Kolomey was freed from the evil ones. The Soviets entered Jablonow, Kosov, Kitev, Tchernovitz, and even Peczenizyn. But we were five kilometers from Jablonov and we weren't free yet.

The peasant's wife came to us joyfully to tell us that she was getting ready to bake bread for us to take with us on our way home. Not for home, because we no longer had a home, but for freedom. Freedom to live, freedom to breathe. What we felt then could only be understood by those who had no freedom. But we still could be disappointed. The Soviets did not really know how anxiously we waited for them.

The peasant told us that we mustn't go out until the Soviet army arrived since a Ukrainian nationalist group named "Banderavtzi" had been organized. They were against everyone; they fought against the Germans, they had killed several high Soviet officers, generals, when that army moved out. In the confusion that followed, the Banderavitzi had also caught all the Poles they could, many of whom spoke Ukrainian as their native language or were from mixed families. They killed Jews, Poles- whoever they happened to catch. We were aware of such incidents when they tied up Poles with barbed wire and slaughtered Poles. Some dead bodies lay near our stable and they couldn't be buried for several days. The peasant told us that they were stationed along all the roads and forests looking for Poles, and if he let us go out, by the time we went one kilometer, they would stop us and certainly kill us. At that time and even later after the Soviet army had arrived, they killed Jewish survivors.

But in the meantime, our wait was in vain. The Soviets did not come to us. The area of Delatyn-Stanislov was still occupied by the Germans and and the Soviet strategy obviously did not require them to march here right away.

We waited each day for the Soviets to come, and suddenly big tanks arrived from Delatyn and Mikulitchin with Hungarian troops. They established camps all over the forest and the villages, and requisitioned all the houses. Our stable was full of Magyars. Over us, on the leaves lay perhaps 200 men. They made their beds on the leaves and lay down to sleep over us. We could barely let ourselves breathe. Even the slightest move could give us away. Not far from us, they dug in heavy cannon, and all around the woods, they dug trenches.

And battles went on day and night. There was shooting all around us for four months. Our situation became more precarious and frightening each day. The inhabitants of the neighboring village had been evacuated and our village was scheduled to be evacuated as well and we might finally be discovered because of that.

Then the situation changed, and the evacuation order was cancelled. The whole area was occupied by the Hungarian army and in our peasant's house there were five Germans who ran a radio post. The peasant used to give us their army rations since they ate more homecooked meals at his house.

In this dangerous, anxious state of affairs, we regretted more than once that we had not left there when no one was there. It would have been risky, perhaps, but maybe we might have succeede in running away. And we were tired of the peasant.

I would like to add that when we looked through the boards of our hiding place, we could see that the Hungarian army had many Jewish workers who were assigned by the Magyars to special divisions. They were sent to work in the worst places.

And suddenly, one morning in August 1944- we noticed a feverish retreat by the Hungarians and heard heavy shooting. Our peasant and his family and their animals also fled into the woods behind the house, and they told us that in case one of us met with a bullet, we should be quiet. It went on this way until evening and soon we saw the first Soviet soldiers creeping out of the woods. We saw them crawling on their stomachs out of the woods and we breathed more freely. We wanted to run to them but the hail of gunfire didn't allow that. And finally- our peasant wouldn't allow it.

We couldn't sleep all night and we prepared to go out in the morning. The peasant stopped us again. He wanted us to remain hidden away longer. But he saw that he had no choice with us so he took us out to the woods.

We were fired at from the front, and from the other side of the hill by the Magyars. All around us were bullets and fire but we came safely to the woods. The path was all shot up and the peasant led us through the woods and later left us alone.

We went out of the woods and soon went through the fields and "talakes" [meadows]. We came upon abandoned, half ruined peasant huts. Most of the population had been evacuated. We went down the hills to the former Jewish town of Jablonow (Stopchet). We met Soviet soldiers and we greeted them with tears in our eyes, "Zdrastvoitye!" [Hello!] They answered us in a friendly manner. We came to the highway. All the houses and the courtyards were filled with Soviet soldiers. Most of the houses were damaged. But what difference did it make since most of the people who had lived in these houses were no longer alive. We went on the road to the market and then we planned to go further to Kolomey.

Suddenly we were stopped and were told: "Zaiditye padjoloiste!" [Come, please]. They asked us to come into a house. We went in and saw that we were in a command post of the N.K.V.D. [Soviet secret police]. We looked very shabby. They could see what they had to deal with. There were five of us: Dr. Tillinger with his wife and their ten year old daughter Fraydele, and I and my wife. Their manner toward us was warm and courteous. They asked us to be seated. We all sat down, and one of them, an official, came to us: "Vi skazhiteh tchto vi za yedni-Banderavtzi?"- he asked us with a little smile. I answered him as if to say: you see who we are. "Da-" I said to him- "Banderavtzi ale Yevreyski". [Yes, all Jews are Banderavtzi.] The conversation between us was a warm one. Across from us, next to the official, stood a young man, a captain. It was a pleasure to look at him. I said to my wife that he must be a brother. He smiled at us. They asked us for all the details and we told them our troubles. The officer told us that since it was already past noon and would soon be night, it was not wise for us to go further, since the road could be dangerous.

The Jewish captain took charge of us. He wanted to arrange for us to go to a peasant overnight but we begged him to let us go free because we couldn't trust anyone. So they took us in among the soldiers, near the kitchen, and invited us to eat and drink.

We didn't want to drink very much, only a little. And they gave us as much food as we could eat. I would have liked to keep on eating forever but we couldn't. I had never in all my life picked fruit from a tree, but that day I climbed up a tree and picked good ripe sour cherries.

At night our captain came and led us to a barn full of straw and we lay down to sleep there. He stationed a Tshasavai (a guard) outside and we heard him say: "A ti atvietchayes za etikh ludei". ("And you are responsible for these people with your head.")

The soldier guarded us all night. In the morning our captain (Yakubovitch from Leningrad) came and brought me a pair of army shoes; I had no shoes since they had rotted in the ditch where we hid. He also brought us all kinds of canned goods, gave us a "Bumageh" (a document) and apologized very much for not being able to escort us to Kolomey; he had been ordered to move on further. And in the meantime they were marching out a great many Hungarian prisoners. I and my wife prepared to set off on the road to Kolomey. I asked the captain how I could repay him. So he asked me to write a letter to his elderly father. I took his address and made sure to write his father about how his son had conducted himself with Jewish survivors.

We went toward Kolomey. A difficult journey. After lying in a bunker for 18 months, our feet didn't want to carry us. So we walked heavily. We kept going. We met native peasants who greeted us quite heartily: "Dobre dzien." [Good day.] On the way we met a captain on a a a horse. We gave him a lively and friendly greeting. I said once more to my wife in Yiddish, "It's a brother." As soon as he heard that, he quickly turned his horse around, "You are Jews?" "Yes," we answer, "Jews." He sprang quickly off his horse, embraced us as though we had known each other from somewhere sometime. We kissed each other and he put his arms around us: "Come, my children, come! Tell me how it all happened. Where are you from?"

All three of us, I, my wife, and the Soviet Jewish captain sat down together. We told him what we had been through, and he told us how he was one of six brothers who went off to war. Four of them were killed in battles against Hitler's hordes.

We waited until a few automobiles came from his detachment and we were driven to Kolomey.

At the beginning of August, 1944, there were no longer any Jews in Kolomey except for Isaac Feuerstein, the Neiders, Spiegel, and the Gottfrieds. We stayed overnight at the home of my wife's former teacher.

The city of Kolomey was mostly burned, ruined, empty, vacant everywhere; streets and the courtyards were paved with gravestones.

After a year went by, we went away to Poland and from there, in 1948, to the land of Israel.

Translator's note:

1.   Words in square brackets, [_] are explanations or translations by the translator of transliterated Polish, Ukrainian, or Russian words. Round parentheses are from the text. For street and town names, the Polish spelling is used in many instances and the transliteration of the Yiddish pronounciation in others. The same is true for the names of people mentioned. Sam Goldin helped with the Polish and Ukrainian spelling and meaning. More information about the author of this narrative and any corrections are welcome.

[Pages 414-419]

In Kolomey between 1944 and 1946
by Lusia Borten (Tel Aviv)

Translated by Claire Hisler Shefftz
with reference to a previous translation by Adele Miller

Donated by Dr. Ben Nachman

With frightful feelings of dread and apprehension, we sat in open boxcars on cannons and boxes of ammunition in September 1944, as we neared our our former home, the city where we once lived.

At the railroad station, the ruins could be seen right away. Destroyed houses without windows, doors, and roofs brought back memories of their former owners. In some houses, gentiles lived, the heirs and perhaps the direct or indirect murderers of their owners. Former servants had taken over the houses of their employers. We walked on the railroad street. We saw the the big building of Yonah Zager's prayer shawls factory with the sign high up under the roof printed in Polish and Yiddish.

But there was nothing left of the factory except for the sign; the sign was the only reminder of Yiddishkeit. The large windows gleamed with emptiness. The prayer shawls factory had been transformed into a cannery.

Here was the essence of the great destruction. There are no Jews- we don't need any prayer shawls. Never again would the skillful hands of the renowned talis makers provide Jews all over the world with their traditional needs.

We went further. We met Christians, former good friends. They were so happy to see us that they wanted to kiss us. Where were they in Hitler's time?

Why had they been silent onlookers who let the killing go on, or did they themselves do the killing? Their greeting was:

"You're alive? Where did you come from? Thank God!" Not one of them said, "Come in, put your packages down, have a sip of water." After a exhausting journey of two weeks of cold and misery, shabby, and with two packs on our shoulders, we did not look our best.

We were told that there were Jews in the city. We walked with difficulty toward the city. Everything is frightful. We are like strangers. We don't see any Jews. There is a chill in our souls. But we still have a spark of hope left. Approaching Valava [Walowa] Street and not meeting any Jews, we suddenly, without realizing it, walked into our own street.

The street was overgrown with high grass and bushes. Aside from the corner houses which had belonged to the Eifermans and the Hegers and were occupied, all our houses were ruined and full of dirt. And soon, soon, we came to our house where I was born and lived all my years. It was the only house in the street that was still intact. It looked clean and swept as though someone had left only a few hours ago. Some doors and windows were missing. Maybe someone had just left, after hearing that we were coming.

I went through the whole house. It was still. I could only hear my own heart beat. I went up to the attic with only one thought: perhaps somewhere there will be sign, a letter, maybe a farewell letter could be found? Flying feathers from torn bedding were the only signs of the former inhabitants. If only the feathers could talk and tell...

I found other signs of the former inhabitants: a photograph of my brother, a picture of my sister-in-law (drawn by my other brother) and a mezuzah. These treasures accompanied me through all the twists and turns of my travels to Israel (the mezuzah hangs on our door). From above, I glanced down to the open cellar. A terrible feeling kept me from touching anything. It turned out later that it was the right thing to do. Someone went there afterwards searching for valuables. He found the skeleton of a child of about ten years of age.

With a heavy heart, I left my house. We took our packages and went to look for Jews. Near the ruined market place, we found a Jew. The Jew showed us the house of the Premingers in Zalevska Street, where Jews lived now.

Mr. Shnabel greeted us heartily. The dwelling consisted of one room and a kitchen. A few people were there already. For the first time, we sat at a warm stove, worn out and shivering with cold after our day's experiences. We were five people sleeping on a straw sack on the ground, satisfied that we were in a Jewish house among Jewish people

This was in September 1944. The enemy was not very far away but everyone hurried to return home. Every day several people came back, believing that they might find someone from their families who was still alive. All the Jews stayed together in a few houses on these streets: Zalevska, Valava [Walowa], Shevtchenka [Szewczenki], Piekarska, Kamienietzka [Kamionecka]. Ten to twelve people lived in one house. All of them arrived ragged, hungry, and without money. All of them were miserable and didn't know how to begin again.

Slowly some people started working, others traded. They had to live. Others came to take a look and went away.

Our first trip was to the cemetery. The gate was closed, the burial house had become a locksmith's shop. We walked from the gate, going step by step, from grave to grave. We wanted to find just one grave of one of our relatives or friends. But the whole cemetery was covered with recent nameless graves. Only seldom, seldom did we see a gravestone with a name. A gravestone along with others had fallen on the Hamer family grave.

Dr. David Hamer perished on his 50th birthday. Two small tin tablets, put up by the community, mark the graves of Miriam and Moti Horowitz. They say that they committed suicide. We went further and saw an open uncovered mass grave. The wall between the cemetery and the railroad had been knocked down. Cows graze there. Many stones are missing, many lie overturned, but most of them are still there. Due to the initiative of my husband, the city government covered the grave, rebuilt the wall, forbade cows to graze there, and only permitted entry to cut the grass.

We Jews often went to the cemetery. Once we went there with two doctors, Dr. Haber and Dr. Seller. They found what we had not seen. They gathered together the bones of poor little Jewish children and buried them.

A second time, we were there with Dr. Hubschman, known as Pusch, and we still found human bones scattered there.

My husband was the only Jew who went to the Szeparowice Forest and saw the five mass graves. There were buried almost 72,000 Jews from Kolomea and from neighboring towns who without pity, dead or half alive, were thrown into the pits. The mass graves were fenced off and watched by the city government. No one wanted to go there. The route was dangerous because Ukrainian hooligans were in that area.

The old cemeteries were a sorrowful sight. There was no sign of the brick wall which once surrounded the cemetery on Tarnovska Street. The old gravestones were taken down and carried away. One part of the emptied area was turned into a garden.

The same can be said about the old cemetery on Kamenker Street, behind the city hall. Everything is destroyed, broken; only a few gravestones with their old inscriptions remain. The torn out gravestones from our holy ground were used to pave the courtyard of the S.S. on Krashevska [Krazewskiego] Street, Dr. Herer's courtyard, the courtyard of the city hall and other places.

We walked through the former Jewish streets, and went up to former Jewish synagogues, and Jewish houses. Everywhere there were signs of Jewish suffering. Flying feathers, a little rag, a shoe, a broken pot, a broken plate, a candlestick, human excrement.

We saw whole streets that were burned together with their inhabitants. The densely populated Jewish streets between Valava [Walowa] and Lenyanava [Legionow] Street and the Ring Platz, the former first ghetto with the Talmud Torah, Bais Hamidrash, the Kosover Synagogue, the Vizhiner, the Boyaner, and little shuls along with the large and renowned Great Synagogue- they were all destroyed.

There isn't much to say about the areas of the destroyed ghettos. They existed- they're gone. A white line on the surrounding buildings remained as a sign of the three ghetto borders.

The beautiful center in Kolomey, where once thousands of Jews traded, the Rynek, the so called "Canal", the Hai Platz, Pilsudski Street with its many stores: all are empty.

The gentiles that I formerly knew are almost all here. Market Day looked as it did before (only without Jews). Many good things were for sale. On display for sale were old furniture, bedding, clothing, underwear, entire Jewish households- even candlesticks and prayer shawls. And everyone bought. Jews had no choice. They spent their first and last earned groshn. They were in effect, naked and barefoot. They were afraid for their lives. A Jew couldn't go to a village. Their lives were in danger. Once we were shot at in the middle of the city. Luckily, the bullet missed my husband's ear.

The Soviet adminstration had taken swift action to round up and punish the murderers and the Nazi collaborators. The jails and barracks were overflowing with them. A Jewish Kolomear boy, 17 year old Herzl Terner, known as "Grisha", was actively involved in the revenge movememt. Afterwards he immigrated to Israel and sacrificed his brave young life in defense of the Jewish State.

Those in power at that time showed some understanding of Jewish concerns. A "Jewish Affairs" committee with four members was established. A member of the City Council who was a Russian was assigned to this committee.

Very moving letters began to arrive from within the country and from abroad. They were searching for fathers, mothers, brothers, sisters, and children. The committee answered all the inquiries addressed to it. Letters that were sent to private addresses went unanswered. The residents were no longer there. At my husband's request, they assigned all the private letters to us. We worked day and night looking for information, putting together a list of those who were still alive, and we sent it to the Kolomear organization in America and asked them to publish it in the newspapers.

The great day finally arrived, May 8. [1945] The war was over. A great joy over the whole world. The worn out remaining Jews in the concentration camps were free. They left the barracks.

A huge crowd had gathered in front of the "Mars" movie theater. After hearing the official announcemment over the loudspeaker, they broke out in a wild jubilant celebration. People were kissing and dancing. We Jews cried bitterly. There wasn't one of us who hadn't lost his whole family. We gathered in a little shul which was in good condition, and carried there the books and sidurim (prayer books) we had found. There we held a heart rending memorial serice. The survivors poured out their hearts. Every one remembered father, mother, brother, sister, husband, wife, child, grandfather, grandmother, friend; scream, weep - they are no more!

In order to illustrate how few Jews there were in Kolomea then, I have to tell this story:

There was a day afterwards when a great portion of the Jews had just left Kolomea to be repatriated in Poland. Walking along Pilsudski Street before noon, I met an acquaintance. Once he was a cheerful young man. He gives me a bitter smile and says, "It's good that I met you. I have been walking along the street already for quite some time and have not yet found a Jew to whom I can say 'Gut Morgn.'" [good morning]

In the winter of 1945, Mrs. Reitzes died in the house of the Christian woman who had saved her. The Jews were notified. Burying her according to Jewish law was a big problem. She lay for two days. After that three men went to the cemetery and dug a grave for her and two women attended to the ritual cleansing. Three Jews and a Christian (Mr. Dolinski) as a fourth carried the body out and laid it in a wagon. My husband drove the wagon through the city and two more men and three women accompanied it to its final rest. We could not get a minyan together. [10 men]

It was was not possible to live in this once very Jewish city or even to die there.

At the end of May 1946, we left Kolomey with great sorrow.

———————

[Page 420]

The "Judenrat"
and its Chairman Markus (Motek) Horowitz

Translated by Claire Hisler Shefftz
with reference to a previous translation by Adele Miller

Donated by
Dr. Ben Nachman

It is difficult to provide an accurate and reliable account of the Jews who were members of the Judenrat. Reports of eyewitnesses are contradictory. If the Judenrat had wronged one of the surviving witnesses, the reports of that witness would be one hundred percent negative.

On the other hand, if the Judenrat had helped someone, he would understandably have a favorable opinion.

They never speak only in personal terms. One never says: they abused me, or they did me a favor, only: "They helped the Nazis destroy the Jews," or "They tried to save Jews whenever it was possible."

We have a negative report about the Judenrat and its chairman, Markus (Mordechai, Motek) Horowitz from a Jew named Hirsh Birnbaum.

Hirsh Birnbaum now lives in Caracas, Venezuela. As a well established resident of the nearby town of Gwozdiec, he arrived in Kolomey on September 3, 1941, and remained in the ghetto there with his family until June, 1942, nearly nine months. Then, he was fortunate to be able to escape to Chernowitz. Hirsh Birnbaum's accounts of the Kolomeyer Judenrat and its chairman are almost entirely accusations.

Hirsh Birnbaum has written his report in the form of a long poem with 27 stanzas. The positive aspect of his negative report is that it reveals to us the names of the members of the Judenrat.

According to the poetic report of Hirsh Birnbaum:

1. The Head of the Judenrat was
   R' Motek Halevi Horowitz

> Carrying out his chairmanship with ease
> To his four ready cabs
> That stood at his door each day
2. The vice-chairman-
> Dr. Moshe Hutschnecker,
> A Stanislav lawyer,
> Who during the Soviet occupation
> Returned to Kolomey
3. Their personal assistant,
> That fellow Lazar Biber,
> In every hole and pit.
4. The secretary:
> Judge Isser Reichman.
5. The head of appropriations:
> Sheike Frish.
6. The head of housing:
> Hershl Chayut.
7. Liaison between Judenrat and Gestapo:
> (as Birnabum named him)
> Joel Jacobi and his helper
> Itzele Ganeva.
> (It is not clear from Birnbaum's account if they were members or merely
> appointed by the Judenrat.)
8. The head of materials production:
> Herr Fish.
9. Members:
> Solomonovitch and fellow dealers
> Each time on a different hunt, registrations,
> Taking Jewish belongings, profiteering.

In his footnotes, Hirsh Birnbaum tells that Solomonovitch was originally from Tchekia from the city of Mehrish Austroi and had been deported to Poland in 1938. Solomonivitch arranged work cards for Jews.

Hirsh Birnbaum emphasizes that the majority of the Judenrat members were not from Kolomey. Jacobi, the Hutschneckers, Fish, Solomonovitch, and also Mandelgreen, the head of the Jewish Police, arrived during the Soviet or the Hitler occupation.

Hirsh Birnbaum had no favorable opinions of anyone in the Judenrat. All of them, according to his account, were out to do evil and make money.

About the chairman of the Judenrat, he says:

> The head of the community Horowitz,
> His behavior coarse, brutal, cruel,
> Inflicted upon Jews terrible misery.

A completely contradictory report about the head of the Judenrat, Motek Horowitz, is given by Eliezer Unger in his book, "Zkhor" (Tel Aviv, 1945, pp. 59-64). Unger lived in the Kolomeyer ghetto from June 1941 until November 1941, and then from December 1941 until May 1942, also nearly nine months.

Eliezer Unger writes:

"When Chaim Ringelblum refused to be chairman of the Judenrat, the German district commander, Folkman, appointed a Jew by the name of Horowitz to take his place. Markus Horowitz was a grandson of the respected and brilliant Reb Meshulam Horowitz of Stanlislaw. He was the owner of a large factory and a man of great initiative and energy. In normal times Kolomeyer Jews had wanted to elect him head of the community and for city council. But Horowitz refused. In these critical difficult times, however, he agreed to accept this obligation. He handled very difficult matters. The people from the "Death Organization" broke his right hand while he worked as supervisor at the railroad tracks. They held him in prison and sentenced him to death. These incidents weakened his will. Horowitz accepted the enormous and responsible position of chairman of the Judenrat with good intentions and some pride. And from the day he began, he devoted all his time and thoughts to the work of the council.

The Judenrat included about three hundred employees amd workers. They were exempt from slave labor. But they lived in constant fear of the frequent visits from the Gestapo. The direct and frequent contact with the Gestapo and their threats led the chairman of the Judenrat to believe that the Jews must fulfill the Gestapo demands since trying to evade them would only make things worse. The Jews in the city were afraid of Horowitz and obeyed his orders promptly. Markus Horowitz gave away his entire wealth to the treasury of the Judenrat and proposed that other wealthy Jews should do the same. When the Gestapo required payments from the Kolomeyer Jews, Horowitz personally went to the homes of the wealthy Jews to collect the required sums.

Motek Horowitz who had been a wealthy man all his life and had associated only with those of his own kind, now, as chairman of the Judenrat, paid attention to the poor. He was concerned about the poor in the city and tried to help them as much as he could. If a poor man called him "Herr Horowitz", he rebuked him and told him to say "Du", "because don't you see that we have ceased being Herren and have all become slaves and brothers in misery?"

When he became chairman of the Judenrat, his family life ended. He moved to the Judenrat building and ate with all the poor people in the soup kitchen. He was not a religious Jew, but when he became chairman of the Judenrat, he changed completely. He began to pray every day with a minyan in his office even though putting together a minyan was dangerous. He also became a frequent visitor to the Kosover rabbi, Rabbi Chaim Hager, who had fled from Kosov and was hiding in Kolomey.

From time to time, the members of the Judenrat had to go to the Gestapo to give reports about the work of the Judenrat, the changes in Jewish life, the deaths and births among the Jews of the city, and the slave labor work. The Judenrat members were always filled with fear when they had to go to the Gestapo office. Horowitz always walked erect, well dressed and without the least bit of fear. More than once, Frost, the district head of the Gestapo, pointed his revolver at Horowitz's chest, but Horowitz was not frightened. It was as though that freed him from the fear of death. His confident bearing even evoked some respect from the Gestapo. Feelings of harshness and pity flowed together within Horowitz. When he stood in the square in the morning watching thousands of Jews assemble to go to their slave labor as ordered by the German labor commander, Horowitz would shout and swear at some Jews, but very often he would cry like a child when he saw Jews led to off to work like slaves.

It was told about him that on September 12, 1941, when the Gestapo rounded up two thousand Jews in Kolomey with Horowitz's wife among them, friends advised him to go to the Gestapo to ask that she be released. Horowitz refused: " If I can't free other Jews," - he said - "I do not want the exclusive right to free my wife." His wife never returned.

At the beginning of November, 1942, when there were only three thousand Jews left in Kolomey, Motek Horowitz and his sister Miriam were found dead in the Judenrat office. They had both poisoned themselves. Horowitz left a letter in which he wrote that he had hoped to save at least a part of his community, but since he saw no possible chance of achieving that, he would rather be dead.

When the Gestapo Frost heard about Horowitz's suicide, he smiled cynically and said: " A proper Jew, he was. He saved us work and a bullet."

Which of these reports tells the truth: Birnbaum's or Unger's?

The one thing that cannot be denied is that Unger's report, shows not only the desire to speak favorably, but also to be objective.

Translator's note:

1. The Judenrat were Jewish councils, a form of "self government" that the Nazis imposed upon the Jewish communities of occupied Europe. For a complete examination of the topic, read Judenrat by Isaiah Trunk, originally published in 1972 and reprinted by the University of Nebraska Press in 1996. Markus Horowitz is listed in the index.

Trunk believes that Unger's description of Horowitz's suicide is not accurate since two other survivors who were in Kolomey at the time (one is Hanna Weinheber-Hacker's account in Pinkas Kolomey) report an unsuccessful suicide attempt in November 1942, followed by a succesful one later. Unger was not in Kolomey in November 1942 since he had left the previous March. Horowitz and his sister Miriam were buried in the Jewish cemetery; Lusia Borten's "In Kolomey Between 1944 and 1946" in Pinkas Kolomey, mentions seeing two small tin tablets that marked their graves.

———

[Page 425]

The Murderers of the
Martyred Jewish Community of Kolomey

Translated by Claire Hisler Shefftz
with reference to a previous translation by Adele Miller

Donated by Dr. Ben Nachman

The main murderers of the Kolomear Jews were the chief of the Gestapo in the Kolomear district, Peter Leideritz, and the head of the Shupo (Shutzpolitzei), Herbert Hertl.

According to testimony gathered by attorney Yaakov Sack for the Center of Jewish Documentation in Vienna, Kolomeyer Jews in Germany recognized Leideritz on the street after the war. He was arrested and sent to Poland and there he was sentenced and hung. And that was the end of him.

Whether the hand of justice also reached the second murder commandant, Herbert Hertl, we do not know.

But about fifteen "smaller' murderers were arrested in Vienna in 1947. The accused and the witnesses were questioned and everything was written down. However, the Soviet Union required the deportation of the lawbreakers and the prisoners were repatriated to Russia at the end of 1948. One of them, Leopold Winkler, who was the in charge of the prison in Kolomey during the years of evil, hanged himself in his jail cell just before he was to be deported to Russia. The others were sent back to Russia for a mere seven years and returned to Vienna in November 1955.

When the organization of "Former Inhabitants of Kolomey and Vicinity" found out about the return of the murderers to Vienna, they insisted that they be brought to justice.

The organization, under the direction of the well known Tuvia Friedman of the Vienna Historical Documentation Center, and with the help of Israel Zweig from the World Jewish Congress, had published a copy of the German collection of testimony and documents several months earlier (Haifa, 1957). This was the basis for the trial of the murderers. To this material, Tuvia Friedman added a strong preface about those who were the murderers, how they were found and questioned, and the procedures used to bring them to justice.

Here is a short version of Tuvia Friedman's report:

Among the refugees who lived in Vienna from 1945-1948, there were also a few Jews who were survivors of the Kolomeyer ghetto.

In the summer of 1947, several Jews came to the office of the Jewish Historical Documentation Center in Vienna, and said that they had lived in the Kolomeyer ghetto from 1941 to 1943 when there were about 60,000 Jews there and that of that number, only two hundred survived. The described the atrocities committed by the Nazi murderers and gave several names that they remembered.

The refugees who survived the Kolomeyer ghetto were: the brothers Joseph and Moshe Schliesser, Herman Zener, and the cousins Mordechai [Markus] and Itzik [Jsak] Krauthammer. Later a few more witnesses appeared.

In 1941 and 1942, the witness Itzik Krauthammer was a servant for the Shutzpolizei in Kolomey and was a bootblack for Police Sergeant Alois Steiner. Krauthamer also remembered the names of the chief police commandant Hertl and of police officers Kleinbauer, Gall, and policemen Steiner, Schipany, and Pernek. The Schliesser brothers and the witness Zener named other policemen.

According to this evidence, the first division of the district police of Vienna brought in : 1. Alois Steiner, 2. Franz Schipany, 3. Jahan Gall, 4. Franz Pernek, and 5. Otmar Kleinbauer. They were questioned and arrested. From their interrogation, they obtained more names of those who took part in the murders of Kolomeyer Jews.

More Kolomeyer Shupo people were arrested: 6. Franz Stanka, 7. Franz Straka, 8. Karl Gross, 9. Josef Ruprechtshofer, 10. Jacob Uitz, 11. Leopold Winkler, 12. Reisenthaler, 13. Layer.

Leopold Winkler had been the prison governor in Kolomey and after his return from the war, he was a prison inspector in Vienna until September 1947. Franz Stanka and Franz Straka and a few others also served in the Vienna police until their arrest.

More than twenty extermination actions were carried out in Kolomey: in the slaughterhouse, in the Jewish cemetery, and in the Sheparovitzer [Szeparowce] forest. Although the main orders to deport Jews to the death camps came from higher officials, the local murderers killed about a third of the Jews in Kolomey.

Oberlieutenant Kleinbauer told how he carried out the liquidaton of the Jews at the cemetery. Schipany, Pernek, Steiner and Uitz admitted that they personally had killed Jews. Others further declared that they were present at all liquidations and deportations.

In Sheparovitz Forest, where the liquidations were carried out by the Kolomyer Gestapo and Shupo, no one was left alive.

The Gestapo and Shupo of Kolomey also carried out the deportations and killings in the nearby towns of Kitev, Kosow, Jablonow (Stopchet), Pistyn, Peczenizyn, Horodenka, Czernilicia, Gwozdiec, Zablotow, and Zabie. Forty thousand Jews were killed in these towns.

One of the master murderers, Shupo chief constable Franz Shipany, declared during his interrogation, "Yes, I know I am a murderer." Shupo Oberlieutenant Otmar Kleinbauer stated during his interrogation that he used dum-dum bullets during the liquidations which caused pieces of of the victims' brains to splatter on his face. As he spoke, the accused murderer wiped his face as though he were still wiping away the brain fragments.

During the questioning at the Vienna Police Bureau, the murderers quarreled with each other and each one tried to accuse the other of his crimes. If there was anything ugly missing from the description given by the murderers, each of them added to the ugliness during his interrogation and with his arguments.

The Shutzpolizei who "worked" in Kolomey, together with other war criminals from Boryslaw, Drohobycz, Stryj, Stanislaw, and Lemberg (Lwow) were deported to Russia at the end of 1948.

When they returned to Vienna in November, 1955, some of the Vienna newspapers as well as the world press, demanded that they be brought to justice.

The organization of Kolomeyer Jews in Israel went to the Austrian ambassador in Tel Aviv in 1956 with a petition signed by 130 former Kolomeyers requesting that the lawbreakers who had returned from Russia be brought to trial. To the petition was attached a list of of Jews who had lived in the Kolomey ghetto and were ready to be witnesses and testify.

Through the intervention of the Vienna Community Council and the World Jewish Congress, the Austrian Ministry of Justice agreed to question the witnesses in Israel, and postponed the trial until their testimony was completed.

In February, 1957, the first witnesses were questioned in Tel Aviv, Jerusalem, and Haifa and one could be sure that the entire testimony reached the Austrian Justice Ministry in April.

It is difficult to understand - writes Tuvia Friedman - why only six of the murderers were put on trial, since in 1947 fifteen had been arrested. Winkler committed suicide. That left fourteen. Why wasn't Oberlieutenant Otmar Kleinbauer, who admitted that he took part in two liquidations, put on trial?

Also difficult to understand is why Jakob Uitz was not among the accused (unless he did not return from Russia). He admitted during questioning that on the 15th of September, he personally shot twenty Jews.

The photocopied collection of testimony begins with a "We accuse!" signed by the "Organization of Kolomeyers in the State of Israel". We reproduce only a part of the accusation in Yiddish translation. This is no doubt a fitting ending to the Holocaust section of "Pinkas Kolomey."

"In the name of thousands of men, women, and children who were killed in Sheparovitz Forest and in the Jewish cemetery in Kolomey; in the name of the last ghetto orphans who were left without a roof over their heads and died of hunger or were shot in the streets of the ghetto; in the name of the elders and little children who died of hunger, thirst and exhaustion in the trains on the way to the Belzec concentration camp; in name of thousands who were dragged naked from their beds and driven to their deaths; in the name of all who were shot trying to escape,

WE ACCUSE THE MURDERERS!

New York, May 17, 1957

[Pages 431-441]

In Everlasting Memory

List of Kolomeyer, who together with millions of other martyrs, perished in the great khurbn [destruction] TSh- TSh"H [5700-5705] [1939-1945]

To the names of Kolomeyer martyrs given to us by their surviving relatives, we include the thousands and thousands of other cut off lives of the sons and daughters of our city, who left not a single remaining heir or relative.

Let Pinkas Kolomey serve in place of a gravestone on the symbolic grave of their scattered ashes.

Their memory will never be erased from our memories.

Kolomeyer Memorial Book Committee

We Remember Those Killed in the Khurbn Years TSh- TSh"H
[5700-5705] [1939-1945]

A [aleph]

Lazer Auster:
His slain family.

Paula Aizenhammer:
Her father Shlomo Shvamenoi, mother Berta, sister Sala, brother Adolf Shvamenoi.

Ulye Aizner:
Yaakov and Toibe Aizner.

B [bet]

Zanvl Beiser:
Brother- Yitzchak Beiser, sisters- Miriam, Kaile, Pesie, and Mantshe.

Yosef Birnberg:
His father Menachem Birnberg, mother Esther Birnberg.

Shlomo Bickel:
His aunt Feyge Kreisel, her husband Yeshaye and their children; his aunt Frume Vagenberg, and her husband Nachum and their three daughters; his uncle Yankl Bickel, wife and daughter.

Yetta Bickel:
Her sister Fanny Goldstein, born Sheffer, and her husband Heinrich and their daughters Gerta and Rena.

Buchalter brothers:
The slain family.

Charles Findur and Wife:
Remember their family.

G [gimel]

Fani Gitterman:
Shmuel and Pearl Hirsch.

Sadie Geller:
The family Isidore Geller.

S. Gellis:
His uncle, Moshe Hecht-Zorger and the family, his sister Gitzye Eiferman and the family, his relative Shmuel Eiferman.

H [hey]

P. Hacker:
The slain family.

Lazer Horn:
Father, Israel Horn and mother, Pesye-Rechl.

Pearl Hisler:
Brother-in-law, Yitzchak- Avraham Lindauer, his wife and children.

Miriam Hisler, born Shuster:
Brothers, Joseph Shuster, Avraham Shuster, his wife Pearl, their child Anschl; sister Malka
Shuster.

Lottie Herman:
Father, Pichas Waller and his wife Brucha

Chaim Hecht:
Parents, Moshe and Osna Hecht; brothers and sisters, Zvi, Koppel, Sholom, Friedl, Shayne
Yente, Yosef, and Hentzie.

Wolf and Sholom Hacker:
Father, David; mother, Fayge; brothers, Yitzchak and Moshe; sisters, Shaindl and Frimeh
Hacker.

A. Heller:
His slain family.

Simon Hecht:
The slain family.

Charles Hager:
My friends from the Kolomeyer gymnazye. [high school]

Rozia Herman:
Her father, Alfred Herman; mother, Lara Herman; brother, Bernard Herman; uncle, Shlomo
Balk.

V [vav, vav] - [turns to "w" in English; Yiddish has no "w" letter]

D. A. Wolf:
The slain family.

Ethel Walder:
Her parents Zalman and Rivtze Tacker and her brother-in-law Avraham Walder and his wife.

Fishel Weiser:
His wife Chaya, his daughters Gitl and Batye, his father Itzik Tsaderer, his mother Sasye, his
brother Shaye Tsaderer and his wife Gitl, their son Velvel; Moshe Weiser, his wife Rivke, their
son Avraham Gershon and daughter Batye.

Fayge Weissman and Runke Hirsh:
Their parents Joseph and Chaya Eisler.

Gertrude E. Weber:
Julius Ellenbergen

Yitzchak Wechter:
Parents, Herman and Yehudis Wechter; sisters, Lottie and Regina; and aunt Tanya Kanfer.

Z [zayen]

Miriam Zorger:
Her family- Shprintze, Adela, Shmuel, Yitzchak, Max, Aaron, Gusta, Bertha, and Fayge- Feuer.

M Zinger:
The slain family.

Gabriel Zeidner [also spelled Seidner]:
The family Zeidner and Blum.

L [lamed]

Charles Lander:
The family Wolf, Genya and Renya Hausknecht.

I. Latner:
The slain family.

Rosa Lazar:
Bayle Bruche Graf and her children Sarah, Chaya, Hersh, Meshulam, David, and Oyveneh.

Max Langer:
The Hirsch family; Sarah, Naftali, Gershon, Sonia and Golda Langer.

Fyvush Lieber:
Parents Mayer and Esther Lieber; father-in-law and mother-in-law Moshe and Chava Shapiro;
brtoher and sisters, Israel Lieber, Frume Lieber, Sarah Lieber, Avraham Shapiro, Nathan
Shapiro, Malka Shnebalg, Bayle Ruchel Lieber.

Yitzchak Likworknik:
The Likwornik family.

M [mem]

Helen Miller:
Her father- Dr. Joseph Zilberman, mother- Anna Zilberman.

Mintzer:
The slain family.

N [nun]

Golde Neger:
Parents- Aharon Yankl Reich, mother, Sarah; brothers- Yose Litman-Hersh, Shmuel- Lazar, Baruch and sisters, Blimah- Dvora, Yetta, and their children.

S [samech]

Dr. Saul Sokal and his wife, Dr. Tika Sokal:
Uncle- Yekl Sokal and wife Mirel.

Mary Smolinski:
The family Max and Esther Susskind.

E [ayin]

Abraham Ettinger:
Parents- Hersh-Wolf and Hannah Ettinger, brother- Yosef, sisters- Mina Zeidman, Bertha ettinger and Regina Frish.

David Eckerling:
His slain freinds, gymnazistn [high school classmates] from Kolomey.

P [pay]

Joseph and Adela Preistag-Yuris:
Their family- Yuris, Kreisel, and Zilber.

Shmuel Push:
The family Leibtzye and Ruchl Push.

F [fay]

Roza Feuerstein:
Her father- Yehuda Baruch Feuerstein, her mother- Nettie, her sister- Minka Kahn-Feuerstein, her brother-in-law - Dr. Leon Kahn, nephew- Jerszy Kahn, her sister Malvina Grossfeld-Feuerstein, her brother-in-law,- Morris Grossfeld, her brothers Gabriel and Tselu Feuerstein.

Yaakov and Isaac Feuerstein:
Their brother- Herman Feuerstein, sister-in-law -Frieda, nephew- Morris, sister- Adela Habicht, brother-in-law - Hersh Habicht, niece- Dania Habicht, brother- Simon Feuerstein, sister-in-law- Frieda Feuerstein, nephews- Gershon, Chaim and Mayer Feuerstein, brother- Moshe Feuerstein, sister-in-law- Olga Feuerstein, nephew- Pinchas Feuerstein.

Julia Feuerstein:
Her father- Yaakov Wizschnitzer, her mother- Clara, her sisters- Rosa Tsigler, Frima and Ruchl Feuerstein, her brother-in-law- Herman Tsigler, nephew- Israel Tsigler, uncle - Joseph Lachs, aunt- Bertha Lachs, cousin- Leon Lachs, cousin- Yehudis Lachs.

Mayer Feder:
The family Eliezer Mordechai Feder and Kalman Ber Hager.

F. Feingold:
The slain family.

Feivl Frantzas (Sydney, Australia):
Father- Yeshaye, mother- Chana Frantzas and sister- Ruchl.

K [kof]

M. Kalkshtein:
The slain family.

Shaye Kaner:
His parents Lazer and Gitl Kaner.

Leah and Michal Klier:
Brothers and sisters- Israel, Shlima, Leah, Anna,Dora, Sarah, Clara, Mina, Herman, Malka, Ephraim Zelig.

R. Kleinfeld:
The slain family.

Morris Kesten:
His sister Regina, her husband Oscar Ellenbogen and their children Clara and Nathan.

Yosef, Hersh, Sima, Itzik, Baruch and Bayle Kesten:
Father- Moshe, mother- Tila, youngest sister Ethel Weiss, her husband Shlomo, their child Batye.

R [resh]

Clara Rosenbaum:
Her father- Yosef Wachs, mother- Leeza, brothers- Avraham and Chaim Wachs, uncle Avraham Wachs, aunt Chana Wachs.

Hershel Ruhm:
His slain family.

Emil and Yosef Raisel:
Parents- Jacob and Amalia Raizel, sisters Dorothea Raizel and Dr. Shaye and Regina Raizel [or Rizel]

I. Reiter:
The family.

Susan Reynolds:
Her father- Abba Fishl, mother Yetti Fishl

Sh [shin]

Avraham Shapiro:
His parents Nachum and Chana, his sisters Vicky and Chaya-Tziye Shapiro and his brother
Zalman with his wife and children.

Julius Shomer:
Slain Family.

Tamara Schwartz:
Her father Herman and her step-mother Tama Alweil, sister Adela and brother Natsia Alweil,
sister Clara Alweil- Schwartzfeld, her husband and two daughters.

H. N. Shtahl [Stahl]:
Joseph, Hersh, Itzik, Baruch, Sima and Bayle Kesten, his mother Tilye Kesten, Moshe Kesten,
sister Ethel Weiss and her husband Shlomo, their daughter Bertha.

M. Shteigman [Steigman]:
The Steigman family.

Mordecai Sheinfeld:
His parents Yehezkiel and Chana Sheinfeld, sister Leah, brother Michal, uncles- Ezriel,
Shmelka, Yosef, David Arye, Mendl Arye, their wives and children, cousin Joseph Rosenfeld,
aunt Tosher and family. David Arye's son, Ephraim, was killed in Lithuania.

Joseph Schliesser:
His wife, Toybe Schliesser, his children, Mayer and Lola, his brother, Isaac Schliesser, sister-
in-law Ruchl and children.

Lusia Schliesser:
Her parents, Moshe and Bayle Shafel, and brothers and sisters.

Moshe Schliesser:
His parents, Moshe and Bayle Shafel, and brothers and sisters.

Brothers Moshe [Max] and Joseph Schliesser:
Their parents, Zindl and Blima Schliesser, their brother Isaac and his family, Nettie Schliesser,
her son Mendl and daughter Paula.

Sally Schlesinger:
Mother Brucha Waller and her husband Pinchas, uncle Hersh Leib Kris [Kresz?].

M. Schneck:
The slain family.

[The following are in boxed form in the book- a border is drawn around each remembrance.]

Benjamin Preminger, Sao Paulo, Brazil:
His sister Gitl (Tova) and her husband Yaakov
Bitter and their sons Nathan and Gedalia:
His sister Roiza Kretz, her husband and their daughter.

Dr. Mark Glinert:
Brother- Moshe, sister-in-law Dina Fish:
Their daughter Nina Socher and her husband,
sister- Frimke, her daughter Musia, son-in-law
and grandchild, sister- Matilda, her husband Mark
and their son Arthur.

Aaron Hisler and his sister Henche (Ann) Beiser:
Brother- Benjamin Wechter, his wife Esther and their
children- Rivke [Regina], Avraham Yosef [Yoshe], Gitl
[Giza], Mendl, Berl-Mayer, Sureh, and Chaya Hugeh.

Leib Weitz (Meisler):
His father Aaron, his mother Leah, father-in-law and
mother-in-law- Joseph and Pearl Kagan, his brothers-
in-law and sisters-in-law Mottel and Dina Shapiro, their
two children; Yitzcak and Nechama Kagan with their
son; Chana Weitz with her twin Munia; his uncle and
aunt Moshe and Prive Konig.

Yitzchak Isaac Susskind and sister Tzili Gottfried:
Their mother Ethel, sister Elsa Schwartz, her husband
Avraham and her child; their brother Isser Susskind
and his wife Regina.

Roiza Susskind (born Hibner):
Her mother Brucha Waller with her husband Pinchas.

M. Taback, Sao Paulo, Brazil:
His mother. Roza Komet-Taback,
uncle Mendl Komet and their two sons.

Blima and Avraham Yitzchak Reichbach:
Their children Moshe, Lazer,
David (Dutsye) and Leah (Lottie).

David Marksheid:
His brother Itzik and his family; his sister Sosye,
brother-in-law Gedalia and their daughter Laria; his
brother-in-law Lazer Muntchik and child.

Isaac Feuerstein:
His wife Genia, his daughters Tzivia and Rivke,
his son Yeshaye.

Gershon Frish:
His parents- Benjamin and Regina Frish, his brother
Yaakov, his grandfather Hersh-Wolf Ettinger and other
relatives: Joseph and Gita Ettinger, Shmuel and Berta
Ettinger, Alexander and Mina Zeidman.

Bertha Sturm, Yaakov Biger,
Etta Scherr, Sylvia Recht:
Their mother, Hentzia Biger, brother Lazer with wife
and three children, sister Toiva and her husband,
brothers Avraham and Leib.

Fred and Collete Sheffer:
The family of their grandfather Fishl Glinert and of their
grandmother Clara Glinert, born Rap: Sarah Glinert
and children, Sita Rap, Roka Osterer and children, Dr.
Isaac Rap and children, Dr. Beno Rap and children,
Anschel Rap with his wife and children,
and Karl Rap with his wife and children.

[Page 442]

Those Who Fell in the Soviet-Nazi War

When the German-Russian war broke out in the summer of 1941, and before the Soviet army withdrew from Kolomey, the Red Army mobilized a number of Jewish young men. Others joined voluntarily to go fight against the Nazis.
Of the hundreds of Kolomeyer Jewish youth who fell on the battlefields, we know, unfortunately, the names of only twelve of them. Let these twelve, then, be memorialized in "Pinkas Kolomey" as a symbol for all the others.

[black line forms a box around the names of the twelve arranged in two columns of six]

Mayerl, the young Rabin's son	Yankele Kegler
Moishele Glazer	Herman Gottlieb
Sumer Feigenbaum	Moshe Feuerman
Nachman Brettler	Mechele Mandel
Israel Feder	Hersh Mozberg
Hersh Gutshiess	Gedalia Buchman

[Pages 444-448]

Kolomeyer Organizations in New York

Translated by Claire Hisler Shefftz

The Joint Kolomear Relief

In 1944, when the war was close to its end, the Joint Kolomear Relief was organized under the initiative of the "Kolomear Jewish Center." All the existing Kolomeyer organizations took part in the "Relief." The organization intended to get in touch with Kolomey as soon as the war was over in order to help rebuild the Jewish institutions that had been destroyed during the war. No one could imagine then that the outcome would be so horrible and tragic.

In the meantime, the Relief started to raise money. There were many Kolomeyer Jews who put a great deal of effort and work into collecting a substantial amount of money so that it would be there when it was needed. The tragic news that Kolomey and its Jews had been destroyed discouraged everyone. But individual cries for help began to arrive. Soon food packages were sent to Kolomey. The pleas for help increased and came not only from Kolomey but from Kolomeyer landsleit scattered and spread out all over the world. Requests for help came from Rumania, Poland, Hungary, Russia, Austria, Germany, Israel, and Italy, and help was sent. In the three years from 1948 to 1951 the Relief sent food packages for a sum total of about twelve thousand dollars. [CARE packages cost $10 each then.]. The Relief was flooded with letters from Kolomeyer, sick and broken people, who needed medicines that were not available where they were. So the Relief bought the medicines that were needed and air mailed them to the those who were suffering. And thus a good number of landsleit were saved. About two thousand dollars was spent on medicine alone. With great devotion, women especially, worked to collect clothing and linens for the Kolomeyer who desperately needed them. And here we would like to single out for special praise the Gellis family, who spent many days and nights packing and sending the clothing packages.

When most of the Kolomeyer landsleit went to Israel, the relief work went there also. It soon became a tradition for the relief to send packages before each holiday whether the recipients had asked for it or not. Even in 1952, when the Relief's work had nearly ended, 120 packages for Passover were sent to Israel.

A special chapter in the Relief's work was to welcome Kolomeyer landsleit who came to America. The newcomers were visited by representatives of the Relief in their homes. A hundred immigrants were given material aid.

Finally, we would like to remember the names of of the people who undertook so much:

The presidents, William Renner, Charles Kleinman; the treasurers, M. Sobel, L. Sher, and S. Gellis; the financial secretaries, A. Weinstock, M. Suss, A. Hisler; the recording secretaries, L. Diener, L. Weitz, and R. Feuerman.

This report summarizes the commendable work and effort of good Kolomeyer landsleit for their suffering brothers.

A. Hisler

[Note: Aaron Hisler was my father and our whole family helped with the Joint Kolomear Relief. I remember addressing envelopes asking for donations and seeing the air letters that came to our house from landsleit in D.P.(Displaced Persons) camps in Italy and Rumania. With a second-hand typewriter, we typed names and addresses for CARE packages. Letters came from HIAS inquiring about relatives of survivors. Many families were reunited through the Relief and its caontacts with landsleit and my parents gained the deepest satisfaction from these reunions even though their families had not survived. I was an overprotected teenager then and met many survivors but never heard their complete stories. -Claire Hisler Shefftz]

The Kolomear Jewish Center

By noting the organizations which made the publication of the yizkor book possible, we wish to remember the Kolomear Jewish Center, which organized the book committee, under whose name we met at first. The Kolomear Jewish Center also gave us our first contribution, which made it possible for us to begin our work.

Kolomear Branch #528 Arbeiter Ring [Workmen's Circle]

A group of youthful Kolomeyer landsleit in New York organized a relief group during World War I to meet the needs of those Kolomeyer who had suffered during the war. A few years after that war, the Kolomeyer Relief achieved the noble purpose its members had intended. From the more eminent among them came the idea to remain organized as a branch of the Arbeiter Ring [Workmen's Circle] and Kolomear Branch 528 was formed.

The story of Branch 528 Arbeiter Ring is an open book of uplifting and splendid undertakings, not only for its members but for the entire Arbeiter Ring organization. That which the Arbeiter Ring is noted for, for being the finest Jewish folk organization on the American continent, is what the Kolomear Branch realized during the 37 years of combined activities.

During this period in the Kolomeyer Branch, thanks to the loyalty of its members and the good administration, there was great enthusiasm in the clubs, which we call workmen's circles. The Kolomear Branch carried out its work under the leadership of its parent organization which brought to gether the scattered immigrant masses into an experimental united collective.

Today the Kolomear Branch is an active participant in Israel Bonds; the Branch serves as an aid organization for its members; the Branch took part in building an Arbeiter Ring home for the elderly; it takes part in worker's committees and aid activities in other Jewish organizations

The 1957 officers of the Branch are:

Nathan Stahl - President;
Harry Feingold - Vice-President;
Ida Gutman - Financial Secretary;
Ella Busch - Recording Secretary;
Harry Teicher - Hospitaler;
Gussie Goldin - Treasurer;

Members of the Executive Board are:

Fanny Feingold, Fanny Zaiger, Hillel Newmash, Seymash Hecht, Matis Busch.
Julia Busch- Secretary of Relief Fund;
Matis Busch- Treasurer.

Kolomear Friends Association

A group of young men who had recently come over from Kolomey, met in the home of Jack Hagler's parents on Rivington Street in New York in 1904 and decided to form an organization called "Kolomear Friends Association." The purpose of the organziation was not just mutual support, the basic idea behind other such organizations which were formed in those years by young Jewish immigrants, the new Kolomeyer organization specified in its program the important goal of helping the socialist movement and also the workers back home in Kolomey. This was the first Kolomeyer organization of this kind in the new world.

In 1905, shortly after the organization was founded, the historic strike of the talis workers began in Kolomey. The Kolomear Friends Association organized a mass rally of Kolomeyer landsleit. An appeal at the rally collected fifty dollars- a significant sum in those times. The money was immmediately sent to Kolomey for the striking workers who enthusiastically welcomed the brotherly help from their landsleit in America.

Later on, the organization sent an annual contribution of three hundred fifty dollars a year to the Kolomeyer orphan's home for many years. The goals of the organization were not only

limited to relief work. From its beginning, the Kolomear group worked with the socialist movement back home. In 1907, the organization arranged a spirited celebration in New York in honor of the famous victory of the Austrian Social Democrats in the parliamentary elections of that year. In 1908, the organization sent fifty dollars to the Social Democrats' campaign in Lemberg,

Until this day, the Kolomear Firends Association, is the largest and strongest of the Kolomeyer groups and organizations.

The current officers are as follows:

A. Feuer - President;
L. Ellenberg - Vice-President;
L. Blumenthal - Recording secretary;
H. Unger - Financial Secretary;
M Gischner, D. Wasserman, D. Stemzer, S. Kramer, M. Shakby, and S. Weissman - board members with various duties.

In Memory of Our Dear Loved Ones

They Served us Faithfully and We Will Always Remember Them with Honor:

Sam Schwartz, d. July 1, 1922;
Irving Feldberg, d. May 18, 1926
Molye Weinstein, d. January 31,1929;
Isidore Saltzhauer, d. April 26, 1929;

Louis Eisner, d. November 7, 1929;
Israel Hundert, d. August 8, 1933;
Louis Cohen, d. October 3, 1935;
Sam Schneck, d. July 25, 1937;
Nathan Hilsenrath, d. March 16, 1942;
Sam Kramer, d. June 2, 1942;
Simon H. Singer, d. August 7, 1944;
Harry Manger, d. December 1, 1945;
Sol Konigsberg, d. December 8, 1945;
Saul Eisner, d. April 9, 1946;
Harry Kerker, d. August 2, 1949;
Abba Singer, d. April 23, 1950;
Alexander Tarasov, d. December 19, 1950;
Sam Eisner, d. February 4, 1951;
Harry Daitchman, d. July 16, 1951;
Nathan Goodman, d. August 6, 1952;
Joe Lindauer, d. July 24, 1953;
Jacob Stein, d. October 9, 1953;
Frieda Zegenreich, d. August 11, 1954;
Beatrice Kesten, d. February 28, 1955;
Sam Busch, d. November 26, 1955;
Philip Hoshkes, d. December 20, 1956;
Sam , d. March 15, 1957.

NAME INDEX